Play Therapy with Children in Crisis

PLAY THERAPY WITH CHILDREN IN CRISIS
A Casebook for Practitioners

Edited by

Nancy Boyd Webb, D.S.W.
Fordham University
Graduate School of Social Service

Foreword by Howard J. Parad, D.S.W.

THE GUILFORD PRESS
New York   London

© 1991 The Guilford Press
A Division of Guilford Publications, Inc.
72 Spring Street, New York, NY 10012

Printed in the United States of America

This book is printed on acid-free paper.

Last digit is print number: 9 8 7

Library of Congress Cataloging-in-Publication Data

Play therapy with children in crisis: a casebook for practitioners /
   edited by Nancy Boyd Webb.
        p.   cm.
   Includes bibliographical references and index.
   ISBN 0-89862-760-5   ISBN 0-89862-151-8 (pbk.)
   1. Play therapy—Case studies.   2. Crisis intervention
(Psychiatry)—Case studies.   I. Webb, Nancy Boyd, 1932-
   [DNLM: 1. Crisis Intervention—in infancy and childhood—case
studies.   2. Play Therapy—infancy & childhood—case studies.   WS
350.2 P7227]
RJ505.P6P56   1991
618.92′891653—dc20
DNLM/DLC
for Library of Congress   91-19756
                                                                  CIP

Dedicated to
DR. MARY ANN QUARANTA
Fordham University, Graduate School of Social Service

*Inspiring Dean, whose special appreciation of childhood
and of the importance of child and family therapy
has stimulated my teaching, writing, and practice.*

—N. B. W.

Contributors

Teresa Bevin, M.A. Formerly, School Based Mental Health Program, Children's Hospital National Medical Center, Washington, D.C.; Presently, Montgomery County Government Crisis Center, Bethesda, Maryland

Joyce Bluestone, M.S.W. School Social Worker, Westchester County, New York; Adjunct Instructor, Fordham University, Graduate School of Social Service, Tarrytown, New York

Joan S. Doyle, M.S.S.A. Director of Treatment Center, Berea Children's Home, Berea, Ohio

Victor Fornari, M.D. Director of Clinical Services, Division of Child and Adolescent Psychiatry, North Shore University Hospital, and Assistant Professor of Psychiatry, Cornell University Medical College, Manhasset, New York

Robin F. Goodman, Ph.D. Team Leader, Pediatric Hematology and Oncology Services, Steven D. Hassenfeld Children's Center, New York University Medical Center, New York, New York

Jill Hofmann, M.A., L.M.F.C.C. Coordinator of Clinical Services, Santa Cruz County Mental Health, Project COPE, Santa Cruz, California

Dermot J. Hurley, M.S.W. Assistant Director, Child and Adolescent Center, Children's Hospital of Western Ontario, London, Ontario, Canada

Mary Ellen Johnston, C.S.W., C.A.C. The Children's Alcohol Resource and Education Center, Freeport, New York

Cathy Dodds Joyner, M.Ed. Child and Adolescent Services, CAMH, Charleston, South Carolina

Carol P. Kaplan, Ph.D., B.C.D. Assistant Professor, Fordham University, Graduate School of Social Service, New York, New York; Former Director of Adolescent Treatment Unit, Rockland County Community Mental Health Center, Pomona, New York

Corinne Masur, Psy.D. Assistant Clinical Professor, Widener University, Chester, Pennsylvania; Adjunct Assistant Professor, Temple University Medical School, Philadelphia, Pennsylvania; Clinical Associate in Psychoanalysis, Philadelphia Psychoanalytic Institute and Society, Philadelphia, Pennsylvania

Howard J. Parad, D.S.W. Professor Emeritus, University of Southern California, School of Social Work, Los Angeles, California; Former Dean and Professor, Smith College, School for Social Work, Northampton, Massachusetts

Jane E. Price, M.S.W., A.C.S.W. Formerly, Child and Adolescent Crisis Intervention Team, presently, Acute Adolescent Inpatient Unit, Bronx Children's Psychiatric Center, Bronx, New York

Steven E. Reid, Ph.D. Psychologist/Consultant, Herbert G. Birch Children's Center, Brooklyn, New York

Joyce M. Remkus, M.S.W. Formerly, Early Years Preventive Services, presently, Sound Shore Community Services, Rockland Children's Psychiatric Center, Orangeburg, New York; Adjunct Instructor, Fordham University, Graduate School of Social Service, Tarrytown, New York

Howard Robinson, M.S., M.S.W. Coordinator, Child and Family Counseling Center of Southern Westchester, and Assistant Director, Postgraduate Certificate Program in Child and Adolescent Therapy, Fordham University, Graduate School of Social Service, Tarrytown, New York

Pam Rogers, M.A., M.F.C.C. Santa Cruz County Mental Health, Project COPE, Santa Cruz, California

Sallie Sanborn, M.S., C.C.L.S. Senior Child Life Specialist, Bellevue Hospital Center, New York, New York

Barbara Saravay, M.S.W., B.C.D. Northern Westchester Guidance Clinic, Mt. Kisco, New York; Adjunct Instructor, Fordham University, Graduate School of Social Service, Tarrytown, New York

David Stoop, M.S.W., M.Div. Coordinator, Secure Treatment Center, Berea Children's Home, Berea, Ohio

Virginia Strand, D.S.W., B.C.D. Director, Child Abuse and Neglect Training Center, and Assistant Professor, Fordham University, Graduate School of Social Service, Tarrytown, New York

Nancy Boyd Webb, D.S.W., B.C.D. Director, Postgraduate Certificate Program in Child and Adolescent Therapy, and Professor, Fordham University, Graduate School of Social Service, Tarrytown, New York

Susan Wojtasik, M.A., C.C.L.S. Director, Child Life Department, Bellevue Hospital Center, New York, New York

Foreword

Consider this casebook as a drama of childhood suffering and struggle enacted on a vast stage. The stories are those of at-risk children and their families and of those who help and support them. Like all serious drama, the children's predicaments reflect much tragedy. But they also attest to the resilience of the child's spirit and his or her ability to cope with—and in triumphant moments to master—some of the most wretched crises that victimize children in today's world: physical violence and sexual abuse; the dislocation of being a refugee; temporary and permanent loss of parental attachments and supports; AIDS and other catastrophic illnesses; substance abuse; desertion, divorce, death; and natural and man-made disasters.

Crisis intervention is an increasingly accepted and effective part of the human service professional's therapeutic repertoire for helping people respond to the threats and challenges of overwhelming stress. While considerable attention has been given to crisis therapy with adolescents and adults, much less attention has been focused on crisis intervention techniques with young children ages 3 to 11. This casebook makes a highly significant contribution toward filling this gap. Not content with condensed case summaries, which often conceal more than they reveal of the actual clinical encounter, Dr. Webb, with the collaboration of 21 mental health professionals, takes us behind the scenes, so we can have a clear understanding not only of what the child (or parent) says, does, and feels, but also of what the clinician says, does, and thinks during the process of therapy.

Dr. Webb's introductory chapters provide a comprehensive framework for assessing the child in crisis (with thoughtful attention to family and other sociocultural influences) and for appreciating the meaning and use of play, as well as the special role of the play therapist in crisis intervention.

This volume commends itself to a wide readership. While especially useful to faculty and graduate students in social work, psychiatry, psychology, education, and nursing training programs, it also can be very valuable to the clinician on the firing line who has to deal with diverse crises. With their authentic hands-on approaches, the contributors invite us to share the psychosocial experiences of children in crisis, attuning us to the child's private world of fantasy and reality.

Do not expect therapeutic dogma or absolute truths to be espoused in the pages that follow, for you will find that most of the contributors are pragmatically eclectic in their treatment approaches, integrating psychodynamic, cognitive-behavioral, and art therapy perspectives. The authors' thoughtful study questions will promote your critical thinking about each case, as well as enhance your awareness that child therapy is an art form, subject to many nuances of interpretation. You will, I believe, be informed and stimulated and, I hope, inspired by these poignant in-depth case accounts, as I was in reading them.

HOWARD J. PARAD

Preface

This book focuses on helping children in a variety of crisis situations through the modality of play therapy. The need for the book became apparent in teaching social work graduate and postgraduate students who wanted detailed examples of how to conduct play therapy, once they understood the theoretical framework that guides such practice.

In addition to demonstrating a wide range of play therapy techniques with children from ages 3 to 11 in many different settings, this book attempts to elucidate the inner world of the therapist/clinician during the therapeutic process. Based on the conviction that play therapy is as much art as science, the attention to the therapist's thoughts and feelings during the work with the child invites students and practitioners to consider what *they* might have said or done at certain points in the treatment. Use of a double-column format in presenting the cases facilitates the dual focus on child and therapist which is ideal for teaching purposes.

Although the book emerged from social work practice and teaching, many of the authors come from other mental health disciplines that also teach and practice play therapy with children. It is fascinating to see the commonalities of practice among child therapists of different professional backgrounds. Thus, the book is appropriate for training child therapists in the fields of child psychiatry, clinical psychology, art therapy, child life therapy, psychiatric nursing, child welfare, special education, and pastoral counseling, in addition to clinical social work.

All the authors are experts in their specialized fields and have selected cases to demonstrate play therapy with children in the midst of specific crisis situations. The cases have all been disguised to protect the confidentiality of the children and families.

The understanding of clinical practice depends on an appreciation of the subtleties and intensity of therapeutic interaction. For this, we need real examples of actual practice. Child and family therapy occurs behind closed doors, and a summary of what happened is not sufficient to train someone to become a therapist.

I am deeply grateful to the clinicians who have been willing to expose their work to the analysis and scrutiny of child therapists and practitioners in training, for the future benefit of countless children and families. We have all learned from our clients, even as we help them, and we now hope to learn from each other.

NANCY BOYD WEBB

Contents

Play Therapy with Children in Crisis

PART I

Introduction

CHAPTER 1

Assessment of the Child in Crisis

NANCY BOYD WEBB

Children, like adults, experience crises in the normal course of their lives. Contrary to the myth of the magic years of childhood as a period of guileless innocence and carefree play, the reality of the preteen years, like that of later life, includes stressful experiences that provoke anger, jealousy, fear, and grief as well as joy and pleasure. The parent who protests, when confronted with his child's problems, "But these are supposed to be the best years of his life!" has forgotten that negative fallout from stress affects the young as well as the old.

Although stress in itself is not harmful (Selye, 1978), it may precipitate a crisis if the anxiety accompanying it exceeds the individual's ability to adapt. Anxiety that paralyzes or seriously interferes with usual functioning propels the individual (child or adult) into a state of crisis.

People have different levels of stress tolerance, however, and different modes of responding. Psychological defenses and symptom formation are the usual outcomes of attempts to "fight" the anxiety or flee from it (the "fight or flight" responses; Selye, 1978). Since the coping repertoire of young children is limited because of their youth, immature defenses, and lack of life experience, they are particularly vulnerable to stress and often require assistance to obtain relief from their anxiety and to learn new coping methods.

This book recognizes the vast range of stressful events that may impair everyday functioning and cause emotional pain to young children. In this chapter, the focus is on making an assessment of the child in crisis. This assessment includes an evaluation of individual and family factors as these interact with the particular crisis situation.

DEFINITION OF CRISIS

An underlying principle of crisis intervention theory maintains that crises can and do occur to everyone (Gilliland & James, 1988; Golan, 1978, p. 62). No previous pathology should be assumed when, for example, a rescue worker discovers a child in a mute, stunned condition following an earthquake that destroyed his home. Although individual differences influence personal vulnerability to breakdown and the form and timing of the disturbance, no one is immune from the possibility of such an occurrence in the aftermath of a crisis. Situations of extreme stress cause overload and create malfunctioning to the system.

Gilliland and James (1988, p. 3) summarize five different sources in their definition of crisis: "a perception of an event or situation as an intolerable difficulty that exceeds the resources and coping mechanisms of the person. Unless the person obtains relief, the crisis has the potential to cause severe affective, cognitive, and behavioral malfunctioning."

Emphasis on the *perception* of the event, rather than on the event itself, appropriately draws attention to the unique underlying meaning of the situation to each individual. Different people experience the same situation differently, and idiosyncratic factors determine their separate perceptions of the crisis. For example, following the news of the sudden death of their classmate in an automobile accident, a group of third-grade children exhibited anxiety reactions ranging from mild to severe. All the children in the victim's class displayed some degree of shock, concern, and curiosity about the death, but individual reactions varied greatly. One child told his teacher the next day (falsely) that his father had died suddenly the previous evening. Another child complained of headaches and stomachaches for a week with no physical cause, and a third child had frightening nightmares for several weeks about being chased by a monster. Most of the children in the class did not develop symptoms and did not appear to be traumatized by the death, according to opinions of the teachers and school social worker. The child with the nightmares had been a close friend of the dead child; their favorite activity had been playing war games, involving chasing and killing. This child benefited from brief therapy in which the dynamic of winning and losing and acceptance of the unpredictable were played out symbolically. The child's symptoms disappeared after four play therapy sessions.

Anna Freud (1965, p. 139) states that "traumatic events should not be taken at their face value, but should be translated into their specific meaning for the given child." Green, Wilson, and Lindy (1985, p. 59) elaborate further by pointing out that "different poeple who are present at the *same event* will have different outcomes because, not only will their experiences differ, but the individual characteristics they bring to bear upon the psychological processing are different, and this processing may take place in differing recovery environments."

For the child in crisis, the "recovery environment" holds particular significance because of the child's dependence on family members and other adults to provide support and guidance. Thus, the assessment of the child in crisis includes an analysis of individual factors interacting with the resources of the family and the social support network in the face of a particular crisis situation.

TRIPARTITE CRISIS ASSESSMENT

Analysis of an individual in crisis focuses on three interacting profiles: (1) the nature of the crisis situation, (2) the idiosyncratic characteristics of the individual, and (3) the strengths and weaknesses of the individual's support system. Figure 1.1 illustrates the components of this tripartite crisis assessment and suggests how the impact of a specific crisis situation depends on the balancing of the interacting influences among the three sets of variables.

THE NATURE OF THE CRISIS SITUATION

Although the individual's perception of a crisis takes precedence over the objective circumstances of the event or situation, nonetheless analysis of the specific components of the crisis situation aids understanding of its impact. For example, a child subject to harsh and repeated beatings at the hands of a drug-abusing father did not become dysfunctional until the father threatened to kill himself and the entire family. It is important to learn as many details as possible about both the precipitating event and the background of the crisis situation. In this example, the father's threat was the precipitating event, occurring to a child already vulnerable as a result of the chronic abuse.

Severity of Psychosocial Stressors

The revised third edition of the *Diagnostic and Statistical Manual of Mental Disorders* (DSM-III-R; American Psychiatric Association, 1987) provides for measurement of the severity of psychosocial stressors on axis IV. The intent is to rate the severity of the stressor "based on the clinician's assessment of the stress an 'average' person in similar circumstances and with similar sociocultural values would experience from the particular psychosocial stressor(s). This judgment involves a consideration of . . . the amount of change in the person's life caused by the stressor, the degree to which the event is desired and under the person's control, and the number of stressors" (American Psychiatric Association, 1987, p. 19).

Additional information required by DSM-III-R about the stressors includes their duration: *acute* events are those of less than 6 months' duration, whereas *enduring* circumstances are those lasting longer than 6 months. DSM-III-R ranks psychosocial stressors on a scale of 0–6, with 6 being catastrophic (see Table 1.1).

Other Factors

The rating of psychosocial stressors provides an objective foundation for analysis of the nature of the crisis situation. However, information about other contributing factors (as listed in Figure 1.1) also should be considered. These are:

- Anticipated versus sudden crisis
- Single versus recurring crisis events
- Solitary versus shared crisis experience
- Presence of loss factors
- Bodily injury or pain
- Presence of violence (witnessed or experienced)
- Degree of life threat (personal/family/others)

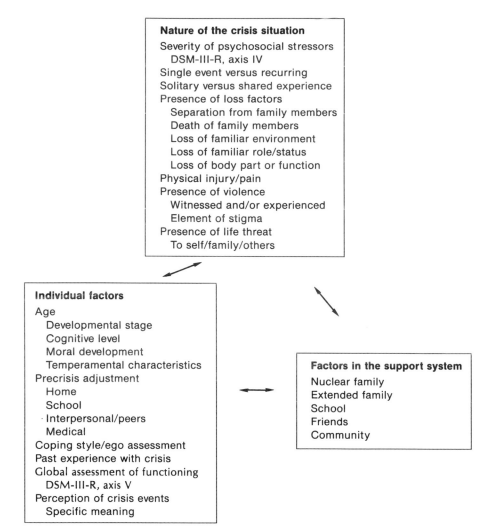

FIGURE 1.1. Interactive components of a crisis assessment.

Anticipated versus Sudden Crisis

The Scout motto, "Be prepared," implies, by contrast, the undesirability of unpreparedness. Arkin (1974, p. 11) notes in referring to sudden death that "what human beings dread most is being taken by surprise, which they feel unprepared [for] and unable to master."

Some events that lead to crisis are, by their nature, unpredictable. Examples include natural disasters with no preliminary warning, the sudden death of a parent who was previously well, and the killing and injury of innocent bystanders in a wanton shooting episode. These contrast with other situations that gradually

TABLE 1.1. Severity of Psychosocial Stressors Scale: Children and Adolescents

Code	Term	Examples of stressors	
		Acute events	Enduring circumstances
1	None	No acute events that may be relevant to the disorder	No enduring circumstnaces that may be relevant to the disorder
2	Mild	Broke up with boyfriend or girlfriend; change of school	Overcrowded living quarters; family arguments
3	Moderate	Expelled from school; birth of sibling	Chronic disabling illness in parent; chronic parental discord
4	Severe	Divorce of parents; unwanted pregnancy; arrest	Harsh or rejecting parents; chronic life-threatening illness in parent; multiple foster home placements
5	Extreme	Sexual or physical abuse; death of a parent	Recurrent sexual or physical abuse
6	Catastrophic	Death of both parents	Chronic life-threatening illness
0	Inadequate information, or no change in condition		

Note. From the *Diagnostic and Statistical Manual of Mental Disorders* (3rd ed., rev., p. 11) by the American Psychiatric Association, 1987, Washington, DC: Author. Copyright 1987 by the American Psychiatric Association. Reprinted by permission.

build up to a crisis. Examples of anticipated crises include a family move to another community, the departure of the father from the home as the beginning of a marital separation, and the terminal illness of a family member. Stressful events that develop toward a predictble outcome present the opportunity for gradual comprehension and assimilation of the impending transition or loss. The ego does not have to absorb abruptly the painful reality of an irrevocable event.

Janis (1977), in studying the reactions of preoperative surgical patients, found that a moderate amount of anticipatory fear about an impending operation permitted patients to develop effective inner defenses, in contrast to situations in which the patients did not worry beforehand and were later less able to cope with the pain and discomfort following surgery. Janis postulated the concept of the "work of worrying" and concluded that "a person will be better able to tolerate suffering and dysfunction if he worries about it beforehand, rather than maintaining expectations of personal invulnerability (Janis, 1977, p. 284).

We do not know how this concept applies in nonmedical stressful situations, nor do we know how applicable it is to children. Many well-meaning adults deliberately try to shield children from worry, and they avoid exposing them until the last minute to situations they believe will prove upsetting. This prevents children from psychologically bracing themselves for the upcoming assault.

There is a growing body of children's literature (Fassler, 1978) dedicated to helping children, through the medium of stories, to master stressful life events such as a grandfather's death, going to the hospital, parental divorce, and moving. The crisis techniques of "role rehearsal" and "anticipatory guidance" (Parad & Parad, 1990) help clients prepare in advance for future stressful situations. The child who has advance knowledge, through pictures and explanations, about surgical masks and medical procedures, for example, shows less anxiety when confronted with these in the hospital. Kliman's (1968) concept of "psychological immunization" proposes that "mastery in advance" through reflection or fantasy provides enhanced coping in future stressful situations. A folk saying claims that "a job well dreaded is more than half done." Even though the dreading is unpleasant, it permits anticipatory problem solving and psychological prepara-tion. Since sudden crises lack this opportunity, they arouse more debilitating stress than crises that have been anticipated.

Single versus Recurring Crisis Events

The notion of the last straw that breaks the camel's back suggests that the accumulation of stress weighs so heavily that not even minor additional stressors can be tolerated. Thus, the precipitating factor in a crisis may not be as significant as the events that preceded it and created a "vulnerable state" for the individual (Golan, 1978). In the previous example of the child who suffered repeated physical abuse, a relatively minor occurrence such as a scolding from a teacher could precipitate a crisis because of the child's vulnerable state.

Individuals have different levels of stress tolerance, but multiple crisis events exact demands for adaptation that eventually deplete emotional reserves, even in individuals with high tolerance levels. Although successful resolution of a crisis may result in stronger, more versatile coping, psychic assaults from repeated, multiple crisis events will ultimately result in disorganization and fragmentation of even adequate coping abilities.

Solitary versus Shared Crisis Experience

If "misery likes company," then we would expect the sharing of crisis experiences to afford a degree of comfort and support that is absent when an individual undergoes a stressful crisis alone. Certainly, the dynamic of guilt (Why me?) and issues of personal responsibility (How could this crisis have been avoided?) are irrelevant or greatly reduced in situations of shared crisis. Although every crisis is experienced ultimately on a *personal* level, the knowledge that others also are enduring similar turmoil may reduce the stigma of victimization. For example, the child victim of incest may gain extraordinary benefits from participation in a group of similarly victimized children.

However, the commonality of a shared crisis event does not automatically lead to bonding among the individuals involved. Terr (1979), reporting on the aftermath of the kidnapping of a school bus of summer school students, found that the traumatized youngsters avoided contact with one another after the horrible experience was over. As if to escape the memories of their ordeal, this group assimilated into the community and stayed away from their fellow students, who would remind them of the frightening experience.

When the crisis situation conveys stigma, the individual understandably avoids being identified with it. Violent deaths by murder or suicide often burden the survivors with the shame of stigma, added to the stress of tragic loss.

The extent to which sharing of crisis helps children necessarily depends on their age. Preschoolers are normally narcissistic, and peers begin to exert influence only during the latency years. Thus, the impact of the shared versus solitary crisis experience seems valid mainly from latency onward, with qualifications, based on the uncertain impact of stigmatized crises.

Presence of Loss Factors/Physical Injury and Pain

Loss plays a major role in many crisis situations, and the attendant reactions of confusion, anger, and desperation may be understood as mourning responses connected to the loss. When losses include the death or separation from a family member, grief and mourning are appropriate. Less obvious losses occur in situations such as moving or school promotion. These involve giving up a familiar location or status and developing new relationships. Teachers attest to the high level of anxiety in September until children become comfortable with the expectations and people in their new grade. This anxiety usually does not cause a state of crisis for most children, but it can put them into a "vulnerable state" in which their ability to cope is reduced temporarily.

The converse of loss is attachment. If no positive bonding existed, no mourning would be necessary. Bowlby's (1969) seminal work on attachment highlighted the biological source of the need for proximity in human relationships, with the prototype of attachment the mother–infant relationship. Although object constancy permits the mental retention of loved persons and places in the memory, nonetheless a child whose parents separate suffers the loss of daily contact with both attachment figures. This loss of the intact nuclear family often also includes a change of residence, school, and life style, but the loss of contact with the attachment object (parent) represents the most serious deprivation. Multiple losses cause multiple stressors, adding to the potential for crisis.

Illness, although a common occurrence for children, introduces a number of temporary or permanent restrictions on the child's life, which the child experiences as losses. The child with a terminal illness, for example, must adapt to bodily changes, environmental restrictions, changed expectations for the future, and changed relationships based on the altered perceptions of others about him or her. These all constitute losses, which also prevail to a minor degree for the child who remains home from school for a week with chickenpox. Physical injury or pain constitutes a serious threat to the child's basic sense of body integrity, compounding the other stresses associated with medical treatment. The family has an important role in helping the child cope with a serious medical crisis.

Losses comprise a central part of any crisis assessment. Both losses that are "vague," such as the loss of the sense of predictability about the environment (as during a flood or earthquake), and more evident losses, such as the death of a pet, should be enumerated. A crisis assessment must include past as well as present losses, since memories of past experiences of loss and bereavement typically reawaken in current loss situations. This is discussed further in the section on assessment of individual factors.

Presence of Violence/Degree of Life Threat

We live in a violent world that does not shield children from graphic exposure to conflict in all forms and locales, including the family, school, and community. Star (1980) states that American society maintains a high baseline tolerance for violence and that within the family this takes the form of child abuse, spouse abuse, incest, and other assaultive episodes. Pynoos and Eth (1985, p. 19) believe that "children who witness extreme acts of violence represent a population at significant risk of developing anxiety, depressive, phobic, conduct, and post-traumatic stress disorders." The child witness experiences traumatic helplessness and cognitive confusion when confronted with human-induced acts of violence. The child witness who, in addition to observing violence, also suffers personal injury may develop subsequent dissociative symptoms and multiple personality disorder, according to Putnam, Post, and Guroff (1984).

When violence results in death, and the community and newspapers sensationalize the surrounding events, the people involved may feel overwhelmed by an emotional battery of reactions including shame, hatred, and guilt (Shneidman, 1981, p. 350). The family can help or hinder the child in these circumstances, which all too often cause the family to close ranks and create a barrier of silence around the traumatic events (Eth & Pynoos, 1985, p. 177).

Summary

The nine-item Crisis Situation Rating Form (Table 1.2) facilitates a review of the components of the crisis situation, which have been discussed separately. This rating form can assist intake workers and others involved in forming a comprehensive overview of the crisis situation in a compact format. Rating of the crisis situation must combine with an assessment of individual and support system factors in order to obtain a full understanding of the crisis in all its complexity.

ASSESSMENT OF THE INDIVIDUAL CHILD IN CRISIS

"The susceptibility of any child to psychic trauma is a function of several parameters, including genetic, constitutional, and personality makeup; past life experiences; the state of mind and phase of development, the content and intensity of the event; and the family circumstances" (Eth & Pynoos, 1980, p. 286). Having

TABLE 1.2. Crisis Situation Rating Form: Webb

1. Severity of psychosocial stressors: DSM-III-R, axis IV
   Severity: Mild _____ Moderate _____ Severe _____
   Code (1–6)—Duration: Acute _____ or Enduring _____
   List stressors _____

2. Anticipated _____ or Sudden _____ crisis (check where appropriate)
   Amount of preparation _____

3. Single _____ or Recurring _____ crisis events
   (List discrete crisis events)
   a. _____   c. _____
   b. _____   d. _____

4. Solitary _____ or Shared _____ crisis experience
   Number of other individuals involved _____

5. Presence of loss factor
   a. Separation from family members (list relationship and length of separation) _____
      _____

   b. Death of family members (list relationship and cause of death) _____
      _____

   c. Loss of familiar environment (describe) _____
      _____

   d. Loss of familiar role/status (describe; temporary or permanent?) _____
      _____

   e. Loss of body part or function (describe, with prognosis) _____
      _____

6. Physical injury or pain (describe, with prognosis) _____
   _____

7. Presence of violence: verbal and/or physical
   a. Witnessed _____ Verbal _____ Physical _____
   b. Experienced _____ Verbal _____ Physical _____

8. Degree of life threat
   a. Personal (describe) _____
      _____

   b. To family members (describe, identifying relationship) _____
      _____

   c. To others (describe) _____
      _____

9. Other components of the crisis situation _____
   _____

Note. This form is one of a three-part crisis assessment, which also includes an assessment of individual and support system factors.

focused first on the content and intensity of the crisis situation, we turn now to a review of the individual factors that comprise the tripartite crisis assessment.

The standard diagnostic assessment of the child assumes knowledge of normal child development, child psychopathology, and of a diagnostic classification system such as DSM-III-R. According to Chethik (1989, p. 37), "the purpose of the assessment is to shed light on specific problematic areas and explicate the underlying forces that have created the difficulties," Mishne (1983, p. 25) clarifies further that "the objectives in an assessment are to determine how, and in what areas, the child differs from others of the same age; to assess the chronicity of the child's problems; to appraise areas of strength in the child and the child's family, and to aid in conceptualizing some hypothesis about possible contaminating factors—be they past, present, constitutional, or family induced."

In a situation in which a family seeks help for a child about a chronic problem, the assessment process typically consists of several interviews with the child and the parents (separately and in different combinations) in order to gather historical and observational data on which to formulate a dynamic assessment and treatment plan. Information from sources such as school psychologists, pediatricians, teachers, and child psychiatrists also contributes to the assessment, depending on the particular circumstances of each case. The completion of a thorough assessment of a child is a time-consuming process that frequently takes several weeks.

The Crisis Assessment

Situations in which the child and family are in crisis usually do not lend themselves to this methodical, thorough data collection process. According to Gilliland and James (1988, p. 35), "the crisis worker generally does not have time to either gather or analyze all the background and other assessment data that might normally be available under less stressful conditions. . . . [Therefore,] the ability to make a quick evaluation of the degree of client disequilibrium and immobility— and to be flexible enough to change one's evaluation as changing conditions warrant—is a priority skill."

The pressure on the crisis therapist is intense. If the family and/or child is disorganized and in panic, the therapist must not join with these feelings. The challenge to formulate an assessment in crisis permits some abbreviation of the assessment process, but the crisis therapist still must strive to understand the meaning of the crisis to the client. This usually requires a thorough exploration of both the precipitating event and past events that were similar.

In some instances this review process, which may take several hours, has a calming influence on the family, especially when they begin to connect their feelings about past losses and the present crisis. For example, a 5-year-old boy began bedwetting when his stepfather of 6 months was hospitalized suddenly for an appendectomy. In the assessment interview with the child, the play therapist set up a doll play situation in which the father doll had to have an operation. The child played out a fantasy scene in which the stepfather was going to die and in which the little boy doll was "bad" and had to be punished. It seemed probable that this child's unresolved feelings about the death of his biological father were being evoked in the current situation because of the stepfather's medical emergency. The child's mother readily understood this connection during the evaluation interview, and she later was able to reassure her son that the stepfather's operation would be minor and not fatal. This reassurance stressed the difference between the current, relatively minor medical procedure and the serious heart attack of the child's father, thus serving to further the child's understanding about his father's death.

The crisis assessment differs from the standard assessment by permitting the judgment of the therapist to determine the specific type and timing of information to be obtained. This judgment assumes a knowledge base that views the present crisis situation from the perspective of child development and the typical individual and family responses to stress. The crisis therapist works from the same knowledge base as other child therapists but, because of time constraints, applies this knowledge selectively.

For example, in a situation of a 6-year-old's refusal to separate from the mother following the brutal murder of a favorite babysitter, the crisis therapist focused the assessment inquiry on the child's caretaking history, past reactions to separations, and previous experiences with death. The parents' reactions to this horrible event also required exploration. The process of obtaining school and medical reports, on the other hand, was postponed in favor of dealing with the parents' urgent concerns about how much to tell the child about the murder and whether to take the child to the funeral.

Individual Factors in the Assessment of the Child in Crisis

Six factors comprise the assessment of the child. They may be recorded on the form Individual Factors in the Assessment of the Child in Crisis (Table 1.3), which affords a summarized overview of the child's development, level of functioning, and past experience with crisis. The specific individual factors are as follows:

- Age/developmental factors
- Precrisis adjustment
- Coping style/ego assessment
- Past experience with crisis
- Global assessment of functioning: DSM-III-R, axis V
- Specific meaning of crisis to the child

Age/Developmental Factors

The child's age at intake automatically places him or her into a specific developmental stage, with corresponding expectations about the child's probable level cognitive and moral development. For example, a 4-year-old whose 2-year-old

TABLE 1.3.   Individual Factors in the Assessment of the Child in Crisis: Webb

1. Age _____ years _____ months   Date of birth _____
                                                     Date of assessment _____
   a. Developmental stage   b. Cognitive level
       A. Freud _____   Piaget _____
       E. Erikson _____
   c. Moral development   d. Temperamental characteristics
       Kohlberg _____   Thomas and Chess _____

2. Precrisis adjustment
   a. Home (as reported by parents) Good _____ Fair _____ Poor _____
   b. School (as reported by parents and teachers) Good _____ Fair _____ Poor _____
   c. Interpersonal/peers Good _____ Fair _____ Poor _____
   d. Medical (as reported by parents and pediatrician)—describe serious illnesses, operations, and
      injuries since birth, with dates and outcome. _____
      _____
      _____
      Past or current use of medications _____
      _____

3. Coping style/ego assessment (as reported by parents and observed in interviews with child)
   a. Degree of anxiety High _____ Moderate _____ Low _____
   b. Ability to separate from parent High anxiety _____ Some anxiety _____
      No anxiety _____
   c. Child's ability to discuss "the problem–crisis situation" Good _____ Fair _____
      None _____
   d. Presence of symptoms (describe, including the extent to which these bind the anxiety) _____
      _____
      _____
   e. Defenses (list, indicating appropriateness) _____
      _____

4. Child's past experience with crises _____
   a. Previous losses (list, giving age) _____
      _____
   b. Major life transitions/adjustments (list, giving age) _____
      _____
      _____
   c. Past experience with violence _____
      _____
   d. Other (describe) _____

5. Global assessment of functioning: DSM-III-R, axis V
   Current _____ _____   Past year _____

6. Specific meaning of crisis to the child: Why is this crisis situation so difficult for *this* child at *this*
   time? (describe) _____
   _____
   _____

sibling drowned in the family pool is, at age 4, already struggling with the tasks of Erikson's (1963) stage of initiative versus guilt while cognitively explaining most occurrences in concrete, egocentric terms (Piaget, 1969) and operating on the principle of imminent justice, according to Kohlberg's (1964) view of moral development. The crisis of the sibling's death is superimposed on the child's normal developmental process. Mowbray (1988, p. 198) warns that "combined with young children's egocentrism, their primitive sense of moral development may have some serious consequences for how they react to traumatic events . . . if something bad happens, then *they* must have deserved it." In the crisis situation as described, the intake therapist with a solid knowledge of child development would consider that the child's presenting symptoms of nightmares were probably related to the child's anxiety connected to his distorted thoughts about blame and causality. This would, of course, have to be explored and confirmed in a play interview with the child. Although the child may need help in alleviating his feelings of guilt, the presenting symptoms "make sense" in the context of the child's age and developmental stage.

Anna Freud (1962, pp. 149–150) states that "the diagnostician's task is to ascertain where a given child stands on the developmental scale, whether his position is age-adequate, retarded, or precocious . . . and to what extent the observable internal and external circumstances and existent symptoms are interfering with the possibilities of future growth." In the previous example, the danger existed that the stress from "external circumstances" (the death of a sibling) would interfere with the child's developmental progress; therefore, therapy was indicated.

The therapist who understands Anna Freud's concepts of developmental lines (Freud, 1963) can use this framework for viewing childhood disturbances. Erikson's view of development as consisting of discrete tasks to be mastered during specific stages of development is another useful tool for the diagnostician, as is knowledge of Piaget's (1969) stages of cognitive development and Kohlberg's (1964) stages of moral development. The reader who is not familiar with these theories may consult the citations on the reference list at the end of the chapter.

Another individual factor that impacts on a child's reaction to stress and therefore merits assessment is the child's temperament. Thomas and Chess (1981) in several decades of research have isolated nine dimensions of temperament, which Wertlieb, Weigel, Springer, and Feldstein (1987, p. 242–243) analyzed for the relationship between stress and behavior. They concluded that temperament may moderate a person's reaction to stress and that it interacts with contextual factors such as social supports.

It seems logical that a child who was jumpy, distractible, and an intense reactor prior to a crisis would respond with an exaggeration of these behaviors when confronted with the stress of a crisis. Three distinct profiles of child temperament synthesize Thomas and Chess's nine dimensions of temperament. (Chess & Thomas, 1986); these are the difficult child, the easy child, and the slow-to-warm child. These general categories of temperamental style are determined from parental reports during the assessment process. More information regarding the interview scoring procedure for the assessment of temperament may be obtained from Chess and Thomas (1986; Thomas & Chess, 1981).

Precrisis Adjustment

Information about how the child had been getting along at home and at school and with peers prior to the crisis helps gauge the impact of the stress on the child. For example, the child who was unhappy, withdrawn, and performing poorly in school prior to a serious fire that destroyed his home might become seriously depressed in response to this crisis. However, another child who was functioning well at both home and school might respond to the same fire with irritability and loss of concentration in school but without major disorganization. Since we view stress as an onslaught that depletes emotional reserves, we need to estimate the precrisis status. Parents, and sometimes the child himself or herself, can truthfully answer the question, "How were you getting along at home (or in school or with friends) before this terrible thing happened? Would you say our adjustment was good, fair, or poor?" This can be indicated on the form, together with a record of any serious illnesses, operations, or injuries and the year of occurrence and the outcome. Use of medications also should be recorded.

Coping Style/Ego Assessment

This category also relates to the child's precrisis adjustment and temperamental style. It assesses, in particular, the child's current level of anxiety, ability to separate from the parent(s), ability to discuss the problem–crisis situation, and the presence of symptoms. It also indicates the child's use of defenses.

The ego development of the child is in a state of growth, and a complete ego assessment requires more information than generally is available to the crisis therapist. Usually, a complete ego assessment, including an analysis of object relations, drive regulation and control, and autonomous and synthetic functions of the ego, is not possible or appropriate when the child and family present themselves in a crisis situation. Furthermore, since crisis is characterized by disorganization, a tentative evaluation based on the history of previous functioning and selected information usually must suffice.

It is of great interest to note how completely the child's symptoms bind the anxiety and what defenses are utilized. Some typical defenses of children in situations of severe psychological trauma were reported by Pruett (1984, p. 611) as denial through fantasy, projection, passive aggression (turning against the self), hypochrondriasis, somatization, and acting out. When a 9-year-old depressed boy denied that he still felt troubled by his mother's suicide 2 years previously, it was difficult for the crisis therapist to challenge this defense until she began to refer to his school underachievement as "self-destructive" behavior. Usually, when individuals come for help in the midst of a crisis situation, they feel overwhelmed by stress and are open to help. In time, their defenses rigidify, and it is more difficult to challenge the denial effectively.

Child's Past Experience with Crisis

The experts differ about whether past experiences with crisis strengthen or weaken the individual's capacity to cope with subsequent crises. Parad and Parad (1990) and Kliman (1968) believe that success in coping with crises has an ego-strengthening effect insofar as new coping strategies have been learned, which build up the individual's "immunity" to future breakdown. On the other hand, Anthony (1986, p. 304) states that "we do not know whether a hard life steels the child . . . or sensitizes him to adversity." Referring to Terr's (1979, 1981) work following the kidnapping and burial of a school bus with 26 school children 5–14, Anthony (1986, p. 304) states that "an experience of overwhelming anxiety is *not* a potentially toughening experience but rather poses a significant and persistent burden on the child's personality development." Garmezy (1986, p. 386) comments that "we are very much in an early and less sophisticated stage of research on children's responsiveness to severe stress." This is because of the multiplicity of influencing variables, the difficulty of following children longitudinally, and the problems in attempting to utilize longitudinal experimental designs. Nonetheless, children continue to be exposed to a variety of crisis situations, and we must continue with our evaluation and treatment efforts, despite the fact that these may be less precise than we would like.

As a guide to understanding a child's possible vulnerability to present and future crises, the assessment form identifying individual factors provides an opportunity to record the child's past experience with loss, with violence, and with major life transitions. Allan and Anderson (1986, p. 144), reviewing a major study by Sandler and Ramsay (1980), state that "loss events (e.g., death of a parent, sibling, or friend; divorce and separation) were the main eliciters of crisis reactions in children, followed by family troubles (e.g., abuse, neglect, loss of job). Lower on the scale were primary environmental changes (e.g., moving, attending a new school, or when mother begins work), sibling difficulties, physical harm (e.g., illness, accidents, and violence), and disasters (e.g., fire, flood, and earthquakes)." A review of the child's history helps the crisis therapist understand and evaluate the child's current level of anxiety.

Global Assessment of Functioning: DSM-III-R, Axis V

The Global Assessment of Functioning Scale (GAF) rates an individual's overall psychological, social, and occupational functioning at the time of the evaluation and during the previous year. The rating scale assumes a hypothetical continuum of mental health–illness from a rank of 90, indicating good functioning in all areas, to 1, "expectation of death." See DSM-III-R (American Psychiatric Association, 1987, pp. 12, 20) for a description of the scale and how to use it.

Ratings for two time periods, current and past year, help indicate the need for treatment based on comparison between the two. The assessment of highest level of functioning during the past year gives an indication of the prognosis, since most individuals return to their precrisis level of functioning following crisis resolution.

Specific Meaning of Crisis to the Child

Just as an intake worker often questions, "Why is the client coming for help *now*, rather than a month or a year ago?" the crisis therapist must try to understand what it is about *this* particular crisis situation that makes it intolerable for this particular child at this particular time. Obviously, some crisis events are so horrendous that an extreme reaction is appropriate. Nonetheless, every individual will attach *personal* meaning to the horrible event, and this needs to be explored in order for treatment efforts to focus appropriately.

In a shared disaster experience, for example, such as destruction of an apartment complex by fire, one child may be consumed by guilt because he escaped unharmed while his brother suffered a broken leg and smoke inhalation. An important component of the child's guilt was the fact that the boys had been fighting just before the fire alarm went off and the injured boy accused his brother of being selfish. After the fire, the uninjured 7-year-old felt convinced that his brother was right and that if he had done "the right thing," he might have saved his brother from injury.

Questions that help uncover the hidden meaning of a crisis to the individual child are the following:

- Do you remember what you were doing just before (the crisis event) happened?
- Do you think there is anything that you could have done to have avoided (the crisis event)?
- What have you been thinking about most since (the crisis event) happened?

Sometimes the child can clarify the personal meaning of the crisis. In the example of the brothers in the fire, the worker might state to the uninjured boy: "I wonder if maybe you're worrying about not having saved your brother, and about why he was hurt and you were not." When the conflict is close enough to the surface, the child may acknowledge it openly. Other times, it is not possible or desirable to seek confirmation, since this might be too threatening. Whether openly acknowledged by the client or not, the underlying meaning of the crisis must be understood by the crisis therapist so that treatment goals can be appropriately established.

FACTORS IN THE SUPPORT SYSTEM

A crisis situation occurs to a specific individual in the context of his or her social and physical environment. We now consider some of the features of the surrounding environment that either help or hinder the individual in crisis. Assessment of the support system is particularly important when dealing with children in crisis, because their youth and dependency make them especially reliant on others to assist them.

Nuclear and Extended Family

The genogram is the starting point for identifying all the family members who potentially can provide support to the child in crisis. In the process of creating the three-generation genogram with the family at the time of intake, the crisis therapist learns not only the names of family members but also their geographic location, the frequency of contact with each member, and something about the quality of the various relationships. It is helpful to ask in completing the genogram: "Of all these various family members, which ones do you consider most important to the child?" The response sometimes reveals the influence of an aunt or uncle in the child's life, which might not otherwise be known.

The demographic characteristics (e.g., age, social class, level of education) of the family and their cultural characteristics often impact on the particular way in which they respond in crisis. For example, Gleser, Green, and Winget (1981) found that better-educated people seem to make a better adjustment following a disaster, and Lindy, Grace, and Green (1981) pointed out that the cultural backgrounds of different groups influence the way a crisis event is perceived and the nature of the response.

These variables are complex and difficult to evaluate. For example, better-educated people may have more financial resources that may contribute to their improved response. Anthropologists have been attempting for several decades to identify specific values typical of distinct cultural groups and the impact of these values on the family system (Kluckholm, 1958; Spiegel, 1982; McGoldrick, 1982). McGoldrick states categorically that "the language and customs of a culture will influence whether or not a symptom is labeled a problem . . . [and that] problems (whether physical or mental) can be neither diagnosed nor treated without understanding the frame of reference of the person seeking help as well as that of the helper (McGoldrick, 1982, p. 6). Thus, an assessment must identify and weigh the significance of cultural factors related to the family's reaction to the crisis situation.

Freud and Burlingham (1943) commented on the relevance of the parents' reactions in a shared traumatic situation to the nature of the child's response. Benedek (1985), however, recognizes that this places a great burden on parents who, themselves, may be traumatized. Even in a noncrisis situation, "financial constraints, absorption in professional development, moves, or deaths of significant relatives can . . . significantly encroach on the adult's available energy to parent effectively" (Chethik, 1989, p. 33). Thus, we identify available resources besides parents in the support system of the child in crisis.

School, Friends, and Community Supports

The Eco-Map (Hartman, 1978) provides a diagrammatic tool for illustrating the available components of supports surrounding a family or household (see Figure

1.2). This is an excellent means for analyzing potential resources in a child's network of friends, church, school, health care, and other institutions. The Beatles song refers to getting by with a little help from their friends; Benedek (1985) stresses the importance of significant, caring human relationships in situations where the child and parents have been traumatized together. It is not surprising that more supportive environments tend to be associated with a better adjustment to stress (Green et al., 1985). However, individual characteristics ultimately may determine how well available supports are utilized. For example, an individual who is in a vulnerable state as a result of an "overdose" of past crises may be unable to cope even when excellent supports are available.

Summary

The complete crisis assessment analyzes the interaction among the various components of the tripartite model: the nature of the crisis situation, individual factors, and factors in the support system. The assessment tools useful for this purpose are the crisis situation rating form, the individual factors in the assessment of the child in crisis form, plus the genogram and Eco-Map. A complete crisis assessment includes an abundance of data that these four assessment tools organize and summarize in a compact, useful format.

TERMINOLOGY UPDATE: DISTINCTIONS BETWEEN "CRISIS" AND "POSTTRAUMATIC STRESS RESPONSE"

The selection of the term "crisis" rather than "trauma" for the title of this book reflects the editor's deliberate intent to focus on crisis situations that may or may not result in subsequent symptom formation. At the beginning of this chapter, I presented a definition of crisis in terms of "an intolerable difficulty" with "the *potential* (my emphasis) to cause severe affective, cognitive, and behavioral malfunctioning." Thus, crisis intervention not only brings with it the opportunity for helping the troubled individual enhance his or her coping ability, it accomplishes this in a timely fashion, *before* anxiety and conflict result in symptom formation.

Crisis intervention services are usually short term because most crises, by their very nature, are time limited. "A minimum of therapeutic intervention during the brief crisis period can often produce a maximum therapeutic effect through the use of supportive social resources and focused treatment techniques" (Parad & Parad, 1990, p. 9).

In discussing crisis, we often refer to stress overload. This overload causes distress to the individual, which, if not relieved, may lead to a psychiatric disorder such as posttraumatic stress disorder (PTSD). McFarlane (1990, p. 70) states that "the degree of distress caused by an event is the major factor determining the probability of the onset of psychiatric disorder. Therefore, a crisis intervention approach that aims to lessen the distress of traumatized people and bolsters their coping strategies is likely to be useful for the primary prevention of PTSD."

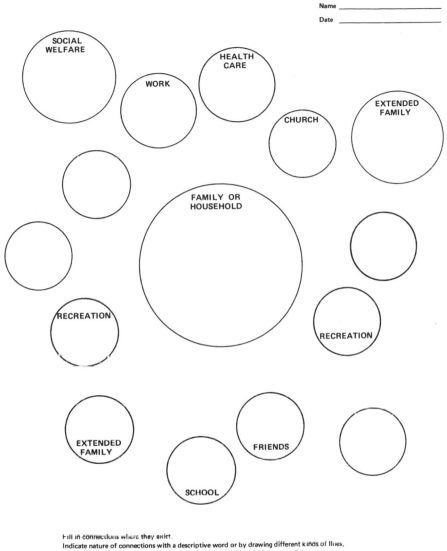

Name _____

Date _____

Fill in connections where they exist.
Indicate nature of connections with a descriptive word or by drawing different kinds of lines,
————— for strong, — — — — — for tenuous, +++++++ for stressful.
Draw arrows along lines to signify flow of energy, resources, etc. →→→
Identify significant people and fill in empty circles as needed.

FIGURE 1.2. Eco-Map. From "Diagrammatic Assessment of Family Relationships" by A. Hartman, 1978, *Social Casework, 59,* 465–476. Copyright 1978 by Family Service Association of America. Reprinted by permission.

TABLE 1.4.   DSM-III-R Diagnostic Criteria for Posttraumatic Stress Disorder

A. The person has experienced an event that is outside the range of usual human experience and that would be markedly distressing to almost anyone, e.g., serious threat to one's life or physical integrity; serious threat or harm to one's children, spouse, or other close relatives and friends; sudden destruction of one's home or community; or seeing another person who has recently been, or is being, seriously injured or killed as the result of an accident or physical violence.

B. The traumatic event is persistently reexperienced in at least one of the following ways:

   (1) recurrent and intrusive distressing recollections of the event (in young children, repetitive play in which themes or aspects of the trauma are expressed)

   (2) recurrent distressing dreams of the event

   (3) sudden acting or feeling as if the traumatic event were recurring (includes a sense of reliving the experience, illusions, hallucinations, and dissociative [flashback] episodes, even those that occur upon awakening or when intoxicated)

   (4) intense psychological distress at exposure to events that symbolize or resemble an aspect of the traumatic event, including anniversaries of the trauma

C. Persistent avoidance of stimuli associated with the trauma or numbing of general responsiveness (not present before the trauma), as indicated by at least three of the following:

   (1) efforts to avoid thoughts or feelings associated with the trauma

   (2) efforts to avoid activities or situations that arouse recollections of the trauma

   (3) inability to recall an important aspect of the trauma (psychogenic amnesia)

   (4) markedly diminished interest in significant activities (in young children, loss of recently acquired developmental skills such as toilet training or language skills)

   (5) feeling of detachment or estrangement from others

   (6) restricted range of affect, e.g., unable to have loving feelings

   (7) sense of a foreshortened future, e.g., does not expect to have a career, marriage, or children, or a long life

D. Persistent symptoms of increased arousal (not present before the trauma), as indicated by at least two of the following:

   (1) difficulty falling or staying asleep

   (2) irritability or outbursts of anger

   (3) difficulty concentrating

   (4) hypervigilance

   (5) exaggerated startle response

   (6) physiologic reactivity upon exposure to events that symbolize or resemble an aspect of the traumatic event (e.g., a woman who was raped in an elevator breaks out in a sweat when entering any elevator)

E. Duration of the disturbance (symptoms in B, C, and D) of at least one month.

   Specify delayed onset if the onset of symptoms was at least six months after the trauma.

Note. From the *Diagnostic and Statistical Manual of Mental Disorders* (3rd ed., rev., pp. 250-251) by the American Psychiatric Association, 1987, Washington, DC: Author. Copyright 1987 by the American Psychiatric Association. Reprinted by permission.

The concept of PTSD was first included in the third edition of the *Diagnostic and Statistical Manual of Mental Disorders* (DSM-III) in 1980 to describe "characteristic symptoms following a psychologically traumatic event that is generally outside the range of usual human experience. The characteristic symptoms involve reexperiencing the traumatic event; numbing of responsiveness to, or reduced involvement with, the external world; and a variety of autonomic, dysphoric or cognitive symptoms" (American Psychiatric Association, 1980, p. 236). According to DSM-III, "the disorder can occur at any age, including during childhood (American Psychiatric Association, 1980, p. 237).

Table 1.4 lists the diagnostic criteria for PTSD as these have been more fully elaborated in the 1987 revision (DSM-III-R; American Psychiatric Association, 1987). It is noted that younger children may experience dreams of monsters and of other threats, rather than distressing dreams that replicate the traumatic event. Also, DSM-III-R points out that young children may relive the trauma "in action, through repetitive play, without the sense that they are reliving the past," and they may also "exhibit various physical symptoms, such as stomachaches and headaches," as part of their response to trauma (American Psychiatric Association, 1987, p. 249).

Critics of the PTSD concept point out that "the distinctions between persons with the normal stress response and those with PTSD are blurred, particularly soon after the event" (McFarlane, 1990, p. 71). Trimble (1985, p. 12) states that "the concept that the traumatic event should be outside the range of usual human experience is limiting." With regard to the applicability of the concept to children, Garmezy (1968, p. 391) cautions against "assigning to children popular diagnostic labels used with adults. Posttraumatic stress disorder may not be a wholly appropriate diagnosis for children's anxiety reactions to stress."

For all of these reasons, and especially for its wider applicability and possibilities for primary and secondary prevention, I prefer the crisis intervention treatment approach and the terminology "crisis," rather than "trauma," in dealing with children under extreme stress.

REFERENCES

Allan, J., & Anderson, E. (1986). Children and crises: A classroom guidance approach *Elementary School Guidance and Counseling, 21*(2), 143–149.

American Psychiatric Association. (1980). *Diagnostic and statistical manual of mental disorders* (3rd ed.). Washington, DC: Author.

American Psychiatric Association. (1987). *Diagnostic and statistical manual of mental disorders* (3rd ed., rev.). Washington, DC: Author.

Anthony, E. J. (1986). Children's reactions to severe stress. *Journal of the American Academy of Child Psychiatry, 25*, 299–305.

Arkin, A. M. (1974). Notes on anticipatory grief. In B. Schoenberg, A. C. Carr, A. H. Kutscher, D. Peretz, & I. K. Goldberg (Eds.), *Anticipatory grief* (pp. 10–13). New York: Columbia University Press.

Benedek, E. P. (1985). Children and psychic trauma: A brief review of contemporary thinking. In S. Eth & R. S. Pynoos (Eds.) *Post-traumatic stress disorder in children* (pp. 3–16). Washington, DC: American Psychiatric Press.

Bowlby, J. (1969). *Attachment and loss: Vol. 1. Attachment.* London: Hogarth Press.

Chess, S., & Thomas, A. (1986). *Temperament in clinical practice.* New York: Guilford Press.

Chethik, M. (1989). *Techniques of child therapy.* New York: Guilford Press.

Erikson, E. H. (1963). *Childhood and society.* New York; W. W. Norton.

Eth, S., & Pynoos, R. S. (1980). Psychiatric intervention with children traumatized by violence. In D. H. Schetky & E. P. Benedek (Eds.), *Child psychiatry and the law* (pp. 285-309). New York: Brunner/Mazel.

Eth, S., & Pynoos, R. S. (1985). Interaction of trauma and grief in childhood. In S. Eth & R. S. Pynoos (Eds.), *Post-traumatic stress disorder in children* (pp. 171-186). Washington, DC: American Psychiatric Press.

Fassler, J. (1987). *Helping children cope: Mastering stress through books and stories.* New York: Free Press.

Freud, A. (1962). Assessment of childhood disturbances. *Psychoanalytic Study of the Child, 17,* 149-158.

Freud, A. (1963). The concept of developmental lines. *Psychoanalytic Study of the Child, 18,* 245-265.

Freud, A. (1965). *Normality and pathology in childhood.* New York: International Universities Press.

Freud, A., & Burlingham. D. T. (1943). *War and children.* London: Medical War Books.

Garmezy, N. (1986). Children under severe stress: Critique and commentary. *Journal of the Academy of Child Psychiatry, 25,* 384-392.

Gilliland, B. E., & James, R. K. (1988). *Crisis intervention strategies.* Pacific Grove, CA: Brooks/Cole.

Gleser, G. C., Green, B. L., & Winget, C. N. (1981). *Prolonged psychosocial effects of disaster: A study of Buffalo Creek.* New York: Academic Press.

Golan, N. (1978). *Treatment in crisis situations.* New York: Free Press.

Green, B. L., Wilson, J. P., & Lindy, J. D. (1985). Conceptualizing post-traumatic stress disorder: A psychosocial framework. In C. R. Figley (Ed.), *Trauma and its wake: The study and treatment of post-traumatic stress disorder* (pp. 53-69). New York: Brunner/Mazel.

Hartman, A. (1978). Diagrammatic assessment of family relationships. *Social Casework, 59,* 465-476.

Janis, I. L. (1977). Adaptive personality changes. In A. Monat & R. S. Lazarus (Eds.), *Stress and coping* (pp. 272-284). New York: Columbia University Press.

Kliman, G. (1968). *Psychological emergencies of childhood.* New York: Grune & Stratton.

Kluckhohn, F. R. (1958). Variations in basic values of family systems. In N. W. Bell & E. F. Vogel (Eds.), *A modern introduction to the family* (pp. 319-330). New York: Free Press.

Kohlberg, L. (1964). Development of moral character and moral ideology. In M. L. Hoffman & L. W. Hoffman (Eds.), *Review of child development* (Vol. 1, pp. 383-431). New York: Russell Sage Foundation.

Lindy, J. D., Grace, M. C., & Green, B. L. (1981). Survivors: Outreach to a reluctant population. *American Journal of Orthopsychiatry, 51,* 468-478.

McFarlane, A. C. (1990). Post-traumatic stress syndrome revisited. In H. J. Parad & L. G. Parad (Eds.), *Crisis intervention book 2: The practitioner's sourcebook for brief therapy* (pp. 69-92). Milwaukee: Family Service America.

McGoldrick, M. (1982). Ethnicity and family therapy: An overview. In M. McGoldrick, J. K. Pearce, & J. Giordano (Eds.), *Ethnicity and family therapy* (pp. 3-30). New York: Guilford Press.

Mishne, J. M. (1983). *Clinical work with children.* New York: Free Press.

Mowbray, C. T. (1988). Post-traumatic therapy for children who are victims of violence. In F. M. Ochberg (Ed.) *Post-traumatic therapy and victims of violence* (pp. 196-212). New York: Brunner/Mazel.

Parad, H. J., & Parad, L. G. (1990) (Eds.) *Crisis intervention book 2: The practitioner's sourcebook for brief therapy.* Milwaukee: Family Service America.

Piaget, J. (1969). *The psychology of the child.* New York: Basic Books.

Pruett, K. D. (1984). A chronology of defensive adaptations to severe psychological trauma. *Psychoanalytic Study of the Child, 39,* 591-612.

Putnam, F. W., Post, R. M., & Guroff, J. J. (1984). *One hundred cases of multiple personality disorder.* Paper presented at the annual meeting of the American Psychiatric Association, Los Angeles.

Pynoos, R. S., & Eth, S. (1985). Children traumatized by witnessing acts of personal violence. In S. Eth &

R. S. Pynoos (Eds.), *Post-traumatic stress disorder in children* (pp. 19-43). Washington, DC: American Psychiatric Press.

Sandler, I. R., & Ramsay, T. B. (1980). Dimensional analysis of children's stressful life events. *American Journal of Community Psychology. 8*, 285-302.

Selye, H. (1978). *The stress of life.* New York: McGraw-Hill.

Shneidman, E. S. (1981). Postvention: The care of the bereaved. *Suicide and Life-Threatening Behavior,* 11, 349-359.

Spiegel, J. (1982). An ecological model of ethnic families. In M. McGoldrick, J. K. Pearce, & J. Giordano (Eds.), *Ethnicity and family therapy* (pp. 32-51). New York: Guilford Press.

Star, B. (1980). Patterns in family violence. *Social Casework, 61*(6), 339-343.

Terr, L. (1979). Children of Chowchilla. *Psychoanalytic Study of the Child, 34,* 547-623.

Terr, L. (1981). Forbidden games: Post-traumatic child's play. *Journal of the American Academy of Child Psychiatry, 20,* 741-759.

Thomas, A., & Chess, S. (1981). The role of temperament in the contributions of individuals to their development. In R. M. Lerner & N. A. Busch-Rossnagel (Eds.), *Individuals as producers of their development* (pp. 231-254). New York: Academic Press.

Trimble, M. R. (1985). Post-traumatic-stress disorder: History of a concept. In C. R. Figley (Ed.), *Trauma and its wake: The study and treatment of post-traumatic stress disorder* (pp. 5-14). New York: Brunner/Mazel.

Wertlieb, D., Weigel, C., Springer, T., & Feldstein, M. (1987). Temperament as a moderator of children's stressful experiences. *American Journal of Orthopsychiatry, 57*(2), 234-245.

CHAPTER 2

Play Therapy Crisis Intervention with Children

NANCY BOYD WEBB

Play therapy ingeniously undertakes the hard work of child psychotherapy in the appealing guise of play. Since children behave and think differently from adults, the approach to working with them must reflect this difference. Play therapy has adapted its methods to accommodate to the world of childhood, using the medium of play as the means for communicating symbolically with the child.

Few children willingly admit that they have "problems," even when their parents are at their wits' ends because of the child's nightmares, shyness, or aggressive behavior. These children may agree to come for therapy only because they have no other recourse in the face of their parents' or teachers' complaints about their behavior. Once in the therapist's office, however, these children, and the small number who may initially admit to their own fears or unhappiness, cannot endure a discussion about their "problem" with a strange adult. The well-meaning but inexperienced therapist who asks a youngster the typical open-ended question appropriate for adults—"So tell me about what brings you here today"—had better be prepared for a blank stare, a shrug of the shoulders, or, at best, "My mother said you wanted to talk to me!" If it is hard for adults to seek help and discuss their emotional distress in therapy, how much more so is it for children! Fortunately, play therapy techniques come to the rescue, providing initial enticement for engaging the child, and ongoing appeal during the process of treatment.

Play has been used in child therapy since the 1920s, when Anna Freud (1926/1946) employed games and toys as a way to build a relationship with her child patients. Another child analyst, Melanie Klein (1932), used the child's play as the basis for interpretations to the child. Other play therapy pioneers include David Levy (1938), who helped the child recreate a traumatic event through a structured play format, and Frederick Allen (1942), Claude Moustakas (1959), and Virginia Axline (1947), all of whom emphasized the power of the therapeutic relationship in conjunction with the child's natural growth process as key to helping the child individuate and develop basic self-esteem (positive regard). Achievement of these goals in nondirective play therapy occurs through recognition of the child's feelings as expressed in the play and through the therapist's belief in the child's strengths and potential for growth and change.

The considerable differences between the theoretical perspectives and working procedures of these early play therapists have been reviewed elsewhere (James, 1977; Mishne, 1983; Schaefer & O'Connor, 1983; Woltmann, 1955) and are not repeated here. It is remarkable that, despite their differences, these therapists all recognized the unique meaning of play to children and the importance of understanding the symbolism of the child's play language. The operating assumption is that "through play the child will reveal meaningful information regarding his or her emotional problems" (Johnson, Rasbury, & Siegel, 1986, p. 8).

Bettelheim (1987, p. 35) comments that "the child's play is motivated by inner processes, desires, problems, and anxieties . . . play is the royal road to the child's conscious and unconscious inner world; if we want to understand his inner world and help him with it, we must learn to walk this road."

DEFINITION AND PURPOSES OF PLAY THERAPY

What Is Play Therapy?

Definition

Play therapy is a psychotherapeutic method, based on psychodynamic and developmental principles, intended to help relieve the emotional distress of young children through a variety of imaginative and expressive play materials such as puppets, dolls, clay, board games, art materials, and miniature objects. "The assumption is that children will express and work through emotional conflicts . . . within the metaphor of play" (Reid, 1986, p. 261). The play therapist not only helps bring about relief of clinical symptoms (important as this may be to parents and child) but also works toward removal of impediments to the child's continuing development so that the prospects for the child's future growth are enhanced (Enzer, 1988).

An example of these dual play therapy goals is helping a 10-year-old child with a sleep disturbance by encouraging her to plan a number of self-soothing activities that she could employ other than going into her parents' bedroom when she wakes up in the middle of the night. The successful outcome in this case (which also employed a series of planned rewards from the parents when the child did not disturb them) resulted not only in cessation of the nighttime waking but also in an increase in the child's confidence about her ability to deal successfully with her internal distress. The case illustrates both symptom alleviation and enhancement of coping abilities. The play therapy with this girl utilized art techniques to help her externalize her fears on paper and portray her anticipated positive mood at a future time when she would no longer feel afraid.

In ways that will become clear in the various detailed case examples in this book, the *therapy* of play therapy involves far more than merely playing with the

child. Through the interpersonal interactions with the therapist, the child experiences catharsis, reduction of troublesome affects, redirection of impulses, and a
corrective emotional experience (Enzer, 1988). In the safety of the permissive
environment of the playroom, the child can express his or her feelings in fantasy,
thus permitting eventual working through and mastery (Reid, 1986), which then
may carry over to the child's everyday life. Chethik (1989, pp. 48–49) points out
that "play, in itself, will not ordinarily produce changes in the therapist's office
any more than it will in the schoolyard. [It is] the therapist's interventions and
utilizations of the play [that] are critical."

Balance between Verbal and Play Interactions

Many of the therapist's interactions are verbal as well as behavioral (play).
Indeed, Enzer (1988) believes that assisting the child toward greater verbalization is one of the primary goals of play therapy. Obviously, the child's ability to
verbalize depends on his or her age and level of cognitive development. Erikson
(quoted by Woltmann, 1955/1964, p. 31) states that "the child uses play to make
up for defeats, sufferings, and frustratons, *especially resulting from . . . limited
use of language*" (my emphasis). Winnicott (1971, p. 39) reminds us that "the
child does not usually possess the command of language that can convey the
infinite subtleties that are to be found in play." Play, however, must never in play
therapy become an end unto itself. I repeatedly instruct child therapy interns and
beginning child therapists that when the child can talk about his or her anxieties,
we should encourage this verbalization. Playing serves as a safe refuge when
anxiety mounts and the child needs to retreat from verbalized connections to his
or her own life. Play also frequently serves as the means for establishing the
therapeutic relationship. My usual procedure in the initial session with a child is
to say that I am a doctor who helps children and families with their troubles and
their worries and that *"sometimes we talk and sometimes we play."* This gives
the child permission to use verbalization according to his or her own ability and
level of comfort.
      Bettelheim (1977, pp. 56–57) warns about interpretation from the symbol-
ism of the play (fairy tale) to the child's own life, since he believes that making
the child aware of the meaning behind the play will create confusion and deprive
the child of a needed symbolic (fantasy) outlet. It has been my experience, as
illustrated in the Michael case (Chapter 3), that work in a displaced fashion (e.g.,
through family dolls) can bring symptom relief without any interpretation from
the play to the child's life. This is especially true in work with preschool-age children.
      By late latency, the child's verbal communication skills have usually in-
creased, and there is less reliance on symbolic play (Sarnoff, 1987). Kaplan in
Chapter 18 demonstrates the shifting balance among verbalization, large muscle
play activity (Nerf ball and skateboard), and doodling in the case of an 11-year-old
boy whose anxicty in discussions about his illness propelled him away from

verbalization in preference for physical activities that permitted him to deny the possible serious implications of his blood disorder.

Up to What Age Is Play Therapy Appropriate?

As the preceding discussion suggests, play therapy is an appropriate treatment modality through late latency, with the likelihood that the balance between verbal and play interactions will shift gradually through years. Play usually dominates over verbalization in the preschool years, whereas the opposite situation will probably prevail as the child approaches puberty.

There is no hard and fast rule about this. Art techniques, for example, may be used as a medium for therapy throughout the life span, as can some board games and visualization techniques. On the other hand, some play therapy materials such as dolls may be spurned by latency-age boys who consider them "girls' toys," whereas these same boys will engage in puppet play with animal puppets (see Doyle & Stoop's case of 10-year-old Randy, Chapter 6, who constructed an elaborate cartoon lifeline, utilizing animal puppets and drawings).

Terr (1989) notes that "traumatized youngsters appear to indulge in play at much older ages than do nontraumatized youngsters." Therefore, the opportunity to play must be available to facilitate the symbolic expression of experiences that are too horrible to verbalize. This may have been an operating factor in the Randy case (Doyle & Stoop, Chapter 6). The sensitive therapist observes the child for clues as to his or her play preferences while always seeking to help the child toward the maximum level of articulation to which he or she is capable.

Purpose of Play Therapy

The purpose of play therapy is to help troubled children through the medium of play in the context of a therapeutic relationship. The therapist's conscious direction of the child's play activity gives it purpose, meaning, and value in treatment, according to Amster (1943).

Amster outlines the following six purposes served by play therapy:

1. Aids diagnostic understanding
2. Helps establish the treatment relationship
3. Provides a medium for working through defenses and handling anxieties
4. Assists in the verbalization of feelings
5. Helps the child act out unconscious material and relieve the accompanying tensions
6. Enlarges the child's play interests for eventual use outside of therapy

Each child's situation is unique, and, therefore, the work with individual children will have different emphases, depending on the specific assessment of the child's problem situation. Since the focus of this book is on play therapy with children in *crises*, the discussion that follows focuses on the special play therapy approaches that deal with traumatized children.

PLAY THERAPY IN CRISIS SITUATIONS

Erikson viewed play as the child's means of achieving mastery over traumatic experiences (1950/1964, p. 3). The make-believe element, according to Woltmann (1955/1964, p. 24), "eliminates guilt feelings which would appear if action could result in real harm and damage and enables the child to be victorious over forces otherwise above his reach and capacity." Thus, the child who has been subjected to painful medical procedures may earnestly play out giving injections and other treatments in doll play.

In crisis situations, the child has felt helpless and afraid. Through replay of the crisis experience the child transforms the passivity and impotence he or she experienced into activity and power. Instead of being the hurting patient, he becomes the administrator of pain, in fantasy. Mishne (1983, p. 272) comments that "traumatic experiences are repeated to achieve *belated* mastery . . . the painful tension of the original trauma is relived, under somewhat more favorable conditions (e.g., in play) . . . that is under the control of the child." Quoting Walder (1933), Mishne (1983, p. 273) elaborates that "when an event is too difficult or large to assimilate immediately, it must be chewed again and again; in this way, a passively experienced event is converted into an actively experienced one." Just as the mourning adult needs to review over and over the details surrounding the death of a loved one, a traumatized child may repeatedly seek to reconstruct a crisis experience symbolically through play.

However, when posttraumatic play takes the form of secretive, monotonous, ritualized play, it may fail to relieve the child. Terr (1983) describes this type of play in children who were overwhelmed with anxiety following a sudden and intense traumatic experience such as that experienced by 23 children in Chowchilla, California, who were kidnapped and buried for 16 hours in a schoolbus. Based on her work with these children, and on a review of the literature, Terr (1983) believes that the severely traumatized child needs to *verbalize* as well as to play. She recommends a form of child psychotherapy using preset or prearranged play in which the therapist deliberately encourages the child to reenact the trauma by providing the child with play materials suggestive of the traumatic experience. This psychotherapeutic reconstruction includes a verbal review of the traumatic experience in which the therapist helps the child obtain relief from the guilt and fear associated with the trauma. Examples of present or prearranged play in this book are Strand's work with a victim of sexual abuse (Chapter 4) and Bevin's work with a 9-year-old refugee (Chapter 5).

David Levy's (1938, 1939) early work with traumatized children, which he termed "release therapy," "abreaction therapy," and "control play," represents landmark treatment using preset or prearranged play. Unlike Terr's (1983) approach, Levy did not use verbalization, nor did he interpret the child's feelings during the play. "In release therapy the interpretive function of the therapist is reduced to a minimum and may be absent, especially in children age 2, 3, and 4" (Levy, 1939, p. 716). Terr believes that Levy's abreactive treatment remains currently applicable and valid in situations containing a "stressful, if not 'traumatic' effect" (Terr, 1983, p. 314). This may characterize my case of the 4-year-old child witness of parental violence (Chapter 3) who needed to abreact repeated replay of his experience through family doll play reenactment but who resisted "corrective denouement" play (Terr, 1983), which would have allowed me to change his violent story ending. The child's symptom relief in this case occurred primarily through abreaction and gradual mastery of the associated anxiety.

RANGE OF PLAY THERAPY METHODS

Whether the treatment philosophy of the therapist results in a nondirective or a prearranged play therapy approach, the well-trained play therapist employs a variety of play therapy materials and techniques in working with children in crisis. Although few playrooms are equipped with *all* of the play therapy materials listed below and described in case examples in the book, it is important that a variety of choices be available to the child. The therapist must be sufficiently familiar with the materials to maintain focus on the child and his or her communication through the play material.

The discussion that follows reviews some of the major play therapy methods, with suggestions about necessary materials.

Art Techniques

The graphic and plastic arts have broad application and appeal to children and adults of all ages. Rubin (1984, pp. 269–273) states: "it is the peculiar power of art to be able to symbolize not only intrapsychic events, but interpersonal ones as well, and to collapse multileveled or sequential happenings into a single visual statement . . . the art therapist combines both an intuitive, inspired approach with a rational analytic one, alternating and integrating them in tune with the needs of the situation."

There are numerous examples in this book of play therapy using art techniques. Both the immature "scribble" drawings of a preschooler's nightmare (Saravay, Chapter 9) and the elaborate cartoon lifeline of a 10-year-old boy (Doyle & Stoop, Chapter 6) illustrate visual portrayals of feelings that neither child could adequately express verbally. Talking about the drawings permits the feelings to gradually enter conscious awareness, and the child is relieved of the pressure to continue repress them.

In the *Draw-a-Person* and *Draw-Your-Family* exercises (DiLeo, 1973), the play therapist learns about the child's perceptions regarding his or her own body as well as about family relationships. When the child has a physical illness, he may convey this through a self-portrait even when he verbally denies the significance of the diagnosis (see the case example in Goodman, Chapter 16). Robinson's analysis of a 10-year-old's family drawing (Chapter 11) provided important diagnostic clues regarding the boy's sense of impending disaster, in which no family members were portrayed by the child in a protective role.

Winnicott's (1971) *"squiggle technique"* is an excellent ice breaker with children who claim they cannot draw. In this situation the therapist tells the child that no drawing ability is necessary, since the game involves taking turns making pictures out of the previous person's scribble. Employed as a projective technique, the child subsequently can be asked to select his or her favorite squiggle drawing in a series and then to make up a story about it. Hofmann and Rogers (Chapter 19) demonstrate the use of group squiggles with children in the setting of a shelter following the Santa Cruz earthquake.

Modeling clay provides a safe outlet for aggressive feelings, since the clay often requires pounding, poking, squeezing, and cutting to achieve the form the child desires. This modality lends itself to family and group play as well as individual therapy, since each member may create an individual project or the group may work on a joint product (Oaklander, 1988).

Hurley (Chapter 12) illustrates a young girl's anxious use of Plasticine following her father's suicide by gunshot. The child created several heads that corresponded to the members of her family; then she several times mutilated one head and then anxiously turned to other play activities. She was not ready to *talk* about her father's death, but she was expressing her feelings in her play.

Soft Play-Doh is easier for younger children to handle than is modeling clay, and its greater malleability lends it to being squished between the fingers, thus offering an additional sensory experience.

Suggested Art Supplies

- Colored markers; crayons; Cray-Pas
- Paper of different colors; construction paper (full color range)
- Scissors; glue; paste; Scotch tape; stapler
- Water colors; finger paints
- Doilies; magazines for cutting pictures for collage
- Modeling clay (assorted colors), Play-Doh (Kenner), rolling pins, cookie cutters, and assorted modeling tools

Doll Play

This method has particular appeal to preschool children of both sexes and to latency-age girls. Latency-age boys frequently choose to play with army men or soliders, together with trucks and assorted army equipment (see Robinson's case example in Chapter 11).

Miniature bendable family dolls lend themselves to reenactment of exchanges the child has witnessed in his or her own family. The therapist can learn a great deal from watching and listening to the child's play with the family dolls. Often the preschool child unabashedly names the family dolls to correspond with his or her own family members and/or selects their hair color and size to match those in his or her own family. In situations like these, as in my work with Michael (Chapter 3), the child's identification with the family doll play seems indisputable.

Anatomically correct dolls are now routinely used in the assessment of sexual abuse, following a carefully sequenced line of questioning that encourages the child to demonstrate with the dolls experiences that happened to him or her (Shamroy, 1987). Strand's work with a 6-year-old girl (Chapter 4) illustrates the use of anatomically correct dolls.

Stuffed animals sometimes take the place of human figures in children's representational play. The child displaces onto the toy the feelings and conflicts that he or she may previously have repressed. An example of play therapy using a toy mother and baby stuffed panda bear is demonstrated in Masur's work (Chapter 8) with a 6-year-old child whose mother had died when he was 18 months old.

Suggested Supplies for Doll Play

- Bendable 6-inch family doll set (including mother, father, girl, boy, baby, grandmother, grandfather, teenager, woman, and man). These doll sets are available with skin color to correspond to various racial groups.
- Set of doll furniture including kitchen and bedroom or complete play house (Fisher-Price)
- Life-size infant doll with bottle
- Stuffed animals: monkey, bears, "monster"
- Army men (miniatures) and assorted war equipment
- "Trouble" dolls: miniature set of seven dolls in a tiny box. (Explanation suggests that one doll each day of the week will "magically" work on resolving child's problems during sleep.)
- Medical kit (including complete kit with stethoscope, reflex hammer, pill box, tongue depressors, thermometer, injection "needles," bandages)

Puppet Play

Use of puppets, like the use of dolls in play therapy, rests on the assumption that the child (1) identifies with the doll or puppet, (2) projects his or her own feelings onto the play figure, and (3) displaces his or her conflicts onto the doll or puppet. Both doll and puppet play allow the child and therapist to talk about feelings and thoughts that "belong" to the doll or puppet and that the child, therefore, does not have to acknowledge as his or her own. According to Woltmann (1951/1964, p. 398) "puppets are capable of representing specific personalities, either directly or indirectly, or specific sides or aspects of personalities." However, fantasy also prevails when using puppets; as Woltmann (1951/1964) points out, a puppet that is beaten does not feel real pain, and simulated aggression and killing allow puppetry to go far beyond the limits of biological life. Another very important feature of puppet (and doll) play is the opportunity to repeat over and over the traumatic experience and its various outcomes. Use of puppet play in this book occurs in two examples of grief work: Saravay's (Chapter 9), involving bereaved preschool brothers, and Bluestone's (Chapter 13), involving two dramatized play sessions of latency-age girls who each suffered sudden parental death. Puppetry also facilitates a life review process in Chapter 6 (Doyle & Stoop).

Puppet play has been used extensively in hospitals, particularly because of the video examples and published work of Susan Linn (1977, 1978). Alger, Linn, and Beardslee (1985) discuss the use of puppets to demonstrate feelings common to children hospitalized for a wide range of illnesses and procedures. Because of the distancing possible through puppet play, the child can create a separate person that expresses thoughts and feelings the child cannot express directly. The play therapist, through symbolic play, encourages such expression while also helping the child (through the puppet) find constructive ways to cope (Alger et al., 1985).

Suggested Supplies for Puppet Play

- Family hand puppets (mother, father, boy, girl)
- Animal hand puppets (an assortment that permit a range of emotions, e.g., "neutral" characters such as rabbits or squirrels and puppets with more "aggressive" characteristics such as lions or alligators)

Although the use of any puppet will vary in the hands of different children, the provision of a variety of puppets gives the child choices and permits a range of emotional expressions.

Insect hand puppets—ladybug, spider, bee, and grasshopper puppets—provide useful opportunities for children to master through play their fear of insects, and to express in fantasy their "superiority" over the "small" creatures that stimulate fear in their peers.

Storytelling

From the time of the Bible, stories have captured the imagination through creative use of fantasy. Stories may be told, read, or watched, depending on the circumstances of the historical moment. All methods involve distancing, identification, and projection. Children, in listening to stories, learn to exercise the power of their imaginations as they envision animal or human characters coping with situations similar in some respect to those in their own everyday lives. Children who watch television may similarly identify with the characters portrayed.

Richard Gardner's mutual storytelling technique (Gardner, 1971) combines the appeal and distancing component of storytelling in a play therapy approach that helps the child consider alternative solutions to problem situations. In Gardner's method, the child tells a story to which the therapist responds with an adaptation using "healthier conflict resolution," involving the same story characters and themes as in the child's story. As an additional enticement to the child's participation, Gardner uses audio and videotape recordings, which allow the child to subsequently hear or see himself or herself telling the stories.

Although Gardner's approach is highly structured, it lends itself to various adaptations, as demonstrated in this book by my work in Chapter 3, in which storytelling is combined with family doll play. The therapist sets a scene in a kitchen, for example, using family dolls and miniature doll house furniture; after introducing the doll family, the therapist invites the child to act out a family interaction by asking the child to demonstrate "what happens next." Saravay (Chapter 9) uses mutual storytelling in a sentence completion format with a preschool child as an aid to identifying feelings associated with a parent's death.

Other adaptations of storytelling involve writing down the child's stories and putting them into a "book," with a cover drawn by the child on construction paper and the pages stapled together. Hofmann and Rogers (Chapter 19) describe the use of this technique in a crisis group following an earthquake.

The therapist can, when appropriate, encourage the child's written fantasy by suggesting that the child write down his or her stories at home. I often give "blank books" to latency-age children as birthday gifts in order to provide them with an outlet for their written story creations, which they can later bring to the therapy session and read aloud.

As with other creative media (i.e., art), the therapist's use of the child's story productions depends on the assessment and treatment goals of each situation. An analysis of the repeated themes in stories or art provides diagnostic or added information to the therapist related to the child's conflicts and feelings. The extent to which the therapist uses the information gained from these indirect techniques depends on the unique factors of each situation. Play therapy is both an art and a science, dependent on the skills and judgment of the therapist either to use the fantasy material with the child in a displaced manner, keeping the disguise, or to question whether the child notices some resemblance between the fantasy he or she created and his or her own life.

Although the techniques for uncovering the child's inner world through art and stories may seem deceptively simple, the therapeutic management and response to the child's revelations depend on a thorough understanding of child development, typical responses of children to stress, and the nature of symbolic communication. As Rubin (1984, p. 300) cautions, "proceed with open eyes, and with respect for the value of the child, as well as the power of art." Regular supervision is essential for beginning therapists.

Board Games

As fantasy play naturally and gradually recedes in middle childhood when the child becomes more reality oriented, organized games begin to take precedence over imaginative play. Interest in games with rules comes to the fore when the child has achieved the level of cognitive development between 7 and 11 years characterized by logical and objective thinking (Piaget, 1962). Game playing requires observance of self-discipline (waiting for one's turn), cooperation, and obeying rules (Schaefer & Reid, 1986). These ego control functions are beyond capabilities of most pre-latency-age children.

Schaefer and Reid (1986) comment that "few clinicians are aware of the therapeutic potential of games for school-age children and teenagers . . . most therapists associate play therapy with the clinical use of sensory–motor and pretend play with young children" (p. ix).

In recent years there has been growing awareness of the value of using board games with latency-age children because of increased knowledge about its potential effectiveness as demonstrated in the professional literature (Schaefer & Reid, 1986; Nickerson & O'Laughlin, 1983). Game play is now viewed by knowledgeable child therapists as a means to refine diagnosis (by observing how the child plays the game), as an opportunity to enhance ego functions (helping the child master frustration tolerance and self-control), and as a natural route to improving the child's socialization skills (Schaefer & Reid, 1986).

Board games that hold special appeal to latency-age children include both standard commercial games and games that have been designed specifically for therapy purposes. Examples of the former are "Life," "Clue," and "Connect Four"; examples of therapeutic games are "The Talking, Feeling, and Doing Game" and "The Ungame." These are listed below, with names of manufacturers.

In this book, Price (Chapter 10) used an original board game to help an 8-year-old child identify and talk about his feelings.

The concept of winning and losing is implicit in most board games, through accumulation of token "chips" or by progression around a track based on the chance roll of the dice. Children's reactions to winning and losing, and their occasional attempts to change the rules and even to cheat, all become matters for therapeutic discussion. Although most games do not elicit extensive fantasy material from the child, their utility in providing an interactional experience that can be simultaneously enjoyed and analyzed ultimately proves ego enhancing to the child.

Suggested Board Games

Standard
- Battleship (Milton Bradley)   Ages 8 to adult
- Clue (Parker Brothers)   No ages specified (probably best for 9 to adult)

- Connect Four (Milton Bradley)   Ages 7 and up
- Life (Milton Bradley)   Ages 9 to adult
- Sorry (Parker Brothers)   Ages 6 to adult

"Therapeutic"
- Stress Strategies (Stress Education   Ages 8 to 14
  Center, Libertyville, IL)
- The Talking, Feeling, and Doing Game   Ages 6 to adult
  (Creative Therapeutics, 155 County
  Road, Cresskill, NJ 07026)

- The Ungame (P.O. Box 6382, Anaheim,   Kids (ages 5–12); teens;
  CA 92816): five versions   family; couples; all ages

Other Assorted Play Therapy Techniques

The possibilities for using play therapeutically are limited only by the imagination and creativity of the child and therapist. Insofar as *any* object may be used symbolically and/or idosyncratically, it would be impossible to discuss comprehensively or demonstrate, even in a book devoted in its entirety to play therapy, an exhaustive inventory of play therapy techniques. In more than 25 years as a play therapist, I continue to "discover" new activities to use creatively and therapeutically with children. Examples of some of my more recent discoveries include (1) the use of sand play (the Erica method, which originated in Sweden in the 1940s but is not widely practiced in the United States; see Lowenfeld, 1967, and Dundas, 1978), (2) the use of photographs in therapy (see Krauss & Fryrear, 1983; Sedgwick, 1980; Weiser, 1988), and (3) the use of seeds, plants, and gardening. These methods have been very effective with physically ill children as a way of counteracting their own frustrations about their illness (see Wojtasaik & Sanborn, Chapter 15).

Other, less "novel," play therapy materials include the use of construction toys, such as building blocks and Lego sets, toy telephones, miniature farm animals, and miniature "villages."

A Cautionary Note

No therapy office can or should resemble a toy store! This would be overstimulating to most children and countertherapeutic. Many years ago, when renting office space on an hourly basis, I learned that it is possible to carry "the basics" for play therapy in a large satchel. This included paper, markers, scissors, tape, stapler, a few puppets, family dolls, one board game, and a small tape recorder. The selection of materials varied with the ages and interests of the particular child clients. Children will use their imaginations when allowed to do so, and sometimes simplicity brings benefits that diversity may confuse and obscure.

ROLE OF THE PLAY THERAPIST

In play therapy, as in every form of psychotherapy, the therapist tailors his or her interventions to the needs of the client and the specific treatment goals of each case. Ross (1959/1964, p. 121) states that "depending on the manifest needs of the child, the therapist should either take a passive observing role or an active, participating one."

Following thoughtful consideration about the implications of his or her attitude and actions on the child, the therapist chooses among the following alternative roles:

1. *Participating.* The therapist plays along with the child, being careful to follow the child's lead and not jump ahead of the child.
2. *Limiting.* The therapist serves as auxiliary ego, attempting to strengthen the child's own ego functioning by emphasizing rules, encouraging frustration tolerance, and setting limits.
3. *Interpreting.* The therapist gently makes connections between the child's symbolic play and his or her own life. This approach should be used cautiously and only after a positive treatment relationship has been established.

Enzer (1989) enumerates the following functions of the play therapist, which also apply to other forms of psychotherapy:

- Develop a therapeutic alliance
- Help the client with understanding
- Link understanding with feelings
- Reduce troublesome feelings
- Work through defenses
- Find more acceptable modes of expressing affect

In carrying out these role functions the play therapist may engage in the following activities sequentially, simultaneously, or selectively, according to Enzer (1988):

- Observe the child's play
- Ask the child to describe the play activity
- Suggest motivations or feelings in the context and metaphor of the play
- Focus on the child's affect or behavior
- Become part of the play itself
- Set limits when the need arises

It is clear from this, and from the many examples in this book, that the role of the play therapist consists of far more than that of playmate.

TRAINING IN CHILD THERAPY

Just as the child psychiatrist must first demonstrate competence in treating adults before undertaking the board examinations for child psychiatry, in the opinion of this author, mental health practitioners seeking to become child therapists also should do so only after some solid experience working with adults. Because of their youthful dependency, work with children inevitably includes work with adults, and a family focus often is essential. Child therapists must be able to relate helpfully to parents and child caretakers as well as to children; all too often, treatment failure translates to failure to engage the parents adequately as allies in their child's treatment.

Many schools of social work offer elective courses in treatment of children and adolescents, and the internships of such programs on both the undergraduate and graduate level often involve work with children and families. Fortunately, close supervision is a hallmark of these internships, since the challenges and pitfalls of working with child clients, parents, and families demand the careful attention of seasoned practitioners. Mishne (1983) views child therapy as a specialty requiring lengthy ongoing training, experience, and supervision to "acquire a therapeutic objective empathic response . . . that controls against regression and acting out through and/or with patients (p. 13).

Some child therapy training programs in different areas of the United States are listed at the end of this book. A supervised internship is an integral part of these programs, regardless of the number of years of experience or educational background of the trainees. Because of the complexity and special demands of child therapy, supervision is essential for identifying and monitoring counter-transference (Webb, 1989).

GROUP AND FAMILY PLAY THERAPY

Many of the same techniques and materials appropriate to play therapy with the individual child can also be used effectively with the child and his or her family and in play therapy groups. Several chapters in this book demonstrate play therapy with children in crisis groups: Hofmann and Rogers (Chapter 19) illustrate the use of art techniques in a group following an earthquake. Joyner (Chapter 20) includes three sessions of a children's support group in addition to family and individual treatment of a child following Hurricane Hugo. Johnston (Chapter 14) also combines individual, family, and group approaches in her work with a 7-year-old boy in a family characterized by chemical dependency.

In a review of techniques for treating psychic trauma in children, Terr (1989, p. 3) states that "no generally accepted research study has established one certain technique as standard. . . . Among the individual treatment modalities available, play therapy, psychodynamic psychotherapy, cognitive and behavioral therapies, and medication hold the most promise. *A combination of several of these treatments would, in most cases, be the best program available today*" (my emphasis).

By far the majority of chapters in this book describe parent counseling, family therapy, and/or children's group therapy in addition to individual play therapy with the child. When an entire family has experienced a crisis, it is logical to treat them together to implement mutual support and enhance coping skills in addition to offering individual therapy as indicated. Since children live in a family system, a crisis experienced by one member necessarily reverberates to others.

The fact that this book focuses on play therapy as a method for treating *individual* children in crisis by no means denies the validity and necessity of utilizing family therapy and group therapy approaches in conjunction with individual play therapy. Readers who want more information regarding family play therapy may consult Griff (1983), Irwin and Malloy (1975), and Ziegler (1980). An overview of children's group therapy can be found in Schiffer (1984) and Slavson and Schiffer (1975).

Parent Counseling

When the child client lives with one or both parents, the therapist must include them in the treatment plan as a vital component of the child's treatment. Lieberman (1979, p. 225) maintains that "unless parents collaborate in treatment, little can be done to help the child." Arnold (1978, p. 12) clarifies that "it is the *parent's* relationship with the child that is essential for the child's mental health, not the professional's relationship with the child." "An effective parent is the child's most important therapist" (Arnold, 1978, p. 6).

Conveying to the parent that he or she will serve as an essential ally of the therapist forms the basis for the parent–therapist alliance. Many child therapists keep this alliance vital by meeting with the parent once a month to discuss the child's behavior and reactions and by establishing a telephone policy inviting the parents to notify the therapist about any matters of concern about the child. The therapist respects the confidentiality of the child client by refraining from reporting verbatim comments made by the child in treatment and by discussing with the parent only *general* issues related to the child's treatment.

Sometimes it is appropriate for the child's therapist to meet with the parent(s) in the child's presence. This should occur following advanced planning and involvement of the child with regard to the purpose of the meeting. An example of a planned parent–child–therapist meeting occurred in the case of the 10-year-old girl with the nightly sleep disturbance that required a treatment approach involving individual play therapy with the child and child–parent–therapist sessions to implement a behavior modification approach as a supplement to the play therapy.

The ultimate method of parent involvement in the child's treatment is filial therapy (Furman, 1979). This method includes a diagnostic study and interviews with the child and subsequent work with the parent(s) alone as the mean of assisting the pre-latency-age child. As a therapy with limited goals, the parent(s) work with the therapist to help the child, who does not receive individual professional treatment.

VERSATILE APPLICATION OF PLAY THERAPY

The play therapy approaches described in this book are generally applicable to children up to 11 years of age. They can be used in a variety of health, child welfare, educational, and mental health settings by a wide range of play therapists, such as school social workers, child life specialists, early childhood educators, disaster workers, pastoral counselors, pediatric nurses, and child welfare workers in addition to child therapists from the mental health professions of psychology, clinical social work, and psychiatry. Many of these professionals do not have formal training in play therapy, although they may have knowledge about normal and pathological child development.

Our hope is to spark the interest of these professionals in delving into the world of childhood and becoming more knowledgeable and comfortable communicating with the child through the symbolic language of play as a means of helping the child overcome the effects of crises and achieve optimal growth.

REFERENCES

Alger, I., Linn, S., & Beardslee, W. (1985). Puppetry as a therapeutic tool for hospitalized children. *Hospital and Community Psychiatry, 36*(2), 129–130.

Allen, F. (1942). *Psychotherapy with children.* New York: W. W. Norton.

Amster, F. (1943). Differential uses of play in treatment of young children. *American Journal of Orthopsychiatry, 13*, 62–68.

Arnold, L. E. (1978). *Helping parents help their children.* New York: Brunner/Mazel.

Axline, V. (1947). *Play therapy.* Boston: Houghton-Mifflin.

Bettelheim, B. (1977). *The uses of enchantment: The meaning and importance of fairy tales.* New York: Vintage Books.

Bettelheim, B. (1987). The importance of play. *The Atlantic Monthly, March*, pp. 35–46.

Chethik, M. (1989). *Technique of child therapy: Psychodynamic strategies.* New York: Guilford Press.

DiLeo, J. H. (1973). *Children's drawings as diagnostic aids.* New York: Brunner/Mazel.

Dundas, E. (1978). *Symbols come alive in the sand.* Aptos, CA: Aptos Press.

Enzer, N. B. (1988). *Overview of play therapy.* Paper presented at the annual meeting of the American Academy of Child and Adolescent Psychiatry, Seattle, WA.

Erikson, E. (1950). Toys and reasons. In *Childhood and society* (Chapter 6). New York: W. W. Norton. (Reprinted 1964 in M. R. Haworth (Ed.), *Child psychotherapy* (pp. 3–11). New York: Basic Books.)

Freud, A. (1946). *The psychoanalytic treatment of children.* London: Imago Press. (Original work published 1926)

Furman, E. (1979). Filial therapy. In J. Noshpitz (Ed.), *Basic handbook of child psychiatry* (Vol. 3, pp. 149–158). New York: Basic Books.

Gardner, R. A. (1971). *Therapeutic communication with children: The mutual storytelling technique.* New York: Jason Aronson.

Griff, M. D. (1983). Family play therapy. In C. E. Schaefer & K. J. O'Connor (Eds.), *Handbook of play therapy* (pp. 65–75). New York: John Wiley & Sons.

Irwin, E. C., & Malloy, E. S. (1975). Family puppet interview. *Family Process, 14*, 179–191.

James, D. O. (1977). *Play therapy.* New York: Dabor Science Publications.

Johnson, J. H., Rasbury, W. C., & Siegel, L. J. (1986). *Approaches to child treatment.* New York: Pergamon Press.

Klein, M. (1932). *The psychoanalysis of children.* London: Hogarth Press.

Krauss, D. A., & Fryrear, J. L. (1983). *Phototherapy in mental health.* Springfield, IL: Charles C. Thomas.

Levy, D. (1938). Release therapy in young children. *Psychiatry, 1*, 387–389.

Levy, D. (1939). Release therapy. *American Journal of Orthopsychiatry, 9*, 713–736.

Lieberman, F. (1979). *Social work with children.* New York: Human Sciences Press.

Linn, S. (1977). Puppets and hospitalized children: Talking about feelings. *Journal for the Association of the Care of Children in Hospitals, 5,* 5–11.

Linn, S. (1978). Puppet therapy in hospitals: Helping children cope. *Journal of the American Medical Women's Association, 33,* 61–65.

Lowenfeld, M. (1967). *Play in childhood.* New York: John Wiley & Sons.

Mishne, J. M. (1983). *Clinical work with children.* New York: Free Press.

Moustakas, C. (1959). *Psychotherapy with children.* New York: Harper & Row.

Nickerson, E. T., & O'Laughlin, K. S. (1983). The therapeutic use of games. In C. E. Schaefer & K. J. O'Connor (Eds.), *Handbook of play therapy* (pp. 174–187). New York: John Wiley & Sons.

Oaklander, V. (1988). *Windows to our children.* Highland, NY: The Center for Gestalt Development.

Piaget, J. (1962). *Play, dreams, and imitation in childhood.* New York: W. W. Norton.

Reid, S. E. (1986). Therapeutic use of card games with learning-disabled children. In C. E. Schaefer & S. E. Reid (Eds.), *Game play* (pp. 257–276). New York: John Wiley & Sons.

Ross, A. O. (1959). *The practice of clinical child psychology.* New York: Grune & Stratton. (Reprinted 1964 in M. R. Haworth (Ed.), *Child psychotherapy* (pp. 121–125). New York: Basic Books.)

Rubin, J. A. (1984). *Child art therapy* (2nd ed.). New York: Van Nostrand Reinhold.

Sarnoff, C. A. (1987). *Psychotherapeutic strategies in late latency through early adolescence.* Northvale, NJ: Jason Aronson.

Schaefer, C. E., & O'Connor, K. J. (Eds.). (1983). *Handbook of play therapy.* New York: John Wiley & Sons.

Schaefer, C. E., & Reid, S. E. (Eds.). (1986). *Game play.* New York: John Wiley & Sons.

Schiffer, M. (1984). *Children's group therapy: Methods and case histories.* New York: Free Press.

Sedgwick, R. (1980). The use of photoanalysis and family memorabilia in the study of family interaction. *Corrective and Social Psychiatry Journal, 25*(4), 137–141.

Shamroy, J. A. (1987). Interviewing the sexually abused child with anatomically correct dolls. *Social Work, 32,* 165–166.

Slavson, S. R., & Schiffer, M. (1975). *Group psychotherapies for children: A textbook.* New York: International Universities Press.

Terr, L. C. (1983). Play therapy and psychic trauma: A preliminary report. In C. E. Schaefer & K. J. O'Connor (Eds.), *Handbook of play therapy* (pp. 308–319). New York: John Wiley & Sons.

Terr, L. C. (1989). Treating psychic trauma in children: A preliminary discussion. *Journal of Traumatic Stress, 2,* 3–20.

Walder, R. (1933). The psychoanalytic theory of play. *Psychoanalytic Quarterly, 2,* 208–224.

Webb, N. B. (1989). Supervision of child therapy: Analyzing therapeutic impasses and monitoring counter-transference. *The Clinical Supervisor, 7*(4), 61–76.

Weiser, J. (1988). Phototherapy using snapshots and photointeractions in therapy with youth. In C. Schaefer (Ed.), *Innovative interventions in child and adolescent therapy* (pp. 339–376). New York: John Wiley & Sons.

Winnicott, D. W. (1971). *Playing and reality.* New York: Basic Books.

Woltmann, A. G. (1951). The use of puppetry as a projective method in therapy. In H. H. Anderson & G. L. Anderson (Eds.), *An introduction to projective techniques and other devices for understanding the dynamics of human behavior.* New York: Prentice-Hall. (Reprinted 1964 in M. R. Haworth (Ed.), *Child psychotherapy* (pp. 395–399). New York: Basic Books.)

Woltmann, A. G. (1955). Concepts of play therapy techniques. *American Journal of Orthopsychiatry, 25,* 771–783. (Reprinted 1964, as Varieties of play techniques, in M. R. Haworth (Ed.), *Child psychotherapy* (pp. 20–32). New York: Basic Books.)

Ziegler, R. G. (1980). Task-focused therapy with children and families. *American Journal of Psychotherapy, 34,* 107–118.

PART II

The Crisis of Violence

CHAPTER 3

Observation of Parental Violence
Case of Michael, Age 4

NANCY BOYD WEBB

Parental fighting, divorce, and remarriage occur with great frequency in American homes despite the pain and disruption that accompany these events. Such familial upheavals seriously threaten children's sense of security. Factors such as the child's age, his or her previous level of adjustment and coping ability, plus the current environmental support all shape the specific response of each individual to stressful events. The preschool child, whose developmental stage is characterized by narcissism, often believes that his or her behavior caused the parent's fighting. Furthermore, when one parent leaves the home, the young child fears similar abandonment by the other parent. This anxiety can overwhelm an immature ego and precipitate a crisis state.

The case presented in this chapter depicts such a crisis in the life of a 4-year-old boy whose brief life history resonated with family turmoil, causing him to experience emotional and behavioral breakdown. The child's inability to adapt to an unraveling sequence of crisis events seriously compromised his development and interferred with his ability to relate to peers. Play therapy with the child utilized art, family dolls, and tape-recorded storytelling to encourage ventilation and verbalization of the child's anger in the playroom. This resulted in eventual reduction in aggressive outbursts and the child's improved ability to cope with his anger.

Often crises occur as multiple rather than singular events. The term "crisis" in this chapter refers to an upset of a steady state in which the individual's usual coping is inadequate to meet the perceived demands of the situation (Parad, 1977). In the case of Michael, age 4, the crises that were identified during the initial evaluation included:

1. Witnessing of parental violence: Mother reported being beaten by father five times in the child's presence when Michael was between 18 and 30 months of age
2. Father left the home: Michael, age 2½
3. Parents were divorced: Michael, age 4
4. Move to home of mother's fiance: Michael, age 4
5. Mother's impending remarriage: Michael, 4½
6. Threat of exclusion from day care program because of Michael's aggressive behavior

Any one of these crises could precipitate emotional turmoil in a preschool child. Their combined impact caused Michael to feel tremendous anger, which he turned against himself and others. Without therapeutic intervention, he seemed headed for a future of acting-out behavior as previewed in his unpredictable and uncontrollable outbursts and aggression toward other children in his day care program.

The literature on the intergenerational transmission of family violence warns that the male child who witnesses paternal abuse of the mother is at high risk for modeling similar behavior when he becomes a husband (Rosenbaum & O'Leary, 1981; Hershorn & Rosenbaum, 1985). Data from a nationally represent-ative sample showed that "observing hitting between one's parents is more strongly related to involvement in severe marital aggression than is being hit as a teenager by one's parent" (Kalmuss, 1984, p. 11).

In addition to potential *future* repercussions stemming from witnessing parental violence, more immediate aftereffects for the witness take the from of adjustment difficulties similar to behaviors and reactions found in a group of children who were physically abused by their parents (Jaffee, Wolfe, Wilson, & Zak, 1986). Problems reported on a child's behavior checklist (Achenbach & Edelbrock, 1981) included destroying things belonging to self or others, fighting, disobedience at home or school, and feelings of being unloved and lonely. Jacob-son (1978) reports that the parental behavior most closely associated with a child's poor adjustment or dysfunction is physical violence.

Even very early trauma was remembered in behavior and was reenacted in play in a study (Terr, 1988) of 20 children who were under the age of 5 at the time of documented traumatic events. Terr (1988, p. 103) concluded that "traumatic events create lasting visual images" that later may be verbalized or reenacted in play, which often "converts passive into active experiences." This appeared to be the operating dynamic in the case of Michael, who surely felt helpless in witness-ing his parents fighting and whose play in therapy enabled him to identify with powerful, destructive fantasy figures.

In addition to the traumatic experience of witnessing parental aggression, Michael had to endure the loss of his father, initially in his father's departure from the home and subsequently in the father's frequent failures to appear for scheduled visits. The attachment literature documents the significance of the child's attachment to the father as well as the mother from the age of 8–12 months of age (Kotelchuck, 1972; Lamb, 1976). It is probable that Michael was attached to his father and that he experienced a sense of loss when his father left the home when Michael was 2½, since his father had been his regular caretaker while his mother was working. Bowlby's research demonstrated that children as young as 6 months of age displayed sadness and grief following the loss of loved objects (Bowlby, 1960, 1961). Kelly and Wallerstein (1975) found that 44% of children aged 2½ to 6 years old in their study were designated as in "significantly deteriorated psychological conditions(s)" 1 year following parental divorce. Michael came for therapy a few months after his parents' divorce was final. Although he cognitively could not comprehend the true meaning of the divorce because of his young age, he nonetheless had experienced the loss of his father. His aggressive behavior conveyed his confusion, helplessness, and fury.

Following the death of a parent, children may attempt to compensate for the loss through identification with the interests, mannerisms, traits, and behavior of the dead parent (Gardner, 1983). In Michael's case, his father was not dead but was absent from him because of divorce. Michael, however, still loved his father and wanted to be strong like him. Through identification he could keep his absent father with him, and by assuming the ferocious, powerful role he witnessed and admired in his father, he could banish the helpless and powerless feelings of a 4-year-old.

The treatment of a child such as Michael must respect the child's feelings of grief and encourage appropriate expression of the loss, both symbolically through play and verbally. In Michael's case, his therapy also needed to provide a safe place for expressing the confusion, helplessness, and anger related to his witnessing of violent behavior between his parents. Terr (1989), referring to David Levy's (1939) "abreactive therapy," states that Levy's approach, which involves no interpretations by the therapist of the child's spontaneous play, works well with very young externally stressed children. When the therapist enunciates the accompanying feelings being played out by the child, abreaction can occur, according to Terr (1989, p. 14), and "an entire treatment through play may be engineered without stepping far beyond the metaphor of the 'game.'" Much of the early therapy with Michael involved such abreaction, with statements by the therapist naming the feelings he was expressing without making the connections to his own life. Michael's pressured need to "play out" his experiences dominated the first phase of therapy, conveying his need to discharge his tensions in a safe place where he was accepted. Eth and Pynoos (1985), referring to the impact of violence on a child's emerging pattern of identification, suggest that long-term psychodynamic therapy may be necessary to free a child from the disabling legacy of violence. Michael's therapy, which lasted a year and a half, not only resulted in symptom reduction, which facilitated a healthier adjustment for him in his present life, but also strengthened his coping ability by demonstrating alternative methods for expressing his anger.

THE CASE: MICHAEL SPIVAK, AGE 4

Presenting Problem

Michael's mother, at the insistence of his day care teacher, consulted the author, a child and family therapist, about her 4-year-old son. The teacher was concerned because Michael bullied other children, had frequent tantrums, and was verbally abusive to his teachers. Mrs. Spivak, who had been recently divorced from Michael's father after an 18-month separation, shared the teacher's concern about Michael. She was worried about his bad temper and tendency to cry a lot at home.

Family Information

Mrs. Spivak and Michael had recently moved in with her fiance. Mother's remarriage was to occur in 4 months. Michael's father, who was living with another woman and her teenage daughter, visited Michael erratically, according to Mrs. Spivak, and had been physically abusive to her in front of Michael on several occasions prior to the separation. The family composition at the time of the initial evaluation was as follows:

Michael	Age 4 years 3 months
Mrs. Spivak	Age 32; divorced; employed as a bank teller; engaged to Mr. Carbone
Mr. Carbone ("Bill")	Age 66; divorced; father of three adult sons with whom he runs a restaurant business; has several grandchildren Michael's age
Mr. Spivak	Age 35; divorced; employed by telephone company; visits Michael erratically; living with girlfriend and her teen-age daughter

First Interview (Parents)

When a problem involves a child under 10 years of age I usually see the relevant adults alone prior to seeing the child in one or more subsequent evaluation interviews. The purpose of the initial interview is to obtain detailed history of the problem and a developmental history of the child. It is also important to discuss with the parent(s) how to prepare the child for the upcoming evaluation. The therapist instructs the parents to state clearly and nonpunitively to the child that they are concerned about how best to help him or her and that they have already spoken with someone who helps children and families.

In this case I wanted a fuller description of the range and intensity of the presenting problem, including the response of the school personnel and the parents to Michael's outbursts. In addition, I wanted to know more about the extent of the parental fighting that Michael had witnessed, as well as what Michael had been told about the reason for the separation and divorce. Another important factor to be evaluated was the quality of the child's relationship with both his father and his future stepfather.

Mrs. Spivak and Mr. Carbone came together for the intake interview. Mrs. Spivak presented as an attractive woman, whose eyes teared up frequently as she spoke of her concern for her son. Mr. Carbone, a kindly, grandfatherly man, conveyed his affection for Michael whom he had known for over a year and whom he described as "spunky," "strong-willed," and very bright.

Michael's developmental history was unremarkable except for speech, which occurred early (6 months) and was "advanced," according to the mother. Mrs.

Spivak had worked until the day of Michael's birth, and she returned to work when he was 4 months old. Michael was cared for sometimes by his father (who worked nights) and sometimes by a sitter in the sitter's home. He entered day care at age 3½.

According to Mrs. Spivak, Michael's father lost his job several times and alternated between working 7 days a week and being at home unemployed. He was drinking excessively and physically abused Mrs. Spivak five times in front of Michael. One fight occurred in the kitchen and resulted in both parents falling on the floor on top of Michael, who was 18 months old at the time. Mrs. Spivak's injuries caused facial bleeding and necessitated a trip to the emergency room. Mother believes that Michael's present fear of the sight of blood originates from witnessing this fight.

Currently, Mr. Spivak has visitation privileges every other weekend. However, he frequently disappoints Michael by not appearing for a scheduled visit. Mother has told Michael that the reason she and his father were divorced is that they don't love each other any more. Michael knows that his mother and Mr. Carbone, whom he calls "Bill," plan to be married, and he says, "Then, I'll have two daddies." Mr. Carbone stated that he likes to read to Michael at night and that they spend time together taking care of several dogs Mr. Carbone is raising to enter in dog shows.

Mrs. Spivak says that she disciplines Michael either verbally or by withholding privileges (TV). Mr. Spivak never hit Michael. Sometimes, when Michael is angry, he scratches his face and pulls his eyelids down on his cheek, or pokes himself in the eye with his finger.

Bedtime is frequently a problem, and the teacher has told mother that she thinks Michael is overtired. Mother believes that Michael "resists" falling asleep, and at night he often cries out and moans in his sleep. His favorite play activities include space ships, robots, and army men. He does not have friends in their neighborhood and usually plays alone.

The day care teacher elaborated on the presenting problem in a telephone conference. She described a child who seemed "angry all the time," who either ignores his peers or yells at them, shaking his fist menacingly. When he is frustrated, he paces up and down or stamps his feet and cries. He also is destructive and has threatened to cut his sneaker or the tablecloth with scissors. The day care director views Michael as a very bright but immature and explosive child who loses control easily.

First Interview (Child)

Mother had prepared Michael according to my suggestions. A cute boy with excellent speech, Michael brought a Mickey Mouse doll with him and showed no separation anxiety about leaving mother to come with me into the playroom. I told Michael that I was a doctor who helps children and families with their troubles and their worries. Michael responded that he has "lots of worries" and elaborated by mentioning headaches and stomach-aches. I clarified that I was *not* a medical doctor, saying that I help children sometimes by talking and sometimes by playing.

Michael displayed age-appropriate knowledge of numbers and colors, and he spoke clearly with an excellent vocabulary. He conveyed a sense of "bravado" in the session, flexing his muscles, inviting the therapist to feel his biceps, and referring to himself as "big and strong." He denied any fears or feelings of sadness and denied that he fights with other children, although he remembered that his parents used to fight, and he admitted to trying to fight his daddy.

Preliminary Assessment and Treatment Plan

This case portrays a 4-year-old in crisis—a child who repeatedly witnessed his parents' violent relationship during the first 2½ years of his life and who, chronologically in the Oedipal stage, now faces the task of affirming his male identity with a father who physically hurt his mother and frequently disappoints him by erratic visits. Michael's show of bravado in flexing his muscles and referring to himself as "big and strong" suggests that he views muscular strength as very desirable. Indeed, this is the fantasy of many 4-year-old boys. However, in Michael's case, achieving this identity implies hurting others, and this puts him into conflict with the adults he most wants to please—his mother and his teachers. In a paradoxical, no-win situation, he vents his anger at himself in self-destructive behavior (poking at his eyes) or in futile foot-stomping rages at day care.

Michael witnessed the physical abuse of his mother between the time when he was 18 months and 2½ years of age. This age spans the separation–individuation phase of development (Mahler, Pine, & Bergman, 1975), when the young child is developing object constancy and learning that "good" and "bad" qualities can be fused in the same person. In Michael's case his father was sometimes the "good" parent (when he took care of him) and other times was aggressive and "bad" toward his mother. The father eventually left the home and frequently failed to visit when Michael expected him. The undependability of the attachment object (father) creates intense anxiety and feelings of insecurity in the child, which, in turn, provoke rage. Michael has no suitable outlet for his anger. He admits that he tried to fight his father, but his father is seldom present now, and so his aggression becomes turned toward either himself or others.

Currently, a new and different father figure has entered Michael's life. This circumstance promises another view of masculinity—one that includes kindness to animals and people. When Michael says proudly, "I will have *two* daddies," I realize the danger of the child's splitting his perceptions into the "good Daddy" and the "bad Daddy." The mother's obvious pleasure at her upcoming marriage and choice of husband seems to bode well for Michael's future well-being. However, the uncertain role of Michael's father in the child's future requires further exploration.

The *treatment plan* included weekly play therapy sessions for Michael and once-a-month parent counseling session with the mother and future stepfather. In addition, an observation visit with the day care was planned, including an offer by the therapist to be available for telephone consultation to the day care director and Michael's teacher. Finally, I planned to contact Michael's father to offer him the opportunity to meet with me to obtain his views about his child's development and to help me assess and encourage the father's plans for future involvement with Michael.

Specific *treatment goals* in working with Michael included:

1. Helping the child realize that the divorce was not his fault
2. Reassuring the child that his mother would not abandon him
3. Helping the child express his anger verbally and symbolically through play
4. Helping the child toward a masculine identity that includes both strength and kindness

Recommendations for Michael's mother and future stepfather were that they should convey to Michael:

1. Reassurance about their love for him and their wish to have him in their new family
2. The understanding that hitting is not permitted but verbal expression of anger is encouraged
3. Support for his desire to see his father, with no negative verbalization from them about the father

Play Therapy Sessions

First Eight Sessions: Summary

The early work with Michael involved developing the treatment relationship and obtaining a fuller understanding of his conflicts. I usually began the sessions by asking routinely about day care, about visits with his father, and about how he was sleeping. Michael knew that these issues were connected to coming to therapy, and he sometimes would admit to being involved in a fight at school (day care) or to having trouble sleeping because of ghosts, the existence of which he never doubted because of the *Ghostbusters* movies and the toy replicas.

Michael's ability to discuss his "problems" and "worries" was understandably quite limited because of his age. Therefore, after 5 or 10 minutes of conversation and snacks, which usually began the session, Michael would ask to draw or play, and the therapy moved to the level of symbolic communication.

Michael's most frequently chosen activity during the first eight sessions was drawing, accompanied by a steady stream of commentary, which he liked to have the therapist write on the drawing as he worked. The subjects of Michael's art included space capsules, robots, whales, sharks, and space invaders. War and violent destruction were constant themes, as good and bad "Voltrons" with long swords attacked one another and became obliterated in blood and whirlpools. (See sketch on book jacket.) Often it was difficult for me to keep up with the fast-paced violent action, with body parts being chopped off and almost always the "bad" fantasy figure defeating the "good."

Michael's absorption in the imaginary violent world he created on paper was impressive. The robots were vividly real to him, and he would become exasperated with me when I occasionally interrupted to ask for clarification or repetition of details. After finishing a drawing that, following a 20-minute battle scene, consisted of a mass of red and brown scribbles, Michael would ask me to read the story connected to the drawing. As I began to read, Michael would correct my abbreviated version, adding details with an annoyed voice suggesting that I was not fully capturing the richness of the violence as he conceived it.

This was true. It literally was impossible to keep up with the pressured portrayal of this child's primitive rage fantasies. He seemed to feel driven to produce violent scenes, and he resisted vehemently any of my attempts to offer a "different ending" with the good-guy hero winning.

I wondered at times if Michael's steady outpouring of blood and gore provided beneficial relief to him. Was it a "playing out" of his conflicts just as an adult in therapy "talks out" his or her pain? How much of this violent play would be necessary before a move toward more "constructive" solutions? Was Michael "stuck"? And was there a danger that playing destructively in sessions would fan the fires of Michael's aggression and cause it to spread uncontrolled into his real world?

I also analyzed my own feelings about the child's destructive play. Was I trying to move Michael away from the violence because it made me uncomfortable or because I doubted the validity of cathartic expression? It certainly was true that sessions with Michael were intense and often left me feeling that a whirlwind had blown through my office. This despite the fact that Michael was *not* hyperactive and, in fact, had an excellent attention span for his age. He really *worked* in therapy. I realized that Michael's play stimulated in me some of the confusion he felt about his own life, in a parallel process. He made me feel overwhelmed.

As a means of exploring the tenacity of Michael's need to express violent themes, I decided to introduce some new play materials into the next session. I planned to offer Michael a set of eight bendable family dolls and some dollhouse kitchen furniture. I also decided to tape record the session as a means of analyzing Michael's verbalizations. Michael had been introduced to the family dolls in the evaluation session but had not played with them subsequently.

Ninth Session

The session began with the usual snack and review of Michael's week. Michael did not report on any matters which seemed to require exploration. I then told Michael that I had something different today: the doll family Michael already had seen plus some kitchen furniture and a tape recorder. If Michael wanted to make up some stories about the family I would record them and then we could play them back and he could hear his own voice. This appealed to Michael, and he spent about 5 minutes experimenting with the use of the tape recorder. (The doll family consisted of a mother, father, little boy, little girl, grandfather, grandmother, teenage girl, and adult woman [teacher/babysitter]). A small rocking horse and a set of kitchen furniture was on the play table.

Content of Session	Rationale/Analysis
THERAPIST (*speaking into tape recorder*): This is Michael, and he's going to make up a story.	
CHILD (*in falsetto voice*): The little boy is going to ride on the rocking horse. Ohhhhh! (*Puts boy doll on miniature rocking horse and rocks it vigorously. The doll falls off. Imitates crying sound and then puts little girl on rocking horse and repeats.*) Now I'm going on the rocking horse (*crying noises*).	
T: They're *both* crying. Now the Mommy's coming in (*holds Mother doll*). What's she going to say? (*moving Mother doll toward child dolls*)	
C: (*continues to make crying sounds*)	
T: Oh, you children! You're crying, you're crying!	
C: We fell off the rocking chair.	
T: Oh (*comforting tone*), that's too bad! You just come and sit on my lap and you'll feel better.	Trying to see how child will respond to comforting.
C (*in normal voice*): I feel better (*laughs*).	
T (*commenting on child's play actions*): Now they're getting on the horse again. Two together.	
C: Rock, rock, rock, rock (*sing-song*). (*Then they fall off again, and child doll starts crying again; then Michael abruptly falls off the chair in which he is seated and looks at therapist with a very surprised expression.*)	Did Michael want to sit on therapist's lap???
T: Whoops! You just fell, too! Are you all right? I'm sorry. You fell down.	
C: I'm all right. (*Sings cheerfully and briefly, no words; resumes playing making the two child dolls fight.*)	He seems reassured but moves to more aggressive play.
C: This is the new karate. Boop!	
T: Are the kids playing karate?	Checking to see if understood correctly.
C: Yeah! Bop. Ugh (*grunting noises*).	

T: One kicked the other one. In comes the Daddy (*holding father doll*), and he says, "What are you kids doing, kicking each other?"

C: We're doing karate!

T (*in father's voice*): I don't want you to hurt each other!

C: We're not (*then crying sounds as doll play fight continues*).

T: The little girl is crying because the little boy kicked her! Now what's going to happen?

Let the child control the play.

C (*crying sounds continue*): The father's going to come and pick her up and spank the little boy.

T (*taking part of father*): You shouldn't have kicked her. You're a bad boy. You shouldn't have kicked your sister. I'm going to spank you. Bum. Bum. Bum (*Father doll spanks boy doll*).

C: (*Cries; says in an aside, "This will be my room."*)

T (*in father's voice*): You go to your room, and you stay there. (*to child*) What's the daddy going to do to the little girl?

Again asking child to direct play.

C: Pick her up.

T (*in father's comforting voice*): You poor sweetie! Do you feel better now?

C (*in normal voice*): When I get a baby sister, I'm going to give her a hug, and I'm not going to hit her. We're going to play with my "pewter."

Michael departs from play and identifies girl doll as his future baby sister.

T: "Pewter"??

C: It plays games [i.e., "computer"].

T: You're going to let your baby sister play with it?

C: Yeah! Only when she's 4.

T: And then how old will you be?

C: Same age as her.

Preoperational thinking.

T: Really? I thought you might be older because you have a head start on her. How can you be 4 and she be 4 when she's not born yet?

C: She's not born yet! When we get the new house I'm going to have her.

Sounds as if there has been some planning for the future.

T: Later on.

C: Today I'm not getting the new house. (*Returns to doll play; picks up girl child doll and says in falsetto*): I feel better, Daddy.

T: The little girl feels all better. What about the little boy? He's still up in his room.

C: He doesn't like his room (*motions to therapist to resume playing with the father doll*).

T: What's the Daddy going to say to the little boy?

C: He's [the little boy] going to say (*falsetto*) I'm sorry, Daddy. I won't do that again.

T: And what does the daddy say to him?

C (*in strong, "male" voice*): If I see you do that again, you're going to get a real spanking. (*in falsetto voice*) I'm sorry, baby sister. (*Then makes little girl doll kick little boy doll, and little boy begins to cry.*) Wa-a-a-a!

T: Now he's crying! And now what's the daddy saying? What's going on here?

C (*falsetto*): First he kicked me, now I kicked him.

T (*in father's voice*): Oh, you children are impossible! I don't know what to do with you!

C (*aside*): Put me in my bedroom.   Child identifies male doll as self.

T (*in father's voice*): You have to go upstairs and go to your room at once.

C (*crying sounds*): She kicked me!

T (*in father's voice*): See that's what happens when you kick people. It hurts, and you get hurt yourself.

C (*normal voice*): Guess how many [times] I got   Sudden transition.
lost from my mom?

T: How many?

C: Twice.

T: You got lost?

C: Yup.

T: Where were you? In a store?

C: (*No response; silence.*)

T (*repeats question*): Where were you when you got lost?

C: I got lost twice. And I don't want to tell you.

T: You don't want to tell me? Were you afraid? It's not fun to get lost!

C: Yeah. I couldn't find my mom.

T: What did you do? Did you speak to someone? Did you say to someone, "I'm lost"?

C: Yeah.

T: Did they help you find your mother?

C: No.

T: They didn't!!

C: No.

T: Did your mommy find you?

C: (*Nods yes.*)

T: And what did she say to you?

C: She said (*funny voice*) Oh! Why did this boy get lost?

T (*repeats*): Why *did* you get lost?

C: 'Cause I love to get lost!

T: You do? (*surprised voice*) Why?

C: 'Cause I like to.

T: You like to?

C: 'Cause I like to find my daddy.

T: You go to find your daddy.

C: Yeah. But he's not there.

T (*repeats sadly*): But he's not there.

C (*quickly and almost unintelligibly*): So I trade him for a new Bill.

T: You're looking for a new Bill?

C: No. The same Bill that I have before.

T: You were looking for Bill and you went the wrong way?

T: You thought you were looking for your Daddy?

(*Interruption: sound of loud fire whistle interrupts session.*)

T: That's that fire whistle again.

C: What happened?

T: There must be a fire someplace. The fire engine's going to go and put out the fire.

C: Why?

Wonder what Michael is defending against.

Will he tell now?

Therapist is confused here.

Therapist has to think quickly re the significance of this sequence.

Interruption in the flow of very significant material. Will we be able to stay with the topic, or will child be distracted??

T: Because people don't want to leave the fire burning. I don't know where it is.

C: Maybe it's coming from my house.

T: I don't think so.

C: Why?

T: Because it's too far away. This fire must be sompleace close by.

> Child lives ¾ hour away from office.

C: No. It's at my house.

T: I don't think so. Is Bill home at your house today?

> Child is egocentric and also has learned to "expect the worst."

C: Yes. Mommy dropped him off first. I was sleeping.

> Trying to offer reassurance that the "protector" is at home.

T: You were sleeping in the car?

C (*returning to doll play; in falsetto; picks up child doll*): Daddy, Daddy.

> Child returns to play with father doll.

T (*repeats, trying to encourage child to continue*): Daddy, please wake up. I want to talk to you.

C (*in Daddy's voice*): What child?

T: What does the little boy want to say to the daddy?

C: Daddy, I love you! Daddy, I'm sorry, I'm sorry! (*Father doll hugs the little boy doll.*) I love you, too.

> Which Daddy is he talking to?

T (*commenting on child's play: he was grasping all the dolls in his two fists*): Everyone's all hugging each other. The daddy and the little boy and the little girl and the mommy and the gramma and grampy are all hugging each other and the teacher [adult female]. And they're all happy and no one's fighting any more. No one is kicking and no one is fighting.

> A very moving scene. The tension level had diminished. Is this forgiveness for misdeeds?

C: We're all the family. Can I hear my voice now?

> This was a natural stopping point.

T: Yes. (*Therapist rewinds tape and Michael listens intently to the entire replay, smiling broadly at the end.*)

It was time to conclude the session after the replay, so Michael and I put the dolls away, and I gave him his appointment card for next week to give to his mother in the waiting room.

Comment on Session. In this session Michael initiated punishment for aggression, apology, and finally, forgiveness. Michael was no longer stuck in repetition of violence, and he was envisioning through his play how he would be forgiven after apology and loved despite his angry acting-out behavior. The change in play material from art to family dolls and tape recorded stimulated reenactment of the child's life situation.

The child's mourning search for the lost father follows his early aggressive play with child dolls. It may suggest that the two events are connected in the child's thinking. Does Michael think he drove his father away because he was bad? This bears watching in future sessions, as does the rapid replacement of the lost father. It was impossible to determine which of the daddies was intended in the concluding reunion scene, but the hope is that Michael was beginning to merge the two male identities.

My role was not to interpret any of the child's play but to participate in the play at the child's direction. The script was the child's, and in my demeanor I attempted to convey acceptance of the child and a wish to understand feelings and his conflicts.

Tenth Session

Prior to this session, Mrs. Spivak had telephoned me to report that Michael's behavior had deteriorated in day care following a weekend visit with his father. Michael had tried to strangle a child, bit another child (drawing blood), and threw rocks when he was on the playground. His teacher was threatening to exclude him from an upcoming school outing. The mother was very concerned about Michael because the day care was so upset and also because the wedding was to take place in 2 weeks and Mrs. Spivak hoped that Michael would not behave like this with Bill's grandchildren at the reception.

When I went to the waiting room to greet Michael, he was sitting with his head on his mother's lap. His mother told me that he did not want to come today. I said that maybe Michael had had a tough week, and I'd like to help him with that. With this mild encouragement, Michael stood up and accompanied me, carrying with him two plastic toys he had brought from home.

Michael put his toys on the floor and then immediately asked for the doll family and began playing with the boy and girl dolls and the rocking horse, as in the beginning of the previous session. Usually when a child brings items from home, the therapist initiates discussion about them, but Michael seemed very purposeful in his intentions to play with the doll family, and I decided to let the play evolve naturally. After a brief segment consisting of the child falling off the horse and crying, the following exchange occurred:

Content of Session	Rationale/Analysis
THERAPIST: What's the little boy going to say to the little girl?	
CHILD: I hate you!	

T: Why do you hate her?

C: Bop! Ohh! Ohh! Ohh!

T: They're fighting. What are they fighting about?

C: Bopp. Bopp.

T: They're fighting. Do you know what's going to happen? This is the teacher, and she's gong to say, "Why are you children fighting?"

Trying to tie it in to events at day care this past week.

C: 'Cause we like to fight all day.

T: Why?

C: Bopp. Whopp.

T: You're going to hurt each other. One of you may start to bleed.

Trying to get close to anxiety material.

C: Bleed. Bopp. Whopp.

T: And then what's going to happen?

C: Ohh! Ohh!

T: And then what's the teacher going to do?

C: I don't know.

T: Does the little girl want the teacher to pick her up? And sit in her lap?

Will child accept comforting adult?

C (*sing-song voice*): The little girl fell down off the cliff (*knocks child doll on floor*).

Ignores therapist's attempt to guide.

T: She fell off the cliff? That's pretty serious!

C: The little boy pushed her off the cliff.

T: So now what's going to happen?

C: He's going to be punished (*sad voice*).

Pursuing concept from last session that aggression has consequences.

T: How's he going to be punished?

C: He has to stay away.

T: He can't play any more (*sad voice*) How does he feel?

Simulating day care events.

C: Bad.

T: He feels very bad, doesn't he?

C: Can I hear my voice now?

T: Yes (*rewinds and replays tape*).

Child elects to distance from bad/ sad feelings.

(*Pause.*)

T: This is the little boy, and he's living with his mommy and he's going to go to

Therapist attempts to explore weekend with father. Therapist

visit his daddy in his house over here. It's
the weekend. This is the daddy's house over
here.

C: Why did the daddy move?

T: Because the mommy and the daddy don't love
each other any more, and they don't live together
any more. But the daddy still loves the little boy,
so the little boy's going to go and visit him for
the weekend, and you tell me what they are going
to do.

C: She's going on the bridge. Ohh! (*Makes child
doll fall again, as in previous story.*)

T: She's going to fall down.

C: She fell down on the cliff. Ohh! (*more—
unintelligible*)

T: Did you go out for a hike over the weekend?
Did you go out on a cliff?

C: Goo, goo, goo (*shakes head no*). The grampa is
sleeping. This little girl wants to sit down and
eat. She's eating her lunch.

T: This is the daddy's house? And is he going to
give the little boy lunch, too?

C: No. It's the *mommy's* house (*emphasis*).

T: So, here's the mommy (*holding Mother doll*).

C: She's going to open something. (*Little girl doll
begins to cry.*) Oh, oh, oh Mommy.

T: What's Mommy going to do?

C: She slammed the lunch apart. She's kicking it
off the table.

T: Why would she do that?

C: 'Cause she has to do it. She likes to throw it on
the table. Ah, oh, oh!

T: Is Mommy upset?

C: No. Mommy's fine. She's happy Ah! Bop! Bop!
Ugh! (*struggling noises*)

T: The mommy and daddy are fighting.

C: (*Knocks down kitchen chairs and table and
continues to make fighting noises.*)

T: Everyone's falling down, and the kitchen is
falling apart.

---

sets up the beginning of a play
scene.

May be asking about the real-life
situation.

Same theme as in earlier story.

Trying to understand derivative of
"cliff" play.

Again, trying to reconstruct the
weekend visit with father.

This is confusing!

Is this a reconstruction of one of
the fights Michael witnessed?

C: (*noises/struggling and grunting noises; continues for 2 minutes with fight scene and noises*)

T: And what's the little girl doing?

C: You mean the big girl, the mommy?

T: No, the little one. Is she still on the floor?

C: She's tired. 'Cause the daddy . . . She punched him on the tush and fell down.

Trying to help Michael verbalize the feelings of the child witness to the parental fight.

C: Can I hear my voice now?

T: Yes you can (*rewinds and plays the tape*).

Child moves away from memory of trying to fight his father.

(*After replay, child resumes fight.*)

T: The little boy and little girl are back in the kitchen fighting.

C: (*fighting noises*)

T: See if you can help them make up and be friends.

Trying to initiate self-control.

C: No. They want to be fighting. Oh. Bam.

T: They already finished their fight. Now they want to be friends.

C: (*Continues the fight.*)

T: How can they be friends?

C: They knock their brains out.

T: That's not very friendly! Imagine this is the babysitter (*introduces new doll*). I'm going to come over and say, "You chidren are fighting too much. I want you to come and sit on my lap."

C: No! We like to fight all day (*continues fighting*). We knock your brains out all day.

T: Come on! Let's have some snacks. Let's go to the refrigerator and get some ice cream. Here's some ice cream for the little girl (*smack, smack*), and here's some for the little boy. The little boy and the little girl are going to sit down at the table. Let's sit down and enjoy our snack.

Deliberately trying to interrupt the fight scene and change the pace.

C: Put all the ice cream on the table.

T: Now we're going to have a little party. What kind of ice cream do you want?

C: Vanilla and chocolate.

T: Yummy. What's the little girl's name.

C: Jessica.

Name of Bill's granddaughter.

T: And what's the little boy's name?

C: Michael.

Identification with boy doll.

T: They like to have a snack.

C: How about she? (*referring to sister doll*)

T: Is she going to have some, too?

C: (*Child nods yes.*) And soon, who comes in? (*holding mother and father dolls*)

T: There's the mommy and the daddy.

C: (*Begins having Mother and Daddy fight.*) Do you want a bash in the mouth? (*loud screams*)

Michael cannot accept oral nurturing for long before moving to oral aggression.

(*Michael now begins playing with the Land Shark toy he brought to the session, putting the child dolls into the Land Shark's mouth and speaking with a very angry voice.*)

C: Yeoww!!

The violence is escalating.

T: You've got the little girl in the Land Shark's mouth. Poor little girl!

C (*making chewing noises and groans*): Mmmmmm!

T: What's the mommy going to say when she sees her little girl in such trouble?

C (*high-pitched voice, unintelligble*): Grampa.

T: Where's my little girl. Help! Help me Grampa. We've got to rescue her.

C: And you saw the big Land Shark coming. Then the Bashasaurus came and to bash his head off, like that (*manipulating a cannon on a string and swinging it to hit any objects in its way*). Ah, ha ha ha (*menacingly*).

T: Well, she's awfully frightened, but I think she's going to be all right.

C (*speaking as Bashasaurus*): With the Land Shark in my way watch out.

Michael seems to ignore therapist.

T: Now what is this daddy and this grampy going to do?

C (*speaking as Father/Grandfather*): They say, "Get that girl out or I'm going to hurt you."

T (*speaking to Land Shark*): Yes. You've got to give us back our child. Open your mouth and let her come out.

C: Hey! Let *me* do this problem. Bash in the mouth. Bimbo! (*Bashasaurus attacks land Shark.*) Bash!

Is Michael identifying with Bashasaurus?

T: He's [Bashasaurus] going to rescue the little girl.

C: (*Continues battle with Bashasaurus attacking the Land Shark; extended fight scene.*)

T: That must be all the Land Shark can take.

C: And this little boy's getting up. (*Child doll punches Land Shark.*)

T: He's going to hit him too. And I think that's the end of the Land Shark. He couldn't still do that after everyone's hitting him like that. That must be the end of him. He must be opening his mouth up, and the little girl is going to say, "Let me out of here. I want to get out of this Shark's mouth."

As Michael hits his father

Attempting to conclude this violent scene.

C: (*Says something menacing and continues to fight, putting boy child in Land Shark's mouth.*)

T: Isn't someone going to rescue those poor children? Now he has two in his mouth. Isn't someone going to rescue them?

Extended fight scene follows in which the Bashasaurus and Land Shark continue to fight. All family dolls are helpless in the battle, and all family members end up again in the mouth of the Land Shark. Michael resumes attacking play with the doll family sitting in the cab of the Bashasaurus, and they are trying to attack the Land Shark. Michael's voice is angry as he repeatedly has the cannonball hit the Land Shark with noisy sound effects.

Content of Session

Rationale/Analysis

CHILD: Do you want a bash in the mouth? Or a bash everywhere? Oh! Oh! He's gonna bash me blank over. Bash. Bang. Now look what you've done! (*Makes music sound.*) Da-da-da-dum. Press the button. Bash! (*singing between hitting Land Shark with basher–cannon*) Press the button.

THERAPIST: We have to finish soon, because our time is almost up.

C (*alarmed*): Our time is almost up? Turn on the flashlight.

T: We see the light shining on the Land Shark.

C (*dramatic*): It makes me sick. My mouth! My

mouth is getting lightning. I hate lightning! I'm getting sick!

T: That's the end of the Land Shark. He fell down on the ground. That's the end of that one.

C: Oh. You idiot! Look what you did again! (*moving Land Shark along rug*) See how his mouth moves?

T: I see how his mouth moves when you drive him on the rug. I'm going to start packing up the furniture, Michael.

Some of this verbalization sounds like "adult" talk. (Maybe verbalizations he heard when his parents fought?)

C: Oh. Why are you going to start packing up the furniture?

T: Because it's time to get ready to go. That's what we do when it's time to go. We get packed up and get ready to go.

C: I want to stay for a little more.

T: A little more. Until I finish packing up.

C: (*Sings. then starts playing with flashlight. Tries to engage therapist in "ghost" play, with shadow on wall.*) Get him! Get him! Hyeena.

T: (*Hits shadow.*) I got him.

C: (*continues*) Get him again.

T: I can't reach it any more.

C: (*Laughing, moves shadow down.*)

T: I got it. Do you have a flashlight in your room?

Changing pace back to reality.

C: A big one. I can't carry it.

T: Can you turn it on at night if you wake up?

C: No. Can I play with the furniture? The family stuff.

T: We're all finished for today.

C (*whines*): Oh. Can I make a picture?

T: No time today. It's 10 to 6, and it's time to stop for today.

C: Why?

T: Next time, if you want to draw, you can. You did a lot of things today.

C: I want to play with the furniture some more.

T: Next time when you come, we'll decide right away what you want to do. OK?

Therapist should comment on how hard it is for Michael to leave today.

C: Guess what? I'm going to bring these two
again (*leaving with the Land Shark and the Bashasaurus*).

Comment on Session. This was a difficult session for several reasons. First, the mother's phone call had aroused some pressure on me to "calm Michael down" so that the day care situation would not get out of hand and so that Michael would "behave himself" for the wedding. Although I knew intellectually that it was not within my power (or anyone else's) to magically diffuse this child's anger, nonetheless, I sincerely hoped to help Michael feel less at the mercy of his rage. Trying to replay some of the frustrating events in Michael's life during the past week, I made several attempts early in the session to tie Michael's play to day care events (introducing the teacher doll) and to the weekend visit with his father (setting up the family doll play situation with the child doll visiting father). The second attempt resulted in the major battle scene in the kitchen that seemed to recapitulate the traumatic fight Michael had witnessed between his parents. I realized how tremendously significant this reenactment was, including the reference to the child doll hitting the daddy. In retrospect, I wish I had said something about the child wanting to stop the fight, but that he was too little. There was *no* verbalization during this fight scene, only grunts and goans, suggesting that Michael was reenacting a visually imprinted memory.

In the second half of the session Michael would not allow me to intervene in situations of repeated violence in which brute force dominated and the family was helplessly victimized by the barrage of primitive oral aggression.

The vehemence and relentlessness of this aggression (summarized here) was difficult to witness. Michael made me helpless by refusing to allow me to intervene and alter the course of events in his fantasy world, just as he had been helpless when he witnessed the fights between his parents and feebly tried to stop them.

A long-term goal for Michael was that he would learn to tolerate his own anger and talk about it but not blindly act it out. It was far too early in his therapy for him to be able to tolerate alternatives to immediate drive discharge. Just as the adult who is enraged by the betrayal of a loved one needs to go over and over his or her feelings of despair and fury before he or she can begin to reconstruct his or her life, so also will Michael need to reexperience the scenes of powerlessness and violence before he can be motivated to behave in a more mature way. It is the therapist's role at this early stage to stand by the child, offering support and giving occasional glimmers that things *can* work out differently.

Postlude to the Tenth Session. Because of the degree of violence expressed in this session, I decided to telephone Michael's father to ask him if any particularly upsetting events had occurred during Michael's weekend visit. I had had one previous meeting with Mr. Spivak in which I had emphasized the importance of Mr. Spivak's regular contact with Michael.

Related to the weekend, Mr. Spivak initially said things were OK. He noticed a "change" in Michael's behavior toward the end of the visit, when he went to play by himself and seemed "distant." At the very end of the conversation Mr. Spivak asked me, "Do you think an argument between me and my girlfriend could have triggered this [Michael's behavior during the past week]?"

I explained to Mr. Spivak that Michael was, indeed, very sensitive about arguments because of the fighting he had witnessed between him and his mother. I suggested that in the future, it would be advisable to avoid, insofar as possible, arguments or fights while Michael was visiting.

CONCLUDING COMMENTS

The two detailed sessions presented here represent a beginning exploration of a child's feelings associated with (1) the crisis of repeated witnessing of physical violence between his parents and the subsequent "loss" of his father and (2) the reawakening of fears and helplessness associated with this, precipitated by witnessing an "argument" between his father and the father's girlfriend.

The concept of a crisis as a single upsetting event clearly is not applicable in this case. This preschool child had been so traumatized by witnessing violence between his parents, and by the subsequent "loss" of his father, that his energies were not available for developing peer relationships even when his present situation was relatively stable. The child remained vulnerable to floods of primitive rage whenever life events stirred up memories of the extreme helplessness he experienced as a very young child.

The early treatment of this child required permitting him to reenact and play out his experience of aggression and helplessness. Much of the work during the first 6 months of treatment focused on the loss of his father (He's too sick to come and see you now. Maybe you'll see him again when you are much bigger.) and on his adjustment to his sister's birth and his new school.

The later treatment included some behavior modification techniques, rewarding Michael for demonstrating increased ability to control his outbursts at home and at school. This segment of work coincided with a very happy period in the mother's life, and because of her own improved circumstances, the mother was able to follow through with the therapist's suggestions for supporting Michael.

This case demonstrates a child's reaction to multiple family crises. It also demonstrates the stabilizing effect of therapy with a young child who already was evidencing disturbed behavior and who, without intervention, probably would have been identified in the future as an antisocial, acting-out, destructive youngster.

His teacher's report at the end of Michael's kindergarten year stated, "Michael likes 'writing' books. His books are very interesting. He shows excellent creative and expressive abilities. He has shown tremendous growth in his social and emotional development."

PLAY THERAPY MATERIALS

- Family dolls; intergenerational family dolls: Child Therapy Resources, P.O. Box 196, Dept. H, Locust Valley, NY 11560
- Doll furniture; doll house kitchen, doll house dining room: Creative Playthings, Princeton, NJ 08540
- Tape recorder

STUDY QUESTIONS

1. Is it appropriate for the therapist to attempt to reduce, interrupt, or provide a "happy ending" to the child's repeated, insistent enactments of violence? How can the therapist help the child make the transition to reality after such violent play?

2. Discuss the effect on the therapist of working with a child who is consumed with rage. What particular pitfalls must the therapist avoid in working with such a child?

3. How can the therapist most effectively consult with the child's day care and/or school when the presenting and ongoing problem involves the child's aggressive acting-out behavior toward other children in the group setting?

4. What do you consider the prognosis in this case? Can you envision any particular vulnerabilities for this child, and is there any way the therapist might help the parents anticipate these.

REFERENCES

Achenbach, T., & Edelbrock, C. (1981). Behavioral problems and competencies reported by parents of normal and disturbed children aged 4 through 16. *Monographs of the Society for Research in Child Development*, 46(1, Serial No. 188).

Bowlby, J. (1960). Grief and mourning in infancy and early childhood. *Psychoanalytic Study of the Child*, 15, 9-52.

Bowlby, J. (1961). Childhood mourning and its implications for psychiatry. *American Journal of Psychiatry*, 118, 481-498.

Erh, S., & Pynoos, R. S. (1985). Psychiatric interventions with child traumatized by violence. In D. H. Schetky & E. P. Benedek (Eds.), *Emerging issues in child psychiatry and the law* (pp. 285-309). New York: Brunner/Mazel.

Gardner, R. A. (1983). Children's reactions to parental death. In J. E. Schowalter, P. R. Patterson, M. Tallmer, A. H. Kutscher, S. V. Gullo, & D. Peretz (Eds.), *The child and death* (pp. 104-124). New York: Columbia University Press.

Hershorn, M., & Rosenbaum, A. (1985). Children of marital violence: A close look at the unintended victims. *American Journal of Orthopsychiatry*, 55(2), 260-266.

Jacobson, D. S. (1978). The impact of marital separation/divorce on children: Interpersonal hostility and child adjustment. *Journal of Divorce*, 2, 3-19.

Jaffe, P., Wolfe, D., Wilson, S., & Zak, L. (1986). Similarities in behavioral and social maladjustment among child victims and witnesses to family violence. *American Journal of Orthopsychiatry*, 56(1), 142-146.

Kalmuss, D. (1984). The intergenerational transmission of marital aggression. *Journal of Marriage and the Family, 46,* 11–19.

Kelly, J., & Wallerstein, J. (1975). The effects of parental divorce: Experience of the preschool child. *Journal of the American Academy of Child Psychiatry, 14*(4), 600–616.

Kotelchuck, M. (1972). *The nature of the child's tie to his father.* Unpublished doctoral dissertation, Harvard University.

Lamb, M. E. (1976). *The role of the father in child development.* New York: John Wiley & Sons.

Levy, D. (1939). Release therapy. *American Journal of Orthopsychiatry, 9,* 713–736.

Mahler, M. S., Pine, F., & Bergman, A. (1975). *The psychological birth of the human infant.* New York: Basic Books.

Parad, H. J. (1977). Crisis intervention. In J. Turner (Ed.), *Encyclopedia of social work* (18th ed., pp. 228–237). Washington, DC: National Association of Social Workers.

Rosenbaum, A., & O'Leary, K. (1981). Children: The unintended victims of marital violence. *American Journal of Orthopsychiatry, 51*(4), 692–699.

Terr, L. (1988). What happens to early memories of trauma? A study of twenty children under age five at the time of documented traumatic events. *Journal of the American Academy of Child and Adolescent Psychiatry, 27*(1), 96–104.

Terr, L. (1989). Treating psychic trauma in childhood in children: A preliminary discussion. *Journal of Traumatic Stress, 2,* 3–20.

CHAPTER 4

Victim of Sexual Abuse
Case of Rosa, Age 6

VIRGINIA C. STRAND

This chapter describes a brief treatment intervention with a child with whom there are suspicions of child sexual abuse. The focus of the initial intervention is to establish whether the child has been sexually abused and, if so, to assess the impact of that abuse and develop appropriate long-term treatment goals. The chapter details techniques for exploration of possible sexual abuse with a 6-year-old child and briefly outlines the design of long-term treatment priorities.

THEORETICAL FRAMEWORK

This discussion draws on the work of a number of researchers and practitioners. The first is that of Ann Burgess (1987). A crucial element of Dr. Burgess's work is the concept that sexual abuse constitutes either an acute or chronic trauma, depending primarily on the length of time that a child is victimized. With this as a basic premise, she then presents the concept of "trauma encapsulation" (Burgess, 1987) with its inherent concept of secrecy, which interferes with normal outlets for the expression of thoughts and affect engendered by the traumatic event. Consequently, the child's thoughts and memories about the actual event or incidents remain in current memory and must be defended against, together with feelings of rage, helplessness, powerlessness, shame, and guilt. The subsequent defensive structure consumes available psychic energy needed to accomplish normal developmental tasks, thereby resulting in emotional and behavioral symptoms widely cited in the literature (Briere & Runtz, 1988a, 1988b; Gelinas, 1983; Summit, 1988).

In order to resolve the trauma of sexual abuse in a healthy way, the trauma must be reexperienced through the retelling of the events in the context of a therapeutic relationship. The therapist must approach this task of helping the child relive the events carefully. Inherent in this approach is the idea of building up defenses before allowing the trauma of the abuse to surface. Hartman and Burgess (1988) have described an approach to the treatment of sexually abused children, which I have adapted in my own practice. The six phases described below parallel but are not identical to those put forth by Burgess.

Developmental Assessment

On referral of a child for treatment, the first task is to complete a developmental assessment. This can be achieved through the combination of a clinical interview with the child and the taking of a developmental history. Special emphasis needs to be placed on gathering information about possible cognitive distortions as well as emotional indicators and behaviors known to be associated with sexual trauma (Jehu, Klassen, & Gazen, 1985–1986). In addition to evaluating the child's cognitive, emotional, and social development, it is also important to make a specific determination about the child's ability to differentiate between the truth and a lie, and between fact and fantasy. This should not be construed to mean that the clinician makes a judgment about whether the child *is* telling the truth in a given case situation, but that a judgment needs to be made about the *child's ability to distinguish fact from fantasy.* The child's mental state becomes especially significant in assessing for sexual trauma, and the inability to distinguish the truth from a lie has significant legal as well as clinical implications. This particular aspect of the evaluation is referred to as a "credibility assessment."

The child's parents and other caretakers are the primary source of information for the developmental history. It is also important to obtain information from others who know the child, such as teachers, counselors, and caseworkers. The history should include information about the child's knowledge of sexuality, including, for the younger child, the child's exposure to sexual activity between parents or other adults and to sexually explicit magazines or videos. In some instances, psychological testing and/or psychiatric evaluation may be an important part of the assessment.

Sexual Abuse History

The second step involves the assessment of the impact of the sexual abuse itself. I have found it helpful to use the conceptual framework known as the child sexual abuse syndrome, developed by Suzanne Sgroi (1984), in organizing the sexual abuse history. The child sexual abuse syndrome is characterized by the following phases:

Engagement

Most children are abused by adults they know. The literature documents that between 80% and 90% of children who are sexually abused know their perpetrators (Finkelhor, 1984; Russell, 1986). Therefore, it is within the framework of a *preexisting* relationship that the adult engages the child in sexual activity. This nonsexual stage sets the stage for the sexual contact that follows. Engagement often takes the form of attempting to disguise the sexual activity by presenting the interaction as a game, an attempt to educate or teach the child, or as concerns about the child's health. The use of pornographic magazines and videotapes to normalize the sexual activity is becoming an increasingly common ploy. All of these approaches are geared toward having the child accept the sexual contact as "normal," thereby decreasing the child's tendency to disclose the activity.

The adult uses his or her authority as a parent, teacher, or other person in a position of power relative to the child to manipulate the child. The child's willingness to please important adults is easily exploited.

Sexual Interaction

Sexual interaction often begins with less intrusive sexual acts, such as fondling or sexual kissing. If the adult has access to the same child over time, this activity often proceeds to more intrusive acts, such as oral-genital contact and penetration, either anal or vaginal. One of the hallmarks of the sexual interaction is the tendency for it to be *frequent* and, as noted above, to *progress* to more intrusive sexual activity over time.

An important qualification in the tendency for progression occurs when the adult appears to be under the influence of drugs—specifically crack or cocaine. In these instances, sexual interaction may move immediately to intrusive acts.

Secrecy

The adult who is sexually engaging a child almost always communicates to the child that the sexual behavior is to be kept a secret. This communication may be covert, through the adult's secretive, furtive behavior, or more overt, through direct statements that the sexual activity is to be kept a secret. Verbal manipulation (i.e., "Don't tell your mother about this, she could not handle it") to outright threats ("If you tell anyone you will be sorry") may be employed by the offender.

Children who know that the adult is a violent or physically abusive person may be coerced into keeping the secret if, for example, they are threatened with being hit or beaten. The adult may not have to resort to physical abuse during the sexual assault to manipulate the child into not telling. Children depend on the adults around them for support and survival, and they almost always understand the message about secrecy and do not reveal the sexual activity.

Disclosure

The disclosure of sexual abuse, when it occurs, may be delayed or unconvincing. Often the disclosure is accidental, as in the case of the child discovered to have gonorrhea, or when another victim or friend of the victim discloses against the wishes of the child who has been sexually abused. Other times the disclosure is purposeful. Initially, only one incident may be disclosed, and it is important for those doing the investigation to realize that the first report is rarely the only incident (Sgroi, 1984).

Suppression

The tendency for a child to retract, recant, or minimize an initial report of sexual abuse is so common that this has been identified as a phase of the syndrome. The pressure for the child to minimize or recant is immense. Much of the pressure is internal in origin. Since most children feel that they are to blame for the sexual abuse, talking about it stirs up feelings of guilt, despair, fear, and embarrassment. Children may fear rejection by the offender or by members of the family. Sometimes these fears are real, for example, when family members apply external pressure on the child to withdraw allegations.

In order to obtain an accurate sexual history, it is often necessary to uncover certain elements of the trauma (details of the sexual abuse) in order to establish the duration and nature of the sexual abuse. Preparing children and parents for this process constitutes the third step in the initial intervention.

Enhancing Ego Strengths

It is especially crucial to enhance the child's ego strengths prior to efforts to elicit details about the sexual interaction. This can be done directly with the child as well as with the parents. It is important to help the child feel safe and protected from further abuse while reducing confused understandings and increasing the child's means of self-comfort. Protecting the child may entail a range of intervention from removing the child from the abusive home, to orders of protection restraining the alleged offender from contact, to supervised contact, or any combination of the above.

Helping the child learn to comfort herself or himself means helping the child identify the activities that make the child feel good, reduce anxiety, or channel aggression. Examples of these activities include searching out people to whom the child can talk, listening to music, writing, learning relaxation exercises, or finding active outlets for aggressive play. The therapist should work with the parent as well as the child in identifying and using these activities.

Surfacing the Trauma and Assessing Its Impact

When the child's ego strengths have been enhanced, and the child has been prepared in a developmentally appropriate fashion for the uncomfortable feelings that may accompany the retelling of abusive incidents, the work of surfacing the trauma can begin. Play, the use of anatomically correct dolls or drawings, the use of specialized workbooks and board games, and art therapy are all useful in bringing out traumatic detail. I use anatomically correct dolls, for example, to elicit the names of the genitals and secondary sexual characteristics with pre-adolescent children. Some of the workbooks provide a useful means not only of helping to surface the traumatic material but also of enhancing self-esteem.

Once the trauma surfaces, it is important to help the child work through the impact of the abuse. To assess this impact, we can draw on the work of David Finkelhor and Angela Browne (1985). Their conceptualization provides a framework for prioritizing the treatment goals. Four characteristics are manifest in victims of sexual trauma (the traumagenic dynamics model): (1) sexual traumatization, (2) stigmatization, (3) betrayal, and (4) powerlessness.

Sexual traumatization refers to the impairment of healthy sexual functioning because of the sexual nature of the trauma. The varying degree of impairment includes confusion between sexuality and affection, confusion about sexual norms, age-inappropriate sexual knowledge and sexual behavior, negative associations to sexual feelings, a tendency to form erotic relationships, sexual dysfunction, confusion about sexual identity, and in some instances reenactment through the sexual abuse of others.

Stigmatization refers to the tendency of the victims to blame themselves for the abuse, to feel shame, guilt, and self-hate. Low self-esteem and poor self-image are often a consequence. Self-deprecating behaviors (inability to assert one's rights or needs), self-mutilating behaviors (inflicting injuries, anorexia, bulimia), and/or self-destructive behaviors (suicidal ideation or gesture, substance abuse) are common manifestations of this dynamic.

The *betrayal* dynamic refers to the betrayal of trust experienced by the victim of sexual abuse. This leads to difficulty in interpersonal relationships, as evidenced by difficulty in forming relationships, guardedness, suspiciousness, ambivalence, and choosing relationships where one is exploited. Antisocial attitudes and behaviors evolve in response to the rage and anger associated with the betrayal.

The fourth characteristic, *powerlessness*, relates to the sense of helplessness and vulnerability engendered in the child victim of sexual abuse. Anxiety symptoms, phobias, dissociative disorders, and regressive behaviors are appropriately clustered with this characteristic.

The therapist evaluates the child along each dynamic and determines the salience of each component. Once this is accomplished, the treatment priorities can be established. If, for example, the child has experienced betrayal as the most debilitating effect, efforts specifically geared toward developing trust should be undertaken first.

Working Through

This is generally the longest phase of treatment. Treatment priorities can now be systematically addressed using the strategies and tools in the section relating to surfacing the trauma. One board game that I have found particularly helpful with the latency-age child is Play It Safe with SASA (Speak Out About Sexual Abuse). This game strengthens the child's self-esteem while also exploring the emotional reactions and cognitive distortions related to the sexual abuse experience.

Resolution

Resolution of the trauma is evidenced when the child is able to talk about the details without the concomitant emotional upheaval and when behavioral manifestations of the abuse have subsided.

THE CASE: ROSA TORRES, AGE 6

Family Information

Rosa Torres, age 6, was referred by Child Protective Services (CPS) for an evaluation and short-term treatment after allegations of child sexual abuse had been reported to New York State Central Registry for Child Abuse and Neglect. The family included Rosa, her mother, Lisa, 34, her father, Roberto, 39, an older half brother, Jorge, 17, and a 2-year-old sister, Sabrina. Rosa, her mother, Jorge, and Sabrina were currently living with Mrs. Torres's mother in the maternal grandmother's home. Mr. Torres was living with his mother and had visitation with Rosa and Sabrina one night during the week and every weekend.

Mrs. Torres had been born in Puerto Rico and came to New York City as a young child with her mother and older brother. This brother had been killed as a teen-ager in a gang fight. Mrs. Torres was a nurse and had married Roberto Torres at age 26. She had never been married to Jorge's father.

Roberto was also Puerto Rican. He had been born in New York City, had graduated from high school, and worked his way up in a mail order business to the position of salesman. He had been married twice before and had two children (both boys) from his earlier marriages. He had no contact with either son.

Rosa's parents had been separated for approximately 6 months at the time of the first interview. According to the CPS worker who referred the child, both parents wanted physical custody of Rosa. Three weeks prior to the first interview, Mrs. Torres had called in a report of alleged sexual abuse against Mr. Torres, reportedly on the basis of a disclosure by Rosa that "Daddy was touching my private parts." Mrs. Torres had also asked the Court to suspend visitation with the father until the CPS investigation was complete. The judge did not suspend visitation but ruled that visits between the father and child would be supervised by the Department of Social Services until CPS had completed its investigation.

Presenting Problem

At the point of intake, the CPS worker had had two interviews with Rosa and had met individually with the mother, the father, and the maternal grandmother. Rosa had not disclosed any details to the worker regarding the alleged sexual abuse beyond saying that "Daddy touched me in my private."

The CPS worker had had the child examined by a physician experienced in child sexual abuse. The examination was inconclusive, and no specific findings were consistent with child sexual abuse.

The purpose of the referral to me was for assistance in evaluating the possibility of sexual abuse, to prepare for testimony in court if that were the case, and to assess and document the ongoing treatment needs of Rosa and/or family members. Since the court views "blind" evaluations as more objective, the developmental history normally gathered from a parent at the beginning of treatment was delayed until after the first interview with the child.

First Interview

Rosa was brought to the first interview by her mother and grandmother. I met them in the waiting room and introduced myself to all three. I asked Rosa if she wanted to come with me to see the toys in the playroom. Rosa was initially reluctant, standing with her body sideways to me and avoiding eye contact. With a little coaxing from her mother and my offer of something to drink, she was induced into going into the playroom. I stopped in the kitchen along the way to the playroom to get Rosa some juice.

Content of Session	*Therapist's Rationale*

THERAPIST: Rosa, do you remember my name?

ROSA: (*Shakes head no.*)

T: Well, it's Dr. Strand. Do you think that you can say that?

R: Dr. Strand (*very clearly*).

T: Do you know why your mother brought you to see me today?

Setting the context for our meeting.

R: (*Avoids eye contact, shakes head yes, moves toward the shelves that hold toys.*) It's about my daddy.

T: Yes, your mother has told me that she is worried that you may have been upset by some things that your father did. I will want to talk with you about that later after we know each other a little better, but first we are just going to spend some time getting to know each other. (*Helps her bring out toy dishes and invites her to set up whatever she wants.*) So, I wonder, could you tell me a little bit about yourself. I know that you are 6 . . .

Moving to nonthreatening subjects to engage her.

R: My birthday is March 13th.

T: I see you know your birthday. Where do you live?

R: Yonkers.

T: And do you have a best friend?

R: Maria; she lives on my street (*busily playing with toy dishes*).

T: (*still playing with dishes—Rosa has asked the therapist to play house with her*) Do you live in a house or in an apartment building?

Taking advantage of play theme to get at potentially significant information.

R: We live with my grandmother, and she lives on the first floor of a house. My aunt and my cousins live upstairs.

T: And where did you live before that?

R: We lived in a big building on the third floor.

T: And where you live now, does everyone have their own bedroom?

R: Well, Sabrina and I sleep with my mommy, and grandma has her own bedroom. And Jorge sleeps on the couch in the living room.

T: What about when your father lived with you, where did you sleep then?

R: I had my own room then.

T: Did your mommy and daddy always sleep together?

R: No, sometimes Daddy slept on the couch, and sometimes he slept with me.

T: Where was the couch?

R: In the living room.

I continue to play with Rosa and pursue information about her daily life, especially about who takes care of her on a regular basis. Through this line of inquiry I learn that Rosa used to go to a babysitter named Diane when her mother worked. Rosa's grandmother takes care of her now after school when her mother is working. Rosa reported that her father used to put her to bed at night. Some of the details of the bedtime routine emerge. It appears that her father would often read Rosa a story and give her juice. He would also get her up in the morning and get her ready for school.

During this conversation, I interweave questions, using the play materials at hand, aimed at establishing developmental information. An attempt is also made to establish the nature of the child's relationships with family members, especially with her father and mother.

Content of Session	*Therapist's Rationale*

THERAPIST: Who would you say that you like the best in your family?

ROSA: My father, but my mother, too.

T: Can you tell me why?

R: He plays games with me and takes me places. My mother used to hit me more, but now she's nice.

T: I know that you do not see your father as much now as before. Do you remember what kinds of things you used to do with him?

R: Well, before, Daddy would pick me up and take me to Mimi's [father's mother] house. It's fun there.

T: And what about now?

R: I miss him sometimes. I only get to see him now in Miss Ramos's office.

I go on to discuss Rosa's feelings about each member of her family. Jorge is "OK" but "won't play with me much." Sabrina "takes too much of Mommy's time," and "Mimi," her father's mother, is favored over "Grandma," with whom she currently lives. From this interchange it appears that Rosa is quite attached to her father and that her mother appears as a more distant and possibly punitive figure than her father.

Before the end of the session, since Rosa appears to be engaged and is playing readily and is more open in answering my questions, I make the decision to broach the issue of sexual abuse. Before doing this, however, I want to know the child's words for the genitals and secondary sexual characteristics. The anatomically correct dolls serve this purpose.

Content of Session	*Therapist's Rationale*

THERAPIST: I'd like to talk with you now about something that may be a little more difficult to talk about. I have some special dolls that I would like to show you. (*pointing to the breasts on the female child doll*) What do you call these?

ROSA: Titties.

T: And this? (*pointing to the vagina*)

R: Vagina.

T: Do you have another word for it, too?

R: I forget.

I asked Rosa if she could identify the buttocks and anus on a male and female doll as well as the penis on the male doll. She used the words "butt," "butt-hole," and "penis" for these parts. When I next asked if she knew what the "private parts" of the body were, and if she could point to them on the dolls, she correctly pointed to the nipples, vagina, buttocks, and anus of the female dolls and the penis, anus, and buttocks of the male dolls.

Content of Session	*Therapist's Rationale*

THERAPIST: Now Rosa, I have to ask you a question that may be a little harder for you to answer. Did anyone ever want you to touch their private parts?

Rosa: No (*moving away from therapist, avoiding eye contact*).

T: Did anyone ever want to touch your private parts?

R: I would not let them.

T: Who wanted to?

R: I forget. (*At this point Rosa has moved almost as far away from the therapist as she can get in the room, and it is clear that raising this material has generated a great deal of anxiety.*)

T: It looks like this is hard for you to talk about, and I can see that you maybe don't know me well enough yet to want to talk about it any more. Would you like to get back to playing for a little while before we stop for today?

Although Rosa is not denying contact, she is not ready to talk.

The rest of the session was devoted to play with the doll house and discussion of nonthreatening material. The session ended about 10 minutes after the interchange around the dolls.

Developmental History

Mrs. Torres was seen separately at the end of the session with Rosa for the purpose of obtaining a developmental history. She reported that Rosa had been 3 weeks overdue and that she had been delivered by cesarean section. Mrs. Torres had been very anxious during the pregnancy, as she had had three miscarriages prior to Rosa's birth. However, Rosa was a healthy baby who walked, talked, and was toilet trained all before schedule. At age 2 Rosa fell and broke some of her front teeth. Aside from that and an accident when she fell and bruised herself badly at 3½, Rosa has had no major accidents, injuries, or illnesses. Rosa entered kindergarten at age 5. This year in first grade, she is having problems including distractibility, poor attention span, difficulties forming age-appropriate peer relationships, cognitive delays interfering with language acquisition, and overall immaturity.

In terms of education about sexuality, Mrs. Torres reported that since Rosa had started talking to her about what her father had done, she had taught her the correct words for vagina and penis. Before that Rosa had used the terms "cookie" and "birdie." Mrs. Torres stated that Rosa had had many questions about where babies come from when she was pregnant with Sabrina. Mrs. Torres reported telling Rosa that when "God was ready for you to have a baby, he helped mommies grow a baby in their stomach." Mrs. Torres stated that she had always taught Rosa not to touch herself "down there" and that Rosa's preoccupation with masturbation over the last few months was very upsetting to her. In terms of exposure to sexual acts between herself and her husband, Mrs. Torres reported that as far as she knew, Rosa had once come into their bedroom when she was 4 when they were engaged in intercourse. Since that time, she had been very careful not to expose Rosa to their sex life. She also discussed the fact that her husband sometimes watched sexually explicit videotapes but she did not want him to have them in the house, and she did not think that Rosa had ever seen these.

Mrs. Torres said that her husband had shared caretaking for Rosa from age 2 until they separated. He got her up in the morning and insisted on putting her to bed at night, even when Mrs. Torres was home. He would also take her to his mother's for breakfast several times a week, and they had used his mother more than hers for babysitting while they were living together. Rosa had been in a day care program since she was 2. Mrs. Torres's mother now takes care of her after school.

Mrs. Torres reported that she separated from Mr. Torres about 6 months ago and moved back with her parents. Visitation with Rosa by Mr. Torres was irregular until 4 months ago, when he began to pick her up every Saturday and kept her overnight at his mother's home.

In terms of age-inappropriate sexual behavior, Mrs. Torres reported that Rosa began to masturbate excessively about a year ago. It was so noticeable that her kindergarten teacher had discussed it with the mother last spring. Rosa was also labeled "provocative" by the teacher, who reported incidents in which Rosa would pull her pants down in front of boys and try to touch their penises. Mrs. Torres also reported that in the last 4 months, Rosa had been pulling at her underpants. She said that this behavior was especially noticeable on Sundays, after Rosa had been with her father. It was so noticeable that Mrs. Torres tried different detergents and bought a different type of underpants for Rosa, thinking that these might be causing the irritation.

Mrs. Torres stated that starting about a year ago, Rosa began waking up with nightmares. Rosa had also become extremely oppositional in the last year. She would stomp her feet and run out of the room when her mother attempted to discipline her. Inattentiveness and difficulty concentrating at school had affected performance in school this year.

Mrs. Torres reported that Rosa was increasingly reluctant to go on visitations with her father, coming up with excuses, saying "I'm sick" or "I don't want to go." She would not get dressed sometimes, and then would want to wear lots of clothes, including pants over shorts. Rose was also evidencing some fear of men. She was reluctant to approach her grandfather, with whom she had previously been close, and seemed anxious about being around men.

Preliminary Assessment

In the initial session, Rosa presented as a child of average intelligence, with verbal skills appropriate to a first grader. She was slight of build, with thin, shoulder-length brown hair and large, dark brown eyes. Her fine motor skills and memory capability appeared within normal limits. Emotionally, there was evidence of depression and heavy reliance on avoidance when confronted with anxiety-provoking material. Behavioral symptoms reported by the mother included regression, fear responses to men, and oppositional behavior. School records substantiated a decline in performance, difficulty concentrating, and behavioral problems with peers.

Although the nature of the child's reaction to the parents' separation and pending divorce had not been explored in detail in this session, there were some clues to the family dynamics and her attachment to her parents. Her father emerged as possibly the more nurturing figure in that he was remembered by Rosa as the one who used to put her to bed every night and the one who took her places and did fun things with her. This dynamic was consistent with the mother's report about the amount of time and attention Mr. Torres had devoted to his daughter.

In Rosa's eyes, Mrs. Torres emerged as the more emotionally distant parent. One of the first things that Rosa mentioned about her mother was that mother spanks her. However, Rosa also disclosed that she now sleeps with her mother and by implication feels safer now that she is with her at night. The interaction that the therapist observed between Rosa and her mother in the waiting room illustrated Rosa's dependence on her mother.

In terms of the sexual abuse allegations, her answers to the questions asked about touching of private parts of the body were striking. Also remarkable is that she does not answer "No" to the question "Has anybody ever touched your private parts?" but says "They wanted to but I would not let them." She also does not deny that someone touched her but says that she "forgets" the name of that person.

Children who have been sexually victimized often feel that they are to blame for the victimization, and in order to avoid the anxiety associated with guilt, they deny the victimization. Although reluctance to talk about her father and ambivalent feelings about him would be normal for any child caught in the middle of a conflicted parental relationship, the response noted above must raise a red flag in the interviewer's mind. However, in the interest of maintaining the therapeutic relationship, which had begun to develop and was clearly threatened by my introduction of this sensitive topic, it seemed wiser to defer pursuit of this issue to a later session.

Second and Third Sessions

In the second and third sessions, Rosa remained very resistant to talking about any of the sexual abuse allegations, continuing to say that she "forgot" if anyone had touched her. I conceptualized my task in these first three sessions as building a therapeutic relationship and beginning to make an assessment of ego strengths. As a result, by the end of the third session Rosa was responding more fully and becoming engaged with me. Rosa perceived her mother as a protective, helping figure some of the time, and Rosa was mature enough in her cognitive and motor development to know how to take care of and comfort herself. Therefore, it was possible to introduce the idea that Rosa could help herself to feel better when she got upset. I clarified that she might become upset when she was asked to talk about things that she did not want to talk about. The concept of using the therapy session for both "work" and "play" was introduced. The "work" was talking about the upsetting things that Daddy and/or Mommy did, and the "play" was playing with anything she wanted in the playroom.

It is important to note that the interviewer asks the child nonleading open-ended questions, in which there is choice, or questions are restated to obtain clarification. However, it is not always possible to avoid asking leading questions, and depending on the context of a line of questions and/or the developmental age of the child, they may be appropriate.

Fourth Session

At the beginning of the fourth session, Rosa was asked if she understood why she was here. She responded, "To work and to play." When asked what the "work" was, she stated that it was "talking about Daddy." Fifteen minutes into this session, after playing with toys of Rosa's choice, I introduced the issue of the sexual abuse allegations.

Content of Session	*Therapist's Rationale*
THERAPIST: I am worried that maybe your father did some things that you are afraid to talk about. I wonder if you could just show me with the dolls what happened, since it is hard to talk about it.	Testing out hypothesis that abuse may have occurred with an invitation to play it out.
ROSA: (*Throws female child doll and adult male doll to therapist.*) Daddy would be in my room a lot.	
T: Do you know why he would come in?	
R: When Daddy was nervous he would sleep with me.	
T: How was Daddy nervous?	
R: (*Stands with her hands at her sides, holds her body straight and shakes all over, demonstrating what could conceivably be an imitation of a person having an orgasm.*)	
T: What would happen next?	
R: The bed would get all wet.	
T: After Daddy got nervous and shook all over, the bed got wet?	
R: Yes.	
T: Would you get wet?	

R: No.

T: What would happen next?

R: He would go to the bathroom to clean up.

T: And then what would happen.

R: I'm tired of talking.   Child's anxiety is building.

T: OK. You know that I said that we would not
have to work the whole time, but I have one more
question. Would this happen a lot or a little?

R: A lot of times. (*Rosa is moving away, fidget-
ing, avoiding eye contact.*)

T: You have done a good job talking about some-   Acknowledging the child's feel-
thing that seems to make you upset. (*Rosa nods.*)   ings.
What would help you feel better now?

R: I want to play "Chutes and Ladders."

The rest of the session was devoted to playing a board game without any
further attempts on my part to reintroduce the subject of her father. By the end of
the fourth session Rosa appeared to have reestablished her equilibrium, readily
enjoyed her snack, and was not anxious to leave when the time was up.

Fifth Session

Rosa started the session by saying that she wanted to play a board game. After
playing two games, I made an effort to engage her in conversation about her
father, which she avoided strenuously.

Content of Session   *Therapist's Rationale*

THERAPIST: Are you scared?   Her feelings about breaking the
                                                          secret may be a major obstacle to
ROSA: (*sitting and looking at floor; no answer*)   discussing the details of the abuse.

T: Can you tell me, are you scared or mad?

R: Scared.

T: Are you afraid that something bad will happen
to you if you talk more about Daddy?

R: Yes (*in a low voice*).

T: Can you tell me what you are afraid of?

R: (*Shakes head no.*)

T: Are you afraid that something will happen to
Mommy?

R: (*Nods yes.*)

T: Can you tell me what you are afraid of?

R: No.

T: Are you afraid that something will happen to Daddy?

R: (*no answer*)

T: Would you like to stop for today and go see your mother?

R: Yes.

T: OK. Let's stop for today.

Child appeared immobilized by the feelings that had been aroused.

When we got to the waiting room Rosa stood silently by her mother's side holding her hand. Her mother gave her a hug, and in response to her mother's gentle questioning, she said that she was scared and upset and wanted to go home.

Mrs. Torres then reported that Rosa had said to her after the last visit with her father that Mr. Torres had told Rosa that he would shoot her mother if Rosa talked about what she and Daddy did. Mrs. Torres said that she had told Rosa that Daddy was saying that to scare her and that he would not really do that. She said to me that although Mr. Torres did have a gun, she did not believe that he would hurt either one of them, although he was capable of saying this kind of thing to scare Rosa.

Prior to the next session with Rosa, which was 2 weeks away because of an intervening holiday, another supervised visit was planned with Rosa's father. I telephoned the CPS worker to discuss what Mrs. Torres had said happened on the last visit. The CPS worker said that Mrs. Torres had told her this also, and that rather than watching the visit between Mr. Torres and Rosa through a glass partition, she would stay in the room with them on the next visit.

After the supervised visit, and before the next therapy session with me, the CPS worker called me to discuss how the visit had gone. She said that she had terminated the visit early because she felt that Mr. Torres was acting inappropriately with Rosa, crying and saying that he loved her and would never do anything to hurt her. The CPS worker said that she explained to Mr. Torres that he would have to "get himself together" so that Rosa did not feel burdened emotionally.

This was important information for planning for the next session. The information from the CPS worker validated the mother's perception that the father was capable of being inappropriate with Rosa and also indicated that the CPS worker could be an ally in the treatment process.

Sixth Session

Rosa again started the session by wanting to play a board game. She appeared relaxed and talked relatively easily. She said that she had had fun over the weekend with her mother and grandmother, who had taken her to a movie. She said that she had seen her father and that she had been glad to see him.

Content of Session

Therapist's Rationale

THERAPIST: You know, Rosa, your mom has told me a little more about exactly what she is worried about that your Dad has done.

ROSA: (*combing a large, stuffed toy dog*) This is a nice dog.

T: Are you still scared to talk about what happened with Daddy?

Exploring to see how Rosa may have been intimidated into keeping a secret.

R: (*Moves to the floor of the playroom, picks at toys on the shelves.*) Yes.

T: Are you afraid of Daddy?

R: (*not looking at therapist*) Yes.

T: Will Daddy hurt you if you tell?

R: Yes.

T: How?

R: He will kill me.

T: How?

R: Shoot me.

T: (*Takes adult male anatomically correct doll, places it on one side of the room, and begins to surround it with toy soldiers, all with guns pointing at the adult male doll.*) You know what? We are going to pretend that this is Daddy, and we are going to put all these soldiers around him to protect you from him. (*Therapist puts down nine soldiers as she counts.*) Do you want to put more?

Decide to try to see if symbolically, through play, Rosa can be helped to feel safe.

R: Yes. (*Rosa takes over, putting every toy soldier in the collection—30 in all—around the figure of "Daddy."*)

T: Oh, and let's put this police car between you and Daddy as well to make sure that you are really safe. (*Places toy police car between soldiers and Rosa, so that soldiers and police car are now in between.*) You know Rosa, not only are you safe here, but in real life, your Daddy can only see you when Miss Ramos is there with you. Do you feel safe with Miss Ramos?

R: Yes, and do you know she made my Daddy leave when he was worrying me.

T: Yes, she did tell me that, and I am glad that she did that. . . . Do you remember how you told me that Daddy gets into bed with you and how he gets nervous?

R: Yes.

T: Does he touch himself?

R: (*Stands up as she begins to talk, looking directly at therapist, gesturing with hands.*) He touches his private parts.

T: With his elbow?

R: Noooo, with his hands. He did it in the living room, too.

An effort to get detail without asking leading questions.

T: Was he standing or sitting?

R: Sitting, like this. (*Rosa squats down and puts her hands between her legs.*)

T: What was he doing?

R: Touching his birdie with his hands.

T: This is a birdie? (*pointing to the penis on the adult male doll*)

R: Yes; and that's a cookie. (*Points to the vagina on the female child doll.*)

T: What happened then?

R: Stuff came out of the end (*Rosa makes a face*), and it got all over the couch.

T: Did he do this in your bedroom, too?

R: (*animated*) Yes, all over the house, all over the house, in his bedroom, too.

T: Did he ever want you to touch his birdie?

R: Yes, he wanted me to, but I didn't.

T: Did he ever want to touch your cookie?

R: Yes, he wanted to, but I didn't let him. (*At this point Rosa is getting very excited. She takes the adult male doll and pulls the pants off, pulling and twisting the penis.*)

T: Why don't we pretend that he [father figure] is dead?

To help her feel safe and reduce tension.

R: Yes, yes, we'll bury him. (*Puts him under the throw rug on the floor and steps hard on the doll.*)

T: I talk to a lot of children whose daddies have done these things. Sometimes children don't want to let their daddy touch them, but daddies are bigger and stronger and sometimes they *make* the children touch them, or put their birdie against their cookie.

Normalizing and reassuring the child.

R: He wanted to put his birdie against me, but I wouldn't let him do it.

T: You would try not to let him do it, but would he ever do it anyway?

R: Yes, but sometimes I would run away.

T: Where would you go?

R: To my secret place and hide. (*Gets up and goes and stomps on the doll under the rug again.*)

T: When your Daddy would put his birdie against your cookie, was it hard or soft?

R: Hard.

T: Would it move or stay still?

R: Move.

T: And would stuff come out of the end?

R: (*Nods yes.*)

T: And would it get on you?

R: Sometimes, and sometimes it got on the furniture, too. Once it got on the couch in the living room, and we had to spray to take the smell away.

T: Did he ever want you to put your mouth on his birdie?

R: I didn't want to, but he wanted me to.

T: Did he ever put anything on his birdie to make it taste better?

Knowledge of how adults attempt to entice children

R: (*Looks up at therapist, surprised.*) Yes, peanut butter, honey, lotion, all kinds of things.

T: Did that make it taste good?

R: No! (*adamant*) No! No!

T: How did it taste?

R: It tasted yucky.

T: Did your Daddy put his finger in your cookie?

R: Yes.

T: Which finger?

R: (*Shows therapist the middle finger of her hand.*)

T: Did it move or stay still?

R: Moved. (*Illustrates by taking her finger, squatting down, and rubbing her finger on her vaginal area over her tights.*)

T: How did it feel when Daddy did that?

R: It hurt.

T: Have you told your mom everything that you told me?

R: No, not the part about his putting his birdie in my mouth and against my cookie . . . only that he *touched* my cookie.

T: Can I tell your mom?   I need to know how safe Rosa

R: (*Nods yes readily.*)   feels with her mother.

During the rest of the session, I reviewed what Rosa had disclosed, putting this review in the context of being sure that I had heard Rosa correctly. This allowed Rosa to reaffirm what she had already said and add or correct details that I may have missed or misunderstood. I also brought up again the issue of Rosa being afraid of her father. Rosa was able to explain that she had seen her father's gun and that she thought that he would shoot her and her mother just as she had seen him shoot a dog once. Despite this fear, she appeared to have been reassured by the developing confidence in her mother's ability to protect her and the increasing closeness of their relationship. The reality of supervised contact with her father, which reinforced feelings of safety without her having to "lose" her father, was also reassuring. The evolution of a trusting relationship with me, coupled with these external factors, enabled Rosa to make a fuller disclosure than had been possible before.

Based on the information presented by Rosa during the first six sessions, it was possible to determine that her presentation was consistent with the child sexual abuse syndrome. *Engagement* was achieved through the nature of the parent–child relationship and the special relationship that the father had fostered through his caretaking activities. He had clearly attempted to normalize the sexual contact by introducing it originally under the guise of a normal bedtime routine. The *sexual interaction* consisted of genital fondling, oral–genital contact, and penis-to-vagina contact. The sensory detail (i.e., the penis *felt* hard, the finger *hurt*, there was a *smell* when "stuff" came out of the end of the penis) and peripheral detail (e.g., he was sitting, it happened all over the house) provide contextual grounding for the sexual acts. *Secrecy* was obtained through manipulation of the child's trust and dependency as well as by overt threats. *Disclosure* was delayed, as is often the case, and *suppression* was evident in the process of the disclosure over the course of the sessions as well as by the fear response in the sessions.

This opinion was communicated to CPS following the sixth session.

Seventh through Ninth Sessions

In the seventh session, I reviewed with Rosa what I had told her mother and the CPS worker. This discussion stimulated Rosa to reenact the "killing" of her father again.

Content of Session

THERAPIST: You are pretty angry at your father for the things that he did to you, aren't you?

ROSA: Yes! (*hitting at father figure*)

T: Well, it is OK to be angry and feel like you would want to kill him.

R: I know. Mommy said she is mad too, and that there is something wrong with him.

T: Well, I don't know if there is something wrong with him. . . . I do know that he made a big mistake in touching you. Do you know what happens when someone makes a mistake?

R: They get punished.

T: Do you think that your dad should get punished?

R: Yes, but I don't want him to go to jail. Mommy says she wants him to go to jail.

T: Well, I don't know about jail, but I do think he needs to learn how to be a better daddy before he takes care of you by himself again. There are places that he can go to get help to learn how to be a better daddy, and that is what I will help him do if he wants to. In the meantime, he can only see you with Miss Ramos.

R: Yes, I know. Would you like to play "Chutes and Ladders"?

Therapist's Rationale

Attempt to reframe the "bad" or "sick" parent to one who has made a mistake.

Rosa was clearly more comfortable with her angry feelings now that she had been given permission to express them and nothing bad had happened. It is important to note that she continued to see her father in supervised visits, which contributed to her sense that she had not "lost" her father by her "betrayal" of the secret.

The mother, by contrast, was enraged when she learned that the details of sexual abuse were more intrusive than she had first realized. She was consequently very unhappy about the continued visits. One of the roles for the therapist was to clarify the strong attachment between Rosa and her father and the importance for Rosa of a continuing relationship with him.

Based on the material that emerged in the next two sessions, it was possible to assess the impact of the sexual victimization on Rosa according to the traumagenic dynamics model. The presence of sexual traumatization was profound. The nature and duration of the abuse had left Rosa with distorted images of sexuality and generated a tendency to inappropriately eroticize relationships. The threat of the use of force had created a sense of powerlessness that was manifest in dissociative responses and regressive behavior. Feelings of betrayal by the more loved of the two parents and by the failure of the mother to protect her had led Rosa to a damaged self-image. Her self-esteem had been further damaged by the shame and guilt associated with the stigmatization dynamic.

For Rosa, the regressive behaviors and fear response engendered by the father's threats suggest that the powerlessness dynamic, along with that of traumatic sexualization, is the most salient for Rosa. Thus, therapeutic interventions aimed at decreasing feelings of helplessness and increasing feelings of success and competency are recommended. Rosa has already begun to incorporate the age-inappropriate sexual contact into her gender identity; the tendency to eroticize relationships and her impulsive, sexualized play suggest the need for therapeutic interventions that allow for the expression of these feelings in the therapy hour, with the aim of gradually reducing the need for this. At the same time, Mrs. Torres and other caretakers need help in setting appropriate limits and helping Rosa to restrain such behavior in her social settings, since this will impair her ability to develop appropriate family and peer relationships. Consequently, strategies aimed at helping Rosa in these areas were the first priority.

CONCLUDING COMMENTS

The goals in intervention in child sexual abuse are to (1) protect the child, (2) restrain the offender, and (3) rehabilitate all family members, if possible. In the instance of emerging and unclear disclosure of sexual abuse, the focus in the intervention must be on surfacing the trauma in order to help establish the *fact* of the sexual abuse.

In this case, as in most cases of child sexual abuse, it is necessary to establish the *fact* of abuse in the family court. This then permits limited and/or supervised contact between the offending parent and the child as a means of protecting the child from further abuse. As a result of my initial assessment, I was asked to testify about my findings in family court. The law in New York State, as in other states, makes it impossible to make a determination of the fact of child sexual abuse if the child does not testify without some evidence that corroborates the child's out-of-court statements. Without any medical evidence, the most powerful corroboration is the testimony of a mental health expert in child sexual abuse as to the consistency and validity of the child's presentation. I testified that Rosa's presentation was consistent with that of other sexually abused children, and the court adjudicated Rosa as a sexually abused child. The supervised visitation arrangement was continued, and all family members were ordered to treatment. In this manner, the court was in effect restraining the father from harming Rosa at the same time that it was demonstrating an understanding of the need for therapeutic intervention with Mr. Torres. Although the family court in New York State cannot force the father to attend treatment, it can make changes in visitation contingent on the recommendation of the treating therapist. This is what the court did in the Torres case. Mr. Torres continued to deny the allegations and did not accept the recommendation to treatment.

However, Rosa was protected from further unsupervised contact. Mrs. Torres continued Rosa in treatment, which proceeded according to priorities outlined above. Mrs. Torres also started therapy for herself and Jorge. This began the process of rehabilitation for the child and her immediate family.

PLAY THERAPY MATERIALS

- Chutes and Ladders: available from Milton Bradley Co. under Berne & Universal Copyright Conventions
- Play It Safe with SASA: SASA & Company, 2008 LaBrea Terrace, Los Angeles, CA 90046 (Ages 4–11)
- Stowell, J., & Dietzel, M. (1982). *My Very Own Book about Me*: Super Kids, Lutheran Social Service, N.1226 Howard, Spokane, WA 99201 (Ages 3–7)
- Teach-A-Bodies (anatomically correct dolls): 2544 Boyd, Forth Worth, TX 76109

STUDY QUESTIONS

1. How can the therapist help the custodial parent understand the child's need to continue contact with a parent who has abused him or her?

2. If Rosa had *not* wanted the therapist to discuss her disclosure of abuse with the mother, how could this have been handled with the child?

3. In the fifth session, when Rosa was so fearful, the therapist terminated the session early. Discuss the advantages and disadvantages of this action in regard to the child's relationship with the therapist and the implications for their future work.

4. The therapist testified in an adversarial proceeding *against* the father. If the mother had not wanted to terminate her relationship with him, what might the implications be for the therapist's alliance with the mother?

REFERENCES

Briere, J., & Runtz, M. (1988a). Symptomatology associated with childhood sexual victimization in a non-clinical sample. *Child Abuse and Neglect, 12*, 51–59.

Briere, J., & Runtz, M. (1988b). Post sexual abuse trauma. In G. E. Wyatt & G. J. Powell (Eds.), *Lasting effects of child sexual abuse* (pp. 85–99). Newbury Park, CA: Sage Publications.

Burgess, A. (1987). Child molesting: Assessing impact in multiple victims (Part I). *Archives of Psychiatric Nursing, 1*, 33–39.

Finkelhor, D. (1984). *Child sexual abuse: New theory and research*. New York: Free Press.

Finkelhor, D., & Browne, A. (1985). The traumatic impact of child sexual abuse: A conceptualization. *American Journal of Orthopsychiatry, 55,* 530-541.

Gelinas, D. (1983). The persisting negative effects of incest. *Psychiatry, 46,* 312-332.

Hartman, C. R., & Burgess, A. W. (1988). Information processing of trauma. *Journal of Interpersonal Violence, 3,* 443-457.

Jehu, D., Klassen, C., & Gazen, M. (1985-1986). Cognitive restructuring of distorted beliefs associated with childhood sexual abuse. *Journal of Social Work and Human Sexuality, 4,* 49-69.

Russell, D. (1986). *The secret trauma.* New York: Basic Books.

Sgroi, S. (1984). *Clinical handbook of intervention in child sexual abuse.* Lexington, MA: Lexington Books.

Summit, R. (1988). Hidden victims, hidden pain: Societal avoidance of child sexual abuse. In G. E. Wyatt & G. J. Powell (Eds.), *Lasting effects of child sexual abuse* (pp. 39-60). Newbury Park, CA: Sage Publications.

CHAPTER 5

Multiple Traumas of Refugees— Near Drowning and Witnessing of Maternal Rape

Case of Sergio, Age 9

TERESA BEVIN

Sergio is a 9-year-old boy from Nicaragua who was referred to the Multicultural School Based Mental Health Program of Children's Hospital National Medical Center in Washington, DC. The reason for referral, as described by his teacher, was a "panic-like reaction" to new situations. After a psychological evaluation and several interviews with the child and his parents, it was determined that Sergio was suffering from symptoms consistent with posttraumatic stress disorder (PTSD, a disorder frequently associated with war veterans) and dysthymia. Under the heading of "Anxiety Disorders," the revised third edition of the *Diagnostic and Statistical Manual of Mental Disorders* (DSM-III-R) describes some of the main criteria that characterize PTSD as:

> The person has experienced an event that is outside the range of usual human experience and that would be markedly distressing to almost anyone. . . . The traumatic event is persistently reexperienced in . . . recurrent and intrusive distressing recollections of the events . . . [and/or] persistent avoidance of stimuli associated with the trauma. (American Psychiatric Association, 1987, p. 250)

"Dysthymia," on the other hand, is described as a "depressed mood . . . for most of the day more days than not" (American Psychiatric Association, 1987, p. 230).

The focus in this chapter is on the key aspects of play therapy used to help a traumatized child process and understand the traumatic events he survived during his migration to the United States from Nicaragua. Sergio's posttraumatic play is described as it occurred spontaneously as well as in situations prearranged by the therapist to elicit the reenactment of traumatic events.

The case history of Sergio is of special interest to professionals concerned with the impact of violence and war on survivors, both children and family members who shared or witnessed the terror, pain, and humiliation of the survivor.

Play therapy has been utilized successfully with children who have been traumatized, either combined with other methods of treatment or as the sole method of treatment to help children work through the emotions associated with the trauma. According to Terr (1983, p. 318), "Those cases in which play therapy alone can be expected to succeed are those in which the trauma is limited and without extensive intrusion past the child's coping and defense mechanisms."

In Sergio's case, as in most cases of psychic trauma, it was difficult to judge the degree of damage to his coping mechanisms inflicted by the trauma. Only time and a trial of therapy would reveal whether play therapy would relieve his symptoms.

There are different directions a therapist may take to explore the meaning of a child's posttraumatic play. Terr (1983) outlines two different approaches: (1) therapeutic reconstruction of the event or events, and (2) therapeutic interpretation based upon observation of the child's spontaneous play. Sergio's treatment was based on both of these methods.

Eth and Pynoos (1985, p. 23) refer to the psychic trauma suffered "when an individual is exposed to an overwhelming event and is rendered helpless in the face of intolerable danger, anxiety, or instinctual arousal." Sergio's case portrays a child who witnessed life-threatening violence to his mother during their immigration. The aftereffects on the child witness, according to Eth and Pynoos, often include intrusive imagery that interferes with learning and posttraumatic guilt connected to his or her imagined failure to intervene. Therapeutic intervention with the child witness attempts to recapture the worst moment of the trauma and gives the child the opportunity to reconstruct the event in play according to his or her wish about how the outcome might have been different (Eth & Pynoos, 1985). This form of reconstructive play facilitates the undoing of a horrible memory and converts the child's role from passivity and helplessness to one of activity and control.

THE CASE: SERGIO MORA, AGE 9

Family Information

Father	Manuel Mora, mid-30s, heavy machinery operator
Mother	Nita Mora, early 30s, cook and part-time babysitter
First child	Sergio, 9, fourth grade
Sister	Raquel, 3

Presenting Problem

A few months after arriving from Mexico with his mother and sister, Sergio, then 7 years old, was placed in the second grade at a District of Columbia public school. (This was 2 years prior to beginning treatment.) Even though his teacher spoke Spanish and was sensitive to the normal confusion and shock of recent immigrants, she could not engage Sergio in most class activities. Whenever she called his name or requested his participation, he would become rigid, shake, and occasionally cover his face with his hands. He appeared completely unable to cope with the simplest challenge of everyday school life.

In addition to his difficulties with his teacher, Sergio would not play with other children. Instead, he would place himself in a corner of the playground as if he were avoiding the touch or even the approach of another child. When one of his classmates confronted him or attempted to engage him in a game, he would sit on the floor and sob uncontrollably, hiding his face. His teacher reported that during a field trip to the National Zoo, Sergio refused to walk over a wooden bridge and had to be left with a teacher's aide on one side of the creek. The aide said that he seemed terrified of the rushing water, pulling away from it, even telling her to go, that he could stay by himself.

Obviously, Sergio needed evaluation and treatment in order to function adequately in his new environment. The disturbance significantly interfered with his academic achievement, his social development, and most activities of daily life that required his interaction with others.

First Interviews

Sergio's Parents

During the first interview with Sergio's parents the reasons for his panic and insecurities became clear.

In 1987, Sergio's father came by himself to the United States to find employment. In Nicaragua, the family owned a small plot of land, which they cultivated, but it was located in an area where gunfight frequently disrupted their life, making it risky for Sergio to walk to school. Nita and the children were to join Manuel as soon as he could send them enough money to pay someone who would help them to cross the Mexican border illegally. Legal immigration was out of the question for a simple family of few means. A "coyote" (usually a Mexican with legal papers to enter and exit the United States) was eventually located to assist them on the trip across the border.

According to his mother, at age 7 Sergio was a normal, fun-loving child who missed his father and wished very much to join him. Manuel had written several letters telling them of the apartment he had rented for them, of how he had learned to work with heavy machines used to construct tall buildings, and how much happier they would be in their new home. He always had a special message for Sergio, which the child asked to have read to him over and over.

The trek across the Rio Grande marked the first truly traumatic event Sergio was to survive. Nita was carrying clothes and food in a basket on her head, while she carried little Raquel, then 1, in her arms. Sergio was to cross by gripping her skirts. Because it was dark, Nita couldn't find the rope that the "coyote" was supposed to have left for her to guide her through a shallow part of the river. The water was much deeper and the current much greater than she expected. She tumbled and fell to her knees, and Sergio, who fell with her, was dragged away by the current. Nita had the lucidity to cross, put the baby on firm ground, place her in the clothes basket, and dive after Sergio, who had managed to hang on to some entangled driftwood not far from the shore. He was terrified and shivering but alive. As soon as Nita pulled him to shore, they changed their clothes, and the "coyote" appeared to take them the rest of the way. However, instead of taking them to safety, he threatened Nita at gunpoint; there was a struggle, and Nita was raped while Sergio watched in terror. As reported by his mother, Sergio did not speak again until he was in the arms of his father 2 days later.

Sergio's entrance into school 2 months after this incident left him ill prepared to face any more strangers. His parents were immediately concerned that he was unable to make friends, to speak up, and to involve himself with any aspect of life outside the home. He would talk with his parents and play with his sister at home, but he would not venture outside by himself or with anyone besides his parents. They were often aware of his walking around in his room during the night. Manuel spoke with tears in his eyes about Sergio's fearful, reclusive attitude when he remembered his son as formerly gregarious and full of mischief. Nita, having ignored her own trauma and distress, wanted nothing more than to have her child's cheerful temperament back. She prepared Sergio for our first interview by telling him that someone who "understood children's fears" was going to talk to him in Spanish and help him sleep better and have a better time in school.

Sergio: First Interview

Sergio had difficulty responding verbally to my questions and used mostly gestures and head movements to agree or disagree. Slightly overweight, he seemed to slump into the chair, and only occasionally did he look directly at me. His voice trembled as he answered single words such as "yes," "no," "sometimes," and "maybe." He was, however, oriented to time, place, person, and situation, resisting distraction while paying attention to my questions. His intelligence, memory, and ability for abstraction appeared to be within normal limits. His thinking as far as could be determined revealed no evidence of hallucinations or other perceptual anomalies and no distortions of body image or disturbances of his sense of self. Although he chose not to describe any of the events reported by his parents, he admitted to having intrusive thoughts and nightmares revolving around the trauma.

My questions were mostly geared toward Sergio's everyday life until I asked him about "bad dreams" and later about "bad thoughts." With his head low, he spoke softly in Spanish, since his English was not yet fluent. He spoke of bad dreams that "came to him" almost every night. When I asked for details, he kept silent. He stated that "bad thoughts" came to him while at school sometimes and that he was afraid someone would hurt his little sister while he was at school. I asked him to draw his family, which he did without hesitation, concentrating on every detail, sticking out the tip of his tongue and pressing hard on the paper (see Figure 5.1). In the drawing, his father, wearing a hard hat, is standing firmly on the ground while his mother, sister, and he have no ground to stand on, and he

FIGURE 5.1.   Sergio's drawing of his family done during the initial interview.

appears as small as his little sister. The fact that he had no trouble drawing gave me hope for this young survivor who could not bring himself to talk about his experiences but could express himself through pictures. Drawing aspects of the trauma was an indirect communication while "speaking" the stories was too direct a confrontation with his own terror. Through drawings, Sergio could release pent-up emotions without fear of hurting others or being ridiculed for having certain feelings.

Drawing helps children uncover attitudes and feelings buried in the unconscious. Ironically, children at different stages of development often express their belief that they "can't draw," which is a learned attitude caused by criticism of early attempts at self-expression. Fortunately for Sergio, his own creative capacity was still intact.

Preliminary Assessment and Treatment Plan

With the information from the family interviews, from Sergio's interviews and drawings, and from his teacher and teacher's aide, our team, composed of two psychiatrists, a clinical psychologist, a child development specialist, and two social workers, estimated that this child was suffering from PTSD. Consequently, I knew that a simple challenge or new experience could trigger at any moment the feelings associated with the original trauma. Furthermore, Sergio's generally depressed and withdrawn mood pointed to dysthymia as well. The combination of PTSD and dysthymia resulted in a total collapse of his sense of security. He no longer could rely on appropriate emotional responses to otherwise normal, everyday events.

Given the severity of Sergio's symptoms, it was agreed that I, a child development specialist, would see him for 1 hour of individual treatment twice a week at school. In addition, I would visit his home one evening a week to allow his parents to participate in family sessions as cosurvivors of the trauma.

The main goals set for Sergio were to increase his speech production and social interaction and to improve his mood while decreasing his panic-like reactions, passivity, and his tendency to worry excessively. The treatment methods would include a combination of drawing, playing, some journal writing, and some guided imagery. Whatever appeared to engage and interest Sergio would become the predominant method of treatment.

The first task was to establish a rapport with him and to gain his trust, so that he could begin, however slowly, to share his deepest fears and perceptions, distorted by the horror of his experiences. The fact that his parents were going to be closely involved made me feel confident that Sergio's prognosis was favorable. I had the impression that Sergio customarily refrained from expressing his feelings to his parents for fear of causing them additional suffering. Furthermore, Sergio expressed some perplexity at the fact that he could not control his emotional responses to simple events that he knew cognitively were not meant to hurt him. He knew he had a problem and seemed to welcome the prospect of working with someone who wanted to help him.

Play Therapy Sessions

After several initial therapy sessions that included talking, storytelling, drawing, and playing guessing games, the more directive play therapy sessions began.

Fourth Session

During the first half of our play therapy session, I attempted to engage Sergio in play with a doll house and family figures. He categorically considered a doll house a girl's toy, finding this sort of play too "sissy" for him, as he had been raised in a Hispanic, fundamentally "macho" culture. He watched with interest, however, while I placed the little people in different rooms; he removed the roof and put it back on, then sat on the floor next to me to watch me "play." I asked him if he had ever seen a grownup sitting on the floor, playing. He shook his head, smiling. I then showed him some cowboys and Indians, which he seemed to find more to his liking. He manipulated the little men without saying a word, stood them up side by side, and later one behind the other, while checking at intervals, looking up to see if I was watching him.

I deliberately refrained from presenting Sergio with toys that related to his experiences or guiding his play in the early sessions. One of the most significant ways in which PTSD manifests itself in children is "repetitive play in which themes or aspects of the trauma are expressed" (Terr, 1983, p. 146). Sergio's spontaneous play did not reflect a repetitive quality but rather seemed focused on motives other than reenacting the traumatic events. As it turned out, the initial sessions helped him feel more comfortable with me, which was the purpose. He was obviously pleased to find out that I would be bringing him out of his classroom twice a week to "play." He seemed to understand that the sessions were in part aimed toward relieving the stress that being in class represented for him.

Fifth Session

I brought a baby bathtub, which I half filled with water. Little Playskool figures were laid outside the tub. I added a flat piece of wood, about 5″ × 5″, which I left floating in the water. It should be kept in mind that all the verbal exchanges between the therapist and the child have been translated from Spanish. The most significant exchanges are as follows:

Content of Session	Therapist's Rationale
THERAPIST: (*Sits on the floor by the tub. Begins to manipulate the Playskool dolls.*)	
CHILD: (*Sits next to the therapist. Observes quietly, with interest. After a few minutes, begins to use the piece of wood as a boat, making it "sail" through the water. He pushes the "boat" with one finger, carefully avoiding a "crash" against the sides of the tub. This goes on for at least 5 minutes, alternating slow and fast movements of the boat. He begins to produce "sound effects" with his mouth, imitating a motor, like a hum.*)	
T: (*Puts one of the dolls in the water and speaks in a falsetto.*) Ooh . . . I love swimming (*holding the doll; makes the doll go under the water as well*).	
C: (*Stops the "boat" to observe.*) I think the water is too deep for him, and people don't like that.	Child is relating to his fear of deep water, as "experienced" by the doll.
T: What is it that people don't like?	
C: Going under water. Only the guys who work under water like it.	
T: How come they like it?	
C: They work there, and they have all the air tanks and stuff.	
T: So you think that the water is too deep for someone without special equipment?	
C: Yes.	

T: Should we drain some water out?

C: Yes.

T: (*Takes the tub to a sink and drains half the water out. Sets it down.*)

C: (*Observes quietly, while holding the wet doll in his hand.*)

T: Do you think it will be OK now?

C: (*Places the doll in the water. Still covers its head.*) It's still a little too deep for him, but I think it'll be OK. (*Places the wooden square back in the water, puts the doll on it, and "sails" from one end of the tub to the other. The sailing is slower, more deliberate, as the "boat" drags a little on the bottom in shallower water.*)

Maybe it is time to begin to approach the river-crossing experience.

T: (*Places two more dolls in the water, making them "dive," "swim," squeal, jump, and then letting them float.*)

C: (*Does not seem to pay any attention at first. Then begins to observe carefully. Pushes the boat in my direction and places one of the floating dolls on the boat.*)

T: What is he doing?

C: Taking him on the boat.

T: Why?

C: So he doesn't get tired.

T: Tired of what?

C: Swimming.

T: Has he been swimming for a long time?

C: Not very long, but he's tired.

T: Was he drowning?

C: No, he was crampy.

T: From swimming?

C: Yeah.

T: Who is the sailor?

C: He's not a sailor.

T: Who is he?

C: The daddy.

T: Hmm.

Perhaps his wish that his father had been with them.

C: (*Sails slowly while looking at the other dolls.*)

Oh . . . (*talking for the sailor*) I have to get them
too! . . . Turn around, turn around. (*Turns the
boat around and picks the other dolls up and puts
them on the boat.*)

T: Who are they?

C: The daddy's kids.

T: Where's the mommy?

C: Right here (*picking one doll*).

T: Where are they going?

C: They're going fishing first, then they go home.

Child is focusing on negative
aspects of water eased by the
presence of someone who can
"save" those in danger.

It was obvious that Sergio was beginning to relax. His speech production
increased remarkably during this session, and his body language was more spontaneous. At times he seemed lost in play, unaware of whether or not I was
watching him.

Sixth Session

Sergio appeared cheerful. The same materials were laid out: the tub, the piece of
wood, and the Playskool dolls. He sat down without being told and began to place
the dolls on the piece of wood. I allowed him to play freely for several minutes. I
had plans for him, however, and wanted to "guide" the play session a little more
than on previous sessions. Terr (1983) states that "preset or prearranged play
therapy allows the child to 'find' toys which the therapist believes are applicable
to the terrifying events." Sometimes, however, providing significant material is
not enough to elicit reenactment, and the situation has to be manipulated as well.
I suggested that we would pretend that the "people" needed to get from one side
of the tub to the other, without a boat, because they didn't have one. He resisted at
first my wanting to dominate the game; I gave in some if he would give in some.
He finally agreed to follow my lead for a while. The most relevant exchanges were
as follows:

Content of Session

THERAPIST: What should the water be . . . the
ocean, or a river?

CHILD: A swimming pool.

T: OK, we can pretend it is a swimming pool
first, and then a river.

C: Back in Nicaragua, my dad caught a real big
fish in the river.

T: Great! . . . What kind of fish was it?

C: A silver fish.

Therapist's Rationale

The child may be resisting an
anxiety-producing scenario.

Child begins to make positive associations.

T: I bet it was tasty.

C: Yeah. We baked it.

T: Mmmmmmm.

C: Mmmmmmm. (*Rubs his stomach.*)

T: Now, what about our game?

C: OK.

T: How are they going to cross?

C: The water is too deep.

T: Do you want to help me drain some of it?

C: I'll do it!

T: Fine, but I will have to help you because the tub is very heavy now.

C: OK. (*The tub is drained.*)

T: Is this better?

C: Yes.

T: I'll watch.

C: OK. (*talking and doing*) The father is bigger, and he's not scared. He is going to help this one first, then come back fast, take the other, then come back fast, then take the mother. Now they are all on the other side.

T: Good. You did that very well. Why don't we try it as a river now?

C: (*Pauses for a moment, in thought. Scratches his ear for several minutes.*)

T: Well?

C: OK, it's a river. But it doesn't look like a river at all. It looks more like a swimming pool.

T: I know. But when you are playing you can make believe anything, even if it doesn't look like it . . . Right?

C: Right.

T: So let's keep playing.

C: OK.

T: Can you make them cross the river?

C: Yeah, that's easy.

T: Can you try not to do it so fast this time, so I can really see?

C: OK.

Although the play is related to water (the topic of the trauma), his thinking is not dominated by it.

Child is eager to take an active part in the preparations.

Again, the anxiety is relieved by the presence of a benevolent, powerful character.

Child is resisting scenario.

Child may have wanted to "rush" through the scene.

T: Let's go then.

C: They need a rope!

T: A rope?

C: So they can hold it, and nobody can drown.

T: I'll find one. Wait for me.

C: OK.

T: (*Goes to find a piece of string. On returning, finds child clutching all dolls, away from the tub.*) Here's the rope.

C: We need to tie it over there (*points to a chair*), and I'll hold it over here. (*Sets dolls on the floor in order to tie the string.*)

T: You are doing a good job.

C: (*Ties one end to a chair close by, holds the other end, and "walks" each doll along the string to the other side, slowly.*)

T: I guess they made it.

C: Yeah. They made it.

T: What happens if they try to do it without the rope?

C: It's dangerous.

T: You know about that, right?

C: Yeah!

T: You didn't have a rope to cross the river, right?

C: Right.

T: What did that feel like?

C: Scary.

T: What did you think could happen to you?

C: I could drown.

T: Do you still think about that?

C: Yeah.

T: But you made it.

C: Yeah, I made it.

T: Do you want to show me how it happened, with the little man?

C: OK. (*talking and doing*) The water is deep. Help! . . . The current is pushing, pushing, pushing. I'm drowning, help, help. Mom! gulp! gulp!

Child may want a delay or seek a way to relieve his anxiety.

Child is anticipating a "difficult" situation.

Child performed actions as if involved in a well-rehearsed ritual.

Moving to recollections of the trauma.

Focus on reality of outcome.

I'm tired! . . . I can't touch the bottom! Help! . .
The water is dirty and it tastes bad! . . . yuk! . . .
help me! Mom!! (*Pauses.*)

T: And then what happened?

C: Mom got me out.

T: She's strong.

C: Yeah, she's strong.

T: What did you feel when you were drowning?

C: I had to cough and cough, and I swallowed a
lot of black water.

T: You have to be very strong to endure that.   Reassurance.

C: Yeah . . . I'm strong (*puffing his chest*).

T: What would you like to do next?

C: Play with something else. I think you have   Child seeks to move away from
Play-Doh in your bag.   painful memories.

T: Yes I do. You must have seen it.

C: No. I smelled it!

T: It does smell funny.   Child focuses on his resourceful-

C: Yeah.   ness.

T: I would like you to show me how your mom
got you out of the water.

C: Later. OK?

T: OK.   Child may have been feeling positive and does not want to be
brought back to the trauma.

Some of Sergio's actions were performed as if he had done the same thing
many times before. He knew exactly how to tie the rope, and the movements of
his hands were almost mechanical. This may indicate that Sergio had repeated the
play privately, even though there was no rope for them during the real events.

Seventh Session

During this session, I used guided imagery for the first half hour. Sergio and I
pretended we were back where it all happened. I began with some relaxation
exercises. Later I suggested to him that he close his eyes to really imagine the
place so well that he could almost touch it, and that I would be with him. I
explained to him that it would be like a game, like walking into a story book, only
this story was not one of his favorites. We had discussed that there are good
stories and bad stories, and that we all have both kinds in our lives. In order for
me to really share in his "bad" story, he had to tell me how everything happened

really slowly, because I might get scared, and I wanted him to hold my hand, as I may not be as brave as he. I did this because I wanted to offer support to the child. This session was a very important one for Sergio. He let go of his guard and gave in to some of the deepest emotions associated with the episode. He took the job of giving me a tour of the horror scene very seriously. He held on to my hand very tightly and cried softly as he talked for much of the period of the guided imagery. However, he did not want to continue when he reached the part in which he, his mother, and little sister encountered the coyote again because he was "very tired." That had to be reserved for another session.

During the second half hour, I convinced him to play with the doll house and pretend the "family" figures were his own family. He showed me what the family would do on the weekends. He indicated that he liked to spend time playing with his little sister, reenacting some of their games. At some point he introduced his cousin, who, according to Sergio, is a bully. There was not a fifth doll, so he used a rectangular eraser he carried in his pocket to impersonate this character. He expressed his distrust for his cousin, from whom he felt he had to defend his sister because he was "never ever going to let anybody push her around."

Eighth Session

For this session I brought three hand-made rag dolls, two males and one female. I started by comparing the rag doll's body to our bodies when we are relaxed. He quickly grasped the idea and related well to the concept of relaxation, which he understood but could not completely achieve until that moment. After he had some time to play freely and to throw the dolls around as if they were performing great acrobatic feats, I decided to attempt a "role play" of his mother's rape. By now, I felt that Sergio and I had established a good enough rapport to reach the part of his experience together that had clearly caused him the most pain. He had not completely understood what had happened, biologically, but he saw his mother in mortal danger, attacked, pushed to the ground, pinned down, and humiliated. This memory was dreadful and became almost unreal to him. Sergio could not completely understand the aggressor's motives, but he knew it was an ugly, violent act. The threat of losing his mother, and perhaps being killed himself, was outside his grasp. The following contains the key aspects of this play therapy session:

Content of Session	Therapist's Rationale
THERAPIST: Sergio, I would like you to show me what happened after you crossed the river and found the "coyote."	
CHILD: (*Grimaces as if faced with an insurmountable task.*)	
T: I know this is difficult for you.	
C: It's boring.	

T: C'mon, you see it as boring because it is something you don't want to remember. You know that you are safe now, your mom is safe. Show me with the dolls. What do you say?

Gentle confrontation plus reality reassurance.

C: Aw . . . OK. (*Sits motionless for a few moments as if gathering strength. He has a male doll at one side and a female doll at the other. Talking and doing.*) He came out of the bushes to talk to my mom. (*pause*)

T: What did he say?

C: I don't know. (*pause*)

T: Then what?

C: He had a gun and he put it on my mom, right here. (*Points to the throat; pause.*)

T: On her throat? . . . That's terrible.

C: Like this (*more graphically*).

T: Go on, honey, you're doing great.

C: He pushed my mom to the ground.

T: Show me with the doll.

C: Then he talked real ugly to my mom; he said bad words.

T: What did he say?

Important to get as many specific details as possible.

C: He said, "You bitch, I know what you want" (*holds the male doll menacingly over the female doll*) . . . but I don't know what else he said.

T: That's OK; go on.

C: My mom told him that she didn't want me to see, but he told her to shut up or she would be sorry.

T: You are so brave, and you are doing so well. Show me what happened. (*Points at the dolls.*)

C: (*Puts the male doll over the female doll. Shows struggle, fighting. Pushes the male onto the female. Presses down as if to crush her. Stops.*)

T: What were you doing when all this was happening?

C: I was crying, with my sister. (*Indicates he had held his sister during the incident.*)

T: What did you think?

C: He was going to hurt my mom.

T: What was that like for you, inside? (*Indicates the heart.*)

C: Scary (*pause*).

T: Was it dark?

C: Yeah. It was dark.

T: What happened next?

C: He pushed us into a truck and drove to a woman's house.

T: And then, what?

C: My mom called my father, and he came the day after.

T: How was your mom after all that?

C: She cried a little bit after he did that to her, but he told her to shut up or he would hurt us (*pause*).

T: Then . . .

C: He opened the door on my mom's side and yelled that if she wanted to be left right there for the *Migra* [Immigration] to find us, he would push us out on the road (*pause*). He was mean.

T: Yes he was. . . . What happened when your father arrived?

C: We went home.

T: Did you tell your dad?

C: No, because my mom said we couldn't until we were at home. She didn't want my dad to kill the man because the *Migra* could send us all back to Nicaragua.

T: I see. . . . What happened when he found out?

C: My mom told him, and he was mad, and he cried, and he squeezed us together. Because we have to stay together.

T: And it's all over now.

C: Yeah. It's all over (*sighs in relief*).

T: And your mom is OK.

C: She's OK.

There was a great sense of satisfaction for me after this session. It was obvious that Sergio had released some of the negative emotions and fears associated with the traumatic event by reenacting it and talking about it for the first time. His mother reported that after this session he told her that he was beginning to forget about it all and wished she could forget as well. This indicates that he was beginning to feel relief and was attempting to share it with his mother, who he knew wanted him to forget.

Ninth Session

This session was devoted to exploring what would have happened if Sergio had been a lot bigger when the "coyote" attacked his mother. Sergio really put himself into this. The same rag dolls were used. Some of the most important exchanges were as follows:

Content of Session	Therapist's Rationale
THERAPIST: "Let's pretend that you could have become anything you wanted when the man came out of the bushes.	
CHILD: OK.	
T: What would you have wanted to be?	
C: A big, big guy. Real big, like my father.	
T: Fine. You can be as big as your father now.	
C: (*Picks up the male doll he has assigned as the "bad guy" and holds the "good guy doll" facing it.*) You are *not* going to hurt her, you hear me? (*Overpowers the "bad guy" while he talks.*) And this is for being ugly, and this is for being mean, and this is for having a big gun. (*Grabs the doll by the feet and hits the floor with its head, repeatedly until he seems tired. Finally, he throws the "bad guy doll" into a corner of the room with a big tumble.*) There, that'll show him.	Child ventilates his anger.
T: You did great! (*Applauds.*)	
C: I finished him, didn't I? (*Grins triumphantly.*)	

Tenth Session

The following session, and several others, were devoted to Sergio's feelings toward the "coyote" as well as his nightmares. His fear had been transformed into anger by now. He thrashed the rag doll on several occasions. He pretended to be a giant, crushing the man, transforming his previously awesome strength into the powerlessness of a child. The reversal of roles seemed to give Sergio the strength to cope with the traumatic events of the past in his new "safe" environment. After reducing the enemy to a more manageable size, all the other threats in his life began to diminish in importance, giving him a new outlook, renewed self-esteem, and, finally, a place among his peers. Furthermore, his new "control" over his emotions helped him continue to learn about the world around him and about his own strength. Sergio understood that he, alone, had dispelled the clouds and had begun the process of burying the beast.

CONCLUDING COMMENTS

Sergio's case is typical of the experiences of many children from war-torn countries who enter the United States. As previously stated, PTSD is not a disorder that afflicts adults and veterans of war only. Those of us who work with war survivors usually refer to entire families as "survivors and cosurvivors." They must learn to use their own self-healing powers while maintaining family cohesion. The very nature of their trauma, ironically, has forced these children and their families to go beyond ordinary efforts to survive, to function, and to master tasks (Flies-Moffat & Moffat, 1984).

In Sergio's case, every therapy session started with a period of relaxation, one of the most important skills that survivors must learn to counteract the everyday stressors that create a domino-effect reaction relating back to the original trauma. Sergio was taught to relax a group of muscles at a time, first contracting them and then letting go. This way he could feel what it was like for a muscle to be relaxed as opposed to contracted. He understood the principle of relaxation almost immediately but had trouble achieving the effect at the beginning. In time, however, he would start his relaxation exercises by himself, without prompting. He learned the process well enough to use it in order to help himself fall asleep.

The acting out of the traumatic events with nonthreatening objects such as toys can help place the events in the perspective of the past, where they belong. This approach accelerates the process of adapting to life after trauma. Through the manipulation of dolls, Sergio subconsciously indentified his own maladaptive coping techniques (such as panicking and crying in order to be left alone), therefore helping him to conceptualize at some level the aftereffect of his trauma and to recognize his posttrauma behaviors and feelings.

The involvement of his parents in therapy, their willingness to work with their child, and their courage to face their own humiliation and anger were of primary importance to Sergio's recovery. He and his mother recalled the events together, and then his father joined in and cried with them. The whole process was difficult for Sergio's father. It was puzzling for him, a Hispanic male raised in a "macho" culture, to see his son incapable of "shaking himself up" from his distress. An uneducated man, he felt very threatened by this and even thought of himself as less of a man for not being able to be tougher with his son, so he would "stop whining." His father's understanding was of great importance to Sergio, who held him high on a pedestal.

Sergio belonged with his family; they were his foundation to continue growing and developing normally. He was fortunate, considering all he had endured, to have parents who, in spite of their lack of education, loved and respected him, and who were willing to participate in his treatment.

When I was faced with Sergio's initial state, that of a pitiful child who could not cope with the slightest stress, it was difficult to determine how far or how fast he could be encouraged to confront his pain. He was difficult to engage at first, but perhaps he could have been pushed harder, sooner. The speed of his recovery and his quick grasp of concepts and ideas as well as his cooperative nature indicate that his regenerative powers were in far better shape than I had initially believed.

More than a year of treatment has passed, and Sergio today participates once a week in group therapy with children who are all survivors. Sergio still has work to do to improve his ability to interact with his peers. He is not assertive and lacks confidence in his own intelligence at times. However, he attends a special class for children who are interested in space and aerodynamics. He continues to make conscious efforts to extend himself, to reach out. I am confident that Sergio is on his way and will succeed.

It would be impossible to identify the one factor that was critical in the management of this case. I attribute most of the credit for the positive outcome to a combination of treatment approaches and methods. By sharing his fear and his humiliation with me in a displaced manner through play, Sergio began to share what he thought was his alone to endure. The play reenactment helped him turn passivity into activity and provided an outlet for his frustration and anger. I was there with him, appreciating his honesty, praising his efforts, and treating him and his experience with complete respect. Sergio, as a survivor, found the courage to persist and face the monster.

PLAY THERAPY MATERIALS

- One 5" × 5" wooden square
- Four Playskool dolls, about 2" each
- One Fisher-Price doll house
- Four Fisher-Price family figures: mother, father, boy, and girl
- One Sani-Toy baby bathtub, approximately 35" long × 24" wide × 13" deep
- Three hand-made rag dolls, two males, one female; gender shown by clothing, not anatomically

STUDY QUESTIONS

1. Would you have handled this case differently as far as sequence, orienting questions, or the materials used?

2. At the end of the sixth session, would you have asked such an open question as "What would you like to do next?" or would you have continued on the same direction? Explain.

3. In your view, can play therapy benefit children of any culture, and how much knowledge does the therapist need to have about the child's culture?

4. How can the therapist explain to the parents the need for reenactment of events and emotional release through play, when their wish is for the child to forget the trauma?

5. Do you think the therapist should have explored Sergio's understanding about the sexual nature of the assault on his mother? If so, at what point and how could this have been addressed?

REFERENCES

American Psychiatric Association. (1987). *Diagnostic and statistical manual of mental disorders* (3rd ed., rev.). Washington, DC: Author.

Eth, S., & Pynoos, R. S. (Eds.). (1985). *Post-traumatic stress disorder in children.* Washington, DC: American Psychiatric Press.

Flies-Moffat, L., & Moffat, J. G. (1984). Families after trauma: An education and human services resources. *MidPoint: Survivors & Families*, 38-39.

Terr, L. C. (1983). Play therapy and psychic trauma: A preliminary report. In C. E. Schaefer & K. J. O'Connor (Eds.), *Handbook of play therapy* (pp. 308-319). New York: John Wiley & Sons.

CHAPTER 6

Witness and Victim of Multiple Abuses
Collaborative Treatment of 10-Year-Old Randy in a Residential Treatment Center

JOAN S. DOYLE
DAVID STOOP

This case study is about Randy, a black boy of 10, whose childhood has slipped away without his ever having known about bedtime stories, teddy bears, ducks in the bathtub, a comforting kiss good-night, or what it is like to be a gleam in his mother's eyes.

Randy is diagnosed posttraumatic stress disorder resulting from chronic, severe abuse and torture. Not even this diagnosis can adequately describe those years of horror when, according to Randy, "nobody helped." What happened to Randy can more accurately be described as "soul murder," the deliberate attempt to eradicate or compromise the separate identity of another person (Shengold, 1989, p. 2).

Born to a heroin-addicted mother, Randy endured from that precarious beginning extreme physical, sexual, and emotional abuse and neglect. Mother, a prostitute, sold Randy at ages 3 and 4 into prostitution in order to support her drug habit. During his early years, Randy frequently witnessed his mother having sexual intercourse with her clients and, on one occasion, her fatal shooting of a "john" who was abusing her. This act resulted in a 10- to 20-year prison sentence for Randy's mother. Randy was also present when his beloved great-aunt had a heart attack and died. At age 7, Randy was kidnapped by members of a satanic cult for ritualistic purposes. They placed him on an altar, bound and gagged him, and abused him sexually. Afterwards, they threw lighted matches at his genitals.

Compounding all of these traumatic events were numerous out-of-home placements for Randy. In his last placement with a maternal aunt, he set fire to her house after receiving a brutal beating from her for misbehaving in church. The fire caused her death in addition to the deaths of her husband and two of

Acknowledgments: We would like to thank Dr. John W. Caddey, Executive Director of the Berea Children's Home and Family Services, for his ongoing support of our efforts at creative programming for seriously traumatized children. We would also like to acknowledge the assistance of Rebecca Vujanov, M.A. in Theatre Arts, who contributed to this case as creative consultant, and Jeannine Kaleal and Janet Turner, who contributed tireless hours typing and proofing the manuscript.

Randy's cousins, a 16-year-old boy and a 6-month-old baby girl. Randy escaped injury by running outside the house to safety. This act of arson resulted in Randy's placement in a children's psychiatric hospital for a mental health evaluation.

During the entire length of his 6-week stay in the hospital, Randy refused to talk to his therapist or to any other member of the treatment team about either the fire or any of the other traumatic events earlier in his life. The discharge recommendation was for intensive psychotherapeutic intervention in a secure residential setting for Randy in order to deal with his increasingly dangerous and dysfunctional trauma-related symptoms and behaviors, which included two other incidents of fire setting, school problems (he could not read), stealing, high-risk behaviors (e.g., playing on train tracks with a train coming), enuresis, nightmares, suicide attempts, runaways, drug and alcohol abuse, sexual provocativeness, extreme aggressiveness, and an inability to identify or express his feelings verbally (only his eyes occasionally mirrored the unbearable pain he had endured).

In accepting this case in a secure residential treatment facility for children, we knew the treatment process for Randy would be long, arduous, and of a serial nature. Randy's dual victim/witness traumatic experiences and his diagnosis of posttraumatic stress disorder (American Psychiatric Association, 1987) necessitated a vareity of collaborative treatment approaches. Terr (1989b, p. 3) lists the following range of possible approaches to treatment of posttraumatic stress disorder in children: family, group, and individual treatments; play therapy; psychodynamic psychotherapy; cognitive and behavioral therapies; and medication.

A sophisticated residential treatment setting, such as the one in which Randy was placed, is able to provide all of the above intervention modalities plus a holistic therapeutic environment that includes cottage milieu, special education in the form of on-grounds classrooms for children with severe behavior handicap/learning disabilities, recreational therapy, physical development, music therapy, woods therapy, garden therapy, as well as nursing, psychological, psychiatric, medical, dental, and other specialized services.

In setting up an effective treatment plan for traumatized children referred to our residential program, it has been our experience that all of the above treatment resources facilitate the healing process. For the purposes of this chapter, however, we focus on the work of the play therapist with Randy.

Recognizing that Randy had been extremely treatment-resistant in the hospital, where he was provided the conventional treatment modalities, we decided to attempt to engage him in the treatment process through use of some innovative play therapy and creative arts approaches. These included puppets, masks, a cartoon lifeline, guided imagery (Dunne, 1988b), and warm-up exercises (Sternberg & Garcia, 1989).

Puppetry has almost unlimited potential as a therapeutic medium because it represents the integration of sculpture, design, movement, expression, and other elements of the arts (Renfro, 1984, p. 16). A puppet helps a child to feel at ease, since it redirects the focus of attention away from the child and serves as a protective shield behind which a child may temporarily take refuge and assume a new persona. The puppet helps the shy or inhibited child to focus on the puppet's rather than his or her own actions or statements. By encouraging emotional release, puppets offer a wide variety of socially acceptable outlets for discharge of stress-related emotions. Additionally, the child through puppet play experiences alternative emotions and actions (Renfro, 1984, p. 20).

In reexperiencing traumatic events, the child may use the puppet to explore hidden fears by instructing the puppet to overcome these fears. By depersonalizing the situation and exploring the same fears through the persona of the puppet, the child is less fearful because the terrible things that have happened to him or her are now happening to the puppet, not the child.

For children like Randy, coming from low socioeconomic backgrounds, damaged by the ravages of racism, and isolated from the outside world by the invisible confinements of ghetto life, play in its purest sense is an unfamiliar activity. Puppets can be used with such children to help them experience some of the childhood they have missed (Pazzanese & Wise, 1984).

Some of the most important benefits to be realized from use of puppets with traumatized children include the following (Renfro, 1984):

1. Role and situation exploration.
2. Improved responsiveness and spontaneity.
3. Development of communication skills.
4. Opportunity for depersonalization or sublimation of problems through projection.
5. Self-esteem enhancement.
6. Provision of needed and appropriate physical contact.
7. Relief of the child's sense of isolation.
8. Increase in the child's ability to concentrate.
9. Improved motor coordination.

Through use of a mask, a child in treatment can reveal feelings and emotions not expressed previously. Historically, the mask was used in healing, but in today's work in play/creative arts therapy, the mask can help a child express repressed or hidden emotions, depict dilemma or conflict situations, release personal creativity, assume various forms of identity in a group, explore dreams and imagery, and demonstrate and model various social roles (Dunne, 1988b).

Another method for sustaining Randy's interest was the use of a *cartoon lifeline*, which also provided us with drawings of psychodynamic significance. Like puppetry, cartooning distances the participant from the conflictual material and provides a creative tool for activating the imagination. In working with cartooning, the therapist uses existing cartoon characters, strips, or single frames or encourages participants to create their own (Dunne, 1988b, p. 39). Use of a cartoon lifeline with Randy stimulated his willingness to talk (through a puppet) about the cartoons he had drawn.

In *guided imagery* the therapist suggests an imaginary scene and asks if the child would like to go there, encouraging him or her to relax, close his or her eyes, and focus on what he or she is doing. Through the use of guided imagery, with the child in a relaxed state, the therapist helps him or her to reexperience past traumas in a less threatening manner. Guided imagery may be used in several ways: for warm-up activities, as an introduction to sensory awareness, in core activities to demonstrate the variety of individual responses to the same stimuli, and in closure, to restore clients to a calmer state after having dealt with very difficult issues (Naitove, 1981, p. 257).

Most of us are familiar with children's stories and adult novels that contain characters who are extremes of very, very good and very, very evil. The endings of these books, after conflict resolution, are generally in the happy-ever-after category. This may be because many of the authors of these books are traumatized individuals who, through their stories, are trying to rework their own traumatic past. Such was the case with Dickens, Kipling, Chekhov (Shengold, 1989), Poe, Hitchcock, Bergman (Terr, 1987), and Stephen King (Terr, 1989a). Rudyard Kipling, in his book *The Light That Failed*, writes the dedication poem about his mother, portraying her as a loving parent. In reality, his mother cruelly abandoned him when he was only 6 years old. The dedication may have been Kipling's creative attempt to defend against his feelings of rage and sadness around his early abandonment and betrayal/loss.

Randy may not possess the literary genius of these renowned authors to enlist in his attempts at trauma integration and resolution. Nonetheless, we believe that he can be helped to find acceptable ways to process and deal with the events in his painful past through involvement in play/creative arts therapy as well as through more conventional treatment approaches. We hope that with much hard work in these areas, over time, Randy, too, will be able to "write" a happy ending to his story.

THE CASE: RANDY, AGE 10

Family Information

Randy is a black youth, 10 years old, who previously lived in housing projects in the "inner city" of a large northeastern American city. His mother was a 17-year-old prostitute when she gave birth to him; Randy never knew his biological father.

Randy was raised in and among the homeless. During his early years he moved from mission to shelter and from condemned building to junk car lot. During this time he was sold into prostitution by his mother to support her drug habit. When he was 4 years old he was removed from his mother and placed in the temporary custody of the Children's Services Board.

For the next 6 years Randy shuttled back and forth among a variety of relatives. He developed a strong bond with his great aunt, with whom he lived after being taken from his mother until he was 5 years old, when she died of a heart attack in his presence.

Subsequently, Randy was placed with a maternal aunt. Unknown to county officials, she was a crack peddler in a part of the city known as "Devil's End." She took Randy with her on her travels into this part of the slum. On one occasion he was kidnapped by satanic cult members, who bound and gagged and then sodomized him as an act of religion. They concluded this ritual by throwing lighted matches at Randy's genitals. The immediate aftereffects of this horrific experience on Randy, according to the record, included nightmares, enuresis, hypervigilance, exaggerated startle response, verbal and physical aggressiveness, and localized psychogenic amnesia. His aunt was later arrested in a drug raid, and Randy, then 8, was removed once again from his family.

Randy was placed with another maternal aunt in a small town 100 miles from his city of birth. This aunt and her husband were in their mid-30s and had two children, a teen-age son and a 6-month-old daughter. They had been able to rise above their own background of poverty into the black middle class.

Randy was illiterate despite being in the third grade. When he began fighting in the learning-disabled class, he was placed in a class for the behaviorally handicapped. His aunt and uncle, steeped in the Baptist tradition, were strict disciplinarians. When Randy began to use obscene language, they would ground him to his room, but this form of punishment worked for only a short while. Randy, at age 9, would simply climb out of his first-floor window and run away. The couple felt forced to use more drastic measures to control Randy's behavior, and they resorted to corporal strapping with a belt. Following a strapping after his caretakers learned of a stealing incident at school, Randy set a stuffed bear on fire in his room. The fire was discovered and extinguished.

A few weeks later Randy misbehaved while attending church. His aunt and uncle were mortified and furious with him for such sacrilegious behavior and on returning home gave Randy a severe beating and banished him to the basement for the night. Randy had a secret stash of matches and a cigarette lighter in the basement. Allegedly, in the early morning hours, he ascended the basement stairs and poured a trail of lighter fluid up the stairway to the base of the bedroom doors. Then Randy set the path of accelerant on fire with a match and escaped through the back door. The entire family perished in the blaze.

Randy was hospitalized in town after he was discovered by neighbors and firefighters in the back yard. He was screaming hysterically and was naked. He was moved back to the town of his birth and placed in a psychiatric hospital for children. After 6 weeks Randy was discharged from the hospital to a secure residential treatment setting.

Presenting Problem

Randy's life of ever-spiraling trauma, including nomadic unsettledness during his preschool years, the witnessing of violence and death to loved ones, and cult sexual abuse, has led to the boy's ongoing struggle to master his anxiety, which was rooted in chronic powerlessness. Randy's frenzied attempts to control his anxiety took the form of aggression in school, flight from punishment, increasing sexualized acting out, suicide attempts, and homicidal fire setting. Once the powerless object or bystander witnessing hostile and incomprehensible acts, now, armed with the fruits of his past, he wages war with the whole world.

First Interview (Summary)

Randy entered my (Stoop) office. As he walked to the chair he appeared to be moving within the rhythm of a rap song. Sunglasses masked his eyes; his T-shirt read "Run DMC." The bottom half of his head was shaved in a semicircle around the back, and the word "bad" was carved as a signature at the nape of the neck.

As I asked basic questions related to his record, Randy increasingly teetered on the back legs of his chair. When I asked him why he wore sunglasses inside, he remarked in the typical voice of a 10-year-old, "You want to know about the fire don't you? I didn't do it. What time is it anyway? How long do I have to stay in here."

I calmly stated, "We're going to get along just fine." "Huh," he replied. "White people give up on black people." "I'll be back tomorrow," I said. "Can I go?" he asked anxiously. I nodded.

The tone in the initial interview in my office was rife with tension. Randy adorned himself in "street" garb and immediately introduced the racial roadblock. As a while male I felt painstakingly conscious of the racial issue and concerned about whether I would be able to bridge these two worlds. I was a bit nervous, thinking Randy might act out in order to fulfill the prophecy of "white rejection." I wanted to avoid verbal and physical confrontation at all costs. I retreated by reassuring him I would be seeing him tomorrow. I admit I was relieved when Randy exited the office.

Of note, my office is located within the 10-resident secure treatment unit. Therapy is regularly scheduled once per week with each of the 10 residents.

Preliminary Assessment and Treatment Plan

Control and power appeared to be the primary dynamic displayed by Randy. The opposite feelings of powerlessness, triggered when Randy becomes anxious or not in control, are buried, albeit not far from the surface, covered by Randy's aggressive style. The traumatic events of abuse, loss through death, and innocent, helpless witness to violence fuel Randy's ever-recurrent compulsion to repeat and replay the drama of power over powerlessness.

Randy's aggressive behavior, like his other behaviors that originated from the severe traumas in his past, meets Randy's need for survival and helps him gain mastery of his victimization. In Randy's case, setting fires may have originally met his need to express rage related to having been sexually abused and then tortured by fire. According to James (1989, Chap. 9), an individual who experiences a great deal of power and relief of tension by the act of fire setting may become addicted to these same feelings, which then leads to dangerous repetition of this behavior. It is possible that Randy, if untreated, could assume such a profile.

The goal of treatment for Randy was to bring his self-destructive, aggressive behaviors under control. Using the concept of traumagenic states (James, 1989, Chap. 3), the clinical team identified the following issues that would have to be addressed in Randy's treatment either in the present or at some future developmental stage: powerlessness, destructiveness, eroticization, self-blame, stigmatization, fragmentation of bodily experience, betrayal and loss, as well as a possible dissociative state.

The treatment intervention, to be described in this chapter, consists of four therapy sessions that address the issues around the traumagenic state of powerlessness—the pivotal event of ritual abuse in a satanic cult. In order to master the trauma, bridge-building exercises were introduced to link fragmented past events and empower Randy through the experience of self-expression in a safe venue. The actual fire-setting incident is dealt with at a later stage in treatment, when Randy's ego strength has been enhanced.

In addition to once-per-week individual therapy sessions, Randy participates in twice-weekly group therapy. These groups focus on development of the following skills: anger management techniques, including the quieting reflex, and breathing/relaxation exercises; success imagery skill exercises; and social skills learned through role play and public practice.

Although family therapy is an active part of the treatment plan for many residents, unfortunately, for Randy, this was not possible because of his mother's imprisonment.

The following four individual therapy sessions demonstrate the use of a cartoon lifeline of Randy's own making and the stories he created about the characters in the lifeline. The first session depicts the formulation of the lifeline. The second session demonstrates a bridge-building exercise between two characters from the lifeline, enlarged on masks. The third session includes a puppetry exercise based on characters in the lifeline. The fourth session introduces a handmade fire puppet to permit the issue of fire to be broached in a nonthreatening space.

Play Therapy Sessions

It took a month and a half to attain the trust necessary to attempt the exercises and activities presented here. I often had to seek Randy out and pursuade him to come to therapy. He almost always resisted but ultimately agreed to come. He has yet to miss a session. These early weeks were rough going, since Randy was frequently verbally assaultive. I believed the only way I could win his trust was to refrain from using my authority to countermand his assaults. In addition, I was always available on a daily basis. I frequently saw Randy on the unit and would often speak to him, using my knowledge of music and sports to engage him in conversation. I used humor whenever possible and always reacted to his humor when appropriate. In a sense, I outlasted his attempts to drive me away.

First Session

Materials needed for this session included the following: a table, large sheets of white paper divided into equal blocks (prior to session), crayons/markers/pencils, and a bagful of magic stick-ons, to be added to the lifeline. The magic stick-ons were prepared ahead of time by the therapist but could be created by the client himself.

The first session contains two parts—Tell a Story, a warm-up exercise enabling the client to enter a state of suspended belief, and the Cartoon Lifeline, a fun, nonthreatening story creation in which fragmented parts can later be brought together.

Tell a Story. Randy entered my office in casual attire, as is his custom, and slouched in the chair at the table. I sat at the table opposite him. His head was down and resting on his hand.

Content of Session

THERAPIST: I'd like to try something different today. Let's you and me tell a story. This is how you do it. I say a line and stop. You pick up where I left off and we go back and forth.

RANDY: (*Sits up straight in his chair.*)

T: I was walking through the woods and . . .

R: I fell into a hole . . .

T: And there was a shadow above the hole. . .

R: And the shadow was a man . . .

T: But then the sun came out . . .

R: And burned down all the trees . . . (*Smiles sheepishly.*)

T: And the shadow called out . . .

R: And the man in the hole yelled back. . .

T: There's a gun . . .

R: And the man died . . .

T: But the man rose up from the dead . . .

R: And died again . . .

T: Dirt fell from the sky into the hole . . .

R: A flower grew up out of the dirt. (*Takes off his sunglasses.*)

T: And it started to rain . . .

Rationale/Analysis

The hole: might represent birth/death cycle or painful event or remorse (a moral event).

Sun = fire = power.

Power of the word.

Randy never said gun was fired also; Randy keeps open whether it was death of shadow-man or man in hole.

R: The flower grew . . .

T: And became . . .

R: A man. The end.

Resurrection metaphor—leads one to hopeful prognosis.

Cartoon Lifeline (see Appendix A). I laid the white sheets of paper out on the table in front of Randy. For filling in lifeline blocks, Randy had the choice of crayons, markers, or a pencil. The magic stick-ons were in a paper bag to be placed on the lifeline later when it was complete.

Content of Session	Rationale/Analysis

THERAPIST: You did very well with that story. Now we're going to do another story in a new and different way. You like the comics in the paper? (*Randy's face lights up.*) This will be our very own comic strip . . . a kind of cartoon. (*I point to each block on the paper and say*) Each block is a year in a life. (*I proceed to write 0 through 11 above the blocks in chronological order.*) Sound like fun? (*Randy nods. His eyes are intent and expressive.*) You have a choice of crayons, Magic Markers, or a pencil. Ready?

Choice = power.

RANDY: I was born ready.

T: OK, great. Draw two characters in each block for each year in the story. After you draw the characters, have them say something to each other like they do in the funny papers. Put your words in a caption or bubble. Got it?

R: Got it, dude.

T: The first block is before birth when a baby is in its mother's tummy.

Randy has had numerous confrontations with a pregnant child care worker named Maggie. Safe displacement of rage. Staff white/mother black.

Outline of pregnant woman in orange. Half of baby's head is orange. Rest of baby is brown. Brown strands connect mother's and baby's heads.

Randy identifies self with fetus.

R: (*Chooses crayon for the first block. Randy teeters on the back legs of his chair and smiles defiantly.*) I hate her [referring to Maggie, female child care worker].

T: OK. Next block. Year 1.

Negative feelings about his mother displaced onto Maggie.

The child has a large open hand ready to receive, but the large figure has a rectangular, closed-off hand, which is apparently unable to give.

Both figures are smiling and are in a greeting mode, possibly symbolizing hope and openness toward future.

R: (*Switches to pencil.*)

T: Who are these two characters?

R: Stick people.

T: Do they have names?

R: No names.

Stick figure—bereft of power.

Names in ancient world are magical keys that unlock the mystery of a person. Namelessness represents powerlessness and meaninglessness.

The large figure is frowning. "NO" appears to be unspoken thought, not spoken words. The large figure recognizes inability to provide for the future.

Hands unable to clasp.

Box-like hand is suspended in midair, connected to neither figure.

T: Keep on. You're doing great.

R: (*Head down, he intently continues.*)

Appearance of large full figure. No hands—unable to give or defend self. Eyes covered. Mouthless, yet able to speak. Phallic or gun-like hat.

Child figure is armless and sad/mad. Armless = powerless = abused.

Child stick figure is now sole focus. Smile might represent "happy" period with favorite aunt.

Ego intact—Randy is still able to declare "I am . . ."

R: I don't want to draw two [characters] any more. (*Remains intent but appears to weary.*)

T: You're in charge.

Year 5 is the year he witnesses death of aunt.

Handless = powerlessness.

Frown covers erased smile—great expectations in beginning of year change to disappointment (now chronic).

T: Why so mad?

R: (*Continues on without conversation.*)

122

II. The Crisis of Violence

The reappearance of the full-figured adult signals an attempt by Randy to empower himself as an adult.

Year 6 represents the end of the spoken word. The future is a question mark.

In contrast to year 3, here the eyes are uncovered, there is a mouth (smile, but there are no feet (unable to move). Power at this age is both enlightening and immobilizing.

T: Ah, he's back.

R: (*Teeters on back legs of chair after drawing year 6. His left arm circles the back of his head, and his left hand covers his mouth from the right.*)

T: Why the question mark?

R: He's a dummy.

Only figure with motion. Motion = power. Power symbolized further in large hands and feet.

Year 7—kidnapping and ritual abuse by sodomy and fire.

T: You're doing very well.

R: (*Does not look up or speak.*)

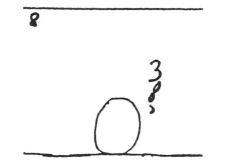

The egg might represent the return to the womb or rebirth (regressive or progressive?).

The onset of suicidal ideation began at age 8, as detailed in Randy's case record.

R: I should have started with this one, but that's OK.

T: Why the number 3?

R: It's my lucky number.

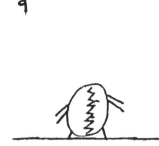

R: (*Randy's head is resting on the table as he draws.*)

The egg is hatching. Hope or despair? Is the egg cracked open from the inside or the outside? Does the ego or the world own the power?

If dissociative, as a result of trauma/abuse, alter ego might be hatching—cracked from inside.

If cracked from outside—moral interpretation? Remorse over death to innocent infant in fire. Randy attempting to raise the dead.

R: (*Raises his head up during the drawing of year 10.*)

Current state of mind.

Empowered as a fire setter, yet troubled at its consequences. Mouth is hidden in the egg—unable to speak.

Still handless and footless despite devouring power of the fire. Revenge always chains one to the past.

The possibility of return to the egg or ego-empowered suicide is erased. Its as if life carries one in its current.

The prospects look bleak for the man-child. Again handless and footless (without motion) and sad. There is sight, however, and the figure appears to be looking back at the split shell.

R: (*Drops his pencil.*) Is it over?

T: Not quite. I've got a bag of magic stickers. I want you to pull the stickers from the bag and place them wherever you want on your comic strip.

R: (*Places the "Invisible Shield" on year 10, current year.*)

T: Why there?

R: To make me safe from getting hit.

The shield could have prevented the fire. Uses "me" identification.

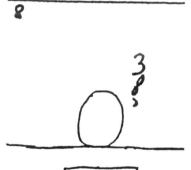

R: (*Next places the "Magic Trunk" in crucial year 8.*)

T: What's in the magic trunk?

R: The egg.

Life itself contains a magical seed of hope, which no amount of suffering can destroy.

Key symbol—egg empowered by magic trunk.

Egg = prefire—identification with aggressor (transferred from abusc).

Egg = postfire grief.

The ship is a rocket-like ship with flames with similar power as the sun. The rocket has the power to exit the earth (split the egg). Randy has really drawn the interior world of the egg in year 8.

Why year 2? Could it be that this is the world created by the mother, who could be the figure in year 2, her last appearance.

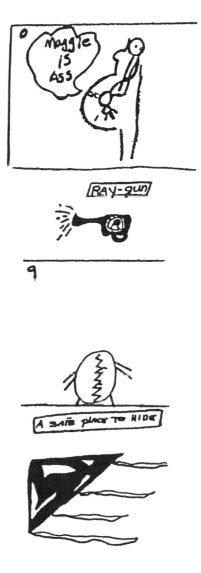

R: (*Picks the blank sticker. He looks puzzled.*)

T: This one's for you to draw "Your World" on.

R: (*Returns to crayons as in the fetal drawing. The world is egg-shaped and pink. Next he draws a box at the base of the world with an arrow pointing upward, box and arrow in pink. Next he draws the sun with rays in yellow. Finally, he draws yellow rays off the base of the arrow.*)

T: What is that in your world?

R: A ship. (*Randy places the "Ray Gun" next in the fetal picture.*)

T: Why there?

R: I need the gun as I get bigger.

R: (*Places "A Safe Place to Hide" under the year 9.*)

T: Why is it safe?

T: It's in the egg. (*Randy looks at me as if I asked a stupid question.*)

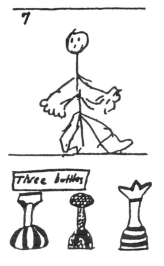

In year 7, year of cult abuse, the magic potion ensures safety via flight.

R: (*Places "The Three Bottles" in year 7.*)

T: What's in the bottles?

R: A potion.

T: To drink?

R: No. To make me grow.

The armless child figure and the large figure are wish and fulfillment of the same mind.

R: (*Places "The Road to Where I'm Going" in year 3.*)

T: Where does the road lead?

R: Power

R: (*Places the final magic sticker in the future year 11.*)

T: Where do you think the door leads to?

R: Back to the egg.

T: Thank you, Randy. You've done an excellent job. Next time we'll do more neat stuff with our cartoon.

R: (*Exits the office in a hurry.*)

Second Session

The second session 7 days later contained two parts: a warm-up exercise, "Pass the Prop," and a bridge-building exercise between 2 years in the Cartoon Lifeline.

Pass the Prop is a game that will enable Randy to enter a suspended frame of mind and ease the anxiety in the subsequent exercise. The material in Pass the Prop can be any object and is handed back and forth between therapist and client. When the object is received and before it can be passed back, the person must define the object as something other than what it really is. In other words, a pencil can be anything other than a pencil.

The second exercise is a bridge-building game. Materials needed are the following: a table, the Cartoon Lifeline from the first therapy session, crayons, pencils, or markers, and paper plates. The purpose of this exercise is to extract two characters from the Cartoon Lifeline and enlarge them on the paper plates and establish a dialogue between the two characters. The dialogue uttered through the paper plates (held up to the face and functioning as masks) facilitates connection between the disparate lifeline characters and years. Our hope is that this will enhance cognitive and emotional integrity within the self-story.

Pass the Prop.

Content of Session	Rationale/Analysis
(*I, along with several child care workers, watch as Randy lies down and rolls the length of the hallway between the classroom and my office. There is a curious mix of raucous laughter and belligerent obscenities emanating from the youth. I coax him up off the carpet and into my office.*)	Randy feeling anxious

THERAPIST: Good to see you, Randy. How was your week?

RANDY: Cool, dude.

T: Great, now let's try something a little different. You see this triangular-shaped game piece in my hand. When I hand it to you, I want you to tell me what you've got in your hand. Now the fun part is it can be anything you want it to be except a triangle. OK, ready.

R: You start.

T: I'm holding half of a baseball diamond.

R: (*Smiles.*) I'm holding half of a pair of shades [sunglasses].

T: I'm holding in my hand a three-cornered hat.

R: I'm holding in my hand a ship.

T: I'm holding in my hand a woman's dress.

R: I'm holding in my hand the power.

T: Good job.

Cartoon Lifeline Bridge Building—Masks.

Content of Session	Rationale/Analysis
THERAPIST: (*I spread the entire lifeline from session 1 on the table.*) Remember the comic strip you made last week. Today we're going to bring your comic strip alive. I want you to take a good look at the story you've drawn. Then I want you to pick two characters from the story.	Choice.
RANDY: (*Scans the lifeline carefully. He closes his eyes and leans back in his chair with an anguished look on his face. He opens his eyes slowly and points toward the large figure in year 3.*)	

T: OK, good. How, on this paper plate I want you to draw your character and fill your plate up with him.

R: (*Jiggles his legs anxiously as he draws on the plate.*)

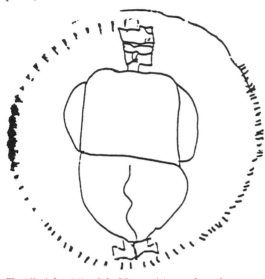

T: All right. Nice job. Now, pick another character.   Choice.

R: (*Scans the lifeline again and then points to the figure in the adjacent year 4.*)

T: OK. Now do the same with this character on this paper plate.

R: (*Proceeds to draw without the anxiety and anguish evidenced in the other mask.*)

T: Abracadabra! Our paper plates have just become masks. Which mask do you want to wear?

R: (*Picks the large figure from year 3.*)

T: (*I hold up the mask of the child from year 4.*)

R: (*Holds up the mask from year 3.*)

T: (*I talk in the voice of a child.*) What's your name?

R: (*Talks in a deep voice.*) The Rapper. What's your's?

T: Slim.

R: (*Smiles.*)

T: How old are you, Mr. Rapper?

R: 18.

T: I am only 4. I live in a house with lots of people. Where do you live?

R: On the streets, dude.

T: Where are you going?

R: Through the magic door.

T: What's on the other side?

R: The power.

T: What kind of power?

R: Just power.

T: Is your mama over there?

R: No, man, power. I said power.

T: Is there a gun?

R: You're starting to bother me.

T: Will you take me?

R: No. (*Randy teeters on the back legs of his chair with his arm.*)

T: I would also like some of your magic power.

R: Look, Slim. There's only enough for me.

T: Will you come back?

R: No. (*The Rapper mask walks off.*)

T: Good-bye.

R: Are we done?

T: We're done. Excellent job.

The power behind the magic door = survival/mastery over the traumas. The power is magical like the power of adults through the child's eye. Yet, there is the implication that it is greater than raw human violence. There is also anxiety over the power's limited supply, which cannot be shared. Randy must leave childhood behind in order to survive.

Third Session

The third therapy session builds on the first two. It consists of two parts: Pass the Prop, a warm-up exercise, and bridge building utilizing puppets and the Cartoon Lifeline. Materials needed are the following: an object to play Pass the Prop, the Cartoon Lifeline, and a variety of puppets.

Pass the Prop.

Content of Session	Rationale/Analysis
RANDY: (*Enters therapy in good mood.*)	
THERAPIST: (*I hold up a plastic egg.*) Let's play, Pass the Egg. Remember, it has to be something other than an egg. (*I hand Randy the plastic egg.*)	I deliberately chose the egg in order to explore the powerful symbol from the lifeline.
R: (*Takes the plastic egg.*) I have a bomb.	
T: (*Randy passes me the plastic egg.*) I have a football in my hand.	
R: A ship.	A ship occurs in the cartoon life-line at year 2.
T: I have a rock in my hand.	
R: A book.	Power of words—sign of hope.
T: A racetrack.	
R: A baby.	
T: A house.	
R: A gun.	

Puppetry/Cartoon Lifeline. Five puppets were set out on the table: a long, yellow furry monster (three times the size of the others), a brown snaggle-toothed walrus, a white monkey, a brown and white bunny, and a rat.

In this bridge-building exercise, Randy will select two puppets (choice) and four blocks/years on the lifeline. These puppets will tell a story about the years on the lifeline. The purpose of this exercise is to engage Randy in an inner-directed dialogue in which Randy expresses feeling and thoughts about the life story. The puppets remove the need to utilize "old" defense mechanisms.

Content of Session	Rationale/Analysis
THERAPIST: I want you to pick two of the puppets.	
RANDY: (*Picks the long snake-like monster and the snaggle-toothed walrus.*)	
T: Which puppet would you like to be?	
R: (*Places the long snake puppet on his hand.*)	

T: (*I place the walrus on mine. In a changed voice
. . .*) Hi, I'm Wally what's your name?

R: (*Places his dark sunglasses over the snake's
eyes. In a changed "high pitched" voice . . .*) My
name's Cool.

T: Cool, are you a boy snake or a girl snake.

R: A boy, dummy.

T: How old are you?

R: Not as old as you, old walrus man.

Hostility in voice.

T: Hey, Cool, where would you like to start in the
comic strip?

(*Cartoon lifeline is on table in front of Randy.*)

R: Here. (*Randy points to year 8 on lifeline.*)

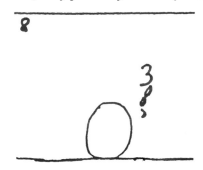

On cartoon line, year 7 represents
death in many facets, since it was
the year of cult abuse. Hence, egg
drawing in year 8 represents need
to return to the safety of the
womb.

T: Cool, what do you think is going on in this picture?

R: It's a safe place to hide.

T: What's inside?

R: I'll never tell.

T: Do you need to hide, Cool, because you're
scared.

R: The world is scary.

T: Cool, why is the egg cracking?

R: A secret is coming out.

T: Can you tell me the secret?

Secret:
  1. Abuse.
  2. Fire-setting confession.

R: The secret is cracked.

T: How can that be, Cool?

R: Let's go on.

T: Tell me about the boy in the egg.

R: He needs the shield.

T: For protection?

R: From them.

T: Them?

R: They hit me.

T: Why?

R: I'm bad.

Cracked secret:
1. Remorse.
2. Fragmented ego.

10

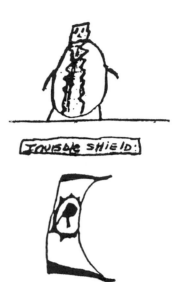

INVISIBLE SHIELD:

11

T: Is that why you're frowning?

R: I don't like the world. I want to go back in the egg.

T: Why don't you?

R: I can't.

HIDDEN DOOR TO ANY WHERE

Fourth Session

In this session puppetry combined with the Cartoon Lifeline will enable Randy to proceed safely through his entire lifeline. Materials needed are the following: a table, Cartoon Lifeline, and puppets. One of the puppets was a "fire" puppet, a specially handmade red hand puppet with matches glued to the face (see Appendix B). On one side of the "fire" puppet, the face is smiling. On the other side, the face is frowning.

A warm-up exercise was utilized to enhance suspended belief in order to set the stage for the lifeline with its powerful story.

Cartoon Lifeline. Ten puppets were used: brown monkey, white monkey, bunny, female child, male child, snake monster, walrus, seal, frog, rat, and "fire" puppet. They were arranged in a row on the desk on the side of the office.

The entire Cartoon Lifeline was spread out on the table.

Content of Session	Rationale/Analysis
THERAPIST: I would like you to choose a puppet for each year in the comic strip.	
RANDY: (*Places a puppet on each block: the brown monkey on block 0, and the frog on 1.*)	
T: Now, here's how it works. You will play the puppet character in year 0, and I will play the one in year 1. We will talk and ask questions to get to know each other better. Then you will take the puppet in year 1 and me the one in year 2, and so on down the line.	
R: (*Picks up brown monkey. I pick up frog.*)	Brown in puppet = racial identification.
T: Tell me about yourself.	
R: I was born.	Frog = leaping ability.
T: What was it like in there.	Mother was IV drug abuser during pregnancy.
R: Sticky.	
T: What's the gun for?	
R: Protect myself.	
[Refer to Panels #1 (frog) and #2 (seal)]	Seal relates to ship drawing in magical sticker.
T: (*seal puppet*) Can I shake your hand?	
R: (*frog*) (*Seal and frog shake hands.*)	
T: I'm sad.	
R: Why are you sad?	
R: Because I'm leaving you soon.	
[Refer to Panels #2 (seal) and #3 (walrus)]	Walrus = adult = empowerment over separation anxiety in loss of mother?
T: Mr. Seal, why are you saying "No"?	
R: Say "No" to drugs.	

T: Have you seen drugs?

R: Yes, Mr. Walrus.

[**Refer to Panels #3 (walrus) and #4 (white monkey)**]

R: (*walrus*) I want your toys.

T: (*white monkey*) Which of you is asking?

R: Both.

T: Both of you are in the puppet?

R: Yes.

[**Refer to Panels #4 (white monkey) and #5 (bunny)**]

R: (*white monkey*) I am happy.

T: (*bunny*) Why?

R: I have toys.

T: I don't have any toys. I want your toys.

R: Here, you may play with some of them.

[**Refer to Panels #5 (bunny) and #6 (rat)**]

T. (*rat*) Are you happy now?

R: (*bunny*) Yes.

[**Refer to Panels #6 (rat) and #7 (fire puppet)**]

R: (*rat*) Why are you smiling?

T: (*fire puppet*) (*I am showing smiling face of fire puppet.*) Because you're happy now.

R: Are you a fireman?

T: That's why I'm running.

R: I'm a dummy.

T: Why do you say that?

R: Because my friend died?

T: Your friend from year 3? (*I point back to year 3.*)

R: Yes.

[**Refer to Panels #7 (fire puppet) and #8 (snake monster)**]

R: (*Places angry/sad "fire" puppet face toward me.*)

T: (*snake monster*) Mr. Fire, are you mad or sad?

R: Sad.

T: Why?

R: The fire.

Randy witnessed world of drugs/prostitution.

Toys = childhood.

Bunny is the antithesis of angry child in year 5.

Smiling fire-face = warmth, comfort, beauty.

Randy's reaction to fire puppet itself—flat.

Death of friend might be death of aunt, death of infant in fire, or death of part of self.

Friend in 3 now missing is small boy.

Snake monster was placed on same block as in session 3.

Identification with aggression—kidnapping/matches trauma at age 7 or grief.

Randy looked at the fire puppet without emotion. He wondered if puppet were a lighter.

T: What fire?

R: The fire that spreads.

A lighter was allegedly used in the fire-setting incident.

T: Where is the fire?

R: (*Gets quiet.*)

Maybe he is immobilized by his conflicting emotions.

T: Do the magic bottles put the fire out?

R: No. They help me run faster.

[**Refer to Panels #8 (snake monster) and #9 (female child)**]

Female child related to female infant who died in fire. Remorse at innocent death.

T: (*female child*) What's it like in the egg, Sammy the snake?

R: (*snake monster*) It's cold in here.

T: Do you need a fire to keep warm?

R: No. I need toys.

[**Refer to Panels #9 (female child) and #10 (male child)**]

T: (*male child*) I want out.

R: (*female child*) But it's not safe out there.

T: But I have to see the world.

[**Refer to Panels #10 (male child) and #11 (red-haired doll)**]

R: (*Chooses a nonpuppet red-haired doll lying in a box in therapy office.*)

T: (*red-haired doll*) What is the dark part in the middle of the eggs?

R: (*male child*) Toys.

Numerous references to toys/childhood.

T: How can you and your toys get out?

R: The power.

May have assumed falsely that power must come from inside.

T: What power.

R: He-Man.

He-Man = TV cartoon character.

[**Refer to Panels #11 (doll) and #7 (male child)**]

T: You can pick any year and go back.

R: (*Places male child puppet at 7 and replaces "fire" puppet.*)

T: (*male child*) Why are you sad?

Reference to frown in Panel 11.

R: (*doll*) The world's not as great as I thought it would be.

T: Do you want back in?

R: Sometimes. (*There is a pause.*) Are we done?

T: We're done. You've done a great job. Thank you.

CONCLUDING COMMENTS

I was surprised that Randy went as far as he did. In retrospect, I might have probed more into the actual fire-setting scenario. Randy may have been readier for it in displaced play than expected from his earlier resistence. The Cartoon Lifeline and fire puppet/puppets will be reintroduced at later stages of therapy. The huge question of limited responsibility must be broached.

Anniversary dates will present opportunities for engaging Randy in "heavy" issues: fire-setting date, death dates, moving dates, abuse dates, and his own birthdate.

Guided imagery and other relaxation techniques will be utilized to balance the "hard work" of therapy when trauma is reexperienced.

In retrospect, the session might have benefited from a better selection of puppets with a wider range of emotion, particularly angry/scary puppets.

From Randy's play I believe that his prognosis is fair. There were hopeful features in the tell-a-story and lifeline responses. There is also much unresolved anger and sadness.

PLAY THERAPY MATERIALS

Crayons, markers, and pencils. Paints could be utilized on a larger-scale lifeline; white drawing paper, paper plates, puppets—variety from any toy/children's store; fire puppet handmade from felt, kitchen matches glued on, yarn for hair glued on.

STUDY QUESTIONS

1. Do you believe that group therapy would be beneficial for Randy? Why or why not? What issues or behaviors should the group therapist be prepared to deal with in regard to Randy?

2. What trauma-related issues should be addressed with Randy when he enters adolescence, young adulthood, marries, has children, finds a job?

3. What spiritual issues are relevant to Randy's case? Do you feel the strict fundamentalist religious disciplinary practices of aunt and uncle contributed to Randy's overall traumatization? In what way?

4. Is Randy so damaged that any form of treatment will be ineffectual? If so, predict his future—homicidal, suicidal, sociopathic, psychotic, or abuser/offender.

5. Discuss the implications of a white therapist treating a black preadolescent boy. How should this be addressed, and what reactions might the therapist anticipate related to racial issues?

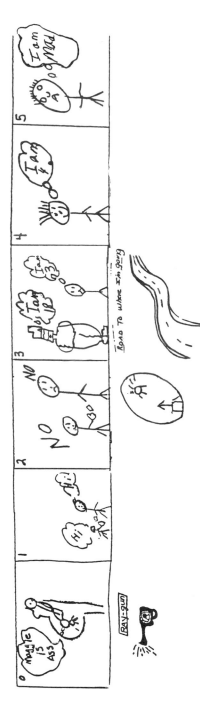

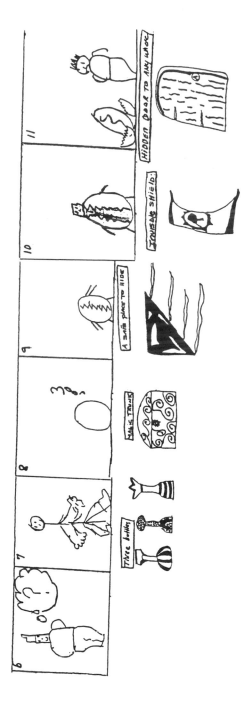

APPENDIX A. Cartoon Lifeline.

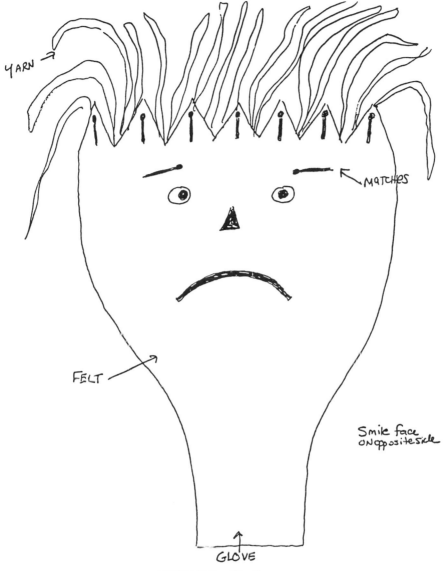

YARN

Matches

FELT

Smile face
on opposite side

GLOVE

APPENDIX B. "Fire" puppet.

REFERENCES

American Psychiatric Association. (1987). *Diagnostic and statistical manual of mental disorders* (3rd ed., rev.). Washington, DC: Author.

Dunne, P. (1988a). Drama therapy techniques in one-to-one treatment with disturbed children and adolescents. *The Arts in Psychotherapy, 15,* 139-149.

Dunne, P. (1988b). *Media in drama therapy: An exercise handbook.* Encino, CA: Center for Pyschological Change.

James, B. (1989). *Treating traumatized children.* Lexington, MA: Lexington Books.

Naitove, C. (1981). A multi-arts approach to drama therapy with adolescents and young adults. In G. Schattnery & R. Courtney (Eds.), *Drama in therapy for adolescents* (pp. 243-259). New York: Drama Book Specialists.

Pazzanese, E., & Wise, D. (1984). Building self-esteem through puppetry. In N. Renfro (Ed.), *Puppetry, language and the special child* (p. 140). Austin, TX: Nancy Renfro Studio.

Renfro, N. (1984). A personal perspective. In N. Renfro (Ed.), *Puppetry, language and the special child* (pp. 16-24). Austin, TX: Nancy Renfro Studio.

Shengold, L. (1989). *Soul murder.* New Haven: Yale University Press.

Sternberg, P., & Garcia, A. (1989). *Sociodrama: Who's in your shoes?* New York: Praeger.

Terr, L. (1987). Psychic trauma and the creative product: A look at the early lives and later work of Poe, Magritte, Hitchcock, and Bergman. *Psychoanalytic Study of the Child, 42,* 545-572.

Terr, L. (1989a). Terror writing by the formerly terrified: A look at Stephen King. *Psychoanalytic Study of the Child, 44,* 369-390.

Terr, L. (1989b). Treating psychic trauma in children: A preliminary discussion. *Journal of Traumatic Stress, 2*(1), 3-20.

PART III

The Crisis of Loss

CHAPTER 7

Repeated Foster Placements and Attachment Failure
Case of Joseph, Age 3

JOYCE M. REMKUS

This chapter presents the case of a 3-year-old child who never formed a secure attachment to his mother because of her mental illness. Failure to do so inhibited the child's cognitive functioning, language development, motor development, and autonomous functioning. His mother's psychiatric condition periodically prevented her from caring for her children, which resulted in their entering the foster care system. When the child was between 10 months and 29 months of age, he experienced several foster home placements, culminating in a preadoptive foster home placement at age 2½. Fortunately, the child's serious developmental delays were noticed at this time, and he was referred for assessment and treatment.

Unfortunately, this case is not unique. Thousands of children have similar histories of poor maternal–child attachment, repeated foster placements, and symptom formation that remains undiagnosed and untreated. These children become the conduct-disordered children in school, the developmentally delayed, the "hard-to-reach" problem children who are so difficult to engage in a trusting relationship with an adult.

The case presentation demonstrates the considerable difference early intervention made in the life of a child, who by age 3 was dangerously at risk of serious future difficulties. A brief review of attachment theory and of the nature of preventive services provides the foundation for understanding the implications and value of early intervention to beneficially stimulate and alter a thwarted growth process.

EARLY MOTHER–CHILD ATTACHMENT

Attachment is essential for survival. Bowlby (1969) defines attachment as an enduring bond of affection, characterized by the desire for proximity to the "attachment object" and protest of any separation from the desired person. Ainsworth and Wittig (1969) point out that the relationship between the child and his attachment figure provides a "secure base" from which the child ventures forth to explore and master his or her world.

A secure attachment bond therefore is the basis for subsequent development. It is through this relationship that the infant learns about trust, love, and social interactions. Failure to establish a secure attachment relationship limits the emotional, cognitive, and social development of the child (Sroufe & Waters, 1977; Sroufe, 1979a, 1979b; Ainsworth, 1979; Ainsworth & Bell, 1971; Mahler, Pine, & Bergman, 1975).

Initially in this dyadic relationship, it is the mother who serves as a monitoring agent and supplier of the infant's needs. Anna Freud (1970) states: "In this earliest partnership in an individual's life, that of infant and mother, the demands are all in one side (the infant's), while the obligations are all on the other side (the mother's)." In this initially disproportionate relationship, it is the mother who must be empathic and in tune to her infant's needs. It is through this early interaction that an attachment relationship develops. Although the infant's propensity to attach is a biological given, it is the mother's response that determines the quality of the attachment. The mother's emotional availability and stability affect the manner in which she interacts with her infant: if she is attentive to her infant's needs and provides comfort to him or her in times of distress, there is a high probability that the infant will develop a secure, trusting attachment relationship. The trust established here later will be transferred over to trust of others (Mahler et al., 1975). Insecure attachment stemming from inconsistent care, on the other hand, takes the form of separation difficulties (Mahler et al., 1975; Ainsworth & Bell, 1971).

Reciprocal Interaction

The mother's attentiveness promotes reciprocal interaction. As the infant matures, he or she increasingly takes the initiative in attempting to engage the mother. Her reactions to his or her gestures are of the utmost importance, since this lays the ground work for future interest in and exploration of the environment. Osofsky and Connors (1979, p. 5) consider that "the quantity and timing of mother's responses to her infant's behavior and the degree of consistency of her responses play important roles in developing and reinforcing the infant's belief that his or her behavior can affect the environment." If, however, the mother is not responsive to the infant's attempts, there exists a probability that this will discourage his or her future attempts to engage the mother as well as limit his or her interest in the outside world (Freud, 1970).

The reciprocal interaction also provides the infant with stimulation (Sander, 1976; Osofsky & Connors, 1979; Rutter, 1972, 1979; Sroufe, 1979a; Sroufe & Waters, 1977) and the rudiments of language development (Lewis, 1977; Bruner & Sherwood, 1983; Ainsworth, 1979; Sander, 1976; Rutter, 1972). Ainsworth (1979) reports that securely attached infants have better language development than infants who were not securely attached to their mothers. The securely attached infants also seemed better able to explore the environment and interact with persons other than mother. Bruner and Sherwood (1983, pp. 42–43) postulate that

> the development of language involves, then, two people working together. The mother must be "finely tuned" to the task and to the skills and needs of the child. It has become quite clear in recent years that language is not encountered willy-nilly by the child; it is instead encountered in a highly structured interaction with the mother, who takes a crucial role in arranging her child's linguistic encounters.

Language development, cognitive development, and curiosity about the environment are interrelated and depend on the amount of stimulation the child receives and the quality of the attachment relationship (Sroufe & Waters, 1977; Sroufe, 1979b; Osofsky & Connors, 1979; Solnit & Provence, 1979; Rutter, 1972, 1979).

The mother–infant relationship actually is a fragile relationship that is frequently impacted on by external forces and individual difficulties. Individual differences, physical or emotional problems in either partner, can set the tenor for disruptions (Osofsky & Connors, 1979; Sander, 1976; Freud, 1970; Emde & Sorce, 1983; Garmezy, 1986; Guttman, 1989; Korner, 1971; Solnit & Provence, 1979; Sroufe, 1979a; Thomas & Chess, 1977). A chaotic environment, marital conflicts, and pathology in the mother can have a devastating effect on the infant's development (Farber & Egeland, 1987; Guttman, 1989; Freud, 1970; Solnit & Provence, 1979; Garmezy, 1986). Children raised in adverse conditions are vulnerable to developmental delays and psychological problems (Guttman, 1989; Farber & Egeland, 1987; Freud, 1970; Solnit & Provence, 1979; Garmezy, 1986; Schroeder, Gordon, & Walker, 1983).

Obviously, when such conditions prevail, the mother's emotional availability is limited, and this, in turn, affects the quality of the attachment relationship and the intellectual and psychological development of the child. Children whose mothers suffer from psychological problems tend to have lower intellectual quota scores, language difficulties, and poor social skills (Rutter, 1972, 1979; Solnit & Provence, 1979; Garmezy, 1986; Osofsky & Connors, 1979). Frequently these children appear retarded (Rutter, 1972; Sander, 1976; Ainsworth, 1979). The dyadic reciprocal interaction tends to be dysfunctional, thus limiting the amount of stimulation (Rutter, 1972, 1979; Sander, 1976; Osofsky & Connors, 1979; Freud, 1970). Sander (1976) considers the early reciprocal exchanges to be the basis for the formation of an individual's sense of autonomy.

MATERNAL–CHILD SEPARATION

Just as the mother's inability to provide adequate and consistent care can have a devastating effect on the child, separation from her can produce additional stress and trauma (Rutter, 1981; Butler, 1989; Garmezy, 1986). Every day numerous children enter the foster care system and thus are separated from their families

(Itzkowitz, 1989; Steinhauer, 1983). Placement occurs as a result of the inability of the parent(s) to provide a safe, secure environment for their children (Itzkowitz, 1989). Frequently these children come into care with developmental delays and psychological problems (Itzkowitz, 1989; Steinhauer, 1983).

Foster care parents, however, may be insufficiently prepared to understand the emotional problems of the children placed in their homes (Steinhauer, 1983). The child in the foster home may present the foster family with problems the family is ill equipped to handle. If the family has difficulty managing the child, or if his or her behavior becomes intolerable, the child may be removed from the home (Itzkowitz, 1989). When this transpires, the child is faced with yet another rejection and separation.

Although separation, even from an emotionally unavailable mother, can be devastating for the child, the provision of a warm, sensitive, caring substitute parent may assist in alleviating the child's discomfort (Ainsworth, 1979; Rutter, 1972, 1979; Freud, 1970; Spitz, 1946). Without such a substitute parent, problems noted prior to placement can become even more accentuated. An attentive, warm substitute parent, however, can effect change in the child's overall functioning (Osofsky & Connors, 1979; Caldwell, 1971; Rutter, 1972, 1979; Mishne, 1979). It is, therefore, the *quality* of care after maternal separation that makes a crucial difference for children in foster care (Rutter, 1972; Caldwell, 1971; Spitz, 1946).

FOSTER CARE PLACEMENT

The philosophy of the foster care system is to provide children with continuous, nurturing care. However, the system is currently designed to provide *temporary* care. This means that the child either returns home, assuming that the dysfunctional aspects of the home have been ameliorated, or the child is placed in an adoptive home (Hess, 1982; Rooney, 1982). This is admittedly a simplified description of permanency planning, but the procedures, policies, and ramifications of permanency planning are beyond the scope of this chapter. Frequently the child develops attachments to the foster family so that either return home or adoption confronts the child with another separation.

Despite efforts to provide the child with a nurturing, warm adoptive home, the child's initial adjustment to the adoptive home often is problematic. The number of placements prior to the adoptive home and the quality of care the child has had in previous placements are important variables that can interfere with the child's adjustment to the adoptive home and the development of attachments to the adoptive family (Butler, 1989; Steinhauer, 1983; Brinich, 1980). The age and cognitive abilities of the child play an important role in this process. Butler (1989, p. 171) states:

> It may be that for some children, multiple changes in the environment before there is adequate language to describe what is happening may leave the child more vulnerable and mistrustful and have profound effects on the adoption

process. It may also be that for some children, having to connect and disconnect repeatedly from caretakers . . . may increase their anxiety and uncertainty as well as that of their adoptive families.

The child may need to mourn the loss of previous attachments before he or she can adequately cathect to a new set of parents. Although the child's ability to form new attachments is one consideration, the response of the adoptive parents is also critical in facilitating this process. The adoptive parents' reasons for adoption, their perceptions about parenthood, and their expectations about the child need to be considered as influencing variables (Butler, 1989; Steinhauer, 1983; DiGiulio, 1987; Brinich, 1980).

EARLY INTERVENTION

The Early Years Program operated by Rockland Children's Psychiatric Center consists of community based preschool intervention programs that were designed to provide evaluation and treatment to children deemed to be "at risk" for developing later developmental disabilities and/or mental disorders. Referrals to the Early Years Program generate from day care centers, Head Start programs, Child Protective Services, Department of Social Services—Children's Unit, pediatricians, and concerned parents.

Evaluation

The evaluation process is based on a medical model and includes interviews with the child's caretaker and play sessions with the child. Typically the child psychiatrist first meets with the parent, while the clinician assesses the child through a play session. In the next screening session, the process is reversed. When the child is already enrolled in a day care or Head Start program, the team then has the opportunity to observe the child in a group situation as well as to obtain information about the child from the relevant child care staff.

At the conclusion of the evaluation process, the clinical staff formulate a comprehensive treatment plan. This plan takes into account the child's needs and the services available and recommends a treatment program to the caretaker. Possible treatment recommendations include family therapy, individual expressive therapy sessions for the child, therapeutic play groups, and a day treatment program, which meets five times per week for 3 hours a session. With the exception of the day treatment program, frequency and duration of services depend on the child's needs and program availability.

Whatever the modality of treatment, therapy with preschool children encompasses a wide variety of activities that are designed to promote mastery and enhance ego development. Typical activities include art projects, music/dance, games, free play, and snacks.

THE CASE: JOSEPH WALKER, AGE 3

Family Information

Biological Family

Father   Calvin Walker, early 30s, unskilled laborer
Mother   Katherine Walker, late 20s, unemployed
Children   (all placed in different foster homes)
           Kenneth Walker, 4, in foster care
           Joseph Walker, 3, in preadoptive foster home
           Mary, 2, in foster care

Preadoptive Family

Father   James Nelson, early 50s, Baptist minister and part-time child care
           worker
Mother   Laura Nelson, early 40s, homemaker; previously employed as a
           data processor
Children   James Nelson, Jr., 21, out of home
           June Nelson, 18, high school student
           Martha Jones, 16, independent living foster child, high school
           student, works part time
           Susan Brown, 7, foster child, student
           Barbara Brown, 6, foster child, student
           Joseph Walker, 3, preadoptive foster child

Presenting Problem

Joseph, a 3-year-old in foster care, was referred for an evaluation by the social
worker at a local Head Start program, who was concerned about Joseph's ability to
function in a Head Start setting. At the time of referral, Joseph's language was
limited to three or four words, and his speech was echolalic, without spontaneity;
at times his utterances were considered "gibberish." There were concerns about
other developmental delays as well, notably his gross motor coordination, which
seemed poorly developed. At times his mood appeared sullen; he cried easily and
displayed temper-tantrum behaviors. The foster mother also reported that Joseph
did not know how to play, nor could he dress himself.

Past History

Joseph's family history (obtained from the foster care agency) revealed psychiatric
illness, mental retardation, convulsions, hypertension, diabetes, alcohol abuse, and
birth defects. Joseph entered the foster care system as a 10-month-old when his
mother arrived at the police station in a state of agitation and confusion with
Joseph and his older brother. A mental health crisis team found that Mrs. Walker

was not oriented to the three spheres, and therefore she was taken to a local psychiatric hospital for an evaluation and observation.

When initially placed Joseph was very distressed by the separation from his mother and became hysterical. He was difficult to comfort and console. His distress became intense at bedtime, and after 2 months the foster mother requested that he be removed from her home. At this time Joseph was also separated from his older brother. Although his behavior in the new home did not differ from that in the previous home, the foster mother seemed more tolerant and was able to comfort him. She was also alarmed about his developmental delays, specifically his inability to perform tasks typical of 12- or 13-month-old children. However, he gradually began to exhibit separation protest when the foster mother departed from his visual range, thereby indicating that he had developed an attachment to her.

Against the advice of the foster care agency, 8 months later the court returned Walker children to their parents' care. Weeks after their return home, Mrs. Walker's psychotic episodes necessitated readmission to the psychiatric hospital. With Mrs. Walker hospitalized, the care of the children became the sole responsibility of Mr. Walker, who, although intellectually limited, was gainfully employed. To assist him with the child care responsibilities, he employed a homemaker. Apparently one day he left for work prior to the homemaker's arrival, and when she entered the home she found all three children in the bathtub—8-month old Mary face down, and the two boys playing. A neglect petition was filed against Mr. Walker, and the children reentered foster care. Shortly after this foster care placement, the parents divorced and surrendered the children for adoption. In view of the family history and his current level of functioning, Joseph was considered "at risk."

The Nelsons had known that Joseph had some problems before entering into the preadoptive agreement. However, they expected him to have made more gains after 7 months in their home. Mrs. Nelson believed that Joseph had been neglected and possibly ignored in the previous foster homes because his behavior had not been troublesome. She felt that his withdrawn and complacent attitude made it easy for him to be overlooked and neglected, with a resulting lack of adequate stimulation. Although the Nelsons accepted Joseph's problems and understood the possible causes, they were becoming increasingly apprehensive about their commitment to adopting Joseph. The Nelsons, therefore, were placing an enormous amount of hope in Joseph's treatment.

First Interview with Child (Home Visit)

Before the evaluation process could proceed the Early Years Program's permission forms needed to be signed by the supervisor of the foster care agency. To facilitate this procedure a visit to the Nelson home was arranged, which gave me the opportunity to meet Joseph and Mrs. Nelson. The following is a segment of that initial meeting.

Joseph was a slim, attractive 35-month-old boy whose expression reflected sadness. His gross motor coordination seemed awkward and underdeveloped.

Content of Session	Rationale/Analysis
THERAPIST: Hello, my name is Joyce. What is your name?	
JOSEPH (*smiling*): Name.	
MOTHER: That's how he talks, but I feel that he understands what happens . . . goes on. Joseph, go get a car. (*Joseph leaves.*) He loves cars but does not seem to know what to do with them. (*Joseph returns. He is smiling, holding a plastic truck.*)	His gait seems wide.
T (*pointing to the truck*): What's that?	Child repeats last word spoken to him.
J (*smiling*): That.	
T (*pointing to the truck*): This is a truck. Can you say truck?	
J: Truck.	
T: Very good, Joseph. Do you want to play?	
J: (*Smiles.*)	
T (*squatting on the floor*): Can you roll me the truck?	Wanted to see if he could follow a simple instruction.
J: (*With a broad smile he rolls the truck to therapist.*)	

I continued this interaction for several minutes. Throughout the exchange Joseph seemed to take pleasure in the play.

Content of Session	Rationale/Analysis
THERAPIST: Can you roll the truck under the table?	Wanted to see if he knew the concept of "under" without any visual clues.
JOSEPH: (*In silence he does so.*)	
T: Very good, Joseph. (*after returning the truck to him*) Can you roll the truck around the table? (*pointing in the direction*)	
J: (*Smiling he does so.*)	
T: Very good. Joseph you listened very well. I have to talk to Mommy now. Thank you for playing with me.	

When I stopped this interaction it was as though a switch went off inside of this child. He froze and his smile disappeared until someone glanced in his direction or uttered his name. During these times he would produce a large smile but remained physically immobile.

From the short meeting with Joseph it did not seem that he neatly fit into the diagnostic category of either pervasive developmental disorder or mental retardation. It seemed more probable that this 3-year-old child was suffering from early childhood neglect and inadequate stimulation. He appeared to need a great deal of stimulation from adults (a high-sensory-threshold child).

Korner (1971, p. 615), in describing her neonatal studies, noted, "infants with high sensory thresholds will show the effects of maternal neglect more acutely than infants who, unaided, are more receptive to environmental stimuli."

Parent Counseling

Following the brief encounter with Joseph and his mother, I decided to give this dyad some very simple tasks that were primarily designed to assist Joseph in language development. I suggested that Mrs. Nelson constantly talk to Joseph throughout the day. I wanted her to focus him on tasks they were performing together (e.g., telling him she was helping him put on his shirt), and I also wanted her to explain to him what she was doing in the course of the day's routine (e.g., "Mommy is ironing Daddy's shirt," "Mommy is cooking rice for dinner"). Since his play was underdeveloped, I asked her to sit down and play with him for at least 15 minutes per day. The final task was that she teach Joseph his name. Mrs. Nelson readily agreed to the suggestions.

Psychiatric Evaluation

Three weeks after the initial meeting, Joseph and Mrs. Nelson came to the agency for a psychiatric evaluation. Since the initial meeting Mrs. Nelson had been following the suggestions previously offered. When the psychiatrist asked Joseph, "What's your name?" Joseph clearly responded, "Joseph." Joseph showed interest in exploring the playroom and seemed delighted in his discoveries. As to be expected because of his age, his primary focus was in the transportation section of the room (cars, trucks, trains). Tentatively and apprehensively he responded to reciprocal play situations, and when the play was terminated, Joseph did not remain "frozen" but rather tenuously continued his exploration. His play, however, lacked symbolic expression and was more appropriate to that of a younger child.

In order to assess the attachment and level of object constancy of this 3-year-old, Mrs. Nelson was asked to temporarily leave the playroom. Prior to the separation, I showed Joseph where his mother would be. He was able to tolerate the separation without any signs of anxiety, and on her return, he shared his new experiences with her.

Despite the numerous gains that had occurred in only 3 weeks, Joseph's speech still exhibited echolalic traits, was poorly articulated, and lacked spontaneity. Although he did not have a repertoire of words for the items around him, he was able to point accurately to specific items when requested to do so. For example, when shown four different pictures, he was able when asked, to point to the picture of the keys.

Psychological Evaluation

Concurrently with our evaluation process, Joseph was given a psychological evaluation at the foster care agency. The tests administered were the Stanford-Binet and the Cattell Infant Intelligence Scale. Both tests placed Joseph's IQ in the high 80s. On both tests Joseph scored very low or failed the verbal response sections. Much like the situation during the evaluation, he was able to point accurately to items and follow simple verbal commands. His ability to do this suggested that his intellectual functioning was greater than his verbal responses and that the IQ scores were not truly representative of his intellectual abilities.

Preliminary Assessment and Treatment Plan

Joseph's history suggests that he had not had consistent or adequate care until he was 29 months old, when he arrived at the Nelson home. It was quite possible that his atypical responses reflected a lack of early stimulation as an infant and maternal neglect.

Joseph's biological mother had had numerous psychiatric hospitalizations and was unable to care for her children. Because of her psychiatric illness, her emotional availability for her son was less than adequate. Emde and Sorce (1983, p. 28) believe "that maternal emotional availability plays a crucial role in infant development since it helps create an atmosphere that fosters enjoyment, curiosity, and enhanced opportunities for learning." Other theorists have also suggested that the reciprocal mother–infant interaction is the basis for language acquisition (Bruner & Sherwood, 1983; Lewis, 1977), social learning, and stability that allows exploration of the environment (Emde, 1985; Sroufe & Waters, 1977; Sroufe, 1979b; Solnit & Provence, 1979; Rutter, 1972, 1979; Mahler et al., 1975), as well as ego development (Blanck & Blanck, 1979).

Joseph's attachment to his mother seemed "anxious" rather than "secure" (Ainsworth & Bell, 1971). In Joseph's case we note that his history was spattered with inadequate care and several separations. According to Rutter (1972, p. 34), "a child's response to a separation experience may be influenced for the better or worse by the nature of previous separations." Furthermore, Rutter suggests that with each separation there seems to be a more difficult or lengthy process for attachment to the next caretaker (Rutter, 1972). This is clearly seen in the difficulties Joseph had in his first foster home as well as during the parent–child visits. The records indicate that during the visits his mother and father would sit back and observe their children without any parent–child interaction, and neither Joseph nor his brother approached the parents to initiate contact with them.

When Joseph was separated from his second foster home to return to his parents at 18 months of age, he became hysterical. It appeared that an attachment to his foster mother had begun when the process was suddenly terminated. This experience duplicated the first separation. After a brief 2-month stay at home, Joseph once again entered foster care. Originally he was placed with the prior foster mother. However, when she became ill, he was placed in another home. By this time it seemed that Joseph tended to withdraw even farther. He seemed to expect nothing of his environment (Rutter, 1981).

By the time he reached the Nelson home, Joseph seemed bewildered and confused. After a short while he began to shadow Mrs. Nelson around. It became apparent that he was attempting to form an attachment to her, but this attachment was anxious and insecure (Ainsworth & Bell, 1971). For several months after he was placed at the Nelson home, Joseph would become hysterical whenever he had to leave the house. He would not calm down until he was safely at home. It seemed that leaving the home produced intense separation anxiety.

Joseph was a child who had received inadequate care throughout his infancy and toddler years, and his life contained a poverty of nourishing, growth-enhancing experience. There was no valid way initially to determine how definitively his early childhood experiences would continue to affect his subsequent development. In other words, how much change could be possible, given the years of deprivation?

Diagnosis

Mental retardation was ruled out by the results of the psychological testing and the gains that Joseph had made in such a short period of time. Although he did not accurately fit the criteria for pervasive developmental disorder, the team felt that more information was needed before this disorder could be categorically ruled out.

The treatment team, composed of a child psychiatrist and a psychiatric social worker, concluded that this child's problems were indeed a direct result of less than optimal early care and a lack of adequate stimulation. The team also assessed that the repeated foster home placements had increased Joseph's difficulties.

Treatment Plan

Because of the extent of Joseph's deficits, a once-a-week hourly expressive therapy session was considered inadequate to meet his needs. The team decided that the most effective model of treatment would be a small therapeutic play group to provide Joseph with stimulation from activities as well as from other children. Ideally, this would consist of a 5-day-a-week day treatment program with a speech and language component. Unfortunately, this ideal was not available, and the best compromise consisted of a referral to a speech pathologist for speech therapy and admission into a 2-hour therapeutic play group that convened twice weekly. The team also ordered a complete audiological evaluation.

The *initial treatment goals* were:

1. To continue to facilitate the attachment process, which was still "anxious."
2. To encourage Joseph's development along normal lines.
3. To increase Joseph's language skills.

Therapeutic interventions with preschoolers encompass a wide range of techniques and are not limited to "pure" psychological interventions. Helping preschoolers learn how to do a puzzle, identify colors, and paint, for example, increases their sense of mastery and ultimately leads to improved self-confidence and self-esteem. For Joseph, the abovementioned activities were necessary for developing mastery as well as for his development. Although his play was improving, it failed to demonstrate a repertoire of play themes. Expansion of play themes is a necessary prerequisite for the normal development of symbolic play. Helping Joseph expand on play themes, therefore, would be an additional treatment objective.

Although physically Joseph appeared his stated age, his behavioral responses were more appropriate to a younger child. It occurred to me that he was slowly going through the missed developmental phases. This idea was shared with Mrs. Nelson, who was informed that as the process proceeded Joseph might enter into the "terrible 2s." This information did not concern Mrs. Nelson, since she viewed it as a welcome progression that would signal the end to Joseph's compliant behavior.

Play Therapy Sessions (Group)

The therapeutic play group consisted of four 3-year-old children. For the first six sessions Mrs. Nelson brought Joseph to the group. During the 2-hour length of each session, initially Joseph would periodically check on his mother's physical availability. This indicated to the team that he was still anxiously attached to her. Eventually he was content to just check the picture of him and her together. Part of our procedure in working with such a young population includes the use of Polaroid pictures of the mother–child dyad in order to assist the child with separations, and thus facilitate a more secure attachment. Since some of our children are also uncertain about the next therapy session, we make a calendar for the parent and child. Here the mother is instructed to mark off each day, with therapy days and times circled in red. I also add other special days, for example, the child's birthday, holidays, and planned trips.

Although Joseph eagerly interacted with his peers, his play tended to be parallel rather than cooperative. Joseph interacted appropriately with his peers, but it did not seem that his development had proceeded to the point where he had a strong sense of "mine." Joseph willingly shared with group members, but they at times would just grab items from him, and he did not object.

Session 7

Mrs. Nelson called before the seventh session (3½ weeks following the initial session) to inform me that she had no way of transporting Joseph to the session.

When she tried to explain to Joseph that he would not be attending group today, he became angry and upset. We decided that I would transport him with the other children. I suggested that she talk with Joseph explaining to him that he *would* be coming to group *but* that she would remain at home waiting for him to return.

I decided that Joseph would be the last child picked up. He was apprehensive about getting into the van, but the other children's greeting to him seemed to ease his fears. My philosophy is that therapy actually begins from the moment of "pickup." As we travel through town, objects (trucks, flowers, etc.) are pointed out for the children to observe and discuss.

When we arrived and were settled in the playroom, the group started with a story. After this the following interaction occurred. Joseph asked for the water table. The other two 3-year-old children, Sarah and David, joined him. Joseph was pouring water from one container into another. (Actually, pouring is very good exercise for him, since he refused to pour his juice at snack time.) As the parallel play was in progress I joined the group.

Content of Session	Rationale/Analysis
THERAPIST: Joseph, can you pour me some water . . . for tea?	Wanted to expand on the pouring theme.
JOSEPH: OK. (*Looks for a cup; then pours some water into the cup.*) Here's your tea.	
T: Thank you. (*pretending to drink from the cup*) This is good tea.	
SARAH: Joyce, want some juice?	Sarah also wants the therapist's attention.
T: What kind do you have?	
S: Apple juice. Want some?	
T: Why yes, please. (*Sarah hands a cup of "juice" to therapist.*) Thank you. (*pretending to drink*) This is good juice.	
J: Want some juice?	
T: What kind do you have?	
J: Apple juice.	
T: Yes, I would like some. Maybe you should ask David if he wants some too.	Attempting to connect David, who looks sad and withdrawn, to the group process.
J: David want some juice?	
DAVID: (*Nods OK.*)	
T: Thank you, Joseph. David do you like your juice?	
D: Yes.	
T: Can you tell Joseph?	
D: Good juice, Joseph.	

This play continued with several variations, including getting dishes, pots, and pans from the kitchen play area. At one point while "cooking," Joseph became anxious and looked sad.

Content of Session	Rationale/Analysis
THERAPIST: Joseph, what's wrong?	
JOSEPH: Mommy.	
T: Where's Mommy?	
J: (*Walks over to his cubby to get his picture.*)	
T: (*Follows, squats, and places arm around him.*) What's that a picture of?	
J: Mommy.	
T: That's right. Who else is in the picture?	
J: Me.	
T: Where is Mommy?	Wanted to see if he remembered
J: Home.	that his mother was home waiting for him (object constancy).
T: That's right, your mommy is at home. (*Sarah also indicates that her mommy is home too.*) Sarah's mommy is at home, and Joseph's mommy is at home. Is your mommy home waiting for you?	
J: Yes.	
SARAH: My mommy is waiting for me.	
T: What about you, David, is your mommy at home waiting for you?	
T: When you get home, let's tell Mommy about playing in the water table. A little later we will draw a picture. You can take that home to show Mommy too.	Attempting to help the children make the connecting link between playroom and home via objects to be taken home and stories to be repeated.
J: (*Places the dyad picture back in the cubby and returns to the water table.*)	

This session demonstrates that Joseph was still anxiously attached to his mother. Periodically throughout the session, he needed to return to his cubby and check the dyad picture. This behavior continued for several subsequent sessions.

Expansion of Play Themes. Whether at the water table, in the housekeeping area, or using other toys, I would attempt to have Joseph expand his play themes. For example, if cars were used, I had the car stop for gas, go to the store, etc. Originally he chose to use only cars, without the people that were part of the Fisher-Price set. I began to include a person in my car. He imitated. When the people stopped at the store, I tried to have Joseph name some items that they might purchase.

Another example of expanding play themes occurred during water table play, which featured washing the "baby." Here I would have Joseph wash all the body parts of the doll, dry the doll, clothe the doll, feed the doll, and then place the baby in the crib. Mrs. Nelson was urged to have Joseph bathe himself with her coaching "wash your face," "wash your arms," etc. Little by little he started to develop some play themes. His language was also steadily improving. By the end of the summer, the Nelsons were pleased with his progress. Mrs. Nelson said, "Before group, if I would ask Joseph to get his shoes, he would just stand still and look at me. Now if I say Joseph get your sneakers or sandals, he goes off and returns with his shoes."

In September Joseph began Head Start. When I met him during the "phase-in" process, he greeted me and informed me that he was playing with the blocks. His speech was still poorly articulated, but now it was spontaneous. Two new 3-year-olds, LeRoy and Brian, were added to the group. Both boys were also in foster care. Late August David returned to his mother and left the area and therefore was no longer part of the group. The first few sessions in the group in a different location produced some regressive behaviors in Joseph. For example, he had difficulty expanding on play themes. He felt more comfortable rotely rolling the cars. This quickly abated, however, he became reluctant to leave the sessions.

Although Joseph had made gains, there were some areas that indicated uneven development. One such area was his intense fear of party favor finger puppet monsters. It should be noted that these puppets did not in any way look frightening, nor did any other child in the program perceive them as frightening. The play room had dinosaur toys, which Joseph did not fear. This session shows the intensity of his fear and his inability to cope when upset.

Session 18

The group had just finished an art project and went off for free play. Joseph went to the transportation area, LeRoy to the kitchen area, and Brian's play was nondirected and scattered, reflecting anxiety.

Content of Session	Rationale/Analysis
LeRoy: (*Starts cooking.*) I'm fixin' some food.	
Therapist: That's a good idea.	LeRoy's play is usually disorganized; acknowledging his direction was a form of reinforcement.
Brian: (*Looking through all the baskets and dumping the contents on the floor.*)	
T: Brian, you don't seem like you know what to play with today.	
B: (*Still emptying the baskets.*)	
T: Maybe you could cook with LeRoy or play cars with Joseph?	Wanted to connect Brian to the others whose play was more di-

L: Brian wanta cook?

B: (*Finishes going through the baskets when he finds the finger puppets.*)

T: What did you find?

B: Monsters. RAH!

JOSEPH: (*Stops his play and looks on.*)

T: These monsters make a loud noise.

B (*in an angry and anxious voice*): RAH! RAH!

T: These monsters seem upset. What is making them so upset?

J: (*Begins to cry.*)

T: (*Goes over and holds him.*) What's the matter?

J: No monsters! No monsters!

T: Are you afraid of these puppets?

B: (*Comes over and in Joseph's face*) RAH! RAH!

J: (*Starts swinging at the finger puppet.*) NO! NO!

B: RAH!

T: Brian, Joseph is afraid of the puppets. He does not like it when you scare him. Maybe you can take them over there (*pointing to the other side of the room*).

B: (*Does not move.*)

L: (*Comes over and takes a finger puppet and interacts with Brian, but relatively close to Joseph.*) RAH!

J: NO!

T: Boys, *I* want the puppets.

L: (*Gives therapist the puppet and returns to the kitchen area.*)

B: They're not real.

T: That's right, they are not, but Joseph is afraid.

B: (*Reluctantly hands over the puppets.*)

T: Thank you. Brian what makes *you* afraid?

B: The monster at night [this has been a constant theme for him].

rected. This would also facilitate group interaction.

Attempt to expand his play beyond RAH.

Brian cannot recognize Joseph's feelings. I am not happy that he continues this behavior. I hope he will not persist.

Decide that I must protect Joseph.

He seems bewildered about Joseph's reaction.

I know that Brian has several fears; therefore, I wanted to see if he could identify with Joseph's feeling.

T: You are afraid at night, and Joseph is afraid now.

L: Let's cook.

T (*still holding Joseph*): What made the monsters so scary?

J: No monsters!

T: I have the monsters in my pocket. No more monsters.

Prior to each group I would remove the finger monsters from the basket containing space people and monsters. On a few occasions, however, I would forget, and Brian would taunt Joseph. On one occasion Joseph told the monsters and Brian to leave him alone. This, however, did not work. Again I felt the need to take the monsters. The subsequent session Joseph dealt with his fear as follows:

Content of Session	Rationale/Analysis
JOSEPH: (*Enters the room and takes the basket of army men. He locates a particularly large figure with a big rifle. He returns the other army men to the basket and goes off to play with Legos.*)	
BRIAN: (*Play is disorganized and aimless. He finds the monsters.*) RAH, Joseph!	I started to intervene but decided to see what would develop
J: Go away.	
B: RAH!	
J: (*picking up the army man*): I'll shoot you.	
B: RAH!	
J: BANG! You're dead, monster.	
THERAPIST: Joseph just killed the monster. No more frightening monster.	Addressed to Joseph to give him a sense of power but also to Brian—that Joseph was not afraid.
B: (*Takes another.*) RAH!	
J (*holding the army man*): BANG! BANG! The monster is dead. (*Each time Brian tries to frighten him, Joseph shoots the monster.*) Now leave me alone. (*He returns to his play.*)	
B: (*Goes off.*)	
T: Joseph is no longer afraid of the monsters.	
J: Right. (*Continues to play, keeping the army man nearby.*)	

From time to time after that Brian would try to scare Joseph. Usually it did not work.

CONCLUDING COMMENTS

After approximately 1 year Joseph seemed to have gone through a complete metamorphosis. From having no language or no developed play, he emerged into a child whose play was more age appropriate. Although his vocabulary had expanded, it was still underdeveloped and poorly articulated. It seemed that his speech and language delays required more intense intervention. The treatment team, his speech therapist, and the Head Start social worker decided to refer Joseph to a preschool language program. Mrs. Nelson was in agreement with the referral. As part of the admission process, the preschool language program administered a complete battery of tests. Joseph's language was assessed at being 12 to 18 months below age level. Intelligence test results indicated that his intellectual functioning was within the normal range. He was accepted into their 5-day-a-week program. It should be noted that at the time of discharge from our program, the Nelsons were no longer ambivalent about adopting Joseph.

Prior to the existence of Early Years programs, a child like Joseph would not have received the services necessary to stimulate developmental changes. By the time he entered kindergarten, the deficits would have increased, and he probably would have been given a label of mental retardation or pervasive developmental disorder. Given the Nelsons' apprehension about the adoption process, Joseph might have suffered yet another loss. Even the loss of neighborhood for a young child is a devastating traumatic experience that can be equated to a major loss or death (Brenner, 1984). Throughout the treatment process, Joseph's preadoptive foster mother proved to be this child's greatest asset. She energetically spent hours assisting him to develop to his potential. Without Mrs. Nelson's level of involvement, the therapeutic efforts would not have had as much effect. She was the catalyst behind the change.

This case presentation is of particular relevance to clinicians who work with preschool children. Although children like Joseph who have numerous and serious delays may not frequent our clinics in large numbers, his story and treatment can encourage us as we attempt to understand the etiology and "undo" the effects of early deprivation and separation experiences.

PLAY THERAPY MATERIALS

- Water table (Childcraft)
- Complete wooden kitchen set: stove, refrigerator, sink, utility cabinet (Childcraft)
- Polaroid camera
- Playskool: house, people, cars, barn, and animals
- Matchbox cars—a vast assortment
- Plastic truck and jeep (Woolworth's)
- Fisher-Price medical kit
- Play-Doh

- Large cardboard blocks (Childcraft)
- Kitchen set at Head Start was a single unit with stove, refrigerators, and sink (Playskool)
- Legos

STUDY QUESTIONS

1. What do you think was behind Joseph's intense fear of the finger monsters? How would you have handled the finger monster play?

2. Discuss the pros and cons of group and individual treatment for a child like Joseph. Would you have changed the modality of treatment from group to individual sessions? If so, at what point in treatment would you have done so?

3. Every day numerous children enter the foster care system and are separated from their parents. Foster care parents and workers are frequently insufficiently prepared to address the needs of the children entering the system. Can you think of any techniques, workshops, or programs to improve this situation?

4. At what age and how might the therapist engage Joseph in discussion about his biological parents? What are the implications of such a discussion for the adoptive parents?

REFERENCES

Ainsworth, M. D. S. (1979). Infant–mother attachment. *American Psychologist, 34*, 932–937.

Ainsworth, M. D. S., & Bell, S. M. (1971). Attachment, exploration, and separation: Illustrated by the behavior of one-year-olds in a strange situation. In S. Chess & A. Thomas (Eds.), *Annual progress in child psychiatry and child development* (pp. 41–60). New York: Brunner/Mazel.

Ainsworth, M., & Wittig, B. A. (1969). Attachment and exploratory behavior of one-year-olds in a strange situation. In B. M. Foss (Ed.), *Determinants of infant behavior* (pp. 111–136). London: Methuen.

American Psychiatric Association. (1987). *Diagnostic and statistical manual of mental disorders* (3rd ed., rev.). Washington, DC: Author.

Blanck, R., & Blanck, G. (1979). *Ego psychology II: Psychoanalytic developmental psychology.* New York: Columbia University Press.

Bowlby, J. (1969). *Attachment and loss: Vol. 1. Attachment.* New York: Basic Books.

Brenner, A. (1984). *Helping children cope with stress.* Lexington, MA: Lexington Books.

Brinich, P. M. (1980). Some potential effects on adoption and self and object representations. *Psychoanalytic Study of the Child, 35,* 107–133.

Bruner, J., & Sherwood, V. (1983). Thought, language, and interaction in infancy. In J. D. Call, E. Galenson, & R. Tyson (Eds.), *Frontiers of infant psychiatry* (pp. 38–52). New York: Basic Books.

Butler, I. C. (1989). Adopted children, adopted families: Recognizing differences. In L. Combrinck-Graham (Ed.), *Children in family contexts: Perspectives on treatment* (pp. 161–186). New York: Guilford Press.

Caldwell, B. M. (1971). The effects of psychosocial deprivation on human development in infancy. In S. Chess & A. Thomas (Eds.), *Annual progress in child psychiatry and child development* (pp. 3–22). New York: Brunner/Mazel.

DiGiulio, J. F. (1987). Assuming the adoptive parent role. *Social Casework, 68*, 561-566.

Emde, R. N. (1985). Assessment of infant disorders. In M. Rutter & L. Hersov (Eds.), *Child and adolescent psychiatry: Modern approaches* (pp. 325-335). Boston: Blackwell Scientific Publications.

Emde, R. N., & Sorce, J. F. (1983). The rewards of infancy: Emotional availability and maternal referencing. In J. D. Call, E. Galenson, & R. Tyson (Eds.), *Frontiers of infant psychiatry* (pp. 17-30). New York: Basic Books.

Farber, E. A., & Egeland, B. (1987). Invulnerability among abused and neglected children. In E. J. Anthony & B. J. Cohler (Eds.), *The invulnerable child* (pp. 253-288). New York: Guilford Press.

Freud, A. (1970). The concept of the rejecting mother. In E. J. Anthony & T. Benedek (Eds.), *Parenthood: Its psychology and psychopathology* (pp. 376-386). Boston: Little, Brown.

Garmezy, N. (1986). Developmental aspects of children's responses to the stress of separation and loss. In M. Rutter, C. E. Izard, & P. B. Read (Eds.), *Depression in young people: Developmental and clinical perspectives* (pp. 297-323). New York: Guilford Press.

Guttman, H. A. (1989). Children in families with emotionally disturbed parents. In L. Combrinck-Graham (Ed.), *Children in family contexts: Perspectives on treatment* (pp. 252-276). New York: Guilford Press.

Hess, P. (1982). Parent-child attachment concept: Crucial for permanency planning. *Social Casework, 63*, 46-53.

Itzkowitz, A. (1989). Children in placement: A place for family therapy. In L. Combrinck-Graham (Ed.). *Children in family contexts: Perspectives on treatment* (pp. 391-412). New York: Guilford Press.

Korner, A. F. (1971). Individual differences at birth: Implications for early experience and later development. *American Journal of Orthopsychiatry, 41*, 608-619.

Lewis, M. (1977). Language, cognitive development, and personality. *Journal of the Academy of Child Psychiatry, 16*, 646-661.

Mahler, M., Pine, F., & Bergman, A. (1975). *The psychological birth of the human infant: Symbiosis and individuation.* New York: Basic Books.

Mishne, J. (1979). Parental abandonment: A unique form of loss and narcissistic injury. *Clinical Social Work Journal, 7*, 15-33.

Osofsky, J. D., & Connors, K. (1979). Mother-infant interaction: An integrative view of a complex system. In J. D. Osofsky (Ed.). *Handbook of infant development* (pp. 519-548). Lexington, MA: Lexington Books.

Rooney, R. H. (1982). Permanency planning: Boon for all children? *Social Work, 27*, 152-158.

Rutter, M. (1972). *The qualities of mothering: Maternal deprivation reassessed.* New York: Jason Aronson.

Rutter, M. (1979). Maternal deprivation. 1972-1978: New findings, concepts, new approaches. *Child Development, 50*, 283-305.

Rutter, M. (1981). Stress, coping and development: Some issues and some questions. *Journal of Child Psychology and Psychiatry, 22*, 323-356.

Sander, L. W. (1976). Issues in early mother-child interaction. In E. N. Rexford, L. W. Sander, & T. Shapiro (Eds.), *Infant psychiatry: A new synthesis* (pp. 127-147). New Haven: Yale University Press.

Schroeder, C. S., Gordon, B. N., & Walker, B. (1983). Clinical problems of the preschool child. In C. E. Walker & M. C. Roberts (Eds.), *Handbook of clinical psychology* (pp. 296-334). New York: John Wiley & Sons.

Solnit, A. J., & Provence, S. (1979). Vulnerability and risk in early childhood. In J. D. Osofsky (Ed.), *Handbook of infant development* (pp. 799-808). New York: John Wiley & Sons.

Spitz, R. (1946). Anaclitic depression. *Psychoanalytic Study of the Child, 2*, 313-342.

Sroufe, L. A. (1979a). The coherence of individual development. Early care, attachment, and subsequent developmental issues. *American Psychologist, 34*, 834-841.

Sroufe, L. A. (1979b). Socioemotional development. In J. D. Osofsky (Ed.), *Handbook of infant development* (pp. 462-516). New York: John Wiley & Sons.

Sroufe, L. A., & Waters, E. (1977). Attachment as an organizational construct. *Child Development*, 48, 1184-1199.

Steinhauer, P. D. (1983). Issues of attachment and separation: Foster care and adoption. In P. D. Steinhauer & Q. Rae-Grant (Eds.), *Psychological problems of the child in the family* (pp. 69-101). New York: Basic Books.

Thomas, A., & Chess, S. (1977). *Temperament and development*. New York: Brunner/Mazel.

CHAPTER 8

The Crisis of Early Maternal Loss
Unresolved Grief of 6-Year-Old Chris in Foster Care

CORINNE MASUR

The ability to love has to be learned and practiced. If, in the course of learning to love, the primary love object is lost—to divorce, illness, depression, abandonment, or, most ultimately and irretrievably, to death—the implications for the child and for his ability to love are critical (A. Freud & Burlingham, 1944). The original alliance between mother and infant is perhaps the most significant of human relationships; it is the wellspring for all subsequent attachments and is the formative relationship in the course of which the child will develop a sense of himself (Klaus & Kennel, 1976); if this relationship is interrupted during the early stages, the effects may be devastating for the young child's future interpersonal relations and personality development. This chapter focuses on the phenomenon of loss of the mother, its effects on the young child, and the manner in which play therapy can ameliorate these effects.

It is believed essential for mental health that the infant experience a warm, intimate, and continuous relationship with his mother in which both find satisfaction and enjoyment (Bowlby, 1980). When the mother dies, the child is in a uniquely dangerous situation because of the special nature of his tie to her. Whereas an adult distributes his love among several meaningful relationships—his spouse, parents, children, friends, colleagues—the young child, by contrast, invests almost all of his feeling in his parents. Only in childhood can death deprive an individual of so much opportunity to love and be loved and face him with such a difficult task of adaptation (Furman, 1974). Therefore, the impact of a parent's death on the individual child and the manner in which he attempts to cope with it assume crucial importance in shaping the course of his future personality development (Bowlby, 1961, 1980; Deutsch, 1937; Fleming & Altschul, 1963).

Death in general, and the loss of a parent in particular, is an experience that crosses all boundaries of ethnicity, race, religion, social, national, and political allegiances. It is a reality that, despite increasing medical and technological sophistication, we cannot avoid. In fact, Volkart and Michael (1957) suggest that the loss of a parent by death or desertion in the contemporary nuclear family is possibly even more traumatic than it was for the child in the traditional extended family setting of the past. The child in the nuclear family does not possess the familial supports such as the live-in grandparents, aunts, uncles, and multiple siblings provided by the extended family. Therefore, as Gelcer (1983, p. 504) stated, "given the dwindling role of active cultural and religious mechanisms, psychotherapy seems to have become the primary mode of helping mourners."

Fulton (1976) stated that the wise management of grief in children as well as in adults revolves around two major factors: (1) the encouragement and facilitation of the normal mourning process, and (2) the prevention of delayed or disturbed grief responses. In the case of young children, facilitation of mourning includes helping the child to identify and correct distortions in the understanding of how and why the death occurred, especially as this relates to the child's beliefs about his or her own role in the death.

MOURNING

There has been considerable debate in the professional literature regarding the question of whether children can mourn. If one adheres to the strict definition of the term mourning as implying a complete detachment of "the survivor's memories and hopes" (S. Freud, 1913, p. 65) from the lost loved one in order to unconflictually be able to reattach to another loved one, then it follows that true mourning cannot occur until adolescence has been completed (Deutsch, 1937). However, since Sigmund Freud himself doubted that complete decathexis is a possible or desirable accomplishment of anyone of any age, it is therefore more useful to consider mourning to be the "painful, gradual process of detaching libido from an internal image" (A. Freud, 1965, p. 67). Thus, it appears possible that a *beginning* capacity to mourn exists after the establishment of object constancy when an internalized image of the mother has been formed.

With this understanding, children by 4 to 5 years of age can be considered capable of undertaking the mourning process if provided with an optimally supportive milieu in which they are encouraged to both experience and discuss their feelings (Furman, 1974).

In early childhood and infancy the child is unable to understand clearly the reasons connected to the death of a loved one. The way in which he experiences the loss and undertakes mourning is affected by his age and stage of development, his characterological makeup, his coping skills (defenses), his capacity for relationships, the quality of his existing relationships, and the nature of his relationship with the lost loved one, the circumstances of the death, as well as the plethora of stressors that accompany any such family crisis.

Moreover, there is a developmental progression to the capacity to mourn. The age and stage of development at which a child experiences a significant loss is particularly important, since this determines both the child's perception of the loss and the range of abilities that are present to help him to understand and cope with the loss. For example, in the case presented in this chapter, Chris's mother died when he was 18 months of age. A child of 18 months has different cognitive ability than a 6-month-old or a 7-year-old. He will understand death more as a disappearance than as a final loss. Moreover, since he is in the anal phase of development and the rapprochement subphase of the separation–individuation process (Mahler, Pine, & Bergman, 1975), the loss will be colored by the egocentricity of this age.

To illustrate this concept further using the psychodynamic and Mahlerian frameworks for development, let us consider what the loss of his mother might mean to an 18-month-old. According to Sigmund Freud, the concerns of a young toddler of this age are organized around the anal zone. During this stage, difficulties typically arise between the mother and the child as a result of the child's normal developmental conflicts and his push toward individuation. Although the child at this age continues to require the mother's investment and protection, he is endeavoring to separate himself from her and to assume some control over himself. Of particular concern around this time is the mother's desire to toilet train the child and the child's desire not to be toilet trained but rather to wet and soil when and where he pleases. The child is caught between the desire to do as his mother wishes in order to maintain her presence and her love and to do as he wants. The loss of the mother at this point in development creates particular difficulties for the child. Given his anger at his mother for her desire to control and limit him, and because of his natural egocentrism and feelings of being all-powerful, he may actually feel responsible for his mother's disappearance (i.e., death). Because he does not understand what death is at this age but rather views it as a leavetaking, he may feel that he caused it to happen. He may link this with his mother's encouragement of cleanliness and toileting and her displeasure with messing and toileting accidents and therefore feel that because he was "bad" or "dirty," his mother wanted to leave him. Or, having frequently felt angry and having had destructive wishes toward her, as all children do, he may feel that it was actually he who hurt his mother or made her ill.

Lopez and Kliman (1979) report on the analysis of Diane, a 4-year-old girl whose mother committed suicide when Diane was 19 months of age. They state that her analytic material demonstrated a "prominence of magical ideas that somehow she had been the cause of her mother's disappearance and grandiose wishful ideas that she could somehow cause her mother to return" (p. 264). A variety of other fantasies may arise out of the loss of the mother at this stage of development, such as ideas involving the powerfulness and omniscience of the parent and the possibility of her continued existence (in heaven or elsewhere).

Another aspect of the child's development at this stage involves his efforts at separation and individuation. According to Mahler et al. (1975), from approximately 15 to 25 months, the child is involved in the rapprochement subphase of the separation–individuation process. At this age, not only are issues of control and independence related to toileting, but they are also related to autonomy in general. With his increasing mobility, the toddler now has the option to leave his mother, and he experiments with this new possibility for independence during this period. At this time the child normally experiences separation anxiety connected to his conflicting and alternating wish to run from the mother and operate independently together with his concern that he not be without his mother when he wants her.

At this time the toddler usually has achieved what has been called object permanence by Jean Piaget (1937/1954); that is, he understands that even when he cannot see an object, it continues to exist. He also has the capacity for evocative recall so that he can bring to mind an image of his mother in her absence. However, according to Mahler et al. (1975) and Kernberg (1975), true object constancy has not yet been established. As a result, loss of the mother at this stage of development can interfere in the development of an integrated internalized image of the mother. The capacity to recall the mother's image in her absence is ephemeral at this age. Although the toddler may be able to do this for hours, days, or even weeks during her absence, over longer periods of time her image will fade, and he needs a real person to comfort him. His internalized representation of the mother will be split into all good and all bad representations, as is normal at this stage, but the orphaned child may have difficulty proceeding to an integrated image of the mother. There are serious implications, therefore, for the development of later psychopathology. Moreover, difficulties may arise later in development around separation and independent functioning.

The case of Chris, a 6-year-old boy, illustrates the effects of early maternal loss and the use of psychodynamically oriented play therapy that allowed Chris full expression of his thoughts and feelings. He was not directed toward any particular play material but was given full run of the office. Chris's play was the expressive medium of the therapy; talking occurred during the play as part of it, not as the main means of communication as occurs in adult treatment. Melanie Klein (1953) stated that in psychoanalytic treatment the child expresses fantasies, anxieties, and defenses through the play. The purpose of this technique is to allow the therapist to understand, clarify to the child, and interpret to him his own feelings, anxieties, and experiences as expressed in the play. This, in combination with the therapeutic effects of the relationship with the therapist and the benefits of the experience of the free play situation itself, comprises the technique utilized in Chris's treatment.

My office was simply furnished with a desk, two chairs, a large toy box, and a doll house. In the box were art supplies, Play-Doh, glue, tape, two play telephones, cars, trucks, Legos, checkers, Parcheesi, a large baby doll, puppets, a large panda bear and its baby, a Nerf ball and bat, a basketball hoop, two toy guns, a Nok-Out bench and hammer, toy soldiers, and farm animals. The large doll house, furnished with furniture and a doll family, was on the floor next to the toy chest. As Woltmann (1955, p. 775) states, "the specific selection of play material in the play room is less important than the child's ability to structure and endow the materials with conceptual and functional content." In fact, this case was selected for presentation because of the child's ability to express his concerns so vividly through the play. As will be seen, Chris actually used very few toys, but those that he used took on great meaning for him. Consequently, Chris was an excellent candidate for this form of expressive play therapy.

THE CASE: CHRIS, AGE 6

Chris was an adorable 6-year-old boy when he first presented for evaluation. He was small and therefore appeared at least 1 year younger than his stated age. For the initial evaluation Chris was immaculately groomed and dressed in the fashionable "preppie" style characteristic of his foster family.

Family Information

Chris was born into a family in which his mother was Catholic and his father Protestant. He had one brother, Billy, who was 4 years his senior and who accompanied him into foster care. By report of the foster care agency, Chris's mother was a habitual drug user and, as a result, did not care for him consistently throughout his infancy, frequently leaving him and Billy in the homes of friends and relatives. When Chris was 14 months old his mother discovered that she had leukemia, and when he was 18 months, she died. During these 4 months she may have spent some time in the hospital, although little reliable history is available for this period of Chris's life.

Chris's father is an alcoholic who lived with Chris, Billy, and their mother sporadically. When the children's mother died, he felt that he could not care for his sons until he "got his life together." As a result, Chris and Billy went to live with their maternal aunt, who was married but had no children of her own at that time. Chris called his aunt "Mommy" as he had called his mother and was reported to have been extremely upset when, at the age of 4½, he was told that because his aunt was about to have a baby she could no longer care for him and Billy. At that time Chris and Billy were placed with a foster family, upper-middle-class Catholics who had four children of their own, ages 18, 15, 12, and 9. The family felt that they wanted to share the love that existed in their family with a foster child and had asked the agency to place a little girl with them, preferably one under the age of 4. Instead, the foster care agency asked them to take Chris, almost 5 years old, and Billy, age 9.

Presenting Problem

When he was first brought for evaluation Chris was encopretic one or more times a day; he was also accident-prone and when hurt would lie on the ground crying without making any effort to get up or help himself in any way. He was unable to concentrate at school; he sucked his thumb frequently and sometimes spoke in a baby-like manner. At other times, however, his foster mother reported that both Chris and his brother cursed "like truck drivers" and had few manners.

It was unclear whether Chris's encopresis was primary or secondary; in other words, it was not known whether he had ever been completely trained. His aunt felt very ambivalent about having given up the boys and, perhaps as a result, was only occasionally available to provide history to the foster care agency or to visit with the boys. She reported that Chris had been toilet trained, although there had been some "accidents" over the years. These become far more frequent upon foster placement. It is likely that the encopresis represented a regression from a previously higher level of functioning.

First Interview

Content of Session

When Chris first met me he was immediately friendly and engaging. He separated from his foster mother with no apparent difficulty, leaving her to wait for him in the waiting room. He went with me to my office, walking backwards part of the way so that he could see me while he talked to me. He said, "You're a worry doctor, aren't you? Well, I have a record at home that makes me cry every time I hear it. That's a worry, isn't it?" Before we arrived at the office he asked if he could bring the record and his record player next time to show me what it was that was worrying him.

Therapist's Rationale

The information gained by observing the child's demeanor and approach to the therapist in the waiting room at the time of the first meeting proved to be very important. Chris immediately demonstrated his capacity to engage with a new adult. His ability to form rapport was excellent; however, the ease with which he separated from his foster mother was of concern to me.

Knowing his history, I questioned the effect of multiple separations on his capacity to form an intimate, trusting bond; I felt that this ease of separation might indicate a degree of neediness and object hunger that might allow people and relationships to be interchangeable. However, I was impressed by his apparently good understanding of the role I could play for him (the "worry doctor") and his immediate use of me in that capacity.

Content of Session

Once in the office, Chris chose a chair and sat quietly for several minutes. I invited him to look at the toys and told him that the purpose of our work together would be to help him to understand more about his worries. I told him that the way that we would do this would be to play and talk together. He immediately began to explore, using the remainder of the session to look at each of the toys in the toy chest, to play with each for a minute or two, and then to look at the next. At the end of this first session, I stated that I would see Chris next week at the same time and explained that we would meet two more times. After that I would talk to his foster parents, and we would decide about future meetings.

Therapist's Rationale

The first session with the child is particularly important in beginning to form a relationship and in setting the stage for future sessions. Since the treatment was to be expressive play therapy, it was important that Chris understand that he did not need to be quiet and polite as if he were at school. Although I usually do not direct the session, I invited him to look at the toys as an introduction to the tools that we would use together. My brief explanation was designed to demonstrate the purpose of our work as simply as possible.

Preliminary Assessment and Treatment Plan

Before seeing Chris for the first session I had met with his foster parents for one session in order to take a developmental history and to learn their concerns about Chris. I also spoke on the telephone with Chris's foster care worker in order to gain as much information as possible about Chris's early life, his family, and his placement with his aunt. I also wanted to form a working relationship with the worker because I viewed her as an ally in Chris's treatment.

Following three sessions with Chris (including the one previously discussed), I met again with the foster parents in order to apprise them of the results of the evaluation and to make my recommendations. I suggested to Chris's foster parents that the loss of his mother at 18 months of age had constituted a severe trauma for Chris, resulting in a developmental interference (Nagera, 1981). The subsequent rupture in his relationship with his aunt at the time of foster placement had been a second trauma of a similar type, that is, one involving the loss of a mothering figure, which caused a recrudescence of the feelings regarding the original loss of his mother.

At this time Chris experienced a partial regression to the time at which the original developmental interference had occurred, resulting in symptoms typical of that phase of development: encopresis, accident-prone behavior, inability to self-soothe, difficulty concentrating, and baby-talking. I explained that these symptoms represented both a return to the age at which the original trauma had occurred and a yearning on Chris's part to have his early unmet needs gratified in the present. In technical terms, at the time of the loss of his aunt, Chris regressed to the fixation point established earlier in the anal period by the loss of his mother. For Chris, a significant amount of libido remained arrested at the anal level, with less energy available for forward development as a result. His foster parents understood that some areas of Chris's development had proceeded appropriately, since he was among the brighter children in his class at school, but in other areas he regressed to functioning almost as a toddler.

Nonetheless, it was difficult for them to be sympathetic to the symptom of encopresis, as the management of this was most unpleasant to them. They wondered how psychotherapy would help and how soon they could expect results. I briefly explained the rationale behind play therapy and recommended twice-weekly sessions. However, because of Chris's foster mother's busy schedule, she was able to agree only to once-weekly visits.

Treatment

Chris's teatment continued for 1¾ years. The play therapy session presented here occurred approximately 4 months into the treatment. It illustrates the use of play as the symbolic representation of his concerns, the loss of his mother during the anal phase of development.

Content of Session	Therapist's Rationale
CHRIS: Panda! Panda! (*As he walks into the office.*) Where are you? Where is he? (*Looking in the toy box.*) Panda! There you are! Did you miss me?	I always allow the child to start the session. This permits whatever is on his mind to direct the session.

In this session Chris immediately goes to find the "Panda," the baby of a mother–baby set of stuffed panda bears. This toy had become very important to him and was one with which he had played for most of the previous six sessions. Chris's searching for Panda at the beginning of the session was not unlike the searching he must have done for his mother after her death. As seen later in the session and as I knew from previous sessions, Panda was often used to represent Chris's mother. The play of the session gave Chris the opportunity to find Panda, as he had not been able to do with his mother. In this way he repeated over and over again the loss of Panda/Mother and was able to effect a happier ending for himself. This is what is called "turning passive into active." Whereas Chris had been the passive victim of his mother's death, he needed to master this experience by turning himself into an active participant in the event. In the play he was able to do this by actively "losing" and then finding Panda. He was also able to bring up the important question of whether Panda missed him between sessions. In doing so he implicitly referred to how much he missed his mother (and his aunt and me between meetings) and his question about whether any of us missed him.

Content of Session	Therapist's Rationale
CHRIS: Now come on! Let's play! Where's the Play-Doh? (*Finding it in the play box.*) Panda wants me to make some food for him! He's hungry! It's been so long since I saw him. Here, Panda, you need to be strong. I'm making him spinach and iced tea. That's his favorite food. HERE! (*Feeding Panda some green Play-Doh.*) Here's your spinach. Here's some more (*putting it against Panda's face*) Oh no! Oh no! I got some on his face. Oh no! Let's get it off! (*Getting some tissues.*) It won't come off! Here, I'll be Panda, "You stupid! You Idiot! KA! KA!" (*He has Panda karate chop him and push him under my desk into the kneehole where my trash basket is.*) He's throwing me in the wastebasket!	Here Chris indicates his concerns over obtaining oral supplies and his own feeling of being hungry and needy. It is also possible that Chris is bringing up a very early memory of his mother's need to be fed and made strong from her weakened state. He may also be referring to one of the activities in which his mother engaged him—his own feeding. I do not interfere in the play by engaging with Chris about the reality issue of one of the toys becoming dirty. It is not of particular concern to me, my only rule being that the child not purposely break the toys or hurt me or himself during the session.

THERAPIST: Oh! Panda's so angry with Chris for messing his face that he's karate chopping him and throwing him away!

C: Wah! (*Pretending to cry.*)

T: Oh! You got thrown away!

C: You be Panda! Yell at me!

T: You got me all dirty! (*Holding Panda so he's looking at Chris under the desk.*) How could you do this to me? You!!! I'm throwing you away because you made me dirty. I'm putting you in the trash where dirty things go! You stay there!

C: Wah! (*Crying.*) Please Panda! I'm sorry! I won't do it again. Wah! Now, call me curse names!

T: You dirty so and so! You got spinach on me!

C: NO! Real curse names!

T: You think Panda's throwing you away because you made him dirty. You're afraid that Panda is so mad at you that he wants to curse you and put you in the trash.

C: (*From under my desk still.*) Say it again.

T: When you got spinach on Panda's face, it was a mistake. You were just trying to feed him and make him strong. But then you got scared that Panda would be mad at you for being messy. You were afraid that he would be so mad at you that he would curse you and punish you by throwing you away and never ever seeing you again.

Here Chris is vividly portraying his sense of having been discarded as a punishment for his messiness. In this case Panda plays the part of his mother and aunt.

Chris asks me to enter the play, and I do so to help him to play out this scene. At the same time I am trying to understand its meaning. The material regarding the Play Doh and the messing of Panda's face is new, and as such I have not had time to process it. On the other hand, knowing Chris's history, I have been waiting for material to emerge regarding both the understanding of his mother's departure and the meaning of the encopresis. As the material is new and I do not fully understand it, and as it is quite early in the treatment, I stay in the medium of the play and do not make any comments to Chris about the relevance of this material to his feelings about his mother.

In a later session, however, after this scene had been played out several times, I was able to make a connection between the play and Chris's belief that his mother left him for being dirty. After several weeks of further play and discussion of this theme, Chris's play took a notable turn toward more phallic–Oedipal themes.

Content of Session

CHRIS: OK! Let's say he helps me out of the trash now. You be Panda.

THERAPIST: Here, take my hand Chris. You can come out. I know it was a mistake that you got spinach on me. I know that boys make messes sometimes.

C: Oh Panda! (*Kissing him.*)

Therapist's Rationale

T: You know, it's almost time for us to end today.

C: Oh! Can I take Panda home?

T: You feel sad to leave Panda every week, but I think this week is especially hard because Panda was so angry with you. Maybe you want to take Panda along to make sure he still loves you.

C: Well, can I?

T: Well, you know what I always say about how the toys have to stay here so that they will be here next week for you to play with.

C: Oh please, just this once! Please??? Oh, OK. Well, let me put him to bed. (*He gets two tissues and makes a bed for Panda on a shelf over the toy box.*) OK. Bye Panda. Bye. . . . See you next time.

With younger children I often give a warning a few minutes before a session is to end. Here, unlike at the time of the initial interview, I can see a demonstration of Chris's separation concerns. Panda had come to mean many things by this time in the treatment: he was a transitional object linking Chris to me and to our work together; he was a representation of both Chris's original mother (needing to be made strong and healthy) and (sometimes) of Chris himself (the Panda was a baby panda and, as in this session, had to be fed and put to bed and cared for in other ways much as Chris wished to be cared for).

However, I did not allow Chris to take Panda home between sessions for reasons of both practicality and principle. For Chris, it was important to have the experience of leaving me and the toys and then to find us just where he left us the week before. This in itself provided a relationship of consistency and continuity unlike that which he had experienced with his mother or aunt. On the practical side, it was important for the toys to stay in the office both because other children played with the same toys and because, when taken home, toys have a tendency to get lost. By allowing Chris to put Panda "to bed" and by attempting to insure that Panda would be in the same position when Chris found him the next week, I both allowed Chris a leavetaking ritual and provided a situation around which to explore his concern about separation. Allowing him to take Panda home would have deprived both of us of the opportunity to learn more about these separation concerns.

Summary of Treatment

Following the session presented, Chris's treatment continued for approximately 1½ years. For the remainder of the first year of treatment Chris continued to play out themes of separation and loss. First, he brought in the record that he had referred to in his first session. It was a Cabbage Patch record, and the song he played for me was about two Cabbage Patch Kids who were lost in the forest and could not find their way back to the cabbage patch where they were born. Through this song Chris eloquently presented me with his own dilemma. Later, through his play with Panda, he portrayed his fear that his relationship with his mother (and perhaps with his aunt and his father) had come to grief because of his messiness. Following a great deal of play, discussion, clarification, and interpretation regarding his mother's death and his own role in this event, Chris's play took on a different quality. Starting at the beginning of the second year of treatment, Panda took on a more aggressive quality. Chris began to represent Panda as he liked to see himself. Panda was no longer apologetic but rather more phallic. He started to drive a jeep and to pal around with an older brother who drove a pick-up truck. He became interested in showing off and fighting. At the same time, Chris's concentration improved; he no longer demonstrated self-destructive or accident-prone behavior, and he was babyish less often.

Despite these improvements, however, Chris's foster parents became increasingly concerned regarding his encopresis. They left him at home with a sitter during family vacations and denied him certain privileges in hope of convincing him to stop soiling. Although I felt that this symptom would remit with further work, I was very concerned about the foster family's feelings. They were able to provide a stable, loving environment for Chris, and I thought it vitally important that his secure home not be disrupted. I was worried that if they continued to feel upset by the encopresis, they might consider terminating their relationship with Chris and his brother. In this way I had concerns for Chris's real security that would not necessarily have been present in the treatment of a child with similar symptomatology who lived with his biological family.

As a result, following much discussion with Chris, I enlisted the help of a behavior modification specialist. With close communication between this adjunct therapist and myself, he began to visit Chris at home during the second year of treatment. He set up a reinforcement schedule for Chris, and within a matter of weeks the encopresis diminished and ultimately ceased. Although I was not accustomed to making this sort of arrangement, in this situation consideration of the foster parents' concern was of the utmost importance.

In the summer before Chris began third grade, his foster mother requested that the treatment be terminated by the beginning of the school year. I had moved from a clinic setting into private practice, and the foster mother was finding it difficult to bring Chris to my office while continuing to take his brother to the clinic and to transport her other children to their many activities. Her request came also, I suspect, in response to Chris's almost complete symptom abatement. I had mixed feelings about terminating Chris's treatment at this time. On the one hand, he had made an excellent adjustment to this foster home and to school. He often called himself by the foster family's last name; he was reported to be "the life" of family gatherings; he had friends at school and was concentrating well. He had begun to talk openly about his "first Mom and Dad" and carried a small photo album with their pictures in it with him. On the other hand, his treatment had been relatively brief, and I felt that there was more work to do in regard to his confronting and understanding the multiple traumatic losses he had suffered. Although we had dealt to some degree with the death of his mother, we had only just begun to talk about and play out his feelings and concerns about his father. During our last session Chris brought his camera and took pictures of me and had his foster sister take pictures of him and me together. We talked about his getting in touch with me in the future should he feel the need, and I gave him my card, at his request, to take with him.

CONCLUDING COMMENTS

In summary, I see Chris's treatment as having been moderately successful. In regard to his adjustment to his new home and school, the treatment was of great help. However, the infrequency of the sessions and the relative brevity of the treatment hampered a more complete working through of Chris's many losses. Ideally, I would have liked to have seen Chris twice weekly, and I would have preferred that termination come about through a mutual agreement between him and me that our work together was done. However, overall, I believe that Chris's play therapy was of help to him in moving forward with his development and in clarifying the important issue of his misapprehension that he had caused his mother to abandon him. As stated, Chris moved nicely into appropriate latency-age play in the second year of treatment, and neither his play nor his concerns focused so predominantly on anal issues. The initial regression with which he had presented had cleared, and Chris appeared ready to proceed with his life.

PLAY THERAPY MATERIALS

- Doll house (Childcraft), doll house furniture (Childcraft), doll house family (Fisher-Price and Childcraft)
- Magic Markers (washable ink), colored pencils, pens, pencils, 8½ X 11" paper
- Play-Doh
- Elmer's glue, Scotch tape
- Two play telephones
- Three Micromachine cars, one plastic pick-up truck, one metal jeep
- Legos, checkers, Parcheesi
- One large baby doll, miscellaneous puppets, one large stuffed panda bear and baby
- Nerf ball and bat, Nerf basketball hoop and ball
- Two toy guns
- Nok-Out bench and hammer
- Plastic toy soldiers, plastic farm animals

STUDY QUESTIONS

1. Discuss the developmental considerations that might influence a 6-year-old's reaction to a parent's death. What is meant by the statement, "There is a developmental progression to the capacity to mourn"?

2. In this chapter the therapist stated that she did not begin the session but rather allowed the child to do so. What are the relative advantages and disadvantages of proceeding in this way?

3. If the child described in this chapter had had the opportunity to complete treatment, what else would you have optimally had him work on in the treatment?

4. How would you evaluate Chris's prognosis? At what future developmental stages would you anticipate difficulties? Why?

5. Discuss the implications of termination in a case where a child has experienced the death of a parent. What factors contribute to a "good" termination in such a case.

6. Discuss the use of a separate therapist to conduct behavior modification focused on symptom elimination. What would have been the pros and cons of the primary therapist assuming this role?

REFERENCES

Bowlby, J. (1961). Processes of mourning. *International Journal of Psycho-Analysis, 42*, 317-340.

Bowlby, J. (1980). *Loss, sadness and depression.* New York: Basic Books.

Deutsch, H. (1937). The absence of grief. *Psychoanalytic Quarterly, 6*, 12-22.

Fleming, J., & Altschul, S. (1963). Activation of mourning and growth by psychoanalysis. *International Journal of Psycho-Analysis, 44*, 419-431.

Freud, A. (1965). *Normality and pathology in childhood.* New York: International Universities Press.

Freud, A., & Burlingham, D. (1944). *Infants without families.* New York: International Universities Press.

Freud, S. (1913). Taboo and emotional ambivalence. In *Standard Edition* (Vol. 13, pp. 18-74). London: Hogarth Press.

Fulton, R. (Ed.). (1976). *Death and identity.* Bowie: Charles Press.

Furman, E. (1974). *A child's parent dies.* New Haven: Yale University Press.

Gelcer, E. (1983). Mourning is a family affair. *Family Process, 22*, 501-516.

Kernberg, O. (1975). *Borderline conditions and pathological narcissism.* New York: Jason Aronson.

Klaus, M., & Kennel, J. (1976). *Mother-infant bonding.* St. Louis: C. V. Mosby.

Klein, M. (1953). A contribution to the psychogenesis of manic depressive states. In *Love, guilt and reparation and other papers, 1921-1946.* London: Hogarth.

Lopez, T., & Kliman, G. (1979). Memory, reconstruction and mourning in the analysis of a four year old child. *Psychoanalytic Study of the Child, 34*, 235-271.

Mahler, M., Pine, F., & Bergman, A. (1975). *The psychological birth of the human infant.* New York: Basic Books.

Nagera, H. (1981). *The developmental approach to childhood psychopathology.* New York: Jason Aronson.

Piaget, J. (1954). *The construction of reality in the child* (English translation). New York: Basic Books. (Also published 1955 under the title *The child's construction of reality.* London: Routledge & Kegan Paul.) (Original work published 1937)

Volkart, E. H., & Michael, S. T. (1957). Bereavement and mental health. In A. H. Leighton, J. A. Clauser, & R. N. Wilson (Eds.), *Exploration in social psychiatry.* New York: Basic Books.

Woltmann, A. (1955). Concepts of play therapy techniques. *American Journal of Orthopsychiatry, 25*, 771-783.

CHAPTER 9

Short-Term Play Therapy with Two Preschool Brothers following Sudden Paternal Death

BARBARA SARAVAY

"Five percent of American children lose a parent through death before they reach the age of eighteen" (Wessel, 1983, p. 125). The death of a parent shakes the young child's core sense of security and arouses fears of being left alone and helpless in the world without a loving caretaker. The stress associated with parental death can seriously endanger personality development, according to Furman (1974), who argues that assisting the child with the mourning process can avert this negative outcome. Gardner (1983) maintains a similar position, as does Kliman (1968), who recommends preventive intervention for children younger than age 4 who experience sudden parental death.

The experts, however, do not all agree about the ability of children to mourn (Anthony, 1940/1973; Bowlby, 1980; A. Freud & Burlingham, 1943; S. Freud, 1917/1957; Furman, 1974; Kliman, 1968; Nagera, 1979; Palombo, 1981; Wolfenstein, 1966). The disagreement centers on whether children are capable of understanding the finality and irreversibility of death and of tolerating the pain associated with irrevocable loss. Wolfenstein (1966) and Nagera (1970) believe that true mourning, which results in decathecting the lost object, is not possible until adulthood. By contrast, John Bowlby (1980) believes that children's reactions of anxious protest, despair, and withdrawal when separated from their mothers are similar to extreme expressions of mourning in adults.

In agreement with Gardner (1983), Bowlby (1980), Kliman (1968), and Furman (1974), I believe that children who have attained object constancy have the capacity to grieve and mourn. Normally, object constancy occurs between 18 and 36 months of age, when the child begins to value the attachment object independent of its need-fulfilling functions. He or she feels denial and sadness when the attachment object is lost (Grossberg & Crandall, 1978).

Acknowledgments: I wish to acknowledge the contributions made to the theoretical section of this chapter by Nancy Boyd Webb, D.S.W., and the helpful comments and suggestions made by Carol P. Kaplan, Ph.D.

This chapter demonstrates short-term play therapy with two adopted pre-school boys following the sudden death of their father. Although their adoption was a factor in their mourning process and may be an issue for the boys in the future, the focus here is on the impact of the adoptive father's death and on the play therapy intended to help the children mourn their loss. Before the case is presented, the factors that influence the nature of the mourning process in children are summarized, followed by a discussion of the role of short-term therapy in facilitating children's mourning.

FACTORS INFLUENCING CHILD SURVIVORS

The manner in which a child copes with the trauma of a parent's death depends on a number of circumstances including:

1. The age, developmental stage, and cognitive level of the child.
2. The child's previous psychological adjustment.
3. The nature of the child's previous relationship with the deceased parent.
4. The response of the surviving parent.
5. The presence of available support in the extended family, school, and community.

This discussion emphasizes the impact of these factors on the *preschool* child.

Age and Cognitive Level of the Child

Lonetto (1980), quoting Nagy (1948), discusses the evolution of children's con-ceptions of death, beginning with the early childhood view that death is a spirit or a person, followed by the more abstract, mature understanding of death that is typical of the 8- or 9-year-old child.

Preschoolers typically believe that death is temporary and reversible. The dynamic pattern of a child's conceptions about death finds its origins in a magical perspective that emphasizes the interchangeability of life and death. Children from 3 through 5 years of age understand death as living on under changed circumstances (Lonetto, 1980, p. 34). The anger that often emerges several months after a death may be the child's reaction to the fact that the dead person has not returned.

The magical thinking and egocentricity of preschool children also impact on their notions of causality. Thus, the Oedipal child who feels a normal range of ambivalence toward both parents may conclude, after a parent's death, that his or her occasional hostile angry thoughts about the deceased parent caused the fatality (Raphael, 1983). Therapists working with children bereaved during the Oedipal stage should be especially alert for indications of guilt associated with the death of the same-sex parent and expressions of idealization connected to the death of the opposite-sex parent (Fenichel, 1953–1954).

The Child's Previous Psychological Adjustment

Obviously a child whose development has been progressing normally is in a stronger position to cope with the sudden loss of a parent than is a child who has exhibited developmental delays or problematic behaviors prior to the death. However, sudden paternal death may place a child at risk from a psychiatric standpoint even when the child did not have a problematic history, according to a study of 25 Israeli children aged 2 through 10 whose fathers died in the Yom Kippur War of 1973 (Elizur & Kaffman, 1982).

The Child's Relationship with the Deceased Parent

With specific reference to *father* loss, Grossberg and Crandall (1978, p. 124) analyze the components of the father's role as related to the development and growth of the young child. They refer to Burlingham's (1973) list of six aspects of paternal function, which obviously are lost when he dies:

1. The father is an early object of love, admiration, and identification.
2. The father gives bodily care to the child.
3. He is a powerful or omnipotent or god-like being.
4. He serves as a comforting protection.
5. He is a threatening castrator and inhibitor of autoerotic and Oedipal wishes.
6. He is an authoritarian figure to be overcome before adulthood and independence can be reached.

Thus, the father's death represents far more than the loss of a person.

The Response of the Surviving Parent

Grossberg and Crandall (1978) maintain that following paternal loss the mother's relationship to the child becomes critical in the child's future development; her reaction to the loss is the model for the young child. "The mother's attitude toward the absent father and her feelings toward men in general will be of paramount importance to the child who now does not have the daily opportunity to experience the 'real' relationship with a father to correct any distortions provided by the mother" (Grossberg & Crandall, 1978, p. 130). Furman (1974, p. 18) adds that the younger the child, the more crucial is the surviving parent's influence.

The Presence of Other Supports

Family, friends, and community representatives play a vital role in offering support, consolation, and comfort to the bereaved. It is unfortunate that children are sometimes deprived of this opportunity to receive support because of the well-meaning efforts of relatives, who want to protect children from the possibly upsetting experience of contact with grieving adults.

When children are not told of the death, they are deprived of the opportunity to share in the grieving process with other family members and to begin to understand that death is a part of life (Kübler-Ross, 1975). Involvement of the child with the grieving family, by contrast, helps the child to develop a trusting relationship with an adult whom he or she can approach with questions both in the present and in the future. This relationship frequently develops with someone other than the surviving parent, who may be too overwhelmed to help the child.

SHORT-TERM TREATMENT FOR CHILD SURVIVORS

According to Lieberman (1979), short-term play therapy is an appropriate treatment to insure optimal development and growth of children coping with specific problems. Short-term play therapy with the young child survivors of sudden parental death as presented here has two major goals:

1. To give the child information, answer his or her questions, and clarify misconceptions.
2. To facilitate the mourning process by encouraging expression of anger, sadness, anxiety, and guilt through both direct (verbal) and indirect (symbolic play) expression.

Clarifying Cognitive Confusion

The repetitive questions of the preschool child about the death indicate his or her need to know the details about how and why the death occurred. This verbal questioning builds a sense of mastery and reassurance that resembles the child's repetitive play in trying to dominate and work through the loss (Fox, 1985). Questions may continue for months and years as the child grows emotionally and intellectually. Even when young children have been exposed to death in their daily lives, they may not have understood the true meaning of the concept because they lack the capacity to comprehend abstract ideas. Because a young child thinks in concrete terms, he or she needs concrete explanations of what has happened in the child's own language, based on his or her cognitive ability to process the information. Specific information reduces confusion and misunderstanding and diminishes the child's tendency to replace reality with fantasy. It also reduces the need for future corrections of misperceptions.

Facilitating Mourning

The term "mourning" in this chapter refers to "the mental work following the loss of a love object through death" (Furman, 1974, p. 49). Essential to the mourning process are the understanding that the dead person will not return and the expression of accompanying feelings that result from this reality. Furman (1974, p. 24) states that "young children need help in tolerating their sad and angry feelings and in distinguishing the objective reality of the parent's death from their own fantasies." Sometimes guilt about the death complicates the bereavement. This can diminish or abate through repetitive play and/or verbal reenactment of memories associated with the dead person, which permit the cathartic expression of the pent-up feelings. Nagera (1970) points out that it may be difficult for the young child's ego to sustain the pain of prolonged and continuous mourning; indeed, Raphael (1983) refers to the "ebb and flow" of mourning in the young child, whose grief often appears to be intermittent.

The play therapist working with bereaved young children helps them articulate their feelings of sadness, anxiety, anger, guilt, and confusion about the death. The therapist may encourage this communication through the use of puppets, dolls, or art in addition to focusing on the child's real-life situation.

Counseling the surviving parent is also an important function of the child's play therapist. The parent may need help in understanding the difference between adult and children's mourning so that the parent does not misinterpret the child's seemingly fleeting moments of sadness. The play therapist also can prepare the parent for numerous questions from the child and encourage the parent to include the child in family discussions about the deceased, even when these are sad. The process of remembering the dead person will help both child and parent.

The task of grief work has been described as that of integrating the loss so that the individual can proceed with other relationships and developmental stages (Fox, 1985). Although the death of a parent will reverberate in the psyche throughout the lives of child survivors, the intent of short-term play therapy is to support and guide the young child toward an acceptance of this cruel loss so that development can proceed along normal pathways.

THE CASE: THE HARRIS FAMILY[1]

Family Information

Mrs. Harris, a 47-year-old widow, works part-time as an executive in the family business. Although a middle child, Mrs. Harris was the caretaker of both her older sister and younger brother. Her father died when she was an adolescent, resulting in her also assuming a caretaking role for her mother. Mrs. Harris currently maintains a friendly and supportive relationship with her siblings and their families and with her mother.

---

[1]This case was seen at The Northern Westchester Guidance Clinic in Mt. Kisco, New York, as part of the C.L.I.F. (Children Living with Illness in the Family) Program. C.L.I.F. provides preventive services for youngsters faced with chronic or terminal illness of a family member or death in the family.

Mrs. Harris was married 10 years ago to a widower with two children. Her relationship with her stepdaughter, now 26, was and continues to be close and supportive, as compared to her relationship with her stepson, age 30, which previously was good but has deteriorated since the death of Mr. Harris.

Unable to have children of their own after 7 years of marriage, the Harrises decided to adopt a child. At this time, both of Mr. Harris's children had married and left the house. When informed that two boys were available for adoption but that they could take only one if they chose, the Harrises agreed to adopt both.

Mr. Harris, 55, died suddenly and unexpectedly of a heart attack when the boys were 3 and 4 years old. He had no previous history of illness. He is described by his wife as an honest, loving, caring, and giving man. Mr. Harris appears to have been a primary caretaker, protector, and comforting presence to his children and to his wife. It was Mr. Harris who would comfort the boys, especially David, when they had trouble sleeping at night. Mr. Harris is survived by three older siblings who have no contact with either the children or Mrs. Harris.

David, 3, and Michael, 4, were adopted at 7 and 19 months of age, respectively. Little is known of their early development. The Harrises were told by the social worker that Michael was a very angry child. As reported by Mrs. Harris, the boys were very dependent on each other and have slept in the same room, by their choice, since coming to live with the Harrises. Reports from nursery school indicate that this year the boys are more independent of each other, have their own friends, and eat lunch at separate tables. It was Michael who woke his mother and then David after finding his father's dead body in the family room of their home one morning when he woke up early.

Presenting Problem

Mrs. Harris sought treatment for herself to help her cope with the sudden and unexpected death of her husband and to assist her children with their loss. With this as a goal of treatment, weekly sessions began approximately 2 weeks after Mr. Harris's death. Parkes and Weiss (1983, p. 225) state that "children at home are themselves at risk following bereavement, and support given to a bereaved parent may also benefit these children." Grossberg and Crandall (1978, p. 132) describe the treatment alternatives following father loss as follows:

1. Work only with the mother in an educative and supportive approach in which she is given specific suggestions and advice.
2. Educate the mother to be the therapist (treatment of the preschool child via the mother).
3. Psychotherapy for the mother alone, with indirect benefits to the child.
4. Direct treatment of the child and mother.

This case began with work with the mother alone. At the time of our initial meeting, the boys were reportedly asymptomatic as a result of Mrs. Harris's ability to continue parenting effectively while working through her own grief.

Mrs. Harris answered her sons' questions openly, honestly, and truthfully, and she was able to express and model feelings appropriately for her children. When the children saw their mother crying, she told them that she was feeling sad because Daddy died. At times the children would say to her, "You feel sad, Mom?" to which she would reply in the affirmative.

One month after therapy began, I requested that Mrs. Harris bring the boys to meet me. This enabled me to observe the interaction between mother and children. The boys appeared to be coping adequately with the death of their father. David was quiet, slow moving, and clinging to his mother while Michael, in contrast, appeared active, inquisitive, and independent.

Some months after this initial meeting with the boys, Mrs. Harris reported that the boys were having sleep disturbances and exhibiting excessive anger. Nightmares have been correlated with insecurity and frightening life changes (Bedell, 1975). Both boys, especially David, had sleep disturbances following their adoption; these had lasted for approximately 6 months after their arrival in the Harris home. Mr. Harris had taken an active role in dealing with the children when they awoke at night and would frequently spend the night in David's bed, comforting him.

Currently David was waking screaming several times during the night. Michael exhibited excessive anger toward his mother and brother as well as some night fears. Michael's anger reportedly bordered on rage and was characterized by the child's clenching his fists and physically shaking. His physical aggression toward his brother escalated since the father's death. Michael's anger toward his mother appeared most evident following his mother's response to his question, "Why Daddy dead?" and his mother's typical response, "He had no choice."

The case presentation that follows demonstrates six sessions of play therapy in an outpatient mental health clinic focused on helping David and Michael with their mourning process.

Mrs. Harris had been advised to tell the boys that she was taking them to meet someone who helps Mom talk about her feelings about Daddy.

First Play Therapy Session

Content of Session

Rationale/Analysis

(I greet Mrs. Harris and the boys in the waiting room. Michael is at a table coloring; David is playing with some toys. Mrs. Harris is seated on the other side of the room.)

THERAPIST: Hello, boys. Do you remember me? *(I sit down on a small chair across from Michael.)*

When working with children it is important to get down physically to their level.

MICHAEL *(not looking up)*: I was here when I was a little boy.

(David looks at me and runs across the room to his mother, throwing himself in her lap and putting his thumb in his mouth.)

T: That's right, Michael. You and David did come here once before. Do you remember my name? (*No response.*) That was a while ago. Now you are older and bigger. I wonder if you know why Mom brought you here? (*Again, no response. Michael continues to color and by this time has accumulated many pieces of paper. David continues to watch us and looks somewhat apprehensive.*) Mom tells me that sometimes David gets up crying in the middle of the night and wakes you up, Michael.

Mrs. Harris and I discussed what she would tell the boys about coming to see me prior to her bringing them to the clinic.

M (*speaking with somewhat of a stutter*): Him have bad dreams. Me too. [Mrs. Harris later told me that she had no idea Michael was having disturbing dreams also.]

T: Can you tell me about your bad dreams? (*At this point David slides off his mother's lap and begins to take a more active listening stance.*)

I chose to remain in the waiting room at this time; I hoped to help the children begin to feel comfortable enough with me so that they would come into my office while their mother remained in the waiting room. From my first experience with them I believed that they would have some difficulty separating from her. Perhaps they were still not sure who I was or why they were here.

M: No.

T: Well, you can draw your bad dreams for me.

M: OK. (*David comes closer as Michael begins to draw feverishly.*)

DAVID: I draw my bad dream too. (*Rushes over and takes paper and crayons and begins to draw.*)

T: Michael, tell me about this bad dream.

M: This man, him have a big stomach. Him not wearing a shirt. Him wearing shorts. [Mrs. Harris later told me that that was how Mr. Harris was dressed when they found his body.] (*At this point, David begins to interrupt Michael and tries to talk about his picture. Both are now competing for my attention.*) My daddy dead. Him have no choice. (*This Michael states quite matter-of-factly.*)

When children cannot talk they can sometimes draw. Information can then be obtained by talking about the drawing.

T: Yes, Michael. Your daddy is dead, and he didn't have a choice. He didn't want to die and leave you and your mother and your brother. (*Mrs. Harris is crying.*) It's sad that your daddy is dead. I wonder if that's why your mother is crying.

I felt it was important to identify and validate mother's feelings, both for her and for the boys.

M: You sad, Mom? (*Still standing at the table and looking toward her. Mother smiles and nods her head in the affirmative. David continues to remain standing at the table with Michael and me.*)

T: People sometimes cry when they are sad. I wonder if you ever feel sad, too? (*No response. Boys return to their drawing*). I wonder what you are going to do with all of these drawings.

M: Take them home. (*He begins to put all the drawings in a pile. David wanders back to Mother, leaning up against her, watching us.*)

Having identified two important themes, death and feelings of sadness, I felt we could move on at this time, as I continued to engage the children.

T: Let's put those pictures in an envelope. It will be easier to carry. Come inside with me, and I'll find an envelope for you. You can come too, David.

(*David holds back, but Mrs. Harris gently pushes him forward, encouraging him verbally in soft tones. Michael follows, half skipping, half running down the hall to my office. David follows with some trepidation. The three of us enter the office, and I give Michael a large envelope for his drawings.*)

T: You know this is a very special place. Children, big children and little children, come here to talk about worries or concerns they have. Sometimes we talk, and sometimes we play. You can say anything you want to here. (*David begins to look around the room at the puppets, chalkboard, and basket full of toys.*)

I give the boys an explanation of this place and what they can do here.

M: I give this to Mom. (*He runs off to the waiting room to give the envelope with the pictures to his mother. Moments later he returns. The boys spend the remainder of the session exploring the room. One of the dolls that particularly interests David is a very muscular male with a beard. Several minutes before the end of the session I announce it will soon be time for them to leave and that we will have to start cleaning up.*)

To allay any feelings of anxiety about separating from their mother, I had left the door to both my office and the waiting room open. I believed this would allow the boys to feel some sense of control and perhaps make it easier for them to return the following week.

T: Mom will bring you back next Thursday, and you can look around some more and play with any of the toys in here that you like. (*They do not respond, but run off down the hall back to the waiting room and their mother. She smiles when she sees them.*) I told the boys I will see them again next Thursday.

(*We all agree. Mother takes their jackets off the hooks and puts them on the floor. The boys dutifully put on their own jackets, David with some extra encouragement from Mom.*)

Preliminary Assessment and Treatment Plan

The boys appeared to be functioning on an age-appropriate level, although exhibiting some separation difficulties. It is not unusual for children who have lost a parent to display some separation anxieties. Reports from the boys' nursery school teacher revealed no marked change in behavior following the death of Mr. Harris. The boys appeared to be able to talk about their father and to have been given appropriate and accurate information concerning his death.

It was my opinion that the children had made a satisfactory adjustment to their new home and parents following their adoption. Discussion of the boys' adoption, begun by Mrs. Harris prior to her husband's death, had temporarily ceased.

The treatment plan was for short-term therapy to facilitate expression of feelings, either verbally or symbolically through play. The expectation was that the incidences of sleep disturbances would diminish as more appropriate ways to express feelings were encouraged. The boys would be seen together, as both had experienced a traumatic loss. I believed it would be comforting to them, and they would be less resistant to leaving their mother if they came together. Assessment would be ongoing, with a modification in the treatment plan in the future if necessary. Mrs. Harris would continue to be seen by the therapist in individual sessions to work on her own grief and mourning and to lend her support in helping her children cope with their father's death. In addition, parenting issues would be explored.

Second Play Therapy Session

Content of Session	Rationale/Analysis
(*I greet the family in the waiting room. The boys are engaged in play, with David in close physical proximity to Mother. Michael immediately holds up a coloring book he is writing in to show it to me. He proudly displays numbers and letters he has made. David hangs back, watching. After a while, during which time Michael engages me by showing me his ability to write numbers and letters, David comes toward us wanting to show us how he, too, can write. I suggest that we can continue to write in my office using either paper or the chalkboard. With some encouragement from Mrs. Harris, the boys run down the hall, Michael stopping in front of my office, appearing proud that he has remembered which one it is.*)	I was particularly interested in assessing separation issues.
THERAPIST: That's right, Michael. That's the right room. You have a big smile on your face. You must be feeling happy that you were able to find the room by yourself.	Identifying feeling and affect.

(*The boys run into the office, David going over to the puppets placed on a table; Michael follows. David takes the bearded, muscular male doll he had seen the previous week. Michael takes the mother and baby puppets and hands them to me.*)

MICHAEL (*to me*): You be the mommy and the baby. I be the daddy. (*David, using the male doll, begins to fight with Michael, who is holding the father puppet.*)

DAVID: I strong. I beat you up.

M: (*Using his puppet to fight back.*) Oh, no you don't. (*The two boys proceed to engage in battle.*)

T: That man seems really angry. (*No response from either boy; they continue to battle with their puppet and doll.*)

Identified and labeled feeling.

T (*as the mommy puppet*): I'll help you. I'll take care of you. (*The mommy puppet then puts herself between the two fighting puppets.*) I wonder if you both are worried about who will protect you now that Daddy is dead.

I believe the strong male doll represented the fears both boys were unable to express verbally concerning who would care for them now that their father was dead.

(*The two do not respond but continue in their play battle. Soon thereafter, the male doll, held by David, lies down. Michael, who seems to have had enough of the play, rushes off to the waiting room to touch base with his mother, leaving David and me alone.*)

In addition, both were expressing the anger that is a normal part of the grieving process. This seemed to make Michael anxious and he returned to his mother for reassurance.

T: That man was really angry, David.

D: Yeah. (*Picks up the doll again and begins to battle with the mother puppet, which I was still holding.*) I strong. (*Tries to overcome the mother puppet.*)

T (*talking through the mother puppet*): I'm strong, too. I'll take care of my children. I won't let you hurt them. (*This battle continues until Michael runs back into the room.*) Michael, I'm glad you're back. (*Michael picks up the daddy puppet, and we again engage in the play. This lasts for several minutes when Michael again ends the play. He then walks to the blackboard and picks up a piece of chalk.*)

M: I draw my nightmare.

T: OK. (*Michael begins to draw. David then goes to the chalkboard.*)

M: I draw my nightmare [see Figure 9.1].

FIGURE 9.1. Michael's nightmare: "Once upon a time there was a scary nightmare. This nightmare has legs. Him has a tail. Him has big teeth that make him bite. Him bite me. When him bite me, I dead. Booboo in his heart. Body in ground. I in heaven."

T: Michael, tell me about your picture.

M: This is a big monster with big scary teeth.

T: That does look scary.

M: Him have big eyes. Him look through the window.

T: It has big eyes and looks at you through the window. I have an idea. Why don't you leave these scary nightmares here? I'll take care of them for

There are many theories regarding nightmares and how to help children cope with them. I decided you and keep them here until next week when you come back.

to try to assess how invested the children were in their dreams.

M: No. I take it home.

D: Yeah. (*Smiling.*) No, no, I take it too.

T: OK. (*The children then run out of the office to the waiting room and their mother, where we say our good-byes.*)

Parent Counseling

Mrs. Harris and I, in individual session, discussed what she did when the children woke at night. She was discouraged from allowing the children to sleep in bed with her. Instead, Mrs. Harris was encouraged to keep the children in their room in their own beds, perhaps staying with them for a while to reassure them of her presence. I prepared her for the fact that it might take time before they stopped waking.

I believe that waking in the night was the boys' way to reassure themselves that their mother, too, had not suddenly left them in view of the fact that the boys found their father dead after they woke from sleep. Another possibility was that they still hoped that their father would return from the dead to comfort them at night.

The mother was given some general information about typical reactions of preschoolers to the death of a parent, including the typical narcissistic belief that somehow they had caused the death. I also discussed with Mrs. Harris the probability that the boys would be especially fearful that they might now lose her as well and that some of their clinging behavior could be understood in this context.

With reference to Michael's questions about why his daddy was dead, I encouraged Mrs. Harris to think about the feelings underneath this question. Eventually, Mrs. Harris was able to recognize Michael's anger and to respond reassuringly and with several different alternatives to her initial response ("He had no choice") such as: "Daddy's heart stopped beating; something went wrong with Daddy's body, and the doctor couldn't fix it."

I encouraged Mrs. Harris to identify and label the boys' feelings as she saw them in her interactions with her sons. Mrs. Harris was very open and responsive to these counseling efforts.

Mrs. Harris showed concern about how to proceed with discussions begun prior to Mr. Harris's death, about the boys' adoption. It was suggested that this, too, could be discussed openly and honestly, as the situation presented itself. For instance when David, one time, insisted that she had not come to him when he cried when he was a baby, she told him that must be a memory from before he lived with her (i.e., before he was adopted). Mrs. Harris responded positively to counseling suggestions, leading me to believe that she would handle this sensitive topic with care and intelligence.

Third Play Therapy Session

Content of Session

Rationale/Analysis

(I greet the family in the waiting room. Mother is reading to David, who is on her lap. Michael is coloring in a book. I sit down on a small chair opposite Michael.)

MICHAEL: Daddy no make French toast for breakfast any more.

THERAPIST: Your daddy used to make French toast for breakfast, but he can't do that any more. *(David looks over at us.)*

M: Him have no choice.

T: That's right. Your daddy is dead, and he didn't have a choice. His heart stopped. He can't make you French toast for breakfast any more, and that's sad. Who makes you breakfast now?

Identified feeling.

M: Mommy.

DAVID: Mommy.

T: Yes, Mommy makes you breakfast. What does she make for breakfast?

M: Cereal.

T: Mommy doesn't make French toast the way daddy did. Mommy makes cereal. *(Michael continues to write in his book, making numbers and letters, occasionally showing me a figure he has made.)*

Reassuring the children that even though Daddy is not there to care for them, their mother can, will, and does take care of them.

D *(to mother)*: Read more.

T: Let's go into my room, and we can read a story in there. *(Michael runs out of the waiting room and toward my office. Mrs. Harris gently coaxes David out of the waiting room.)* Come on David. Let's find Michael.

(At that David gets out of Mrs. Harris's lap, with her help, and runs down the hall toward my office. I close the door for the first time. The pictures of the dreams the children had drawn on the board the previous week are still there. The children begin to look around the room.)

At this point, I felt the children were comfortable enough with me and with the clinic to tolerate closing the door. I did leave the door to the waiting room open. We begin to do a kind of mutual storytelling (Gardner, 1975). I hoped to learn more about the brothers' understanding of death and specifically of their father's

T: Boys, instead of reading a story, let's make up our own. I'll start. *(David seems enthralled by this; Michael less interested. He begins to explore parts of the room he'd not investigated before.)* Once upon a time, there was a . . .

D: Boy.

T: And this boy lived with his . . .

D: Brother Michael.

T: And . . .

D: His brother John. (*Michael leaves the room.*)

T: Michael, David and I are going to make up a story. You can join us if you want to.

M: I go to Mom.

T: OK. You can come back when you want to. (*Returning to David and the story.*) And . . .

D: His sister Alice.

T: And . . .

D: His mother.

T: But the boy did not have . . .

D: A daddy.

T: The boy's daddy . . .

D: Dead.

T: And the boy and his brothers and sister were very

D: Sad.

T: And mother was very . . .

D: Angry.

T: So the children were sad and the mommy was angry because . . .

D: The daddy dead.

T: Sometimes children and mommies are sad, and sometimes they are angry, when the daddy dies. (*At this point Michael comes running back into the room bringing some toys from the waiting room with him.*) Michael, you missed the story. Maybe you'd like to do a story with us.

(*Michael does not respond but goes over to the puppets and takes the father puppet. David takes the male doll. He hands me the mother puppet, and we begin to engage in the play of the previous session: doll and father fighting, mother trying to intervene. As it gets close to the end of the session, I say . . .*)

T: Boys, we're going to have to stop in a few minutes. (*Michael puts down his puppets.*)

death. I decided to allow Michael to leave and continue to work with David. At this point I begin to consider working with each child alone because although their issues are the same, each needs his own time and has his own way of expressing himself.

David's anger at father for leaving displaced onto mother.

Children engage in this repetitive play to gain a feeling of control over what has happened in their lives. Their anger is acted out in their play, an acceptable way to discharge their feelings.

M: I make my nightmare.

T: It's still on the blackboard where you left it last week.

M: I make a new one.

(I give Michael a paper and crayons. He begins to draw. David comes over, gets up on my lap, and begins to draw. The boys start talking at the same time about their dreams.)

M: This is heaven. Daddy in heaven.

T: Daddy is dead. Daddy is in heaven.

D: Him in ground. Him dead.

T: So Daddy's body is in the ground, and Daddy's spirit is in heaven. When Daddy died he was buried in the ground, and you can't see him any more. And that makes you feel sad and maybe angry sometimes. This is hard to understand.

M: When I grow up, I die and go to heaven.

D: I go to heaven too.

T: You would like to see your daddy again. Children usually don't die. Old people usually die, not children. *(The boys do not respond but continue to draw. After a few minutes . . .)* Boys I know it's sometimes hard to leave, but our time for today is up. When you come next time, each of you will take a turn in here alone with me. You can decide which one will go first. Let's go and tell Mom. *(I walk behind the boys as they run down the hall to Mrs. Harris in the waiting room. As we enter the waiting room . . .)*

D *(to Mrs. Harris)*: Next time I go first.

(I explain what we have decided for the following session. Mrs. Harris smiles in acknowledgment and proceeds to help the boys get ready to leave.)

Sometimes it is possible to "save" children's drawings by attaching a note not to erase the blackboard.

The boys know their father was in the ground. Mrs. Harris had taken them to the cemetery to see the grave. The boys were confused as they tried to understand how their father could be in heaven and in the ground too. This *is* hard to understand! Attempted to correct misperceptions: allay worry and/or fear.

Fourth Play Therapy Session

Content of Session

(I greet the family in the waiting room.)

THERAPIST *(to the boys)*: Today each of you will have a turn to come into the office with me. Who is going first?

MICHAEL: I will.

Rationale/Analysis

(*He gets up from the chair he has been sitting on and, taking the book he has been coloring in, runs down the hall to the office. Once in the office, he begins to write numbers and letters in the book. This he does for a short time. He then walks over to the blackboard, now erased clean by a child in another session. Michael makes no comment about his picture of the previous session no longer being there but begins to draw on the board in big sweeping motions. As he works, he looks searchingly around the room. He indicates that he needs something to stand on so he can reach the top of the board. We find a small chair, which he stands up on. He continues to draw using the entire board.*)

T: Michael, you are working so hard. That is quite a picture you're making. Tell me about it.

MICHAEL: A scary nightmare.

T: Michael, can you show me what scary looks like? (*He attempts to make a scary face. I mirror his facial expression.*) Look in the mirror at that scary face. [I have a mirror behind my office door.]

Identifying feeling affect.

(*Michael shrugs his shoulders and smiles in a somewhat embarrassed way. At this point Michael indicates that he wants to go back to the waiting room to see his mother. He opens the door and runs down the hall to the waiting room. I follow.*)

T: Michael, is it David's turn now?

(*Michael nods his head in the affirmative and begins to look around the room for something to play with.*)

T: You did a fine job today, Michael. I'll see you again next week. (*to David*) David, it's your turn now.

(*He runs past me, down the hall, trying to find the office. He stops in front of the open door and looks back to me for confirmation.*)

T: That's it. You found the right one. (*David runs into the room, stops, and looks around a bit. He goes over to an alabaster tic-tac-toe game on a table.*)

DAVID: Let's play this.

T: OK. How do we play? (*He takes the game, sits down on the floor, and takes the circles off the board.*)

D: These mine.

T: I'll take these. (*I take the X's, and we begin.*
We take turns each putting a piece on the board.
When we are both out of pieces, I ask . . .) Who
won? (*David looks up at me with a big smile. . . .*
We were not really playing, merely moving the
pieces.)

D: You.

T: Oh good. I like to win. (*We repeat this sev-*   This repetitive play indicates
eral times, but with David winning every game   David's need to feel in control.
thereafter. Each time he wins he smiles.) You
like to win. I think it makes you happy to win
because you have a big smile on your face. When   Identifying feeling with affect.
people smile it usually means they're happy.
(*We continue this play until the end of the ses-*
sion.)

Reports from Mrs. Harris at this time indicated that the boys' nightmares
had ceased; the boys were still waking at night, but they were not screaming when
they woke. Michael's anger, although still in evidence, did not appear to be
excessive. Because this was planned as short-term intervention as well as a more
in-depth assessment, both Mrs. Harris and I agreed that sessions would cease at
this time. Work with Mrs. Harris would continue to help her cope with her own
issues, help her help her children, and monitor the boys' progress. She was
assured that the boys could return should the need arise. Two more sessions were
planned to terminate treatment: one session with each child individually and one
session with the boys and their mother together. I believed it would be helpful for
Mrs. Harris to hear me explain to the children why they would no longer be
coming to the clinic so that she could answer any questions the children might
have and correct any misperceptions. The boys were told of the format of the last
two sessions beforehand so that Mrs. Harris could reinforce the plan with the
boys on the drive to the session.

Fifth Play Therapy Session

Content of Session   *Rationale/Analysis*

After initial greetings in the waiting room, Michael and I went to my office. Michael was able to
separate from his mother effortlessly. I introduced
the topic of termination as he colored in a book
he'd brought in from the waiting room. I continued by reviewing why his mother had brought
him to the clinic and why children come to see
me. During this time, Michael said nothing. He

sat, coloring and listening. I told him that the next time he came to see me would be the last time but that if he ever wanted to come back, he could. I told Michael that the next time we would all come into the office together, Michael, David, Mom, and me. Michael engaged in drawing on the blackboard during this session. He drew happy and angry faces in response to questions I asked him. Michael did not always correctly identify the affect. At those times I would help him by modeling the facial expression. Much the same thing happened when David and I were alone in session. David had less difficulty leaving Mrs. Harris this session. David said little in response to my stating that we would not be seeing each other after the following session. In his play, he again displayed his need to win, to be in control. We repeated the play of the previous session using the tic-tac-toe game. I, again, was allowed to win the first game. David won all subsequent games. Before ending the session, I told David we would all meet together for our last session: Michael, David, Mrs. Harris, and myself.

Since children this age have an inability to comprehend time, I did not believe it necessary to prolong the termination process. Having everyone in the room at the same time would insure that everyone would hear the same thing. It would also be helpful for Mrs. Harris to hear what I told the children about ending sessions so that she could repeat what I said, should it be necessary.

Sixth Play Therapy Session

Content of Session   *Rationale/Analysis*

(*I greet the family in the waiting room.*)

THERAPIST: Hi, boys. (*David is pulling books off the shelf, looking for one for Mrs. Harris to read to him. Michael is looking around for something to do.*)

DAVID: (*Pulling a book off the shelf.*) Mom, read this.

T: David, I think we talked about all of us going into my office today at the same time. Remember, today is our last time together.

D: No, no, no, no, no. (*Ignoring me and walking toward Mrs. Harris with his hand outstretched holding a book.*) Read.

MRS. HARRIS: (*Smiling.*) Not now, David. I'll read to you later. Remember on the way over here in the car we talked about all of us going into Mrs. Saravay's office together?

D: No, no, no, no, no. Read.

MRS. H: Later, David, I promise. Now we're
going into the office.

T: It looks like you'd really like Mom to read to   Reflecting his feelings.
you. I'm sure she will, later. But now we're going
into my office.

(*With that and Mrs. Harris rising to leave the
waiting room, David joins the rest of us as we
begin to go down the hallway. When we enter the
office, David goes to the tic-tac-toe game and sits
down on the floor with it. Michael begins to rum-
mage through the toy basket and pulls out a puzzle. When David sees Michael with the puzzle, he
wants to play with it too.*)

T: David, I have another puzzle you can play with.   I could have let the boys work out
(*They begin to play with the puzzles.*) You know,   the problem. I chose to intervene
boys, that today is the last time you are going to   so as to get on with the session.
come here.

D: (*With a smile.*) No.

MRS. H: David. Yes you do. We talked about it on
the way over here. (*to me*) The boys want to
know where you are going.

T: (*Smiling.*) I'm not going anywhere. I'll be right
here.

D: You sleep here?

T: No. I have a house with a bedroom with a bed,
where I sleep.

D: You have children?

T: Yes. I have big children. I live in a house; I
sleep there; I have children; and I work here. I'm
not going away. You will not be coming here any
more, though, because you don't need to come
here any more. Do you remember why Mom   Review for children reason for
brought you here to see me? You were having   coming and progress made to
very bad dreams and waking each other up at   date.
night crying.

D: Me still have bad dreams.

MRS. H: You don't wake up at night any more.

T: You may still have bad dreams sometimes. All   I tried to normalize having bad
children sometimes do have bad dreams. And Mi-   dreams. Mother's reports indicated
chael used to get very, very, very angry. It's OK to   that the children were no longer
get angry sometimes. We all get angry sometimes.   waking in the night screaming
                                                            and were waking only occasionally
D: Mom gets angry.   at this point. Again, trying to nor-
                                                            malize feeling.
MRS. H: (*Smiling.*) Yes, I get very angry some-
times. Do you like it when I get very angry? (*No

answer.) I don't think you do because you tell me, "No get angry, Mom."

D: (*Walking over to his mother and putting his face close to hers.*) You bad. You ugly.

Mrs. H: David! What a thing to say. I'm not ugly. Do you remember what Daddy used to say?

MICHAEL: (*Who has been sitting on his knees during this time, playing with the puzzle but listening intently.*) Mom pretty.

Mrs. H: Yes. Daddy used to say I'm pretty.

T: You know, I wonder if David thinks that Daddy went away because he and Michael were bad; because Daddy didn't love them any more.

Mrs. H: Oh, no! Daddy loved us. Daddy wouldn't leave us. He had no choice.

D: Daddy not dead. Him sleeping.

Mrs. H: Oh, no David. Daddy *is* dead! Remember when we passed the cemetery this morning? You told me that Daddy was at the cemetery.

D: (*With a smile.*) Daddy sleeping.

Mrs. H: (*Looking sad and distressed.*) Michael. Tell your brother. Tell him how you found Daddy dead in the room.

D: No, no, no, no, no.

Mrs. H: (*More persistently.*) Michael. Do you remember? You found Daddy and then you came to get me. (*Michael sits on the floor looking at Mrs. Harris and David, saying nothing.*)

D: (*In angry voice.*) And you woke me up. And I was very, very tired and you woke me up. (*Very animated and shaking his hand at his mother.*)

T: David, it sounds like you're very angry because they woke you up. And when they woke you up you went with them and saw your daddy dead. He looked like he was sleeping.

D (*to me*): You have a daddy?

T: My daddy is dead. He died of a heart attack. His heart stopped working just like your daddy's.

D (*to his mother*): What your daddy's name?

> Anger at father for leaving being displaced onto mother.

> Denial of the reality of the death.

MRS. H: My daddy's name was David. You were named after my daddy, and Michael was named after Daddy's daddy.

D: Daddy sleeping.

MRS. H: No, David. Daddy is dead. Don't you remember we touched his hand? How did it feel? (*to Michael*) Do you remember? (*No response.*) It was cold. Daddy was dead.

D: I wake him up. I scream very loud.

T: You would like to be able to wake your daddy. You would like to be able to scream so loud that you could wake him up. And sometimes in the night you did scream very loud, but he didn't wake up.

The belief in the reversibility of death.

D: I scream so loud like this . . . (*Goes over to Michael still kneeling on the floor and yells in his ear. Michael does little to resist.*)

T: But you can't wake Daddy because Daddy can't wake up because he is *not* sleeping.

D: My dream wake him.

T: Your dream will wake him?

D: Him have magic in him's fingers.

T: David. You *wish* Daddy were alive and something could wake him up.

Magical thinking.

MRS. H: But I told you, David. Daddy is dead. He didn't want to leave us but he had no choice.

T: Yes. You did tell that to the boys, but sometimes we have to repeat things for children over and over again. They have to hear it again and again before it becomes real to them. They need to know that each time you will say the same thing. David, Michael, it's sad that your daddy died. Sometimes it makes you angry, and sometimes it makes you sad. You and your mom can talk about feeling sad or feeling angry. I'll be seeing Mom, and she'll tell me how you're doing.

D: You come?

MRS. H: Yes. I talk to Mrs. Saravay. She helps me with my problems and my worries.

T: If you'd like to come back again sometime, you can tell Mom, and she'll tell me. But for now, we will say good-bye.

*(I shake hands with each boy. Mrs. Harris gets up
and we all go down the hall to the waiting room.
The boys get on their jackets. We all say good-bye.
They leave.)*

CONCLUDING COMMENTS

With short-term therapy David's nightmares disappeared, and his waking at night decreased from nightly to approximately once or twice every 2 weeks. Mrs. Harris reported that the pictures the boys had drawn of their nightmares were kept in the envelope in their room. Michael continued to display anger, but it was reduced in intensity.

I had, during therapy, spoken with the boys' nursery school teacher. She reported that the boys played well with their peers, functioned in an age-appropriate manner, and were beginning to separate from each other and be less dependent on each other. She had noticed no marked difference in their behaviors, manner, or play after the death of their father. Sadness in children is often of short duration, and they are easily distracted.

Many of the issues that emerge when someone close dies were evident in the play therapy session with these preschoolers: feelings of anger and guilt; magical thinking; the reversibility of death. Work to correct misperceptions was begun. Honest and consistent responses to questions, reflection and identification of feelings, and permission to feel laid a firm foundation for these children that enabled them to proceed with the developmental tasks of childhood. The possible arrest of their development as a result of the trauma they had sustained was mitigated.

Mrs. Harris proved to be the key factor in the success of the treatment. Her intuition, empathy, caring, her ability to share her feelings and talk openly and honestly with her sons, her willingness to ask for help and follow suggestions were invaluable. An interesting aspect of this case was that two siblings close in age shared this experience. Each served as a catalyst and a sounding board for the other, with each reflecting the other's experience.

If the children need to return for treatment at some future time, I believe their experience of short-term treatment will be viewed by them in a positive way, making return possible. Mrs. Harris, too, will feel confident that treatment can be beneficial, based on her experience.

PLAY THERAPY MATERIALS

- Puppets of family members: mother, father, sister, brother, baby (Child-craft Education Corporation, 10 Kilmer Road, Edison, NJ 08817)
- Crayons (Crayola), small size
- White paper
- Chalkboard
- Colored chalk

STUDY QUESTIONS

1. What was the impact on treatment of the fact that this traumatic event was shared by two siblings? How might the work have gone differently had the event been experienced by one, as opposed to two, children?

2. What are some of the special challenges for the therapist in treating siblings simultaneously?

3. What would have been the advantages and disadvantages to continued treatment for the boys? What do you think about their prognosis?

4. When, how, and by whom should the adoption issue be addressed?

5. Discuss the pros and cons of leaving children's artwork displayed in the playroom between sessions, either on the blackboard or on a bulletin board.

REFERENCES

Anthony, S. (1973). *The discovery of death in childhood and after.* London: Penguin. (Revision of *The child's discovery of death.* New York: Harcourt Brace Jovanovich, 1940.)

Bedell, J. W. (1975). The maternal orphan: Paternal perceptions of mother loss. In B. Schoenberg, I. Gerber, A. Wiener, A. H. Kutscher, & D. Peretz (Eds.), *Bereavement: Its psychosocial aspects* (pp. 191–207). New York: Columbia University Press.

Bowlby, J. (1980). *Attachment and loss: Vol. III. Loss: Sadness and depression.* New York: Basic Books.

Burlingham, D. (1973). The preoedipal infant father relationship. *Psychoanalytic Study of the Child, 28,* 23–47.

Elizur, E., & Kaffman, M. (1982). Children's bereavement reactions following death of the father: II. *Journal of the American Academy of Child Psychiatry, 21*(5), 474–480.

Fenichel, O. (1953–1954). Specific forms of the Oedipal complex. In *Collected Papers I* (first series, pp. 204–220). New York: W. W. Norton.

Fox, S. (1985). *Good grief: Helping groups of children when a friend dies.* Boston: New England Association for the Education of Young Children.

Freud, A., & Burlingham, D. T. (1943). *War and children.* New York: International Universities Press.

Freud, S. (1957). Mourning and melancholia. In *Standard Edition* (Vol. XIV, pp. 243–260). London: Hogarth Press. (Original work published 1917)

Furman, E. (1974). *A child's parent dies.* New Haven: Yale University Press.

Gardner, R. (1975). Mutual storytelling technique. In *Psychotherapeutic approaches to the resistant child.* New York: Jason Aronson.

Gardner, R. (1983). Children's reactions to parental death. In J. E. Schowalter, P. R. Patterson, M. Tallmer, A. H. Kutscher, S. V. Gullo, & D. Peretz (Eds.), *The child and death* (pp. 104–124). New York: Columbia University Press.

Grossberg, S. H., & Crandall, L. (1978). Father loss and father absence in pre-school children. *Clinical Social Work Journal, 6*(2), 123–134.

Kliman, G. (1968). *Psychological emergencies of childhood.* New York: Grune & Stratton.

Kübler-Ross, E. (1975). *On death and dying.* New York: Macmillan.

Lieberman, F. (1979). *Social work with children.* New York: Human Sciences Press.

Lonetto, R. (1980). *Children's conceptions of death.* New York: Springer.

Nagera, H. (1970). Children's reactions to the death of important objects: A developmental approach. *Psychoanalytic Study of the Child, 25,* 360–400.

Nagy, M. (1948). The child's theories concerning death. *Journal of Genetic Psychology, 73,* 3–27.

Palombo, J. (1981). Parent loss and childhood bereavement: Some theoretical considerations. *Clinical Social Work Journal, 9*(1), 3-33.

Parkes, C. M., & Weiss, R. S. (1983). *Recovery from bereavement.* New York: Basic Books.

Raphael, B. (1983). *The anatomy of bereavement.* New York: Basic Books.

Wessel, M. A. (1983). Children, when parents die. In J. E. Schowalter, P. R. Patterson, M. Tallmer, A. H. Kutscher, S. V. Gullo, & D. Peretz (Eds.), *The child and death* (pp. 125-133). New York: Columbia University Press.

Wolfenstein, L. H. (1966). How is mourning possible? *Psychoanalytic Study of the Child, 21*, 93-126.

CHAPTER 10

The Effects of Divorce Precipitate a Suicide Threat
Case of Philip, Age 8

JANE E. PRICE

The impact of divorce on children is as variable as the circumstances before, during, and after the dissolution of the marriage. Even in the best of circumstances, divorce causes stress to all family members. The response of individual children will depend on their general level of adjustment plus the specific factors surrounding the breakdown of the marriage. The rupture of family structure and relationships accompanying divorce usually precipitates major changes in a child's life, frequently involving reduced contact with one parent, possibly a change of residence, and sometimes a change of school. Although the adults may view divorce as a necessary and positive solution to an unsatisfying and untenable relationship, young children experience this changed status as a crisis that seriously threatens their stability and well-being.

The case discussed in this chapter is that of Philip, an 8-year-old black male whose parents have been separated for 4 years and divorced for 2 years, resulting in a 6-year absence of reliable and consistent parenting by two biological parents. He currently resides with his maternal grandmother and mother in a one-bedroom inner-city apartment. Philip was referred to the psychiatric emergency room by his school for an evaluation by the child and adolescent crisis intervention team of a large municipal hospital. The school reported that Philip had expressed his wish to kill himself and that he actually had begun to carry out the threat by opening a window, preparing to jump.

The child and adolescent crisis intervention team, of which the therapist is a member, is composed of two child psychiatrists and four social workers. Cases are referred to our team from a variety of sources such as schools, families, courts, police, other hospital emergency rooms, and ambulance staff. Initial referrals occur either as "walk-ins" or by telephone.

When a child is referred by telephone, the team determines if the case is an emergency requiring immediate evaluation or if an appointment can be scheduled within the next several days. If the child is actively suicidal, homicidal, or psychotic, we arrange an evaluation as soon as possible, since the child is at risk of harming him- or herself or others and may need psychiatric hospitalization. Usually we do not have the luxury of *scheduling* appointments, since the majority of children and adolescents are brought directly into the psychiatric emergency room without any prior notification to the team.

As part of the evaluation process we interview all family members who accompany the child to the emergency room. We interview the child both with his or her family members and alone, since this allows us the opportunity to observe the child's behavior in both constellations. In addition to family members, we interview any other adults who bring the child to the emergency room such as school personnel, group home staff, and foster parents.

The actual face-to-face interview is supplemented with additional information from any relevant source, since it is important to ascertain how the child functions in his or her varying environments and if there have been any noticeable variations in behavior, mood, interactions with others and the timing of that change.

An important factor that we are assessing throughout the entire initial interview with the child and his or her family and support systems is whether the child needs hospitalization or whether outpatient crisis intervention will be sufficient. If the determination is for crisis intervention as the mode of treatment, we avoid a major disruption to the child's life, since this does not separate the child from his or her familiar family and school environment.

Coming to this determination involves a careful assessment of the child's psychological disturbance and his or her potential for harm to self or others. Even when a child is experiencing a significant amount of psychological stress and may actually be psychotic or suicidal, if the family support system is strong and willing to engage in crisis intervention treatment, we will allow the child to remain at home. This assumes that the family is reasonably capable of following through with therapeutic recommendations.

Separating a child from the family is an undesirable option since the separation frequently is traumatizing. An example of a situation in which the separation from the family is therapeutically indicated is the overly enmeshed family where boundaries are so poorly distinguished that a "parentectomy" would facilitate treatment. Another instance is a family that lacks an adequate support system (e.g., the family that is burdened by a myriad of problems and is therefore unable or unwilling to provide the commitment to their child essential during this crisis period).

CRISIS INTERVENTION

Treatment actually begins during the intake process. Once a determination has been made that crisis intervention is the treatment of choice, the length of the initial contact varies from 1 to approximately 4 to 5 hours. As Golan states (1978, p. 81), "Crisis intervention does not lend itself to neat marking off into the study, diagnosis, treatment planning, treatment, and termination/evaluation steps of the casework process. Instead we speak simply of beginning, middle, and ending phases. They may all take place within a single three hour interview or may be spaced out over several months."

The intent of the crisis intervention is to restore the child to his or her precrisis level of functioning, yet we often find that during crisis periods individuals and their families accomplish more than this circumscribed intent. The high level of discomfort during a crisis not only motivates resolution of the presenting problem but also permits exploration of underlying factors contributing to the crisis. Treatment may last from two to eight sessions. These are briefer than the initial interview yet usually longer in duration than the traditional 45-minute psychotherapy session. The initial contact/interview on our team is conducted by the social worker, who consults with the child psychiatrist and/or other team members while the interview is in progress and during daily clinical rounds. The team and/or psychiatrist may also offer diagnositc impressions and may become direct participants in the ongoing interview once it resumes. Crisis intervention in the hospital emergency room is interdisciplinary and collaborative in nature.

Appointments for a follow-up session are scheduled at the conclusion of the initial interview. Occasionally a parent may object either to the particular appointment time or to the frequency of the appointments. This is often an indicator of resistance on the family's part and denial of the seriousness of the crisis. The appointments are made within close proximity to the preceding appointment. The philosophy of crisis intervention dictates a brief amount of time with an intensive effort to resolve the crisis and return the child and his or her family to their prior level of functioning.

Having briefly described crisis intervention approach and its application within a psychiatric setting, we now return to the case of Philip. This case highlights two important issues: the effects of divorce on latency-age children and the management of suicidal behavior in latency-age children.

Philip was 2 years old and in the Oedipal stage of development when his father left the family. During this phase of development the child senses that the mother's attention and her warm soothing touch are not exclusively devoted to him or her. Mother must be shared with Father, and therefore the child is jealous and resentful. He or she would like to be rid of Father. What wish fulfillment young Philip experienced when his father actually left the family at this point in his life, leaving him much to ponder in later years! Did he, himself, cause his father to leave the family? Although Philip was not cognitively aware of the divorce or its significance to his sense of family identity as he would later know it, the foundation for conflict began at this time.

Contradictory feelings of love and anger need to be reconciled during the Oedipal period of development. In Philip's case, it is probable that reconciliation was not achieved because of his father's departure. Thus, feelings of hostility toward his father were not adequately resolved during the Oedipal stage, further complicating his sense of identity as a male.

EFFECTS OF DIVORCE ON LATENCY-AGE CHILDREN

It is common for latency-age children to blame themselves for their parents' divorce (Wallerstein & Kelly, 1980; Wallerstein & Blakeslee, 1989). However, in

Philip's case this seed of blame had been implanted at an early stage of his life, intertwined with a young child's normal narcissistic wish to possess his or her mother all for him- or herself.

This was complicated further by Philip's later wish in latency for his parents' reconciliation. Instead, Philip's mother was dating other men and expecting him to accompany her on these excursions. What a psychological dilemma for a young child, as evidenced by Philip's suicidal ideation and gesture!

Weiss (1979) refers to the negative effects on young children of divorced parents, who learn to suppress their need for their parents' nurturance while becoming prematurely aware of adult concerns. Emery (1988) emphasizes the dynamic of loss and perceived loyalty conflicts when the child lives in a single-parent family. The precipitants to Philip's gesture and expressed ideation appear connected with actual events in his family life that had occurred prior to the incident. These details are discussed later in the chapter.

SUICIDAL THREATS

A suicide threat is always a matter of grave concern, and when it occurs in a latency-age child it merits very careful study. Pfeffer (1986) indicates that although suicide rates for latency-age children have gradually increased over time, the number of suicides in this age group remains low. An explanation for the lower rate of completed suicide among young children includes Schaffer's (1974) view that the association between affective illness and suicide is less prevalent in children than in adults. Another possible theory is that children are basically less isolated than adults and therefore receive greater emotional support, thus reducing their chances of completed suicides. A third hypothesis is that children are not psychologically mature enough to experience hopelessness and despair, since these feeling states develop with abstract thinking in adolescence.

Although suicide in children under the age of 12 is infrequent, suicidal ideas, threats, and attempts nonetheless deserve attention. Children who have attempted or completed suicide do so often in response to what Pfeffer (1986) labels a "disciplinary crisis." A child's suicide threat is often perceived as a desperate attempt to change a frightening situation. This is confirmed and dramatized in Philip's suicide threat and gesture.

A careful assessment of suicidal risk must follow a child's expressed ideation or gesture. The evaluation/interview should consider the degree of risk while exploring with the family the external events that preceded the ideation or gesture. The *meaning* behind the child's gesture must be explored. Often suicide has been referred to as a "cry for help." We must ask, to whom is this cry addressed, and how can we help them listen?

Both verbal and nonverbal modes of interviewing may be employed with the child, yet the verbal interview should be the preferred mode because encouraging verbal expression provides the child with an alternative method to communicate his or her problems other than acting on the impulse, and this may reduce the risk of suicide.

Basic questions need to be explored with suicidal children to assess the degree of intent as evidenced in their suicidal thoughts and behavior. These include the existence of a plan and their access to the means for carrying it out.

It is essential to obtain a promise in the form of a contract with the child not to cause any harm to him- or herself for a specific period of time. It is equally important to secure the family's support in creating a safe environment for their child. We ask that they secure all potentially lethal objects and medications. If there appears to be resistance in either agreeing to the contract or in creating a safe home environment, then it might become necessary to consider the need for hospitalization of the child.

In summary, Philip's case illustrates issues involving a child's unresolved conflicts as a backdrop to his present suicidal ideation and gesture.

THE CASE: PHILIP, AGE 8

Family Information

Philip is a black, 8-year-old male who resides at home with his 32-year-old mother, Jennifer, his 55-year-old maternal grandmother, Vanessa, and his 4-year-old half sister, Tanisha. Both adults are unemployed, and the family receives public assistance. The maternal grandmother is a recipient of Social Security disability, as she has a history of psychosis, which is currently in remission.

Neither Tanisha's nor Philip's fathers provide any financial support for their childrens' care. Tanisha's father never lived with the family and was never married to Jennifer. Philip's father divorced his wife 4 years ago following a 2-year separation. Thus, Philip's father lived with the family until his son was 2 years old. He has not maintained any contact with Philip for approximately 5 years.

Philip's maternal grandmother has lived with the family off and on for many years. She has a long history of psychiatric hospitalization and is currently maintained on antipsychotic medication (Thorazine), which is monitored on an outpatient basis by a psychiatrist. Her most recent hospitalization was 2 years ago. She has resided with her daughter since then on a consistent basis despite being encouraged by others to obtain her own apartment.

The grandmother serves an important primary function in the family. She dresses and feeds the children, which enables her daughter to socialize with her friends and boyfriend. There are no other significant support systems available to the family, and Jennifer relies heavily on her mother's support to take care of her children. It is not uncommon in black families for a son or daughter to share or relinquish primary responsibility for the children to his or her parent. Thus, the grandparent assumes the "parenting" role for a second generation.

At the time of intake, Jennifer had recently met her current boyfriend, and was spending a considerable amount of time with him. She brings both children with her to his house or to her sister's home on the weekends, where they all remain together while the grandmother remains at home in the apartment alone.

This weekend arrangement has been occurring for several months, and the grandmother enjoys the weekends as she is "off duty."

Philip's mother occasionally abuses alcohol and has a history of physically abusing her son, according to Child Protective Services records. She and her son also share a history of being abused by his father with an electric cord. Philip was an infant when this occurred. The incidents were severe and finally necessitated their relocation to an emergency shelter and subsequent separation from the father. Jennifer acknowledges being beaten by her own father when she was a young girl. It is well documented that children who have been physically abused often go on to abuse their own children later in life. The last instance when Jennifer beat Philip was several months ago.

Jennifer's characteristic mode of disciplining involves verbal threats of physical violence. She can be unpredictably violent and hostile toward her son.

The local Child Protective Services agency has been involved with the family since Philip was 4 years old. The case was reopened as a result of the recent allegation of physical assault.

Presenting Problem

The presenting complaint as expressed by the school was as follows: "Philip stated that he wanted to kill himself today while in his classroom. He then left the classroom, promptly followed by his teacher. He ran down one flight of stairs to an empty classroom and began to open a window. He was restrained by his teacher from any further action."

This initial information was obtained via a phone conversation initiated by the school guidance counselor. While on the phone I requested additional information from the counselor. I wanted to know the circumstances that precipitated the event and if there had been observers in the area at the time that the threat was made. Additionally, I wanted to know the floor that the child was on at the time he attempted to open the window and exactly how far the window was opened and how far outside of the window the child actually extended himself.

These questions are important in determining the degree of risk in which the child had placed him- or herself at the time of the expressed ideation. The answers to these questions indicate whether the child needs to be evaluated immediately or if the evaluation can wait until the following day.

In Philip's case, it became apparent that he would need to be evaluated as soon as possible. The guidance counselor informed me that Philip had reported to her that he was beaten with an electric cord 2 days prior to his suicidal gesture. Child Protective Services had investigated the allegation of abuse and found no physical findings. In light of the child's allegation of physical violence that was followed by his suicidal gesture, it was not clear whether there actually had been any actual physical abuse or not. He obviously was troubled, as indicated by his threat of suicide. Somebody was not listening to this child, which indicated that he was still at risk for future attempts.

We requested that Philip be brought in immediately with his parent and grandmother. It is customary to request that the child be evaluated with the significant family members who are involved in his life. This is to gain additional information about the child and to observe how he or she interacts with each member and how the family member interacts with the child while also gathering data about each person.

It is noteworthy that the Child Protective Services (CPS) worker had been in the school at the time of the threat to interview the child in the educational setting as a follow-up to the home-based interview. He also accompanied the family to the psychiatric emergency room.

First Interview

Content of Session

THERAPIST: How do you do? My name is Jane Price, and I am a member of the child and adolescent crisis intervention team. We will be spending several hours together today as I interview Philip with his family and speak to Philip alone. I will also be contacting his school. Would you please introduce yourselves to me.

CPS: My name is Mr. Green, and I was just assigned to the case last week because of a report of violence in the home.

MOTHER: My name is Jennifer. (*Mother's eye contact is poor. She is sitting as far away as possible from Philip.*)

GRANDMOTHER: My name is Vanessa, and I am Philip's grandmother.

PHILIP: I am Philip.

T: Why are you here today?

P: I said I wanted to kill myself today.

T: Oh. I see. How come?

P: Kids in my class said they were going to beat me up today.

T: Philip, you and I will have time to talk more about that in a little while because I really want to hear more about this, but right now I was wondering if your mom or grandmother ever heard you say that before?

G: No. I never heard him say that, and I am with that child a lot. He gets plenty angry sometimes and kicks and screams when he is alone in his

Rationale/Analysis

Introductions to ease the anxiety related to the unknowns of what will be occurring.

Question was not directed at anyone in particular specifically to ascertain who would assume the authority to respond.

Child is remarkably open.

Let the child know he is heard while assessing how much of his anguish he has disclosed to his mother and grandmother.

Grandmother is first to respond to open question.

room when he is mad at me, but I never heard him say he would kill himself.

T: Jennifer, did Philip surprise you today with his actions?

M: No. That child doesn't ever surprise me! I might as well tell you right now that the reason Mr. Green is here is because of what that child said.

Jennifer is glaring at her son.

T: What did he say?

M: He said that I beat him with a cord last week and went to school and told them. Then they called CPS. I never hit him with the cord. I did once before last summer, but not now. His father used to beat him, and that is why we left him.

Mother is feeling defensive and uncomfortable in presence of CPS worker and in current situation.

T: Jennifer, why do you think that Philip tried to hurt himself today?

M: I think he is mad at me for yelling at him. He never does what he is supposed to. I take him with me to my boyfriend's house, and he acts up there. He won't do anything that we ask.

T: Jennifer, I would like to pick up on that thought again after I meet with Philip. I think I have a basic sense of what is going on right now, but I would now like to meet with you individually so that I can best understand the situation and be of most help to you. By the conclusion of the evaluation today, I would like to provide you with a sense of how you can proceed from this point on as well as give you my impressions of the current situation.

This will be a good time to conclude the group interview, since there is enough information now to proceed individually. More confidences may be shared alone with the therapist without fear of reprisal from other family members. I will consult with the psychiatrist on the team now and present the case thus far. I will also call the school to inquire about Philip's socialization with peers and response to teachers. I would also like to know if there has been any change in his overall functioning recently, how his academic grades are, and if there has been any noticeable fluctuation or deterioration in behavior. Prior to meeting with Philip, I will also consult with Mr. Green to gather his impressions of the family and the direction that he sees his agency pursuing at this time.

Interview with Child

Philip eagerly accompanied me to the interview room. I observed that his speech was immature and baby-like. In general he appeared to have an affect hunger and seemed needy of attention and affection. For example, he would place himself in a position where physical contact was inevitable. Philip's clothing was worn and hung shabbily on his small thin body frame. A mental status examination was performed based on both verbal and nonverbal interactions during the interview.

Content of Session	Rationale/Analysis
THERAPIST: What do you think about what your mother and grandmother said while we were all together?	Wonder if child was feeling angry or how he would interpret their comments.
PHILIP: I don't know.	
(*I assist Philip in indentifying his mood through the use of a display of seven boys' facial expressions depicting a wide range of affects. I draw the facial expressions on a sheet of paper while Philip observes with evident interest. I enlist Philip's assistance by requesting that he cut out the affect displays with a scissors.*) *Philip identifies his mood by pointing to the selected affect he has cut out in front of him on the desk.*)	Active engagement in age-appropriate activity to encourage Philip to identify his feelings. An attempt to understand if the suicide gesture coincides with Philip's last recollection of anger toward his mother.
P: I am mad at my mother.	
T: When was the last time you were mad at your mother?	
P: I was mad at her the other day when she was going to take me to Tom's house again, like she always does.	
T: Why don't you like to go there?	
P: There are no toys there for me to play with, and I have no friends there either.	
T: Philip, if you could have three wishes that I could make come true for you, what would you wish for?	Latency-age children often like to fantasize, and this task allows his latent thoughts and desires to be expressed in an ego-syntonic manner.
P: I wish that my mother did not take me to her boyfriend's house any more. I also would want more toys. For my last wish, I would want lots and lots of money.	It is not unusual for a child who is emotionally or environmentally deprived of a supportive and nurturing atmosphere to express the need for objects (toys) as well as the means (money) to supply the exhaustive desire for these objects. Thus, the theme of emotional deprivation is apparent. The first wish Philip stated appeared to be the most significant.

P: My mother said she was going to hurt me with the electrical wire the night before we were supposed to go to Tom's house for the weekend.

The precipitants to the suicidal ideation and gesture begin to emerge. Our explorative play and conversation identify the underlying stressors that contributed to the current crisis that brought the child to the psychiatric emergency room. Philip's gesture, which occurred on Friday, possibly was an attempt to prevent his mother from being with her boyfriend, since this was the customary day for their weekend departure from home. My initial reaction to the threat of physical violence toward this child is that I will not allow any harm to come to him that I can prevent. I also experienced anger toward the mother for even contemplating injuring this child who had already been physically violated in the past.

T: Philip, did your mother hurt you with the wire or her hands or anything else?

P: No.

T: You know, Philip, sometimes parents get angry at themselves or their children, and they might hit them, but it is not OK. Parents should not hit or slap their kids. It is *not* all right.

(*Philip appears more relaxed now as he walks about the room calmly, exploring the environment.*)

P: Sometimes I even tell my mother not to see Tom.

T: How come?

P: It's better at home alone with my mom.

T: Do you ever see your dad?

P: Not for a long time. Maybe a couple of years.

T: How do you feel about that? Does it make you sad or glad?

(*Philip shrugs his shoulders. I offer Philip crayons and paper and ask him to draw a picture of his family.*)

P: I can't draw my family, but I'll draw one person [see Figure 10.1].

Philip needed to hear and understand that physical violence is not supported by other adults and that he is not at fault for being the subject of his mother's aggression.

The "person" appeared to resemble an amphibious creature with

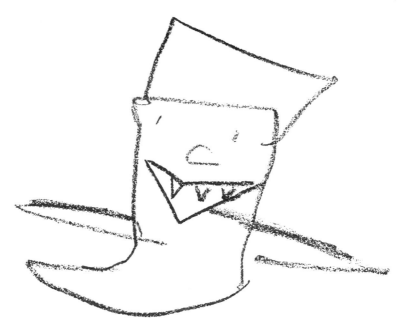

FIGURE 10.1. Philip's drawing of a person.

shark-like teeth displayed through a smile while sporting a baseball cap. The drawing was notably immature for an 8-year-old.

T: Tell me about this "person."

P: This person is friendly but angry.

T: Why is he angry?

P: Because he is not allowed to play with his friends and has to stay alone.

Philip revealed information about himself via the drawing that he would not have been able to do if questioned directly. The game-like orientation involving his imgination allowed Philip to express his subconscious thoughts without fear.

Preliminary Assessment and Treatment Plan

Although we do not as yet have a detailed understanding of the nature of this boy's relationship with his mother, we definitely can state that it appears to be troubled. The suicide gesture can be viewed as a "cry for help" related to the child's fear of being displaced by the boyfriend.

The mental status examination showed no evidence of suicidality, homicidality, or psychosis. His mood was generally angry, and his affect was somewhat constricted. He was cooperative. There was no psychomotor retardation noted, nor were there any sleeping or eating disturbances. His speech was productive and coherent. His cognitive functions and overall intelligence appeared average. His judgment and impulse control were fair.

We assume that Philip was jealous of his mother's boyfriend, Tom, because he robbed Philip of his time with his mother. In addition, the boyfriend caused Philip anguish since he replaced the biological father's role in many respects. Thus, the boyfriend shattered the child's hope of the reunification of his parents' marriage.

Most latency-age children want their parents to reunite and wish for that to occur whether or not the possibility is realistic. Philip's unwillingness to draw a family although he appeared to enjoy drawing suggested some confusion about his family. The drawing of the person confirmed the preliminary hypothesis about Philip's anger. Despite the fact that his parents' divorce had occurred many years ago, the emotional effects were lingering. Philip was angry and felt abandoned by his mother, who admittedly was erratic in her displays of affection and discipline.

Treatment Plan

We decided not to include the grandmother in the subsequent follow-up visit to the emergency room because we believed it was important for the mother to take more responsibility for her son. We reasoned that if the grandmother continued to be involved and solicited by Jennifer, then the child would not receive the reassurance and affection from his mother that he appeared to need so desperately.

The grandmother appeared to be relieved when informed that she did not need to return, and the mother and Philip scheduled another visit. We requested the continued presence of the CPS caseworker, Mr. Green, at the next appointment, since we believed that his presence added to the seriousness of the event and also exerted pressure on Jennifer to recognize the importance of meeting her son's needs. The threat underlying CPS's involvement in the case was that the child could be removed if the home environment threatened the child's safety or well-being.

Second Interview

During the the follow-up visit, Philip and his mother appeared smiling and happier at the beginning of the session. Their overall appearance also seemd to have improved. Jennifer had made a special effort to style her hair and also had applied make-up. Philip was dressed in clean and brighter clothing than in the previous session.

At the beginning of the session Philip sat in his mother's lap. He had attempted to do this during the prior visit, but Jennifer did not permit it. Although this behavior might appear regressive in an 8-year-old boy, in this instance, based on the prior observations of the family dynamics, it appeared to suggest an improvement in their emotional connectedness and in the mother's ability to tolerate the closeness.

Jennifer appeared less angry and more comfortable with me. She tolerated the CPS worker's involvement with her family yet requested that Mr. Green remain outside of the interviewing room, as she had information that she wanted to share with me that she did not want him to know. I said that would be possible and that the only information I would need to share with him would be anything that might endanger Philip directly. Other than that, she would be guaranteed her right to confidentiality. Philip was asked to wait outside the interviewing room while his mother and I spoke.

Session with Mother

Content of Session

MOTHER: You know, Philip reminds me of my ex-husband all the time. That man was just no good. He did not care about anyone but himself. He was selfish.

THERAPIST: I wonder if you are aware of how some of your anger toward your ex-husband seems to be getting spilled over onto your son.

M: Maybe. I love Philip very much and certainly don't want him to suffer.

T: I think it would be a good idea if you began to speak to a therapist on a regular basis, where you will have an opportunity to discuss how you have been feeling, how you can best get along with your son, and any other issues that are important to you.

M: I agree. I could use somebody to talk to that will be there for me. (*Jennifer appears accepting of outpatient therapy at this point.*)

Rationale/Analysis

The traits that she compared were negative in nature and provided the mother with an opportunity to scapegoat Philip. Philip had clearly been a recipient of the unresolved anger and hostility that she harbored toward her ex-husband. Not only did she indicate her hostility by removing him from his house every weekend, but she frequently compared him to his father in a derogatory manner.

Session with Child

Philip and I began our session with a structured task, since he had already demonstrated his reluctance to respond directly to questions about his feelings. We opted for a game that we created together, the "Game of Feelings."

We used a spinner from another board game. We covered up the prior instructions with a variety of feelings such as happy, sad, angry, mad. We took plastic chips from another game and began. Philip was excited with our creation. He sat extremely close to me. The chips were given to the person spinning the dial. The spinner would automatically receive one chip for spinning and a bonus chip for acting out or verbalizing a feeling in some fashion.

Content of Session	Rationale/Analysis

PHILIP: I like you.

I wanted to model the expression of feeling I wanted Philip to express.

THERAPIST: That is nice to hear. I like you also, Philip. I am going to spin first so that you can see how we will play the game. (*I spin dial.*) I have spun "happy." I feel "happy" when I am holding my cat and she is purring.

P: Oh! I understand how to play this game. I'll go now. It is my turn. I spun "scared." (*Philip thinks for approximately 30 seconds.*) I'm scared that when my mommy leaves me in Tom's house alone, that she won't come back for me. (*I promptly reward Philip with his two chips.*)

If in fact Philip was being left alone this needed to be explored with Jennifer and the CPS worker. True or not, Philip's fear of abandonment was real.

T: That is an excellent example of being "scared." I agree that it must be very "scary" to be alone.

P: I haven't seen my daddy for a long time, and my mommy and me had to run away from him because he hit us. We had to run away to a shelter where there were other kids. (*Philip then goes back to the game and spins "scared" again.*) I'm scared that my father left because I was bad and that's why he had to hit me and my mommy.

T: Philip, it is important for you to understand that it is *not* your fault that your parents are divorced. They had problems that were their own.

This prior comment was an initial attempt to relieve Philip of the sense of guilt that he had been experiencing for a long time.

P: I am "mad" that my daddy never came back. Remember the other day when you told me that I could have anything I wanted in the whole world?

T: Do you mean when you were wishing for three of your dreams to come true, if this was a magical world.

P: Yes. I have one more wish that I want to come true that I have been thinking about today.

I had the distinct feeling at that point that Philip was about to reveal his innermost struggle. I wanted to encourage him to proceed with his thoughts and allow him to know that I cared and was listening. He would be safe.

T: Well, what is that special wish? I would like to know.

P: I wish my father would come back.

Comment

Wallerstein and Kelly (1980) point out that it is typical for a child of Philip's age to yearn for an absent parent even when he or she was abusive to the child.

It seemed that Philip was displacing his anger onto his mother since she was the only parent present. This anger might be justifiable if in fact Jennifer does leave Philip for extended periods of time and/or ignores him emotionally. This experience would directly complicate the many expected responses an 8-year-old child would have to divorce. In addition to the anger related to the loss of a parent, Philip also felt guilt connected to a sense of responsibility for the marital break-up. Again, this is a typical response for a latency-age child.

Before concluding this second and final session, we read together *Divorce Happens to the Nicest Kids* by Michael Prokop (1986). Despite the fact that the divorce had occurred 2 years prior, Philip still had many unresolved feelings and emotions related to the dissolution of his parents' marriage and the change in his family. The abrupt absence of his father made Philip's adjustment more difficult.

As discussed earlier, Philip's suicidal gesture occurred the day prior to the customary weekend sojourn at Tom's house. This can be assumed to be one underlying stressor precipitating the gesture, together with the mother's threat to hit Philip with the electrical cord the previous evening. Added to this are Philip's unresolved feelings associated with the absence of his father and the perceived substitution of Tom for his biological father. There are several additional stressors to consider, such as his mother's unresolved anger toward her ex-husband and its projection onto Philip. Yet another possible stressor is the grandmother's history of psychosis and its effect on Philip. Since Philip was often left in her care, it is possible that he feared a recurrence of her decompensation, since he did not know who would care for him in her absence.

Therefore, there are numerous stressors to consider that preceded and possibly contributed to Philips' suicidal gesture. The final precipitant prior to the gesture occurred in the classroom when a peer called Philip "stupid." This was a fairly benign comment that under other circumstances would not have distressed Philip. Yet, given the accumulated effect of the many stressors, he was no longer able to tolerate his anxiety and rage.

I referred Philip and his mother for outpatient treatment. The immediate crisis, the suicidal gesture, appeared to be Philip's means of communicating his "anger" (as he so aptly identified via game play and verbal expression) rather than a true intent to die. The gesture was a means of communicating his anger about the current family situation.

Both Philip and his mother agreed to go for individual and family counseling. The CPS worker, Mr. Green, would maintain his involvement with the family over the next several months to assure that Philip would not be physically or emotionally harmed and that therapy was actually occurring on a regular basis.

Some of the issues that needed to be addressed on a long-term basis were identified as Philip's sense of responsibility and guilt for the divorce and his subsequent anger directed at his mother and Jennifer's denial of her son's needs and the issues underlying her lack of emotional availability to Philip.

CONCLUDING COMMENTS

When reviewing Philip's case at this time, I wonder if other treatment approaches might have proven more useful to the overall family. I acknowledge that Philip was relieved of the acute anguish that he was experiencing and that he and his mother had reunited emotionally via their work together in the emergency room. Yet, had I omitted other important members from our treatment? Should Tom, the mother's boyfriend, have attended a family meeting, since he is an integral member of the reconstituted family?

Another key family member that I had decided to exclude from our treatment was the maternal grandmother. I had done so as a means of drawing the mother into a more responsible role in an attempt to reconnect her with her son while extricating the grandmother from the primary caretaking position.

The primary intent of the outcome of treatment in the emergency room was to relieve Philip of his suicidal ideation and begin to engage the family in long-term outpatient treatment. Although that was accomplished, I still wonder if the same outcome could have been achieved with the grandmother present. If the grandmother had attended the sessions, her role in the family could have been redefined.

All of the aforementioned critique could be addressed in long-term treatment.

PLAY THERAPY MATERIALS

- Self-created materials: "Game of Feelings" (identification of mood via affect displays)
- Paper, crayons, and scissors
- Book: Prokop, M. S. (1986). *Divorce happens to the nicest kids.* Warren, OH, Alegra House.

STUDY QUESTIONS

1. Discuss the intergenerational factors in this family with regard to how the developmental tasks of individual family members may complement and/or oppose those of one another.

2. Discuss the role of the maternal grandmother as caretaker in the black family. Do you agree with the therapist's decision not to involve the grandmother in the child's treatment? What are the pros and cons of this decision for the child, the mother, and grandmother?

3. Consider the psychological tasks typical of a child during the latency period, according to Erikson. Comment on the absence of informtion related to peers and

to extracurricular interests in Philip's situation as this may relate to the presenting problem.

4. How would you assess the degree of risk of suicide in this case at the time of the initial assessment? Critique the therapist's evaluation and state what you might have done differently.

5. Ideally, what kind of aftercare services would you recommend for this family? Consider the needs of all relevant family members and give your reasons for each treatment recommendation.

REFERENCES

Emery, R. E. (1988). *Marriage, divorce and children's adjustment.* Newbury Park, CA: Sage Publications.

Golan, N. (1978). *Treatment in crisis situations.* New York: Free Press.

Pfeffer, C. (1986). *The suicidal child.* New York: Guilford Press.

Prokop, M. S. (1986). *Divorce happens to the nicest kids.* Warren, OH: Alegra Press.

Schaffer, M. (1974). Suicide in early childhood and early adolescence. *Journal of Child Psychology and Psychiatry, 15,* 275–291.

Wallerstein, J., & Blakeslee, S. (1989). *Second chances.* New York: Ticknor & Fields.

Wallerstein, J., & Kelly, L. (1980). *Surviving the break-up—How children and parents cope with divorce.* New York: Basic Books.

Weiss, R. S. (1979). Growing up a little faster: The experience of growing up in a single parent household. *Journal of Social Issues, 35* (4), 97–111.

CHAPTER 11

Visitation with Divorced Father Provokes Reemergence of Unresolved Family Conflicts

Case of Charlie, Age 10

HOWARD ROBINSON

> It is important that a child be able to conquer reality through play. However, even more crucial to his development is the freedom to transform an event of which he was the passive subject into one in which he is the active instigator and controller. (Bettelheim, 1987, p. 206)

Bruno Bettelheim captures the significance of play therapy as a valid and vital method of helping children who have been traumatized. Children subjected to anxiety-provoking events beyond their control and their capacity to cope are plagued by feelings of powerlessness. Even witnessing traumatic events such as family violence, for example, can stir fears powerful enough to overwhelm a child's ego. Play, however, allows children to transform the anxieties and fears of traumatic events into feelings of mastery and control.

Play reveals through symbolic disguise, as do dreams. Winnicott (1964) writes that "play, like dreams, serves the function of self-revelation" (p. 146). The dual nature of play, which reveals and disguises at the same time, allows traumatic material to emerge in nonthreatening form. The "real-life" abuser is transformed into a wolf puppet who is hunted and slain by the woodsman. Battles between Mom and Dad are expressed in the bullying and fighting among barnyard animals. Early abandonment is enacted by the child who protectively "adopts" the vulnerable baby doll and ceaselessly mothers her. Through the modality of play, children communicate events and anxieties too difficult to bear internally. The therapist's attunement to the symbolic nature of the child's expressive material helps create a powerful sense of connection that is deeply satisfying and psychologically reassuring to the child.

Play therapy provides a medium for the enactment of a child's crisis and the forces contributing to that crisis. This chapter presents the treatment of a 10-year-old boy in play therapy whose sense of trauma resurfaced 5 years after the traumatic event of his parents' divorce. This boy was a witness to his father's sadistic attacks on his mother, culminating in a sudden flight from his father and life in a battered women's shelter. He was subjected to aggressive behaviors and chaotic events over which he exercised no control. These experiences occurred when he was at the height of his Oedipal development. As a result, conflicts around power and sexual identity continued to characterize the psychological concerns of this boy, who erupted in crisis after visitation with his divorced father. New developmental needs awakened unresolved family conflicts and ambivalent feelings about his impulsive, violent father.

In my work with children, I have noticed that issues that are repetitiously played out in treatment signal a period in the child's life when trauma occurred. Domestic violence and abrupt parental separation, for example, may halt the child's emotional development. Development remains fixated at the level achieved during the time of the trauma. This 10-year-old was unable to preserve the state of latency because of his fixation on unresolved Oedipal issues. Visitation with his father became a trigger to feelings and conflicts he could not manage alone.

This chapter demonstrates how drawing, play enactments, and other play therapy techniques helped this boy to communicate the unresolved conflicts that propelled him into a state of crisis. Play therapy can provide the therapist, as well, with a tool for communication, empathy, and intervention. Through techniques of play therapy, the therapist can help a child discover the "freedom to transform" events that Bettelheim cites as crucial to a child's development. Traumatized children can gain a sense of control where none existed before. This chapter illustrates how one latency-age boy utilized play therapy in his quest for control over the reemergence of traumatic feelings and conflicts.

Before I present the case, a brief discussion reviews the therapeutic benefits of drawing in play therapy, the special role of the play therapist, and the particular therapeutic values that guide play therapy treatment.

THERAPEUTIC BENEFITS OF DRAWING IN PLAY THERAPY

Drawing is a projective technique that allows a child to construct an image of his world as he experiences it. A drawing often reflects the emotional concerns and preoccupations of the child. One especially valuable aspect of drawing is its potential for allowing the child to place himself in his self-perceived world.

Drawing enables a child to shift his internal world into an external arena permitting communication with others. By drawing, a child can concretize feelings, attitudes, fears, and perceptions that may not yet even have verbal labels. It helps children give form to their internal psychological states, which is the first step to labeling feelings. Transforming feelings into concrete form also allows the therapist and child to interact, providing a bridge to the child's internal world. This helps the child to become aware of his own emotional state and helps the therapist to communicate with him about it.

Drawing provides psychological relief to the child by permitting the internal distress, which children work painfully to keep private, to be externalized. Children in crisis, for example, withhold feelings because they touch on taboo subjects such as sexuality and violence. These subjects provoke overwhelming shame or guilt. Children feel burdened by issues of family loyalty, for example, "telling on" a parent or presenting a parent in a negative light. Drawing is a nonverbal activity that succeeds in distancing the child from such immediate concerns. As a result, the activity maintains the child's capacity to cope.

THE ROLE OF THE PLAY THERAPIST

Maintaining the "play dialogue" with the child is a symbolic activity of particular significance. The therapist's attunement to the child reenacts a developmentally early task of synchrony between parent and child. Brazelton and Cramer (1990, Chap. 14) refer to synchrony as the parental process of attunement to the infant's fluctuating physiological state of attention and inattention. The authors write, "Engaged in the synchronous communication, the infant can learn about the parent as a reliable and responsive being, and start contributing to the dialogue" (p. 122). The dialogue created in play therapy resonates with this early interactive exchange between self and other.

The therapist offers a special form of connection to the child. Through play, the therapist actively attunes to the child's symbolic language. This creates a new and reparative form of "object relationship" in which the adult moves caringly into the child's world. The empathic interaction experienced by the child within the play resonates with the early developmental need for parental attunement and synchrony. Staying within the child's fantasy and using the metaphors offered by the child therapeutically create the sense of attunement.

Therapeutic attunement kindles hope, an essential element for the beginning of therapy. In the act of play, a child may discover a connective bridge between his isolation and the therapist's empathic understanding. The child may feel refreshed and stimulated by this sense of connection. Children who have experienced deprivation and abuse, however, also develop intense and unrealistic expectations of the therapist once the empathic connection is made. A "transferential hope" develops, which the therapist must manage in treatment. The therapist walks a fine line between empathy and indulgence, because children who suffer emotional deprivations attempt to transform the therapist into the missing parent in hope of receiving the alliance, protection, or nurturance missing in their lives.

Transferential hope refers to the child's expectation that the therapist will actively satisfy the child's unmet needs for adequate mothering and fathering. Children perceive the therapist as all-powerful and attempt to recruit the therapist into providing direct reparation or satisfaction of the perceived losses and inadequacies in their lives. Therapeutic interactions are reparative and offer real hope to children that more satisfying relationships can exist for them with others in the future. But the therapist cannot erase the deficits already experienced by the child.

THERAPEUTIC VALUES THAT GUIDE PLAY THERAPY

By accepting and encouraging the expressive elements in a child's play, the therapist implicitly communicates particular therapeutic values that guide treatment. These values include the following:

1. I want to know about you as you honestly perceive yourself and your world to be.
2. Together, we can seek to externalize and share what may until now be held internally and made private.
3. You can tell me your story in your own language, and I will attempt to understand.

The experience of these values is comforting to a child who is released from the pressure of adult compliance and the need for psychic repression. The therapist's ability to understand the child's symbolic code also frees the child to speak his own language. By using the child's "native language" of play, the child can more authentically express his inner affective world.

The therapist's capacity to use and to elaborate the child's own play material constitutes an important therapeutic act of attunement. By keeping verbalizations within the "play scenario," the therapist signals acceptance of the material presented and willingness to interact within the child's level of discourse. This helps to establish the beginning of a therapeutic "play dialogue." The child tosses you his fantasy. You "catch it" and toss it back. As a result, a sense of play emerges between you and the child. The therapist's attunement provides a vital sense of connection that the child may not otherwise experience in his emotional life.

THE CASE: CHARLIE, AGE 10

Family Information

Charlie is a 10-year-old boy presently living in New York with his mother, 7-year-old sister, and maternal aunt. Charlie's parents divorced in California when he was 5. Bea, his mother, fled to New York with her two children a few years after the divorce to escape the violence that chronically erupted between her and Charlie's father.

Bea described her marital relationship as a "hypnotic hell" of sexual degradation, drugs, and physical violence. Charlie's father was addicted to both heroin and alcohol. Bea was victimized by her husband's unprovoked rageful outbursts that were fused with sexual sadism. Bea felt hopelessly trapped and alienated in this violent and life-threatening relationship. With both children in tow, Bea fled to a battered women's shelter advertised in a local TV commercial. She remained there with her children until a separation was implemented. In subsequent divorce proceedings, Bea won custody of the children and maintained an order of protection to curb the potential violence of her ex-husband. A few years after the divorce, Bea moved east to work while living with her older sister Eve.

Presenting Problem

Bea sought treatment for her son in January after "things turned real bad, real fast." Charlie, described as a top fifth-grade student, was behaving violently at home. Bea reported that Charlie hit, kicked, and choked his sister. Bea also described "tantrums" in which Charlie struck at her and screamed "obscene names." Charlie often refused to talk to female relatives. These behaviors reminded Bea of her ex-husband. Bea felt vulnerable and helpless; her own rage was surfacing, and she feared she would be unable to control it. An old and familiar cloud of violence was overtaking the family.

Bea suspected that Charlie's behavior was associated with his relationship with his father. In accordance with the divorce agreement, Charlie visited his father during the summer months. Bea experienced a change in Charlie's behavior when he returned. Charlie, according to Bea, appeared to "lack trust" and "act coldly." He withdrew from friends at school and complained of headaches and stomachaches. In September of the school year, Charlie told his mother, "I might as well just kill myself, 'cause nobody loves me." Charlie's behavior continued to deteriorate, and now the family was torn by Charlie's violent outbursts.

Charlie was a child in crisis; his behaviors signaled the need for help. Charlie's withdrawal and fighting were enactments of his psychological distress, and his retreat from relatives and school friends, his somatic complaints, and his verbalizations of suicidal thoughts were attempts to manage his internal crisis. Charlie was fighting for help with feelings that he could not manage alone. His more violent symptoms succeeded in motivating his mother to seek help for him and the family.

First Session: A Family Portrait

Charlie entered the session with his head bowed remorsefully. He was small-framed and lean with jet black hair. His slow, inhibited gait added to the feeling of his being a condemned prisoner. Charlie remained taut and nonverbal. When asked to draw a picture of his family, however, Charlie energetically drew a spacecraft with all but one of his immediate family aboard (Figure 11.1). He used numerous bright colors and embellished his picture with surrounding stars. He added his name boldly at the top when finished. With a little encouraging prompting, Charlie explained:

Content of Session	Rationale/Analysis

CHARLIE: It's a spaceship. My sister's at the controls. Mom is up here, reading. Dad is sleeping, and Auntie is below, working . . . she likes to be

FIGURE 11.1.   Charlie's family portrait.

away from everybody. This is me. The spaceship
is going to California . . . but we are all going to   Charlie drew a crisis in-the-
crash . . . run into a star.   making!

Charlie's first offering to me as therapist was nothing less than an insightful
depiction of the dysfunctional family dynamics pushing him into emotional chaos.
By drawing, Charlie symbolically represented an untenable psychological dilemma
that he could not successfully resolve. A more detailed analysis of Charlie's drawing helps unveil the multiple meanings of the boy's symbolic communication.

Analysis of Drawing

Charlie depicted himself alone in a world of unavailable adults. His mother is
encapsulated in her own private shell, self-absorbed and seemingly uninvolved
with the tensions existing within the family below. Father, an eerie figure, is inert
and lifeless. He floats dead-like with a capsule covering his head. Father is a clear
presence but is inactive and inaccessible. His lifeless body appears, moreover, to
block contact between Charlie and his mother or sister. Charlie's aunt, the only

other available adult, is unconnected to the family; she flies independently below the doomed spaceship. Charlie stands in the tail of the craft and places one foot in the escape hatch. He is as far from his mother and sister as he can get without leaving the craft. Charlie appears frozen in a posture of choice: stay with the family or escape? But where is he to go? No viable life exists outside the craft; yet, to remain aboard is to crash. Charlie is trapped. This is one dimension of Charlie's crisis.

Other dimensions of crisis are reflected in Charlie's family portrait. Charlie, for example, portrays a family with no effective leader. The power structure of the family, in fact, is rendered topsy-turvy. Charlie's sister, the most vibrant figure in the drawing, is placed at the controls of the craft while his mother, above, remains self-absorbed. In structural family terms, the parental authority of the executive subsystem is subverted by the sibling (Minuchin, 1974). The "executives" of the family, mother and father, are either secluded or "sleeping." Meanwhile, Charlie's sister, the youngest member of the family, mans the controls; the ship (i.e., the family) is in her young hands.

Parental figures, moreover, are depicted as inaccessible and unable to offer help. The ladder to Mom's private perch suggests some hope of movement back into the family. The ladder, however, appears to connect mother and daughter, not Charlie. Mom is clearly distant from Charlie and his concerns. Father is not only depicted in a lifeless state but has a capsule around his head. This provides a further obstacle to discourse and connection with Charlie. Charlie is in trouble; yet he has no bridge to parental figures. Those figures provide no promise of help, for they lack accessibility and power.

Charlie's drawing also has developmental significance. Charlie is on the cusp of preadolescence and needs a father for male identification. Charlie expresses a wish to be with his father in the drawing. The spacecraft, for example, is flying to California. This is where his father and his father's side of the family live. Charlie's drawing, therefore, is the expression of his wish to seek father's presence, to exist where father lives. The wish for father exists symbolically, as well, in the ambiguous placement of the father figure in the drawing. While father appears to block access to Charlie's mother and sister, he also provides a buffer to the female element of the family. Charlie signals a need for some male adult figure to help him individuate as a male within his family of females. Father, therefore, may be needed as a shield so that Charlie can grow safely as a male within the powerful and potentially threatening female household. Charlie appears to need a father who can create enough safe distance between him and his mother to allow his own maleness to emerge.

Charlie experiences something cataclysmic in this wish, however, since the spaceship is destined to crash. Father's stance, moreover, is "off balance" and lopsided, suggesting that he is not on "solid" ground (i.e., is not really a "secure base"). Charlie's distress must continue, since his father is, in Charlie's words, "sleeping" and unable to act vigorously in his behalf.

As we can see, the drawing provides insight into Charlie's psychological distress. He reveals his life situation as he himself experiences it. Charlie's symbolic play language is articulate and dramatic. His drawing narrates his sense of alienation, burden, need, and crisis. Charlie exists alone because the adults are unavailable, inaccessible, and powerless. Mother is narcissistically preoccupied and withdrawn from the family system. Father is wished for but does not actively function. Male identity is sought, but this appears threatening. Charlie is in such deep distress that he contemplates leaving the family as his resolution. Charlie is revealing to the therapist just where he is in his world. Charlie seems to be saying, "This is me; this is my family; and this is my dilemma. Help."

Strategies to Facilitate Expressive Play

When children express anxiety-laden material, it is important, as therapist, to stay within the fantasy of the child. Winnicott (1964, p. 144) has written that "children play to master anxiety." Staying within the fantasy play of the child, therefore, maintains the safety net of the child's self-made "disguise." Play can then continue and be elaborated. As therapist, you might choose, for example, to have Charlie expand the fantasy of his drawing by asking questions that maintain the metaphor and images he himself constructed. Examples of such facilitating questions might include:

1. *What might Mom or Dad do to keep the spacecraft from crashing into a star?* This question would elicit more feelings about Charlie's parents and their capacity, or incapacity, to tune in to his anxiety and needs in a helpful way.

2. *What would happen if Dad "woke up"* Charlie's response might indicate more about his father's interactions with him and the family or provide more specific material about the nature of Charlie's "father" wishes. Charlie's elaborations might indicate what he wants his father to do for him or "be" for him.

3. *What would happen if mother sat down at the controls of the craft?* Responses here might reveal more about the use of power in the family and about mother's feelings. Would mother turn the ship around and head east (thwarting Charlie's wish to be with his father)? Would Sis be unwilling to yield her position of control? Would she rebel or fight with Mom? As hypothetical changes in the scenario are proposed, more family dynamics may emerge.

4. *What would happen if you (Charlie) manned the controls?* If Charlie were in charge, what, in effect, would he choose to do? Such a question magically empowers Charlie and might provoke fantasies concerning the changes he would make to better his situation. If Charlie were "Captain Kirk," what would he do?

5. *What would Mom do if Charlie left the ship?* This question might tap Charlie's fantasy of what his mother feels about him. Would she search for him and attempt his rescue? Cry? Not notice his departure? Become angry? Responses would help to illuminate the parent–child relationship as Charlie experiences or anticipates it.

Questions like those given in the examples above can be used to facilitate expressive elaborations by the child. By staying within the child's own field of fantasy, the therapist can continue to talk about anxiety-provoking material without losing the protective shield of the fantasy itself. This maintains the action of play in treatment and succeeds in opening up the expressive communication of the child.

Therapeutic Functions of Expressive Play

Communicating with the child by using the fantasy, terms, and metaphors of the child also provides a way to strengthen the therapeutic engagement and working alliance. Charlie's drawing was his first therapeutic communication with me. He succeeded in "narrating" his presenting problems using a form of play that was revealing but safe. Charlie initially used drawing rather than words to engage with me. It was then my task to understand his offering.

Responding in the child's own language acknowledges the child's offering and strengthens the child-therapist working alliance. By accepting the child's scenario (i.e., spaceship with the family about to crash) and by posing further questions within this scenario (i.e., "What happens if . . . ?"), the therapist signals his entry into the child's world.

Assessment and Treatment Plan

Charlie entered treatment feeling accused. Because of the hostility he enacted on the family, Charlie experienced himself as the "bad one." Charlie was fearful and nonverbal in his first encounter with me. Children in crisis cannot verbally organize their inner worlds. Drawing, however, provides an organizing process in which it is safe to communicate distress. Charlie was able to use drawing to successfully construct his problem situation and initiate treatment in the process.

Drawing projects the feeling state of the child outward in a form that is safe for the child to apprehend. Charlie's experience of maternal deprivation and his taboo wishes for his father are "secretly"coded in the drawing of his family aboard the spaceship. These are inner feelings that Charlie may be too frightened to voice directly. He may also not be conscious of the feelings he embodied in his family portrait. Drawing helps Charlie to camouflage powerful feelings in symbolic representations that can then be integrated at a preconscious or conscious level.

Charlie was angry at his mother. He experienced her as emotionally withdrawn from him. He also yearned for his father, a source of unresolved hatred for his mother. These two issues were certain to cause conflict between Charlie and his mother in reality. Charlie's physical and emotional dependence on his mother prevented him from exploring or expressing his concerns directly with his mother. But drawing provided a clever disguise that allowed the feelings to emerge without having to personally claim them. The burden of having to repress them was therefore lifted.

As Charlie sees it, his mother cannot leave her own nest of interests to attend to *his* inner needs. He, as child, is forced to accommodate to the parental figure (mother) if he is to maintain any sense of connection. Since Charlie is unable to evoke emotional attunement from his mother, he forces her to recognize him through aggressive acts evoking rage and retaliation. In Charlie's experience, only rage-provoking acts move mother out of her self-absorbed lethargy. Charlie satisfies his need for connection but receives no emotional understanding. He gains his mother's negative emotional reaction, not her empathic responsiveness. For Charlie, conflict is connection, and maternal empathy is lost.

Charlie's drawing depicted his isolation and remoteness from parental figures. His sense of internal crisis mounted because he experienced himself as disconnected from the loved figures on whom he depends for emotional support and understanding. His crisis is exacerbated by having to bear his fear and anxiety alone. Charlie exists in an emotional vacuum symbolized by "outer space" in his drawing. The therapist's attunement, therefore, provides a vital sense of connection that the child does not otherwise experience in his emotional life.

Charlie's drawing succeeded in accomplishing a number of therapeutic functions. Charlie was quickly able to depict his presenting problems to me in a form that was safe and manageable for him. By doing so, Charlie initiated a therapeutic engagement with me. Charlie made a dramatic statement about himself and his family. By drawing, he was able to give form to complicated and diffuse emotional feelings that could later be discussed or elaborated on. Charlie constructed a bridge between his internal feelings and the external world. The crack in his emotional inaccessibility was widened. By drawing, Charlie need not be alone in the wash of his crisis. The communication he established with me was a source of hope. A therapeutic play dialogue had begun, and treatment was initiated.

Charlie was seen once weekly for individual sessions. Initially, I met weekly as well with Charlie's mother, who was in a depressed and psychologically fragile state. Charlie occasionally acted out, which precipitated crisis-intervention sessions. Once, for example, he ran away from home, and another time he became so angry and impulsive that he smashed the glass from a door with his hand.

Bea requested family sessions in hopes of helping both children with divorce issues. She struggled to appease Charlie's sister, who was jealous of his individual treatment. Two family sessions were held during the middle of treatment in which the children, with their mother, were encouraged to reflect on their experiences during the time of the parent conflict and divorce. These sessions also enabled me to observe Charlie in relationship with his sister and mother.

Treatment planning became complicated. The needs of the family were too great for one therapist. The crisis nature of the case, however, led me to use intensive collateral sessions with Charlie's mother to attempt to stabilize the family system. Although this approach risked compromising Charlie's independent claim on me as therapist, I felt that Charlie's welfare was best serviced by enabling mother to function more adequately.

The first goal of Charlie's treatment was to help Charlie engage in the therapeutic treatment process itself. The objectives relating to this primary goal included the following:

1. Charlie will develop a nonthreatening relationship with the male therapist who can help model empathic and controlled behaviors.

2. Charlie will engage in play therapy so that psychological conflicts can be therapeutically enacted in session.

Relationship issues were crucial with Charlie, so that the goal of therapeutic engagement would already help to provide Charlie with a reparative object relationship that might neutralize his aggression and help to modify his intense fears of retaliation.

A second goal of treatment was to help Charlie resolve Oedipal conflicts that sabotaged the developmental tasks of latency (learning without conflict, role identifications, adequate defenses to contain impulses, capacity to sublimate into constructive age-appropriate activities). Objectives in treatment included these:

1. Charlie will express, clarify, and label feelings related to the loss of his father.
2. Charlie will learn to feel safe in the expression of his hostile and aggressive wishes enacted in play.
3. Charlie will learn socially approved ways to cope with his sense of anger toward his mother.

Charlie needed to defuse his aggression. This could be accomplished by playing out and mastering his anger in play. As the threat of retaliation lessened, Charlie might feel safer with his aggression. The aggression itself could be defused by the safety of the play. Charlie might also organize himself psychologically as the source of his anger became clarified. The empathic responses of the therapist as anger emerged would help Charlie to feel understood.

A third goal of treatment was to stabilize the family system so that Charlie's home environment might become more nurturant and less provocative to Charlie. Objectives here included these:

1. Charlie's mother will become aware of the nature of her own conflicts displaced onto Charlie.
2. Charlie's mother will gain more ability to set limits in nonpunitive ways that do not enact anger.
3. Charlie's mother will improve her capacity to interpret and attune to Charlie's feelings and needs rather than project her own.
4. Charlie and his mother will learn concrete ways to deescalate conflict as it emerges between them.

The antagonistic relationship between Charlie and his mother was a major concern of treatment that presented real issues in terms of the management and continuation of treatment. The collaterial and conjoint work was necessary to secure whatever individual gains Charlie might make.

The modalities utilized to achieve these goals and objectives included once-weekly individual play therapy sessions with Charlie, weekly collateral sessions with Bea, and conjoint mother–son sessions as needed.

Play Therapy Sessions

For practically every session, Charlie arrived sporting a hunting cap and army fatigues. His father wore this same attire when Charlie visited. In this nonverbal manner, Charlie expressed his identification with his absent father. Issues relating to loss and identification emerged.

Second Play Therapy Session

Charlie, clothed in fatigues and cap, came to this session withdrawn and sad. Charlie's verbal material did not directly touch on the loss of his father, but the sequence of topics and the context created by his clothing belied the connection between feelings of loss and father.

Content of Session	Rationale/Analysis
CHARLIE: All my pets died when I got back from vacation with my father. First my guppies died, then my hamster. (*angrily*) My aunt flushed my guppies down the toilet. Me and my sister got frogs. But you can't sleep with frogs or cuddle them. . . . When I went to visit my Dad, I got to sleep with my old dog, Benny. Dad bought him for my birthday 6 years ago. He was just a puppy then. Benny only comes when me or my father calls him. (*enthusiastically*) My father and I built a tree house in the back yard with a trap door. We went to a ball game with my uncle, and we swam in my grandmother's pool.	Charlie is in a depressed mood. He begins by talking about the death of his pets. The sequence of verbalizations moves from loss of pets to the dog that he and his father share to happy summer memories with Dad. Charlie's talk of dead pets symbolically expresses the loss of father he experiences on his return from California. Benny represents the special father–son relationship. Charlie expresses his loneliness and alienation in his wish to have "cuddly" pets to sleep with. Charlie yearns for a sense of warmth and companionship. Charlie's depressed tone lifts as he recounts happy memories of his summer with Dad.

Comment. Charlie is dressed in clothing that symbolically resurrects his distant and missing father. Charlie's focus on dead and missing pets is a thin disguise for the feelings of loss related to his father. Yearning for father is consistent with the theme of Charlie's drawing in which he attempts to fly to California. Charlie identifies strongly with his father and mourns his absence.

Charlie attempted repeatedly to have me convince his mother to buy him a dog.

Content of Session	Rationale/Analysis
CHARLIE: Would you ask my mother to get me a dog? She likes dogs.	Charlie wants to recruit me as his advocate.

THERAPIST: What would you want me to say to her?

I invite further elaboration to surface his fantasy and to help identify the role he wants me to play.

C: . . . That I really need a dog. I can take care of it (*pleading, as if to a parent*), and it can sleep with me.

Charlie pleads with me as if I am his mother.

T: What do you think your mother would say?

Continue to invite elaboration.

C: Well, she's said I could have one when she has more money. She says she's been thinking about it, but . . .

I note his affect.

T: You look sad.

I reflect.

C: She *never* does what I want. I ask her all the time, but she just says "maybe" or doesn't pay attention.

Charlie articulates his grievance.

T: You really would like an ally, someone who can fight for you when your mother doesn't pay attention.

I attempt to identify the wish motivating his request for a dog.

C: She might not even let me visit my father again . . .

The need for father emerges.

T: You're angry and sad to be separated from your father. It would feel great to have a father close who could see things your way.

An interpretation that seeks to clarify the transferential wishes underlying our discussion.

Comment. The child's attempt to actualize transferential wishes by recruiting the therapist into the parent role must be caringly acknowledged. When Charlie made requests for me to advocate for his getting a dog, I attempted to solicit and identify the wish motivating the request. One way to do this is to ask what the child would like you to say or do so that the fantasy can be elaborated and not enacted. By identifying the transferential need underlying the child's request, the therapist clarifies the therapeutic issue and creates a frame for the treatment. For Charlie, the loss of his father and the wish for his functional presence became a primary theme of treatment. Charlie's unmet need for a male ally powerful enough to influence and control his mother motivated his requests. To ally with Charlie and help him get a dog was to become the lost father in his real life.

Summary of Sessions 3–13

Aggressive play sessions followed in which Charlie pitched full-scale battles with toy soldiers. Charlie's small army overwhelmed and "slaughtered" the superior forces assigned to me. Charlie transformed the entire therapy room into a battleground. He set up ambushes atop chairs and sofas. He built forts from pillows and blew apart the protective walls. He used bazookas to "waste" individual soldiers. Charlie threw soldiers in the air with accompanying gushes of explosions. Charlie's battles were furious ones.

Charlie identified one soldier as "the Captain." He was a Rambo-type figure who grew in power and stature with each new battle. "Captain" single-handedly defeated any and all adversaries. Charlie celebrated the might of one over many. He exhorted me to develop the strongest attack imaginable and then proceeded to wipe out my forces with his "Captain." Charlie repeatedly played out such battle scenes in a compulsive manner. He appeared active and alive in this play. The aggression delighted him.

Charlie's war games provided a healing opportunity for Charlie to express aggression born from frustration, loss, intrusion, and fear. At home, Charlie felt outnumbered and controlled by females: his mother, sister, and aunt. Charlie's mother expressed her own anger by refusing to grant many of Charlie's requests and had threatened, as well, not to let him visit his father again. As a result, Charlie experienced himself as powerless and defeated. Charlie, likewise, could not control his mother's narcissistic withdrawal. Her distancing was experienced as a hostile rejection of him. Charlie also feared his mother's explosive anger. Charlie felt that he had no protection from his mother's anger when it erupted. In play, however, Charlie could reverse his submissive male role and his powerless circumstances. Where Charlie felt threatened, he now could threaten. Where Charlie felt vulnerable, he now could attack.

Charlie's play was a combination of compensation for psychological vulnerability and identification with the aggressor. Charlie enjoyed destroying my "battle defenses" and rendering me vulnerable and weak. He made me experience the inability to ward off attack; he became the attacker, and I was the victim. Charlie compensated for his feeling of submission by empowering himself. He also enacted on me what he felt was enacted on him. The following dialogue conveys the kind of verbal exchange typical in Charlie's war play:

Content of Session	*Rationale/Analysis*
CHARLIE: I've blown away your bunkers . . . Here come my men to attack.	Charlie destroys my "defenses" and leaves me "vulnerable" to attack.
THERAPIST: I have nothing to protect me; anything can happen to me now.	I verbalize my defenseless predicament. The more I articulate the sense of fear, helplessness, and vulnerability in the play, the greater Charlie's sense that I understand what he experienced.
C: You take all of these men (*gives me the full complement of soldiers*). Captain will fight them all!	Charlie enjoyed being an aggressive male who could freely identify with the power and strength of the Captain figure. Charlie could express his own aggression without fear of retaliation or symbolic castration.
T: The Captain is all by himself; how can he handle all these attackers alone?	I play along by acknowledging the lopsided odds. I praise his power

but insert a skeptical tone to address the sense of unfairness in
his real-life battles.

Playing war with soldiers sublimated Charlie's reservoir of accumulated anger. Charlie channeled his anger safely into toys that could not, in reality, retaliate. Charlie was liberated from any guilt or remorse that might accompany aggression outside of play. Aggressive play in the treatment room was safe. By allowing Charlie to play out aggressive situations with toy soldiers, I communicated to Charlie that his expression of anger was important and safe within the therapy room.

During battles, Charlie also symbolically attacked me, a male authority figure. His attack and control of me continued, as well, in competitive games. Charlie manipulated rules in games such as checkers, Connect Four, ring toss, and cards. He always won. Winning, however, was not generally good enough; Charlie was compelled to "wipe me out." Charlie made rules that led directly to my defeat while creating others that empowered him. The same impulses to destroy, conquer, and control manifest in battle scenes were expressed in his approach to competitive games.

The need to assert power and to control the powerful other are emotional dynamics of the Oedipal child (3 to 5 years old). Charlie's Oedipal aggression appeared in full bloom. Charlie enacted the conflicts and issues of the 5-year-old, Charlie's age when he was abruptly separated from his father. Aggressive themes pervaded Charlie's fantasy play, be it soldiers, board games, or cards. (The card game of choice, of course, was "war"!) Charlie was preoccupied with his own phallic power. Charlie's aggression was quite possibly overstimulated by his father, who showed little control himself. Charlie had also witnessed his father's violent behaviors with his mother, and these behaviors reached their peak during Charlie's own Oedipal development.

Charlie needed an opportunity to express his aggression safely so that he could find ways to both neutralize and master it. Charlie's parents, both capable of exploding in anger, did not provide a role model for control of aggressive impulses. Being able to enact his aggression in the presence of a nonreactive adult was a necessary step for Charlie in the mastery of his own aggression. Charlie's efforts to control me were reparative attempts to control the overly aggressive father or mother whose direct anger and retaliation he feared.

Parent–Child Conflict and Parent and Family Counseling

Charlie's mother was an emotionally fragile woman prone to crisis herself. Her psychological sense of self-integrity was easily (and frequently) shattered, causing her to become emotionally disorganized and panicked. At these times, she sought male figures to take charge of her life. At other times, she spurned intimacy with males and was fearful of male domination and intrusion. Her relationship with males was highly conflicted.

Charlie's aggression at home sparked his mother's own conflicts and made her feel victimized by him. She was incapable of controlling or managing either his anger or her own. Bea reported that Charlie physically resembled her abusive ex-husband, and this alone was enough to trigger her rage. Bea often displaced the rage belonging to her ex-husband onto Charlie. As a result, verbal, and sometimes physical, hostility occurred at home between mother and son.

Bea reenacted aspects of her violent marital relationship of old with Charlie. She had not yet healed the emotional wounds of her marriage in which she had been physically and sexually battered. Charlie's aggressive behavior and physical resemblance to his father provided a powerful stimulus to the evocation of her own repressed anger and rage. As a result, the potential for violence between Bea and Charlie was ever-present.

Charlie, however, was experiencing a need for his father, appropriate to his preadolescent developmental stage. Charlie's developmental need was perceived as a psychic threat to Bea. If Charlie "needed" his father, how would this man, who victimized her, ever be out of her life? Bea also feared losing her son if he decided to live with his father. Bea feared this potential abandonment.

An unconscious battle royal between Charlie and his mother existed. As Charlie began to identify with his father, Bea felt rejected and threatened. At age 12, Bea was literally abandoned by *her* father when he died in a car accident. Bea's anticipated sense of loss and abandonment by male figures originated in her own tragic loss of her father. Bea could not tolerate her son's yearning for his father. His developmental need aroused her own deep unresolved feelings of loss. Bea unconsciously perceived her son, therefore, as a threat to her own psychic equilibrium. This dynamic fueled her readiness for attack.

This parent–child conflict required that the mother, too, be in treatment. She needed to understand the many reasons why her son was a focal point to attack and how her own trauma was being reenacted in the family system. Collateral meetings with Bea were helpful in drawing attention to parallels in Bea's own life and in distinguishing the anger and aggression that were displaced. However, resolution of the parent–child conflict required more intensive therapy of the mother.

Episodic incidents of physical hostility between Bea and Charlie continued to occur. These behaviors needed to be managed for treatment to continue effectively. An intervention was designed to deescalate incipient conflict.

Family Session

Charlie and his mother were each asked to describe how the other acted when angry. This is meant to help the speaker and listener to identify behavioral cues and triggers to angry interactions. Facilitating questions include:

1. How can you tell when your (mother/son) is angry?
2. How does your (mother/son) express anger?
3. What happens when (mother/son) gets angry?
4. What do you do when (mother/son) gets angry?

These questions help "track" the process of conflict. The intent is to particularize every move of the angry "dance" between mother and son. By describing each step of the conflict, and by soliciting each person's perception of the other, we can help an awareness of the dynamics of conflict to emerge. Once this picture is assembled, it can be disassembled to create alternative behaviors. In this way, the conflicted couple can change the behavioral steps of the escalating conflict.

Charlie, for example, was able to verbalize when he first could intuit that his mother was angry. He also became more aware of times when he himself was ready to lash out. He then developed his own solution. He decided that he would separate from his mother, go to his bedroom, and punch pillows. Mother, meanwhile, resolved to go to her study to cool down. We also identified friends she could call to air her frustrations and gain some support.

This approach to conflict implicitly communicates that each person contributes to the interaction and that each person, as a consequence, has the power to control some part of the process. It is important to emphasize the power that each participant has to *stop* the conflict. This intervention can only be used when the child is reasonably old enough to assume some responsibility for his actions. Otherwise you risk making an unempowered and victimized child responsible for the victimization.

Epilogue

Charlie's treatment was prematurely terminated after 7 months. Charlie's strong treatment alliance with me was perceived as a threat of loss to Bea. The family dynamic was projected onto the treatment process itself. Bea felt threatened by Charlie's sense of closeness with me, just as she felt threatened by his close association with his father. The power of this dynamic was too strong to resolve in time to save Charlie's treatment. Bea abruptly ended Charlie's association with me as she had ended his relationship with his father.

Charlie, however, had the opportunity to experience an empathic male relationship, which permitted him expression of feelings that were taboo or negatively sanctioned within his home. Knowing that he could be understood without retaliation served to temporarily allay his crisis state. His positive experiences in therapy would also act as a foundation for treatment at some later date when Charlie might be in a position to chose therapy for himself

PLAY THERAPY MATERIALS

Expressive play materials such as clay, crayons, and paper, pastels, chalk, and board are especially helpful in eliciting nonverbal moods and feelings. Manipulating the materials releases feelings. Warming up clay with the hands and pounding it, for example, can release frustration and anger. Rubbing pastels or coloring vigorously also releases tension. As we saw with Charlie, drawing helped, as well, to unlock his internal sense of burden and initiate the therapy process. The symbolic expressions made with expressive materials that are unstructured can help to frame the treatment approach.

After Charlie communicated issues of loss and helplessness via his drawing, he began to act out his issues therapeutically using *toy soldiers*. Soldiers are manageable toys that he directed and controlled, unlike the rest of his world. He could be certain that "Captain" was victorious in even the most overwhelming circumstances. Play figures such as soliders and animals allow children to create action scenarios that they control. This helps establish predictability and power in their lives. These scenarios also symbolically depict therapeutic issues: situations of vulnerability, quests for power, the sense of isolation, and feelings of being trapped and overpowered. Charlie created play scenarios with soldiers that allowed him to express all of these concerns.

Charlie gravitated to structured *games*, which latency-age children typically enjoy. Games and their rules help preserve order and contain impulses. Their structure is "binding." Although Charlie manipulated "rules," games created a circumscribed arena for his aggressive impulses. Games also help a child to relate in nonthreatening ways to the therapist. Feelings are displaced onto the game and become depersonalized and safe. Charlie's overstimulated aggressive urges were expressed in game play. The rules provided both a disguise and a vehicle for his aggressive feelings. Games are therefore essential play materials for latency-age children.

STUDY QUESTIONS

1. How would you manage Charlie's requests to intervene actively in his life situation? What might be gained therapeutically, and what lost, by satisfying such requests?

2. How would you react to the aggressive onslaughts this child made in therapy? How might you utilize your reactions within the play itself? At what point in treatment might you link his aggressive play to real events in his life? Or would you do this?

3. Discuss the therapist's work with the mother. If you had been Charlie's therapist, how would you have structured the mother's referral to another therapist? What issues would be particularly tricky in making the referral, and how would you manage these?

4. This case was prematurely terminated. Discuss what feelings and reactions you might have as a therapist encountering such an end to treatment. What might the reactions of the child in this case be? What, if anything, might you do as therapist to manage a premature ending such as this?

REFERENCES

Bettelheim, B. (1987). *A good enough parent.* New York: Knopf.
Brazelton, T. B., & Cramer, B. G. (1990). *The earliest relationship: Parents, infants, and the drama of early attachment.* New York: Addison-Wesley.
Minuchin, S. (1974). *Families and family therapy.* Cambridge: Harvard University Press.
Winnicott, D. W. (1964). *The child, the family, and the outside world.* Reading, MA: Addison-Wesley.

CHAPTER 12

The Crisis of Paternal Suicide
Case of Cathy, Age 4½

DERMOT J. HURLEY

Children who are bereaved as a result of parental suicide require urgent intervention to deal with (1) the trauma of the loss and (2) the grieving process, which is affected by the manner of the loss. Traumatically bereaved children require particular sensitivity and understanding on the part of the child therapist, and there are a number of therapeutic approaches cited in the literature for dealing with this population (Pruett, 1984; Eth & Pynoos, 1985). Most authors agree that early bereavement affects later psychological adjustment (Wolkind & Rutter, 1985). There is also evidence that children who lose a parent are at greater risk for suicidal and depressive sequelae than are children in the general population. Studies by Adam (1973; Adam, Lohrenz, Harper, & Steiner, 1982), Brown and Harris (1978; Brown, Harris, & Bifulco, 1986), and Barnes and Prosen (1985) all show a relationship between early childhood loss of a parent and increased risk for suicide and depression, either as a direct result of the loss or as a result of increased vulnerability to the effect of later stress events.

This chapter describes the course of treatment for children who have lost a parent through suicide and who are considered to be in a traumatic grief state. One case is discussed in which a combination of nondirective play therapy and a semistructured play situation decreases the child's resistance as the working through proceeds. The theoretical basis for the therapy rests on a psychodynamic framework with a relationship therapy focus (Moustakas, 1959). Throughout the process, the child therapist is alert to disturbances in the child's ongoing interpersonal relationships as well as to the child's internal psychological conflicts as a consequence of parental suicide. Family relationships can change quite dramatically following a suicide, with varying effects on treatment outcomes for children.

Pretraumatic family conditions are generally problematic in families in which suicide occurs. Children may experience a high level of conflict or, alternatively, a complete absence of overt conflict. Following the loss, family organization is often chaotic, and desperate attempts at reorganization are put into place (Hurley, 1989). Families that reorganize more adaptively are families in which (1) the surviving parent acts competently, not helplessly, (2) a substitute parent figure becomes available in place of the lost parent, and (3) there is a relative absence of stress and conflict in the family (Elizur & Kaffman, 1982).

A grief therapist using the approach outlined in this chapter allows the child to safely explore his or her feelings and the meaning of the experience without overwhelming anxiety or fear. Children can be helped by doing some of the grief work currently rather than postponing it for many years through psychological defenses that compound the problem and interfere with normal development. The emotional climate necessary to do this work is developed by the therapist and child in a nondirective but semistructured play setting that allows the child to express him- or herself freely and come to terms with the meaning of the loss in his or her life. There is no set time frame to predict when mourning will begin in childhood, and many children do not show sadness until circumstances in their life trigger active memories of the deceased.

Suicidal loss can trigger in children an endless search for replacement figures and an emotional flattening or detachment when substitutes fail to provide necessary emotional support. There is often an exaggerated or intensified attachment to the remaining parent or, conversely, a withdrawal from the parent, who may be blamed for the death by the child. The meaning of the parent's death often becomes distorted in the mind of the child, who usually cannot face the "voluntary" nature of suicidal death.

CHILDREN AND LOSS

The following points summarize clinical and research findings concerning children and loss:

1. Loss in childhood affects later psychological adjustment. However, it is not a simple cause-and-effect relationship; much depends on what came before and after the death.

2. Psychological vulnerability in a child is related not only to individual risk factors but also to how well a family resolves loss and regains its stability as a family.

3. A stable family environment is usually not found in cases of suicidal bereavement, either before or after the loss.

4. In traumatic grief as a result of the suicide of a parent, there is often prolonged and intense family disorganization and prolonged unresolved grief.

5. Grief therapy with children requires an understanding not only of developmental issues at the time of the loss but also of complex family processes that interfere with the grieving process.

6. A child's apparent capacity to deal with the death of a parent and to function well in the external world does not mean that the child is without internal conflicts.

7. Frequently the trauma of the immediate loss does not overwhelm the child, but subsequent minor losses or life events reactivate the unresolved original loss.

8. There can be a long time span between the actual loss and the reactivation or reexperiencing of the loss. Time is frozen in the unconscious mind of a child.

9. A child will mourn to the limit of his or her developmental capacity, then discontinue mourning until a higher level of cognitive and emotional integration is achieved, at which time mourning will be resumed.

10. A child who loses one parent becomes emotionally preoccupied with holding onto the surviving parent or parent substitutes. He or she may be constantly vigilant for any sign that some physical or psychological harm will befall that parent. Children may develop somatic complaints, become school avoidant, withdraw from peers, or act in other ways to control, protect, distract, or emotionally activate the surviving parent.

11. Children in bereaved families have difficulties with change and must deal with loss and family reorganization simultaneously. Family roles, routines, and patterns of interaction may change significantly following a death.

Acute loss in childhood triggers an array of childhood defenses including denial, repression, projection, displacement, and splitting. Wolfenstein (1969) found that defensive processes, such as repression and splitting, allow the child to both deny and acknowledge death simultaneously. Dietrich (1985) also confirms that bereaved children employ a variety of defensive operations to maintain the connection with the lost person. Sometimes, however, a child may not be able to remain emotionally connected to the memory of the deceased. Detachment (Bowlby, 1963) can serve as a defense against anger toward the lost person but has significant long-term consequences for interpersonal relationships.

Loss is both public and private in childhood; a loss can be superficially acknowledged by children in the interpersonal world while it is simultaneously denied in the intrapsychic world. Conscious fantasies may include reunion with the lost person and take the form of private communication with the deceased in order to maintain the connection. Many children report seeing the dead parent and communicating with him or her, particularly latency-age children, some of whom cannot be convinced that such "visions" are not real. Wolfenstein (1966, 1969) found that bereaved children commonly display an enduring sense of denial and repetition of aspects of the loss. Dietrich (1985) found that children repress aggression and utilize a number of defenses to handle affect overload. A continual search for the lost object is evident in repetition of aspects of the loss in children's play. Child therapists view such behavior as attempts to gain active mastery of the situation in order to make it turn out differently. Children remain deeply invested in the image of the parent for many years following the parent's death. Fleming and Altschul (1963) found that persons who were bereaved as children remain arrested in part of their emotional development. For example, a 13-year-old boy who lost his father when he was 5 confided to the therapist that he still slept with his stuffed animals and talked to them at night.

In addition to splitting of the ego (Wolfenstein, 1966), in which the child both acknowledges and denies the reality of the parent's death, children show an abundance of death-denying fantasies in play and may become preoccupied with holding onto the parent in fantasy. An example is a 13-year-old boy, whose father died when he was 6 years old, who daydreamed continually of flying fighter planes in which he and his father were the only survivors. Other children replace the lost parent through identification (Lindemann, 1944) and become "parental" or "spousal" children who assume the parents' job and fulfill their family role. Identification may be so complete that the family comes to view one of its members as the living embodiment of the deceased (Poznanski, 1972). Children most at risk may be those children in pathologically grieving families who are identified by the other family members as either being most like the deceased or as a replacement for the dead person (Walsh, 1978; Krell & Rabkin, 1979). Hilgard and Newman (1959) point to the dangers involved for a child identified with the lost parent, particularly around anniversaries, when memories of the deceased and reunion fantasies are more intense.

Grief following Suicide

General consensus seems to be that children have a limited capacity to mourn that is different from adults and is easily aborted and replaced by a variety of defensive operations, which can postpone indefinitely the process of grief. However, the grief of a child under optimal conditions is different from a child's grieving under *traumatic* conditions, particularly when the child is bereaved as a result of suicide of the parent. Children who have been traumatized by suicidal loss must remember the trauma in the process of acceptance and resolution of their loss. This engenders great anxiety. Additionally, a child will have difficulty in mourning if he or she is worried about his or her own survival or that of the surviving parent. Children who have lost a parent as a result of suicide fear further loss. In their 1982 study, Adam et al. found that suicidal trends were prominent where parental loss resulted in long-term disruption of family life. Suicide-bereaved families suffer serious and prolonged disruption of family life. Posttraumatic family reorganization is a crucial determinant of outcome for bereaved children (Hurley, 1989).

Intervention

Therapy deals with three major components simultaneously:

1. The crisis events and circumstances surrounding the death.
2. The child's emotional adjustment in the posttraumatic family.
3. Mourning the loss of the deceased.

A child's resistance to dealing with loss sometimes finds expression through the child's avoidance of dealing with the therapist. The child may at first resist therapy because the therapist, in asking probing questions, reminds the child about the dead parent. A therapist asking any question that begins with "Why" activates resistance in children whose parents have died by suicide, since this is a profoundly disturbing question for children who have not come to terms with the question themselves. Younger children have a tendency to spontaneously reenact, in play sessions, aspects of the trauma they have experienced. Play sessions are rich with emotional material that the young child struggles to comprehend. Preteen children also use play as a way to facilitate therapeutic rapport and they can also be helped to verbalize their experience directly in the session.

The therapeutic relationship establishes the conditions under which mourning can begin. In the initial assessment phase, the child protests the incursions of the therapist into his or her inner space and denies that there are feelings that bother him or her other than the therapist's questions. A typical response is, "I'm doing fine." Sooner or later the child releases other feelings (usually through play or art work, later through direct communication) and is helped to sort out the confused and contradictory feelings about the lost person.

Rutter and Hersov (1985, p. 167) caution that

> the reexperience of painful emotions is not in itself therapeutic . . . what seems important is the use of reexperience to enable children to achieve a more adaptive appraisal of what happened to them during their traumatic experiences, to regain their sense of self-efficacy and self-esteem, and to achieve effective coping mechanisms for their current life difficulties.

As therapy proceeds, the therapist tactfully challenges the child's seeming indifference by normalizing the process and helping the child see that what he or she feels is not unusual. The painful feelings that emerge are frequently projected and/or displaced. Often the child blames the therapist for causing the emotional pain. This may be a particularly difficult moment for the child therapist, who is struggling with his or her own feelings over what the child is experiencing as a result of the trauma. The process is one in which the therapist is interactive and emotionally available throughout the session. The therapist first helps the child work through the trauma of the recent events and then helps the child reconstruct a memory of the dead person that is positive. The child often selects an idealized image of the parent from early childhood. The good picture or image provides the child with a sense of well-being and positive connection with the lost person.

As therapy progresses, idealization gives way to ambivalence, and a more realistic view of the parent emerges. A teen-age girl, whose mother committed suicide, maintained an idealized view of her for the first year following her death. It was only after she failed to acknowledge the first anniversary of her mother's death that she talked for the first time of her mother's disloyalty to her father and her sense of being cheated and lied to by her mother.

Angry feelings toward the deceased are usually very disturbing for children. The child fears that he or she will not be able to tolerate the feelings once unleashed. For prelatency and latency-age children who cannot own, label, or express feelings and who are inhibited in therapy, the sessions allow the feelings symbolic expression in play. One technique to normalize the stages of grief for the child uses a metaphor such as a train and railway station in which the railway stations are the stages of grief at which the train (child) must stop for a while in order to work through the loss (Hurley, 1987). For the preteen child, play facilitates direct communication and working through in progressively less symbolic ways.

In therapy, a pattern of "discontinuous mourning" can occur in which the child may terminate the mourning process prematurely and close off the opportunity for further work until a later time. This conforms to a developmental view of grief in which the child is helped to mourn to the limit of his or her developmental capacity.

PROCESS OF THERAPY

1. *Week in Review.* The child therapist shows concern and interest in the child by reviewing details of the previous session and by providing a sense of continuity between sessions. The reasons as well as the process of therapy are clearly stated, and the child is invited to select the play materials or games.

2. *Maintaining rapport.* The child therapist maintains continuity from session to session by creating a predictable structure for the session and by developing themes from week to week. The child therapist looks for death themes that are communicated repeatedly in verbal and symbolic ways.

3. *Affect Attunement.* The child therapist tunes into the child's immediate experience and makes an empathic connection before exploring the issue of loss. The therapist looks for missing affect and encourages the child to uncover what is being avoided in the session.

4. *Clarification.* Affect and cognitions are repeatedly clarified. Where possible, defenses are acknowledged but not directly challenged. Defenses such as denial, displacement, splitting, idealization, projection, and isolation of affect are accepted by the therapist as understandable and necessary.

5. *Working Through.* When death themes are identified, denial can easily be triggered. It is not usually the denial of the circumstances of the death itself that is avoided as much as the denial of the impact of the loss on the child. The therapist facilitates the working-through process by maintaining an emotional connection with the child and keeping the focus on important themes.

THE CASE: CATHY, AGE 4½

Family Information

Cathy lives with her mother, Mrs. Johnson (34), and two older brothers, Richard (12) and John (8), in a small community. Cathy was referred with her siblings 1 month after the suicidal death of her father. The father had been seriously depressed for 3 months prior to his death and had been admitted to a local psychiatric hospital. He had recently lost money on a major financial investment which had serious consequences for his business.

Mrs. Johnson said that her husband responded poorly to psychiatric medication and that he felt a burden to the family. While in the psychiatric hospital, Mr. Johnson was diagnosed as suffering from a psychotic depression with paranoid features. He shot himself outside the home while on leave from the hospital. Since the death of her husband, Mrs. Johnson reported feeling unhappy and insecure and was receiving "nerve pills" from her family doctor. At the time of the referral Mrs. Johnson stated that she needed help in dealing with her children. The two boys were fighting continually and were rude and disobedient with her, although neither of them had reacted initially to their father's death.

Presenting Problem

Cathy was referred because of her crying and clinging behavior. She was the only one of the children to express any sadness at the loss of her father. John, the middle child, was reported to be the most aggressive of the three children but had always been somewhat physical with both his sister and brother. Mrs. Johnson said that her husband was typically quiet and withdrawn but could be ill-tempered at times. Mrs. Johnson reported herself to be open, straightforward, and increasingly more assertive, especially in the last year of the marriage. Mrs. Johnson reported that the marriage had been a happy one and that her husband's psychiatric problems resulted from serious financial difficulties in his business.

Initial Family Assessment

The assessment team (comprised of a crisis family therapist, a play therapist, and a psychometrist) noted that mother seemed quite functional at the beginning of the session but became increasingly more disorganized as the interview progressed. They also noted that Richard, the eldest, was a sensitive and observant reporter of family events. Richard was said to be suffering from anxiety and disturbing nightmares. John's angry behavior was considered a response to the loss of the father and an expression of his anxiety about the level of dysfunction in the family. He was viewed by all family members as being most identified with father.

There was strong denial and suppression of feelings about the father's death in the session, and a good deal of rationalization about his "sacrifice" on behalf of the family. It was noted that the family belief system incorporated the idea that psychiatric input had been unhelpful to the father and might have contributed to his death. (This is a particularly important point to consider when engaging suicide survivors in the therapeutic process.)

Mrs. Johnson had become extremely busy since the death of her husband and was occupying herself with activities outside of the home. The two boys reported that Cathy was spending more time playing alone with her dolls and was continually crying. She was very attached to her Cabbage Patch doll, saying "I love you" repeatedly to the doll. She had done this more since the father's death. She sulked continually and cried when watching television. Additionally, since the death of her father, Cathy insisted on sleeping with her mother. Previously, Cathy had occasionally slept with the parents. Two months after her father's death, Cathy spent a few days at the home of a close relative but telephoned upset and asked to come home. Cathy was described by John as a nonstop talker who was very "hyper." He said that whenever mother was home, Cathy spent every second of the day with her and attempted to keep mother to herself. Richard, the eldest son, oscillated between being protective of Cathy and annoyed with her for her clingy behavior with the mother. Cathy was considered the closest of the three children to the father. After the father's death, Cathy said to her mother, "Why did Dad play that trick on us? . . . He said he wouldn't take off, and he did. . . . He kept on saying he wanted to go back to the hospital."

The basic goals of therapy following the initial session were (1) to strengthen the mother's position in the family and help her cope with the changes in her life and (2) to prepare the children for grief work.

Interventions

In addition to individual play therapy and weekly family therapy sessions (both of which lasted approximately 1½ years), Mrs. Johnson and the children were involved in a home behavior program to help the mother deal with their behavior more effectively. This was a token system with positive consequences that, for Cathy, included such items as morning hygiene, making her bed, doing a chore, being in bed by a certain time, and sleeping in her own bed. This program was discontinued after a month because of the mother's inability to positively reinforce the children for compliant behavior and because she could not maintain consistency on basic house rules. Mother considered the weekends as "holidays," and she was unable or unwilling to administer the home behavior program consistently. She continued to have difficulty planning and organizing around the children's needs.

In therapy sessions, Mrs. Johnson continued to minimize the loss of her husband and the effects of his death on the family. The eldest son was clearly parentified and was anxious about his mother's well-being. Mother reported that she hated being single and wanted to be married. She said that she has always had to keep busy and that she could not stand being alone. Mrs. Johnson later settled into a relationship with a man with two children. This relationship improved her outlook considerably, and she pursued it with vigor and enthusiasm. Because of this, and because of the nature of her personality, the team decided not to pursue individual psychotherapy for the mother but instead to concentrate on the children's therapeutic needs.

Summary of Interventions

1. A behavior management program for the mother that included six sessions with a behavior therapist.

2. Bereavement counseling for the family, particularly to help the mother begin dealing with loss.
3. Voluntary supervision of the children in the home with a child welfare agency (recommended).
4. Individual play therapy sessions for Cathy and *ad hoc* individual sessions with both boys.
5. Family therapy with the reconstituted family.

Process of Play Therapy

Play therapy sessions took place on a weekly basis. Cathy was seen by a female play therapist[1] in the playroom. Cathy was also involved in family therapy sessions for approximately 1 year.

Initial Session

Cathy came to the playroom easily and talked to the therapist spontaneously about her home life and about missing her father. She remarked that they watched television together, that she would sit on his lap or lie on the couch together. Cathy said that she had some bad dreams but that "One was happy." This was a dream in which "Daddy came out of the coffin," which she said happened "*before* Daddy died." She said that he was standing there stiff and demonstrated this in the session. She said that another dream was scary, but she did not think it would make her feel better to talk about it. She did not talk about it in the session except to say that only she and Daddy were in it. She then picked up a mask from the floor, which she said she did not like because it had no hair. She remarked that "Daddy had lots of hair on his head" and that she liked him "because he was nice."

The therapist said, "Where do you think Daddy is now?" She said, "Heaven." The therapist said, "Do you think he'll ever come back?" She said, "No." She later said, "Yes," then acknowledged, after some clarification, that he would not come back, but she wished he would. "Mommy misses him too. . . . She wants him back too." Cathy said that she cried sometimes but did not feel better afterwards.

Cathy then took a doll and washed it and said how she liked it washed. It seemed very important for Cathy to arrange all the dolls properly in the playroom and to have them all in bed before leaving the playroom. She said that she wanted them to be sound asleep in bed. During this play, Cathy said that she knew how her daddy had died but that her mommy said she did not want her to talk about it. The therapist reassured her about the confidentiality in the session and asked her

[1]I wish to express my appreciation to the play therapist, Ms. Marilyn Brown, who worked with Cathy during her field placement at the Child and Adolescent Centre in London, Ontario, and who assisted with the preparation of this transcript.

if she would like to talk about it. She said that she would, but she could not because her mother said not to.

In summary, the session involved spontaneous play and high verbal content on Cathy's part. She showed appropriate affect in talking about her father, and she seemed to be trying to distinguish the wish for her father to return from the reality of his death. The dream she says she had before he died was really after he died, but he was alive in the dream, so she described it as a "dream when Daddy was here." The therapist was concerned, however, that the child felt inhibited in discussing the manner of her father's death. This needed to be clarified with the mother before the next session.

Session 2

The session began with Cathy acting silly and giggling for no apparent reason.

Content of Session	Rationale/Analysis
THERAPIST: You seem happy today. Are you happy?	
CHILD: No!	Some confusion over what she feels, and perhaps anxiety about entering the playroom.
T: You looked happy . . . but you don't feel happy?	
C: No!	
T: You feel sad?	
C: Yes. (*Laughs and changes subject.*)	The therapist tries to tune in to the child's affect.
T: Where do the giggles come from?	
C: I get them from my babysitter.	
T: Is she a nice babysitter?	
C: Yeah, she is a nice babysitter. I go there every day after nursery school. (*Picks up doll and begins to wash it carefully, paying special attention to the hair, which she rinses in three different basins.*)	A positive identification with caretaking function or a projection of her own need to be taken care of?
T: Do you like nursery school? . . . Have you lots of friends there?	
C: I got lots of friends to play with. (*Looks around for doll from last week.*) Is this the same dress she had on last week? No it's not! (*emphatically*) There it is. (*Cathy then comments on this and on other differences that she has noticed in the playroom. She then begins to play with Plasticine.*) This is just for me to play with . . . not you.	It seems Cathy was looking for her place in the playroom and needed the security of knowing that it would remain essentially unchanged. She may have wanted the therapist to keep some distance and to be in control herself.

T: Is it only for children, not grown-ups?

C: Yeah, I'm making cookie faces. (*She makes five of them in all, with the last one having only one eye and no mouth.*)

T: You're making five faces just like five people in your family . . . with all the parts of their faces.

The therapist (in retrospect) felt that she (the therapist) was moving too fast.

C: This one is much more messy . . . it had all the face parts.

T: Can you say who all the faces are . . . ?

C: I don't know them. I don't know who they are (*Cathy then puts the faces in the bottom of the bowl and throws more Plasticine pieces in on top. She covers the bowl with a piece of paper and then leaves the table and goes over to the water box. She then returns to the bowl, takes out all the Plasticine, and looks for the faces.*) I can't find them all now . . . this is broken . . . they're all messed up. (*Cathy then rolls the Plasticine roughly into one big ball.*) I want to leave the playroom now.

She seems to find the play disturbing and wants to block it out. However, she is not able to do that effectively, and so she returns to the Plasticine.

She wants to block it out and get away from the unpleasant things.

T: It seems you want to leave the playroom now . . . we still have time left to play!

C: (*Stands up and walks quietly over to the sand table, where she is to spend the next 15 minutes. She begins to finger the sand absentmindedly while looking over at the doll house. While fingering the sand, she finds a man buried in the sand.*) Look, I found a man in here.

T: You're surprised to find a man buried in the sand.

C: (*Her attention focuses completely on the sand table now, her eyes focused, and body turned. She proceeds with intent and with a sense of anxious excitement to check the sand very thoroughly with her fingers for more buried men but does not find another. She leans down and picks up a box of army-type men and tanks and dumps them into the sand. She is silent as she works to clear all the sand aside, and, as she works, it becomes apparent to the therapist she is making room for the box to fit.*) I'm making a place for the box to stay.

T: You want it to have a spot there. (*Cathy then takes the tanks out of the sand and places them carefully in the box. With much effort, she piles up the sand and smoothes it up against the box,*

The therapist is aware of the purposefulness of this work and her intense efforts to make it just as she wants it.

wedging and blending it into the sandbox.) It seems you're really working to smooth the sand up to hold the box in place. It's almost like a mountain.

C: (*with pride*) You can see that right! (*She then picks up some of the figures and carefully covers them up with sand with a look of satisfaction.*)

T: Some of the people are buried.

C: Yeah . . . so they can't come out.

T: You want to be sure that they stay buried and no one will dig them up . . . like people in a cemetery are buried and they don't get dug up.

C: Like my dad. He's inside the coffin.

T: In the ground, and no one can dig it up. It stays there in the ground. Is your dad buried in a cemetery too?

The therapist sees this as an opportunity to proceed to talk about her beliefs about her father's death.

C: I think so . . .

T: Where is your dad now?

C: His spirit goes from his body.

T: Where?

C: To heaven.

T: And what about his body?

C: It's in the ground. It's in the ground inside the coffin. The coffin stays in the ground buried. I'd like to see it again.

T: You'd like to see it again, but you can't. That makes us sad sometimes.

C: (*Cathy's affect has been serious throughout this conversation but not visibly upset. She is still standing beside the sand table, fingering the sand. She looks at the sand and then the therapist intermittently. After a moment or two of silence . . .*) I'm finished in the playroom now. I'll have to wash my hands.

The therapist, at this point, feels an excitement and satisfaction in beginning to work through the issue of the death with this child.

T: OK, that's fine.

C: (*still fingering the sand*) It stays in the ground, and we can't see it any more.

T: Sometimes it makes us sad when someone we love is dead and we can't see them any more.

C: (*Leaves the playroom and returns to her mother in the waiting room.*)

The therapist also feels some sadness for Cathy as she says she wants to see the coffin again but cannot. The therapist admires the child's candidness and the way that this 4-year-old is learning to put together the pieces of the puzzle of understanding death.

In reviewing the session, the therapist was impressed with how hard the child had worked to come to terms with the reality of her father's death. Repetition of aspects of the trauma were evident throughout her play, and she was able to communicate symbolically about her fears. The therapist attempted to mirror the child's concerns and remained attuned throughout the session to deeper conflicts that the child was experiencing. The therapist was pleased that some closure was achieved by the end of the session and that the child felt empowered to bring the session to a close.

Session 3

In the next session 2 weeks later, the following interchange took place.

Content of Session	Rationale/Analysis
CHILD: (*playing absentmindedly with Plasticine*) I miss my dad but he won't come back, will he?	The child is still trying to come to terms with the meaning of death.
THERAPIST: You feel sad that you can't see him any more? . . .	The therapist is a little reluctant to respond directly.
C: My mom is sad too. . . . She cries, but I tell her it's OK . . . 'cause I don't like to see her cry. (*She continues to play with the Plasticine and talks about her father and that she is not allowed to say that he shot himself.*)	She is less vulnerable when she takes care of mother.
T: It's OK for you to talk to me about it.	Keeping secrets is an important issue in the family.
C: Yeah, I know . . .	
T: Do you know why he died?	
C: No! I think he just wanted to.	The therapist is probing to see whether there is any blame or guilt.
T: Do you think it was anyone's fault or that anyone did something bad to Dad?	
C: I don't think there was anything bad. (*Cathy then makes a face with Plasticine and comments on the mixed colors she is using. She then makes a nose with flattened pieces and digs into it with the scissors, stabbing it while talking about father shooting himself. She also pounds flat Plasticine and uses scissors to carve out the eyes and the mouth.*) Look, it's not alive if it has no eyes or mouth or nose. (*She then puts those back on the face and starts to make another figure.*)	By playing in this way, she gains some mastery over her fears.
T: Who is it you're making?	
C: My brother. He's mad at himself. My dad used	

to spank him. (*She then proceeds to flatten the Plasticine by stepping on the pieces.*)

First inkling that maybe someone is to blame.

C: This is my brother's body. . . .

T: Do you think he's been bad?

The therapist is probing to see what her associations might be.

C: (*whisper*) Yeah.

T: Do you think he is to blame?

C: (*Puts the Plasticine down and avoids touching it for the rest of the session. She then starts to wash and brush the doll's hair.*) I don't want to say any more.

Clearly, she is upset by what the play is invoking and by the therapist's questions.

T: Maybe you think your dad was mean to your brother . . . or your brother made your dad upset?

The therapist wants to stay with this issue to see what meaning it has for the child.

C: (*standing up, signaling her wish to leave*) Sometimes I don't want to come here.

T: I know it must be hard for you to talk about these things. OK, let's leave it 'til next time.

The child feels intruded on by the therapist and responds by withdrawing from her and the play situation.

Although this is just a fragment of the session, it reveals the serious dilemma for the child and therapist when the parent cannot tolerate a discussion about the dead parent. It leaves the issue of guilt and blame unresolved, with the possibility that deeper emotional processes will remain hidden in the family. There is some evidence in this session that the child is beginning to express anger about the loss of her father and perhaps indicate who she feels is responsible for his death or what circumstances may have contributed to his death. When these ideas and feelings are revealed in therapy, the child is helped to gain some emotional resolution and some cognitive reappraisal of her feelings.

Summary

At the termination of therapy 1½ years after her father's death, Cathy was to start full-time kindergarten. Cathy was reported to be looking after her own care more, to be crying less, and to be more independent of her mother. She was reported to be answering the telephone, brushing her own hair, and helping mother with chores around the home. At the time of termination of therapy, the most pressing issue was the problem of blending the children in the newly reconstituted family.

CONCLUDING COMMENTS

This case reveals a number of important issues for the child therapist working with traumatically bereaved children. Obviously, there are differences in how children express their concerns through play therapy, and although many issues are revealed in the play session, not all are resolved. Clearly, the family's response to the child's attempts at mourning affects what the child will express and how the child will express it.

The case illustrates the traumatically bereaved child's attempt to make sense of her experience and gain mastery over a very critical life event (A. Freud, 1967). Pruett (1984) underlines the importance of understanding the child's idiosyncratic psychic solutions to traumatic events that affect the child's "implicit view of life both in external reality and of the self" (p. 609). This case very clearly indicates how a young child in play therapy struggles to understand the meaning of death, the prohibitions in the family about discussing suicide, and the resultant fear and anxiety for child survivors.

Bereavement in childhood seems to follow the course of adult bereavement, although in more compressed and somewhat less intense phases. The therapeutic work often occurs in short bursts rather than in sustained intensive work. However, childhood defenses are more active, and denial is more frequently and extensively employed by children than by bereaved adults. Children who show prolonged periods of anger and depression, however, can work these through in therapy. I agree with Furman (1973) that a young child has the capacity to mourn if the circumstances allow. In suicidal bereavement, the child has great difficulty beginning the task of mourning because emotional disturbances and confused affects complicate the loss. Frequently, the suicide is the culmination of a number of years of extreme family stress, particularly pathological marital relationships.

In families in which suicide occurs, family myths concerning the deceased help maintain a precarious homeostasis. The tendency of families to replace reality with myth can greatly affect the course of bereavement in children and requires continual clarification in child therapy sessions.

A grief therapist provides a place where a child can safely explore his or her feelings without loss of self-esteem, overwhelming anxiety, or catastrophic reexperience. Children can be helped to do some of the grief work in the present rather than postpone it for many years, sometimes leading to the development of a false self. The emotional climate necessary to do the work is cocreated by the grief therapist and the child.

PLAY THERAPY MATERIALS

- Sand box
- Water basin
- Doll house with furniture (Fisher-Price), little people
- Table with Plasticine, crayons, paper, scissors
- Kitchen refrigerator, cupboards, oven, dishes
- Medical kit
- Ball
- Set of cardboard puppet faces

- Various puppets
- Puppet theatre
- Chalkboard and chalk
- Army men and tanks of two colors

STUDY QUESTIONS

1. In what way did the trauma of suicide interfere with the grieving process for this child? What developmental issues should the therapist consider in relation to the grief of a 4½-year-old child?

2. How realistic is it to expect a child to work through conflicts associated with traumatic loss in a family that cannot allow normal grieving? Is the child psychotherapist expecting too much of a child in therapy when the surviving parent's psychological functioning is impaired?

3. When is it advisable to involve the siblings in treatment, and what are the likely problems for therapists when children are involved simultaneously in individual treatment as well as family counseling?

REFERENCES

Adam, K. (1973). Childhood parental loss, suicidal ideation and suicidal behavior. In E. J. Anthony & C. Koupernik (Eds.), *The child and his family: The impact of disease and death* (pp. 275–297). New York: John Wiley & Sons.

Adam, K., Lohrenz, J., Harper, D., & Steiner, D. (1982). Early parental loss and suicidal ideation in university students. *Canadian Journal of Psychiatry, 27,* 275–281.

Barnes, G., & Prosen, H. (1985). Parental death and depression. *Journal of Abnormal Psychology, 94,* 64–69.

Bowlby, J. (1963). Pathological mourning and childhood mourning. *Journal of the American Psychoanalytic Association, 11,* 500–541.

Brown, G., & Harris, T. (1978). *The social origins of depression: A study of psychiatric disorder in women.* London: Tavistock Publications.

Brown, G. W., Harris, T. O., & Bifulco, A. (1986). Long-term effects of early loss of a parent. In M. Rutter, C. Izard, & P. Read (Eds.), *Depression in young people: Developmental and clinical perspectives* (pp. 251–296). New York: Guilford Press.

Dietrich, D. R. (1984). Psychological health of young adults who experienced early parent death: MMPI trends. *Journal of Clinical Psychology, 40,* 901–908.

Dietrich, D. R. (1985). The bereaved child's psychological health several years later. In G. Paterson (Ed.), *Children and death: Proceedings of the 1985 King's College Conference, London, Ontario* (pp. 91–100). London, Ontario: King's College Publication.

Elizur, E., & Kaffman, M. (1982). Children's bereavement reactions following death of the father: II. *Journal of the American Academy of Child Psychiatry, 21,* 474–480.

Eth, S., & Pynoos, R. S. (Eds.). (1985). *Post-traumatic stress disorder in children.* Washington, DC: American Psychiatric Press.

Fleming, J., & Altschul, S. (1963). Activation of mourning and growth by psychoanalysis. *International Journal of Psycho-Analysis, 44,* 419–431.

Freud, A. (1967). Comments on trauma. In S. S. Furst (Ed.), *Psychic trauma* (pp. 235–245). New York: Basic Books.

Furman, R. (1973). A child's capacity for mourning. In E. J. Anthony & C. Koupernik (Eds.), *The child in his family: The impact of disease and death* (pp. 225–231). New York: John Wiley & Sons.

Hilgard, J. R., & Newman, M. F. (1959). Anniversaries in mental illness. *Psychiatry, 22,* 113–121.

Hurley, D. J. (1987). *Child therapy following the homicidal or suicidal death of a parent.* Paper presented at the 37th annual meeting of the Canadian Psychiatric Association meeting, London, Ontario.

Hurley, D. J. (1989, June 21). *Family therapy following the homicide or suicide death of a parent.* Paper presented at the First World Family Therapy Congress, Dublin, Ireland.

Krell, R., & Rabkin, L. (1979). The effects of sibling death on the surviving child: A family perspective. *Family Process, 18,* 471–479.

Lindemann, E. (1944). The symptomatology and management of acute grief. *American Journal of Psychiatry, 101,* 171.

Moustakas, C. E. (1959). *Psychotherapy with children: The living relationship.* New York: Ballantine Books.

Poznanski, E. O. (1972). The replacement child: A saga of unresolved parental grief. *Journal of Pediatrics, 81,* 1190–1193.

Pruett, K. D. (1984). A chronology of defensive adaptions to severe psychological trauma. *Psychoanalytic Study of the Child, 39,* 591–612.

Rutter, M., & Hersov, L. (Eds.). (1985). *Child and adolescent psychiatry: Modern approaches* (2nd ed.). London: Blackwell Scientific Publications.

Walsh, F. W. (1978). Concurrent grandparent death and birth of schizophrenic offspring: An intriguing finding. *Family Process, 17,* 457–465.

Wolfenstein, M. (1966). How is mourning possible? *Psychoanalytic Study of the Child, 21,* 93–123.

Wolfenstein, M. (1969). Loss, rage and repetition. *Psychoanalytic Study of the Child, 24,* 432–462.

Wolkind, S., & Rutter, M. (1985). Separation, loss, and family relationships. In M. Rutter & L. Hersov (Eds.), *Child and adolescent psychiatry: Modern approaches* (2nd ed., pp. 34–58). Oxford: Blackwell Scientific Publications.

CHAPTER 13

School-Based Peer Therapy to Facilitate Mourning in Latency-Age Children following Sudden Parental Death

JOYCE BLUESTONE

The death of a parent is a tragic and excruciating experience for a child. Children often perceive parents as fountains of love and as their major stable, safe ground in an ever-shifting and sometimes hostile world. Therefore, the death of such a loved one leaves the bereft child with a world that may never again be as secure and safe a place as it was before.

Sandra Sutherland Fox (1985, p. 16) states that "children who experience the death of a parent or sibling have been reported to be at risk for emotional disorders in adult life." Unresolved grief can potentially interfere with a child's emotional and intellectual development.

This chapter's case illustration involves two middle-latency-age children (9½ and 10½). Latency-age children accept the finality of death, and they know that people die and do not return. However, they may not accept that death happens universally, and particularly to themselves. Fox (1985, p. 11) states that

> latency children see death in a personified way—as a ghost or angel or space creature, for example—as something that can come and get you. They believe that death can happen to others, particularly the elderly and handicapped, because they cannot run fast and therefore cannot escape when death comes for them. Most children, therefore, don't die because they can run very fast.

As children move into preadolescence, they begin to recognize that death is inevitable and final and that it will one day happen to them. Although the child intellectually reaches this mature understanding of death, he or she is still struggling psychologically with this concept of finality.

The literature reports (Doyle, 1980; Grollman, 1967; Weizman & Kamm, 1985) that there are three stages in the grieving process experienced by children as well as adults. In the first phase, the typical reactions are shock, protest, anger, and disbelief. The bereaved cannot believe that the person is dead. Often children remain in this stage of denial for several years by continuing the protest, anger at the separation, and refusal to face the finality of the loss. The second stage is one of intense emotion in which the bereaved experiences pain, despair, and disorganization. It is a period of fierce separation anxiety. The last stage is the period of final adaptation. The bereaved begins to organize his or her life without the dead person and seeks new situations with increased ease and feels hopeful and optimistic about her or his future.

The functions of the school social worker include identification, assessment, and resolution of social and emotional difficulties of pupils that interfere with their adjustment and achievement in school. This responsibility includes counseling services—either individual or peer play therapy or group therapy. He or she assists parents to better understand themselves and their children and advises them about school and community programs and services; collaborates and communicates with school staff to help them work more effectively with the children; and plays a distinctive role in the school as the centerpiece of a coordinated system responsive to the needs of troubled students (Johnson & Maile, 1987, p. 230).

In the case discussed, the tasks of the school social worker comprise aiding the latency-age child's development into preadolescence and also dealing with the psychological trauma concerning the death of a parent.

MOURNING IN LATENCY

It is my belief, along with that of child experts (Fox, 1985; Furman, 1974; Grollman, 1967), that the latency-age child has the capacity to mourn and grieve. Yet, because of their special and unique needs, children require reassurance that they will "be taken care of" before they can address themselves to the mourning task.

The mourning process for children is a very gradual, agonizing process. It takes many years to mourn and integrate a loss because children can tolerate only small doses of painful feelings. Children look to adults as role models who will provide guidance and give them permission to grieve openly. The surviving parent or parent surrogate is critical in a child's ability to grieve.

Grieving children frequently express their feelings in indirect, delayed, and disguised ways. They express their grief behaviorally—for example, mischievously, aggressively, rebelliously, by withdrawing, or by displacing their feelings onto undeserving adults. Children need adults to help them attach language to their feelings, to help them begin to understand and grasp the grieving process.

Children experience a range of strong feelings that can overwhelm them when their parent dies, such as anger, sadness, fear, helplessness, guilt, idealizing the deceased, and feeling cheated and regretful. Often children continue to hope for the parent's return, and they may have thoughts and fantasies of reuniting with the lost parent. Children's timetable for grieving differs from that of adults; for example, they may experience shock and denial for a longer duration as a way of protecting themselves from the pain. Feelings of anger, sadness, and guilt often are undifferentiated and confused. Because of this misunderstanding, the child may channel all of these painful emotions through anger and thereby exaggerate and prolong the grief process.

Children may need help to keep their memories alive and conscious because their tendency is to bury them because they are intensely painful. Weizman and Kamm (1985, p. 174) report that "memories are essential for the mourning process due to the individual's need to experience the attachment to the deceased and then separate gradually."

To summarize, adults who are dealing with a latency-age child traumatized by the death of a parent must try to create an atmosphere in which the bereaved child can express attitudes and emotions freely, unhindered by the typical, and usually detrimental, social taboos against such expression.

While keeping in mind the uniquely painful character of the crisis of parental loss, the school social worker should approach this crisis as an opportunity for growth. Confining expectation to age-appropriate levels, the social worker should understand the following special needs of the youthful mourner:

1. The need for security.
2. The child's low tolerance for psychological pain.
3. The need for adult role models.
4. The possibility for suppression and confusion of feelings because of a lack of vocabulary and conceptual development.
5. The need to preserve and foster memories of the deceased.

The case presented involves two girls, each of whom had a parent who died. Cindy is a fifth grader (10½ years old) whose father died suddenly and unexpectedly from a heart attack 2 years ago. Rosa is a fourth grader (9½ years old) whose mother committed suicide by shooting herself.

The death of their parents has been a traumatic experience for Cindy and Rosa. Both have had to deal with the extra burden of the suddenness of their parents' deaths. Their feelings of shock, denial, and disbelief have been extremely intense and contribute to their sense that the respective deaths were wrong and inappropriate.

The suicide has uniquely affected Rosa's ability to integrate her loss. The suicide bereaved may potentially be overwhelmed by thoughts of guilt, blame, shame, horror, anger, rage, or desire for vengeance.

DEVELOPMENTAL TASKS OF LATENCY

An overview of the normal developmental tasks for the latency-age child is particularly helpful in understanding the special value of peer-pairing as an effective therapeutic technique for the latency-age child.

Cameron (1963, p. 79) states that

> the phase of latency occurs when the small child emerges from his home into the wider community, specifically, upon entrance into school. The major social

change in latency is that, while still a member of his family group, the child goes forth alone into the world outside his family, expands his physical and social horizons, and supplements membership in his own family with membership in groups outside it.

Lieberman (1979, p. 98) states, "Cooperation, loyalty, gangs, cliques and organized games are the stuff of middle latency—the age of socialization outside the family." The immediate society of the neighborhood and school exert a major influential force in the developing self-concept of latency-age children. They learn to see themselves as others see them and often according to rather harsh standards.

Simultaneously, the best-friend or special-chum phenomenon becomes an intense and important experience. This relationship usually constitutes the child's first attachment outside the family (Sarnoff, 1978).

Cognitive growth is reflected in the child's play and socialization skills. The latency-age child's play is realistic, constructive, logical, objective, and organized. When socializing with others, the middle-latency-age child can now differentiate between different views and needs; he or she can also consider several viewpoints simultaneously. Socialization is a critical task for the 9- and 10-year-old child. Good socialization skills and positive peer experience encourage strong self-image, solid identity, and intact character formation.

In the case, both Cindy and Rosa have had longstanding problems relating to others. Both girls felt socially isolated, which was exaggerated for each of them by their parents' deaths. Cindy and Rosa's painful task of grieving was superimposed on social adjustment difficulties. Thus, the chosen therapeutic modality was peer-pairing, which in a supportive environment encourages increased social skills and self-esteem and at the same time fosters a developing friendship. This approach is beneficial when group or individual therapy proves to be too overwhelming or threatening.

Mervis (1985, p. 125) states that

pairing is also effective in working with children who feel they are very different from others or who have severe family problems. These children need the opportunity to share feelings and experiences, but it can be too risky to expose them to a group setting in which they might be vulnerable to ridicule or rejection. Through peer-pairing, the children gradually can learn to trust others and to share some of their feelings and experiences in a more controlled and accepting environment. When the sharing becomes mutual, the sense of shame and isolation these children feel can be greatly reduced.

PLAY THERAPY IN THE SCHOOL

In my role as a school social worker, I use play therapy to help children express and understand their feelings. Play is the child's natural way of expressing him- or herself, and play therapy allows the child to communicate in his or her own language. Since children do not easily express their emotions, play helps the child master the conflict, trauma, or anxious situation in his or her life through the act of repetition. Freud termed this the phenomenon of "repetition compulsion," which is the need to relive, again and again, a painful memory. Freud (1914/1958) maintained that the individual unconsciously recreates situations using the conflicted theme as an attempt to gain mastery over the original overwhelming situation. The frequency of the reenactment coincides with the intensity of the trauma.

The child acts out the trauma over and over again in his or her play, and this reenactment relieves tension and leads to catharsis. When this occurs symbolically in a displaced fashion, the child does not have to claim responsibility for his or her actions or feelings ("it's only make-believe"). This potential for catharsis is especially applicable to fantasy play in the form of puppetry. The use of puppetry allows children to grapple with unresolved conflicts and issues in a way in which they can act out or dictate all the parts to be played, trying out different roles, strategies, and outcomes. Puppetry is safe, displaced fun, and the puppets themselves are intriguing and inviting.

The role of the school social worker in puppetry play sometimes takes the form of audience/observer while the child puts on a show with the puppets. The worker may assume a nondirective role and allow the child to play out the scene, deriving therapeutic value from whatever catharsis may occur as the youngster plays out conflictual material. In a different approach the social worker actively participates in the show, taking a turn herself with the puppets and using this opportunity to play out the conflicts presented by the child in a more "therapeutic" form.

Rosa and Cindy were able to express their emotions related to their grieving process through the use of puppetry, drawings, and their spontaneous interactions within the context of their friendship.

In summary, play therapy within the framework of peer-pairing can meet the needs of grieving latency-age children. It creates a safe environment of peer support (friendship) in which each child validates the "normality" of the other's experience of grief and expression of emotion. It also opens up the possibility of subtle therapeutic leadership in the untangling of confused emotions while encouraging the open expression of suppressed emotions. The children gain an element of control through the play activity that provides an ideal setting for the fostering and maintenance of memories of the deceased through shared stories.

THE CASES: CINDY V, AGE 10½ , AND ROSA T, AGE 9½

Cindy

Family Information

Cindy V, age 10½, is in the fifth grade. Mrs. V, her mother, 54 years old, is a full-time homemaker and child care provider for neighborhood children. Two older sisters, ages 25 and 26, live outside of the home.

Presenting Problem

Cindy's father died 2 years ago from a heart attack. Mr. V did not have a history of illness, and his death was very sudden and unanticipated. A couple of months after Mr. V's death, Cindy's oldest sister's baby died at birth, and a friend of the family died as well.

Cindy has a history in her school career of being extremely shy in the classroom setting. Also, since second grade, her teachers have expressed concern about Cindy's weaknesses in reading comprehension and difficulty following directions. The crisis compounds Cindy's withdrawn behavior in the classroom setting and her academic difficulties.

Background

As the school social worker, I counseled Cindy individually and weekly during her fourth-grade year beginning shortly after her father's death. In conjunction with working with Cindy, I counseled and collaborated with Mrs. V and Cindy's teacher. The major treatment issues were developing a therapeutic alliance, encouraging her to grieve openly, fostering assertive behavior, and working with Cindy and Mrs. V to separate more appropriately.

The school psychologist tested Cindy because of her academic difficulties. The results suggested impaired intellectual functioning and a significant amount of psychological tension related to feelings of both anger and sadness.

Cindy expressed anger often and a need to be in control during the counseling sessions. I validated, normalized, and empathized with these feelings and, at times, tentatively connected her anger directly to her father's death. I also used "play" to support and explain her emotions. For example, Cindy enjoyed playing the game "Battleship." In this game, one does not know where the opponent's ships are placed, and the object of the game is to seek out and "bomb" your opponent's ships. Throughout the game, I emphasized life's unpredictability as experienced in surprise attacks and bombers coming without warning. My purpose was to symbolically validate her experience about the suddenness of her father's death and also reassure her that she is a survivor and that most people live into late life.

Cindy had become sensitized to loss and feared her mother's death or disappearance. Children who have lost one parent through death frequently fear the loss of the other parent. Both Cindy and Mrs. V had significant separation problems that became accentuated following the death. Cindy and Mrs. V were sleeping in the same bed. I worked with both of them to encourage separate sleeping, relieving Mrs. V's guilt and reassuring Cindy about her fears.

Addressing Cindy's tendencies to be withdrawn, particularly in the classroom setting, I encouraged and coached her to practice being assertive with her teacher by asking for help and participating in classroom discussions.

The following school year, I continued individual counseling with Cindy. During the summer, Cindy's maternal grandmother died from a long-term illness, and Cindy's sister ran away from home, telling no one of her whereabouts. Cindy and I had two sessions together, and then Cindy told her mother that she did not want to continue counseling. Mrs. V contacted me to let me know that Cindy did not want to continue, but it was unclear why Cindy was withdrawing at this point.

Recalling the last session together, I believe I threatened Cindy by raising family concerns too directly and too soon. Without realizing it, I had spoken about a "family secret" (sister's plight).

I subsequently spoke with Cindy in a nonthreatening manner about what I labeled "a misunderstanding", stating, "It's OK to be angry at me; let's try to work it out," but she was not responsive. For several weeks, I continued to reach out to Cindy in a nonthreatening way through casual contact in the school hallway and letter writing, but her resistance did not soften.

Rosa

Family Information

Rosa T., age 9½ is, in the fourth grade. Since Rosa's mother died, Rosa lives with Uncle Al (mother's brother), 24 years old, a custodian, and Aunt Carol, 25 years old, a sales clerk who is 6 months pregnant.

Rosa eats dinner almost every night and on weekends with Mr. T., her father, 36 years old, a gardener. The parents had been separated for 1 year prior to the suicide. Rosa is picked up from school and spends weekday afternoons until dinner hour with Grandma and Grandpa (mother's parents). The grandparents moved to New York to help take care of Rosa after mother's death.

The family has agreed that Rosa will be living full-time with her father, and maternal grandparents will be helping with child care in the next school year.

Presenting Problem

Rosa's mother committed suicide by shooting herself at the beginning of the school year. Rosa's past school history included problems with peers, feeling isolated and at times scapegoated.

The family was in shock following Mrs. T's suicide, and they decided to tell Rosa her mother died from an overdose of pills. Mrs. T had been psychiatrically hospitalized prior to her suicide and had expressed suicidal thoughts daily, indicating that she would take sleeping pills to kill herself. The school is located in a small community. The adage "Bad news travels fast" applies here, and some children cruelly taunted Rosa by saying, "Your mother shot herself." When Rosa questioned her aunt, she maintained the distorted explanation.

Background

I began seeing Rosa individually and also met with the aunt and uncle. I advised them to tell Rosa the truth, because this would help instill trust between Rosa and her family and prevent future repercussions when Rosa eventually learned how her mother died. The aunt and uncle followed my recommendations, which led to more open communication about their own feelings, fears, and worries about the suicide and loss.

A suicidal death is a stigmatized death. Survivors are susceptible to accentuated feelings of guilt and shame and intrusive images of the disfigured victim (Eth & Pynoos, 1985). Furman (1974, p. 164) states in regard to parental suicide that the difficulty is in coping with anxiety about the circumstances surrounding the death, which the mind cannot master and the environment fails to allay. The concern for the bereaved is that the severe stress interferes with and impairs the mourning process (Burgess, 1975; Eth & Pynoos, 1985).

Rosa has several photographs of her mother that reassure and comfort her despite her recurrent fears about her mother's horrible disfigurement.

After a month of individual contact with Rosa, she expressed interest in talking to other children who had a parent who died.

Formation of Peer Therapy Dyad

I decided to offer a peer therapy experience to meet the needs of Rosa, who was feeling isolated and stigmatized, and Cindy, who was feeling too threatened by the individual counseling. I spoke with each child individually to discuss the proposed therapy, its purpose and value, and to assess their willingness to participate. Each child appeared interested. Cindy was more reluctant and ambivalent but agreed to try it.

The following is a summary of the initial session.

Initial Session

As an introduction, we played a game about our names to break the ice and began to become familiar with each other in a nonthreatening, fun mode.

We then discussed the purpose of this peer therapy: to talk about worries and troubles, to share concerns about having a parent who died, and to make new friends and have fun together. I suggested that the girls share with each other some information about the parent who died—for example, which parent died and when. I also suggested that they each also say one thing about themselves— something they do well. Each made at least one comment about her deceased parent and herself. The girls seemed to be more comfortable.

I then raised the issue of rules and confidentiality. They decided to keep their activities and discussions private except that they wanted to share their experiences with their parent.

I then described my role with them, which would include contact with their parents or guardians because a parent or guardian is an important part of one's life. I explained that my contact with their families would include general themes they raised but never a world-for-word account. The meeting ended on an upbeat note.

I hoped that the peer-pairing modality would provide a supportive atmosphere for Cindy and Rosa to share feelings and experiences about their grieving process. In addition, it would encourage friendship between the girls and thereby promote improved socialization skills and self-confidence.

Preliminary Assessment and Treatment Plan

Rosa is a child who has longstanding peer and relationship problems and low self-esteem coupled with the tragedy of her mother's suicide. Her social problems were magnified by her mother's death, which increased her feelings of isolation and stigmatization. Rosa's family provided good support for her, but her position as an only child contributed to her feelings of loneliness.

Cindy is a child who has a history of shy and withdrawn behavior predominantly outside the family as well as academic weaknesses. She experienced a series of deaths plus more current family crises that increased her feelings of inadequacy, vulnerability, and isolation.

The treatment plan was for Cindy and Rosa to receive play therapy using the peer-pairing technique. The goals for Cindy and Rosa were:

1. To grieve for the dead parent.
2. To provide opportunities to develop increased socialization skills and friendship skills.
3. To develop improved ways to resolve problems.

The play therapy techniques used are puppetry, drawings, spontaneous interactions, and problem-solving methods. The therapy sessions provide a safe environment that permits Rosa and Cindy to mourn openly and freely and to express their feelings of loss.

Regular contact with Rosa's and Cindy's families was maintained as well. For Cindy, the focus with Mrs. V was:

1. To educate her about Cindy's style and pace of grieving and clarify how that differs from adult grieving.
2. To encourage separation between Cindy and herself.
3. To support her to be a more powerful and effective parent.

For Rosa, the focus was helping the family understand the grieving process for a child and, peripherally, providing support for the family's mourning process.

Play Therapy Sessions

Session 4: Excerpt

Content of Session   *Rationale/Analysis*

CINDY: I really miss my dad.

THERAPIST: It must be hard.

ROSA: There's some kids in my class who are always bothering me. I hate them.

C: That's not very nice; they shouldn't do that. I feel bad for you!

R: Yeah, Charles, the boy I sit next to, he's always picking on me, calling me names, and I get yelled at by Mrs. Barron.

C: I'd hate that too!

T: It must be hard. Do you want us to help you figure out other ways to handle it?

R: OK.

T: Good! What do you do when they call you names? Oh, before I forget I just wanted to say that one thing that's really great is that you two really support each other. Cindy, you have a real nice way of supporting Rosa—that's a good friend. So, what do you do when they call you names?

I am pointing out friendship skills and reinforcing positive socialization.

R: I try to ignore it, but then I sometimes call Charles names back.

T: I could understand; it's hard to ignore. It's also really difficult and hurtful to be picked on. It's not an easy problem. Cindy, what do you think Rosa should do?

I am encouraging shared problem solving.

C: I don't know . . . mm . . . maybe switch seats. Yeah, ask the teacher if you can sit next to someone else because Charles keeps bothering you.

T: That's a good idea. What do you think, Rosa?

R: I can try it.

T: Let us know what the teacher says and if it works.

C: I really miss my daddy, but I never cry. I haven't cried once.

I note that Cindy is changing the topic.

T: It sounds like you feel really sad. Do you want to cry?

C: No, I just miss him.

R: I miss my mommy, and I cry when I'm trying to go to sleep.

T: It's really, really hard when a mommy or daddy dies. Naturally, you'd miss them. Rosa, does it help to cry?

R: I don't know. I just cry only in bed—that's when I think about her.

T: It's OK to cry, to feel sad—that's what people feel when someone really close to them dies. It's really hard. It's good both of you can share your feelings with us.	I am normalizing and validating feelings of sadness and how they express their pain.

Session 8: Excerpt

Rosa and Cindy were each completing a family tree picture. The following interaction occurred while they were coloring in their pictures.

Content of Session	Rationale/Analysis
CINDY: I miss my daddy so much!	Cindy is in the throes of her
THERAPIST: It's so hard.	grieving. She is experiencing in-
ROSA: Sometimes I can't believe my mom is dead.	tense emotion—pain, despair, loneliness. (It is near Father's
T: I can imagine it must be difficult to think she's dead.	Day.) Rosa is in the first stage of grieving. She expresses disbelief
C: Why did your mom kill herself?	and denial about her mother's
R: She had problems, was lonely, and kept her problems inside.	death.
T: It's terrible that she could not find another way to deal with her problems.	It is important to give Rosa the message that there are other ways
R: You're lucky your parents are not dead.	to deal with serious problems.
T: Um hm.	
C: Yeah, you don't know what it feels like to have a parent die.	
T: You're right.	
R: It's really hard! Harder for a child than an adult!	
C: My daddy can't see me graduate and won't be able to walk me down the aisle when I get married.	
T: It must hurt so much not to be able to share important things with your daddy.	
R: How would you know? Your parents aren't dead.	
T: I don't blame you for being angry. Sometimes, it must look like I don't realize how lucky I am to have both my parents. I just take it for granted.	It is important to validate their anger. Anger is a natural emotion one feels when a parent dies.
R: Yeah, your parents aren't dead.	

C: How do *you* know what it's like?

T: I'm struggling with this. I need you to help me understand what it's like for *you*. Actually, I think you're letting me know how hard it is, how much it hurts, and how angry you feel.

R: Why do you want to talk about this?

T: That's a good question. I believe it helps children and adults deal with the loss better to share their feelings with others. I am trying to understand. I need your help.

An important message to repeat to Rosa about how people cope with problems and difficult emotions.

C: I love my daddy so much!

T: Um hm.

C: I wish I could die and be with my daddy. I miss him so much.

T: It must hurt to miss him so much and not be able to see him.

C: I wish I could be with him. . . . (*Then on the family tree picture Cindy writes, "I love my Dad so much I wish I could die and be with him." She then shows Rosa and me her picture and then rips it up and throws it in the garbage.*)

T: I'm sorry it's so painful.

R: Sometimes I can't believe that my mom is dead.

T: That's understandable. It is hard to believe that someone so close to you is dead.

I feel scared and overwhelmed by Cindy's death wish. My own feelings make it hard for me to figure out how to respond to Cindy in the session. In retrospect, Cindy's wish might also be a clue that she has unfinished buisness. Another concern I have is how Rosa is interpreting Cindy's death wish.

Immediate Follow-Up to This Session. I was very concerned that Cindy's fantasy was not just a wish fantasy but possibly something she would try, so I asked Cindy to remain in my office following this session. I proceeded to evaluate the seriousness of her risk for suicide. Research by Rosenthal and Rosenthal (1984) reports that children as young as preschoolers can have suicidal thoughts and are capable of suicidal behavior. Fox (1985, p. 16) states that "each bereaved child must be considered potentially at risk for suicide and any kind of communication that suggests such a possibility should be promptly and fully evaluated."

I stated that I could really understand that she would think and wish she could die to be with her daddy because it hurts so much and feels so sad and lonely, but I am wondering what ideas she has about this wish. Has she thought about a way to die? How often does she think about this? Has she told anyone about these thoughts? Cindy's responses were all negative, and I felt reassured that she was not going to act on her feelings. I let her know that it was very healthy that she shared these thoughts and feelings with me and Rosa. "It's important to let people you trust know how you feel."

I also spoke with her mother and teachers (not directly about Cindy's fantasy) to see if Cindy was expressing or acting more morose, angry, guilty, or confused and if there was any noticeable change in her behavior. Neither her teachers nor her mother observed or expressed any concern about Cindy.

I immediately followed up by discussing Cindy's suicidal ideation and the ongoing therapeutic work with a private clinical supervisor in a formal consultation meeting.

Session 15: Summary

Cindy and Rosa decided to put on a puppet show. Their joint decision was prefaced by "We don't want to talk." Both girls felt that I had been pressuring them to express themselves through "talk." Rosa was experiencing denial, disbelief, and shock; Cindy was experiencing intense feelings of anger and sadness. Most often, both preferred and felt more comfortable through play, expressing themselves symbolically rather than directly.

The puppet play was about drugs, and the moral of their story was "Don't take illegal drugs." There were several puppet characters in the play, and all of them either died from taking drugs or were killed by one of the characters who was a drug dealer. It is ironic that children will often state that they do not want to *talk* about difficult feelings and thoughts but then proceed to express their emotions symbolically through *play*. Their feelings of loss are "in their hearts, but seldom on their lips" (Weizman & Kamm, 1985, p. 180).

Session 16

Content of Session   Rationale/Analysis

THERAPIST: (*excited and enthusiastically*) I was thinking about the play you put on last week. Maybe the two of you would like to do a sequel to the first play—you know how there's a Rocky I, then Rocky II. Well, I thought it was a great and creative play, and maybe you would like to put on another one.

CINDY AND ROSA: (*responding simultaneously and enthusiastically*) Yeah!

T: I was even thinking about an idea for your next play. Pretend some of the characters who died or were killed could come back to life.

C: (*with strong emotion; to Rosa*) Wouldn't you like it if your mom could come back?

R: Yeah.

C: This play is about people who died and come back for one day, but their families can't see them, but the dead people were ghosts, and they can see their families. The characters are John and Jane who died. [John and Jane are children.] Mr. and Mrs. Miller are their parents. [Miller is Cindy's teacher whom she adores.] Hello and welcome to our show. This is the continuation of Drug Part II, written by Cindy and Rosa.

R: (*as parent*) Don't you wish our kids were back? I miss them a lot. (*sobbing aloud*)

C: (*as ghost*) I have a good idea. I could ask God to send their children back. Hello, God. How are you? Could you send John and Jane Miller to their parents? (*God says*) Maybe I could. Well probably yes. (*Ghost says*) Because their parents really miss them. (*God says*) I'll send them. OK. (*Ghost says*) Hey, I'm your children's ghost. Do you want to see your children?

R: (*angrily*) Yes, how are you going to get them back to life?

C: Go get your wife, OK? God said they could come back for one more day. You want to see them. (*as daughter*) Hey, Daddy (*very excited and lovingly*).

For Cindy, it is as if she were seeing her own father.

R: (*as father*) Jane! John! (*with disbelief and bewilderment*) I'm dreaming.

C: No, you're not. You want me to pinch you?

R: Yeah—Ouch! Honey, do you want to see the children?

C: (*as child*) Mommy (*full of joy and love*). (*The puppets hug each other tightly.*)

R: Lord, thank you!!! Lord, thank you!!! (*Screams in horror, then relief.*)

I feel deeply moved by Cindy and Rosa's emotional intensity. It feels as if they were each really seeing their dead parents again.

C: We can only come back for one day

R: Thank you Lord. (*Puppets hugging each other tightly.*) Well, what do you want to do? Want to see your friends?

C: Missy! Sandy! [These characters are friends of Jane and John.] Remember us?

R: You're dead!

C: No, were not, we're alive for one day. Let's go to the sweet shop.

[Next scene, sweet shop]

C: (*as drug dealer*) You want some sugar. It's in this little bottle.

R: I don't know. My mom won't let me have sugar.

C: Just take it.

R: She gets so furious when she sees candy in my room.

C: Take it. It's really good.

R: OK.

C: Here's some more.

R: Mmm . . . It's good.

C: Ha, Ha, Ha, Ha. I sold them drugs and they didn't even know it.

R: (*gagging and throwing up*) What kind of sugar is this? This is rotten sugar.

C: Ha! Ha! We fooled you. It's drugs.

R: I have to go to the hospital.

C: (*as announcer*) And so friends, Missy and Sandy died.

R: (*sobbing and screaming aloud*) And their whole family cried. Did you hear what happened to Sandy and Missy?

Throughout the play, Rosa expresses feelings of sadness. This is symbolic of her feelings toward Mother.

C: Yeah, we killed them. And we'll kill you, too. Bang, bang—bang, bang.

R: What are you doing?

C: I'm doing what I was taught to do, Dad. (*with strong anger*)

R: God is going to send you back.

C: God, we don't want to hear any more. Send us back.

T: Is it the end?

R: No! It's not the end. So eat your popcorn.

C: (*kills the parents and says to Rosa*) I hate you, I really do, I hate your guts. Go away from me.

Cindy is expressing anger and rage. Her feelings represent how she feels about her father's death.

R: Is it the end?

C: God, I'm sorry that I asked you to send them down to see their parents because they killed their parents, too.

R: Is it the end now?

C: No! (*starts singing*) I wish I was dead, I can't forget. I really wish I was dead because someone is bothering me about the end of the story. I wish

I believe it is difficult for Cindy to tolerate her feelings of rage and loss, and her death wish surfaces.

I was dead, dead, dead, dead! That pig is such a jerk.

R: (*as pig puppet*) I'm not a jerk.

C: I wish I was dead, dead, dead!

R: So do I because you are a pain in the neck.

C: Well, I'm going to kill myself right now.

R: Oh, don't do that, don't do that, don't do that. (*with pained expression*)

C: Falls down and dies.

R: You know something. This is boring. The End! (*stated forcefully*)

T: That was a strong play. I'm concerned about this last piece when Cindy said she wanted to kill herself and Rosa responded very forcefully. I wonder if it reminded you of your mother?

R: Yes.

C: I'm sorry, I didn't mean that.

R: I want the next play to be in heaven. OK, Cindy?

C: Yeah.

T: This was a very difficult ending, and of course Cindy didn't mean anything about Rosa's mother. Are you OK, Rosa?

R: Yeah. Next week the play is in heaven.

The only thing that will ease her pain is to rejoin Dad.

Instinctively, Rosa tries to save Cindy. Rosa plays out her wish to stop her mother from killing herself. I should have tuned into her feelings of anger and powerlessness.

Rosa creates closure by taking control.

Session 17

Content of Session

THERAPIST: At the end of the last session, Rosa suggested we put on another play about being in heaven. I listened to the last play [it was taped], and it was a *very* powerful play with lots of action, feelings, and surprises. I realized that Cindy really directed the last play and both of you acted in it. Since Cindy was the director for the last play, it would be a good idea to let Rosa be the director this time. OK?

CINDY: All right.

ROSA: Yeah. This play is about someone that goes up to heaven.

T: (*encouraging Rosa to be in charge*) Rosa, you need to give directions to Cindy.

Rationale/Analysis

I strongly suggest Rosa as the director for therapeutic reasons—to help her deal with her feelings of powerlessness and helplessness, which relate to her mother's suicide. She wants to create a play in heaven, perhaps to confront her unfinished business with her mother and her need to understand why her death occurred. Also, the other motive is to en-

R: Cindy, why don't you be the rabbit and bunny. The first scene is in heaven.

C: Rabbit and bunny are eating carrots.

R: I don't know what the next scene should be.

T: What do you want to happen next? You want to describe what heaven's like?

R: Yeah. Heaven's like—it's a beautiful day, everything is all white. It's never nighttime. We can go to sleep when we want to.

C: (*humming in background*)

R: Do you hear something? Who's that? I don't know what to do.

T: Do you want me to help you?

R: Yeah.

T: Why don't you talk more about heaven, and I'll be the person who comes to visit heaven.

C: It's nice up here.

R: What do you want to do today?

C: I don't know.

R: I have no idea.

C: I'll do what you want to do.

R: I'll do what you want to do.

C: It's *your* play.

T: Cindy's being cooperative about letting you be the director. I know it's awkward for you Rosa, but you can do it! Take charge and be the director.

R: OK. Let's go play on the swings.

T: (*as person visiting heaven*) Hi, there!

R: (*fearful*) Who's that?

T: Don't be afraid. My name is Judy. This is my first visit to heaven.

R: How did you get up here?

T: I walked up those imaginary steps to heaven. Can I tell you a little story about myself. I had these really good friends, they both died, and I've been missing them a lot, and every night I pray to God, and I cry myself to sleep, and I think about these friends a lot. I've been really missing my friends so much. I just wanted one more chance to see them. I think God answered my prayers

courage the girls to take turns and share more equally in their play.

Rosa usually follows Cindy's lead, and I purposely encouraged her to take the initiative and assert herself more.

Incorporating Rosa's real-life experience into the play.

and He said, I could come up and see them one more time. I'm looking for John and Jane. *(John and Jane appear.)* Hi, John! Hi, Jane! I'm so happy to see you guys! I couldn't believe you guys had died!

C: Thank you God for letting our friend Judy up here.

R: Yeah, for one day.

C: Are you sure this isn't a dream?

R: Yeah.

T: I've been thinking a lot about you. I've been so lonely and sad without you. I've been feeling terrible.

C: How is it on earth?

T: It is spring on earth. It's beautiful right now. I can't wait for summer—swimming, no school, bicyle riding, playing with my friends!

R: But Judy, we can do whatever we want here.

C: We don't have to go to sleep. You have to go to school, and we don't.

T: Heaven seems like a wonderful place, and I'm relieved because it seems like you're happy and I was worried about you. But I'm really looking forward to earth things—playing with my friends, swimming—I can't wait!

C: Now, you are happy without us! You have more friends!

T: You think I don't miss you. Even though I think being alive is wonderful, it doesn't feel the same without you.

C: Then, why don't you die and come up here and live with us?

R: Up here, if you want it to be spring, you just wish it, and it comes true.

C: We can wish your birthday.

T: I see what you mean. And believe me, part of me wants to be with you. I think it's not the best for me. I really, really wish you didn't die.

C: You can't die up here.

R: Yeah, let's wish for candy.

C: Candy, candy, candy.

Rosa and Cindy raise the question in the bereaved's mind: Is life worth living after someone you love dies? Children need an affirmation of the priority of life over death!

Perhaps I have missed the opportunity to address and identify Cindy's anger toward her father. Cindy feels deserted and abandoned.

T: It's hard, what you're talking about. It's not that I don't want to be with you. I miss you so much it hurts. But one thing I figured out since you died is that my memories, my wonderful memories of you, help me. They really help me when I feel sad. Remember when we went to Great Advertures? Wasn't it great?

R: No.

C: It was boring.

R: Up here you can see all these neat things. You should see the rides up here!

T: Yeah, tell me about heaven! What's wonderful about heaven?

R: You can do whatever you want.

C: You can stay up 'til whenever you want.

R: You don't get grounded.

T: Those are pretty good things.

R: Everyone is nice up here.

T: Aha.

R: No one bosses us around.

T: It makes me feel good to hear that you are so happy.

R: What do you want to do next?

T: I'm really glad to see that you're both OK. I also wanted to tell you a few things I didn't get a chance to say. I really like both of you, you mean the world to me. It really tears me . . .

C: (*interrupts*) Ah, you're just saying that. (*said in disbelief*)

T: Let me tell you something, I wouldn't walk all the way up heaven's staircase if I didn't mean it. Every night I think about you guys . . .

R: (*interrupts and states with bored and annoyed expression*) OK, OK, let's have fun together, enough talking. (*We start dancing and singing.*) Wait a second. I just figured out something. You never have to go down there again because you see . . .

C: (*interrupts and with excitement*) I have a good idea. Let's ask God if she can stay up here forever!

My discussion about realistic memories is intended to guide them through their grief. One needs to remember, then let go to the point of integrating the loss. The children's resistance is a key that I need to slow down and tune into their needs, specifically Rosa's denial.

They are struggling with key questions about death: "What happens to people when they die, where do they go, and what is it like?" "What does it feel like to be dead?"

Both Rosa and Cindy have trouble tolerating the expression of sadness.

T: Wait, wait, I don't think I want to.

R: You don't?

C AND R: (*in unison, both moaning and sighing*) Oh! Oh!

R: Why not?

C: Because she wants to be with her other friends and family.

Cindy is expressing acceptance about the choice of life—a reason to want to live. I am helping them choose life over death, precariously creating a balance between the beauty of heaven and the even better deal on earth.

T: Even though I love you guys so much, and I feel so terrible that you guys are dead, and I'm glad you're happy up here, I want to go back home.

C: Wait a second, let's take a picture of all of us! (*with excitement*)

T: That's a great idea! (*We pretend we are taking a picture and then give each other a copy.*) This is a very, very special picture to me. I just want to clear something up. Jane, we had a fight 2 days before you died, and I was just feeling terrible about it, I just wanted to make sure you weren't angry at me.

I am recognizing any guilty feelings either of them might be feeling.

R: I thought we cleared it up the next day.

T: I was feeling guilty.

R: Don't worry. Let's have a fun time!

C: Let's sing a song. (*We sing some songs together that they learned in the school chorus. Then Cindy writes a song and she sings the song to me.*) Oh Judy you're my friend. / And I wish you could stay, / But it's too far away. / And so I think you're so funny, / And my friend wants to be your honey.

Throughout this play, Cindy in particular is dealing with saying good-bye.

R: Bye Judy. (*crying*)

C: Bye. (*crying*)

T: Just remember I'll never, never forget you! The End.

As a follow-up to creating plays, I state to both Cindy and Rosa that the wonderful thing about making plays is that each of us can pretend and create all kinds of fantasies. We can pretend anything, as we just did—going to heaven and speaking to someone who died. Sometimes pretending and imagining makes us feel better. That is what movies and books are also all about. It is important to remember it is *pretend*, not real life.

CONCLUDING COMMENTS

The therapy sessions were instrumental in encouraging Rosa and Cindy to express their feelings gradually, on a weekly basis, and to begin to work slowly through their loss. One of the key ingredients in helping the children grieve was assuring them of a safe environment in which they can air out their emotions of despair symbolically and still feel accepted. I have learned to create a safe milieu by conveying my unconditional belief in the children's worth and value, by listening carefully to them, and by trusting the client-directed therapeutic process.

Throughout the use of play therapy techniques, Rosa and Cindy were able to express a range of emotions. I was often able to identify the painful emotions and normalize and validate their feelings and anxieties.

The treatment modality of peer-pairing encouraged a budding friendship that both increased feelings of self-worth and improved social skills. Both Cindy and Rosa shared feelings and experiences in this context that allowed them to feel less alone with their suffering. Also in the session, they struggled with new ways to resolve peer and family problems. It was particularly important for Rosa to understand that there are alternative ways to deal with serious personal problems as compared to her mother's suicide.

As stated earlier, the surviving parent or guardian is critical in a latency-age child's ability to work through his or her grief. As Mishne (1983, p. 206) states, "given the child's complete dependency on home and family, the supports or obstacles within the family must be regarded as most significant." Although, I worked with each child's surviving parent/guardian, I did not work with the entire family. The optimal treatment plan should include family therapy so that the therapist can help the entire family work through the stress and symptomology related to sudden death or suicide. By helping the family grieve, we can help the latency-age child to benefit.

However, in a school setting the focus is child centered. The school social worker is greatly limited in his or her opportunities to conduct ongoing family therapy. Nevertheless, as a school social worker, I can provide referrals to families for family treatment with the appropriate mental health agency or community resource.

PLAY THERAPY MATERIALS

- A range of puppet styles and types were used by the children. A set of family puppets consisting of an adult female and male, a female and male child, and a baby, which could be of either sex. These are constructed of a hard rubber material and do not have movable parts. Another set of puppets made of a soft fabric fit on the hand like a mitten. This set consists of animals (pig, rabbit, shark, lion, bear) and people (policeman, fireman, a boy, and a girl). All of these puppets have movable mouths.

- Crayons and white and colored paper
- Tape recorder and cassettes
- Board game: Battleship (Milton Bradley Co., Springfield MA)

STUDY QUESTIONS

1. Discuss the appropriate procedure to follow when a child expresses suicide ideation. Comment on the response of the school social worker with regard to Cindy's
   verbalized death wish.

2. Compare and contrast the therapist's role in the 16th and 17th play therapy
   sessions. Describe the therapeutic value for Cindy and Rosa when the social worker
   assumed a nondirective stance. Explain the purpose of the social worker's more
   directive approach in the 17th session for Cindy and Rosa's treatment.

3. How did the play therapy techniques encourage the children to grieve? Describe
   the function of symbolic communication in the therapeutic process, using specific
   illustrations from the case.

4. If you were the school social worker, how would you have made a referral for
   Cindy's family for family therapy?

REFERENCES

Burgess, A. W. (1975). Family reaction to homicide. *American Journal of Orthopsychiatry, 45*, 391–
398.

Cameron, N. (1963). *Personality development and psychopathology*. Boston: Houghton Mifflin.

Doyle, P. (1980). *Grief counseling and sudden death: A manual and guide*. Springfield, IL: Charles C.
Thomas.

Eth, S., & Pynoos, R. S. (Eds.). (1985). *Post-traumatic stress disorder in children*. Washington, DC:
American Psychiatric Press.

Fox, S. (1985). *Good grief: Helping groups of children when a friend dies*. Boston: New England
Association for the Education of Young Children.

Freud, S. (1938). Remembering, repeating and working through. In *Standard Edition* (Vol. 12,
pp. 147–156). London: Hogarth Press. (Original work published 1914)

Furman E. (1974). *A child's parent dies: Studies in childhood breavement*. New Haven, CT· Yale
University Press.

Grollman, E. A. (1967). *Explaining death to children*. Boston: Beacon Press.

Johnson, S. W., & Maile, L. J. (1987). *Suicide and the schools: A handbook for prevention, intervention
and rehabilitation*. Springfield, IL: Charles C. Thomas.

Lieberman, F. (1979). *Social work with children*. New York: Human Science Press.

Mervis, B. A. (1985). The use of peer-pairing in child psychotherapy. *Social Work, 30*(2), 124–128.

Mishne, J. (1983). *Clinical work with children*. New York: Free Press.

Rosenthal, P., & Rosenthal, S. (1984). Suicidal behavior by preschool children. *American Journal of
Psychiatry, 141*, 520–525.

Sarnoff, C. (1978). *On latency*. New York: Jason Aronson.

Weizman, S. G., & Kamm, P. (1985). *About mourning: Support and guidance for the bereaved*. New
York: Human Sciences Press.

CHAPTER 14

Multiple Losses in Children of Chemically Dependent Families
Case of RJ, Age 7

MARY ELLEN JOHNSTON

In our work with children the theme of loss presents itself with frustrating regularity. In chemically dependent families, loss is pervasive on many levels. There is the loss of a healthy family system, of appropriate parent-child boundaries, and of childhood itself. There are many other losses as well, resulting from change of the family structure from separation, divorce, and sometimes death of the chemically dependent parent. School districts may change along with residences, resulting in loss of a very tenuous peer group. Financial resources diminish if the parents separate, creating the loss of the primary breadwinner. In the chemically dependent family, the child is in a permanent state of crisis, with inconsistency and chaos being the norm.

A tremendous vulnerability exists related to the many associated triggers connected with loss, so that each time the child experiences another loss in any area of his or her life, the *chronic* sense of loss caused by family chemical dependency may be reexperienced. The child of the chemically dependent family feels different and shamed as well. This sense of shame and of being somehow different leads to a loss of the peer group. Latency-age children may then have difficulty in social and academic settings because of their overwhelming sense of shame. They tend to be isolated socially, making group treatment difficult. Studies indicate that one out of four children lives with a substance-abusing parent (Ackerman, 1983), so the sense of shame endures for many children. A psychoeducational group serves, in part, to reduce the sense of isolation and shame common to chemically dependent families and to serve as a major denial reducer in early treatment (Ackerman, 1983).

In the alcoholic family, there are several family survival roles to which a child may ascribe in order to accommodate to a chaotic situation. The roles are the result of unmet needs by the addicted and codependent adults in a dysfunctional system (Black, 1982). In order to maintain the family homeostasis, the children in alcoholic families take on behaviors that meet the needs of the system. Role reversal is common among children of alcoholic families (Ackerman, 1983).

We recognize several primary areas of concern for the physical safety of the child of chemically dependent parents. One is around visitation with the actively substance-abusing parent. Should a child be released for visitation if a parent appears to be using? Should the child continue driving with a parent who has stopped at a bar during the visit with the child? Another concern involves prevention of sexual abuse. The chemically dependent family already has very diffuse boundaries, with role reversals and inappropriate role maintenance by parents, and in such an environment the risk for sexual abuse is common. More information about this is discussed in an article by Mary Lou Jones (1989) on the problem of "double jeopardy" for children of these families.

A careful assessment of the ongoing crises in a child's life must be made to determine the current level of isolation, shame, and depression as well as overall functioning of the child. Some type of educational framework must be established both to provide a much-needed structure for children of chaotic situations and to help children understand the concept of chemical dependency, which they then can apply to future crisis situations. The challenge of play therapy with children of chemically dependent families is both to assist the child in identifying the feelings of loss that are inherent in having alcohol- or drug-addicted parents and also to encourage appropriate ventilation of these feelings so they do not impede the child's functioning to a significant degree. Increasing the child's ability to cope in stressful situations is also a goal.

Parental involvement is crucial in the treatment of the child of a chemically dependent family. Although it may be only the nonaddict or codependent who presents for treatment, efforts should be made to also involve the addicted parent in treatment. Contact should be attempted, even if a face-to-face contact cannot be accomplished. If the addicted person can be engaged in treatment because of concern for the child, he or she may become motivated over time to seek help for him- or herself. If an initial attempt to contact the other parent is made and is met with rejection, this lends credence to the child's belief that there is something terribly wrong to make a parent behave this way, therefore supporting the disease concept. If the therapist could not even get Dad to show up, then Dad must be pretty bad off, indeed. The child then begins to understand that this is a "no-fault" disease. It is always good practice to "begin where the client is" in treatment of chemically dependent children and their families. If a mother needs, at the time of initial contact, to demand that this oppositional child-tyrant be "fixed," then we try to respond to that need. Over time, she can begin to become part of the helping process and be encouraged to explore her own issues in separate sessions. Many spouses of chemically dependent individuals are adult children of alcoholics themselves. They are, understandably, highly defensive about exploration of their own dysfunctional families of origin (Woititz, 1982).

THE CASE: RJ, AGE 7

This chapter focuses on work with a young boy of a chemically addicted father. Through individual therapy, psychoeducational group treatment (family), and participation in a latency-age children's group, he was able to begin to identify the sense of loss he experienced during the ongoing crisis of family chemical dependency. He also began to integrate these experiences of loss without enduring loss of self-esteem. This case demonstrates how engagement and treatment of the child, in conjunction with some well-timed family sessions, served not only the child's treatment goals but as a springboard for the mother's involvement in her own treatment.

Family Information

Mother	Mrs. Jane Sanders, age 30, part-time secretary
Father	Mr. Robert Sanders, age 35, limousine driver, out of home for 6 months
RJ (Robert John)	Age 7, grade 2
David	Age 3
Mr. and Mrs. Cummings	Maternal grandparents, ages 56 and 60, retired bus driver and homemaker

Presenting Problem

RJ presented for treatment around issues of oppositional behaviors at home since his move with his mother and younger sibling to his maternal grandparents' home 6 months previous to entering treatment. RJ's father reportedly had severe alcohol, cocaine, and gambling problems. The precipitating incident to the separation was father's involvement in extramarital affairs as well as violent behavior directed toward the mother. Although RJ was only 6 years old at the time of intake, his mother often spoke of him as if he were a much older child. According to Mrs. Sanders, RJ often hit his younger brother, David, was oppositional around all routines in the household, and talked back to her with no respect.

First Interview

In contrast to many young children of alcoholics, RJ had no difficulty in separating from his mother in the waiting room. Once in the therapist's office, however, he plopped down on the indicated chair and immediately challenged authority.

Content of Session	*Rationale/Analysis*
THERAPIST: Hi, RJ. I'm Mary Ellen.	
RJ (*loudly*): I *hate* this place. I wish my mother didn't bring me here.	
T: You don't even know what this place is all about, and she just *brought* you here, huh?	
RJ (*absorbs this*): What *is* this place, anyway? (*At this point, he begins to get up and move toward the door.*)	

T: I talk with kids who have a mom or dad who drink or drug too much. Sometimes their moms and dads have even split up over it.

RJ (*slowly comes back to table and chair*): Yup, that's what happened to me. But I don't care. I'm gonna go live with my dad soon anyway.

Some acknowledgment of problem, followed by quick denial.

T: It's tough on you without Dad around.

RJ: Yeah, but anyway, I hate this place. (*He spies the markers.*) Can I draw with those?

T: Sure. Can you draw a picture of your family? (*handing him paper*)

RJ: (*Draws a picture of four people: he and his father at the very top of the page, mother and younger sibling at the bottom.*)

Preliminary Assessment and Treatment Plan

Observation of the drawing indicated the reasons for some of the oppositional behavior. This youngster was clearly overidentifying with the aggressor—his father. As it turned out, he had good reason not to trust adults, based on his previous experience in the chemically dependent home. There had been a series of broken promises by both parents, and RJ had often witnessed violence by his father, directed at his mother. In the absence of his father, RJ immediately took on a surrogate spouse role. This created the oppositional behaviors, as he became an angry child in the role of partner. The only role model he had had as a male was his angry, violent, and frequently abusive father. RJ attempted to maintain the balance of the family system by taking his father's place in the only way he could—through acting out behaviors. His strengths included his ability to verbalize feelings and his ability to assess a situation in light of others' needs. Although the means by which he attempted to fulfill the needs of the family were not functional as a coping skill, the behaviors represented his efforts at a protective defense to resolve a difficult situation.

RJ clearly was playing out the survival roles of "family hero" and "scapegoat." Many times the scapegoat is the family hero, as it is he who gets the family to present itself for much-needed intervention. It is important to mention that the changing of survival roles in the alcoholic family should not be considered a treatment goal.

RJ was not an easy child to engage in the therapeutic relationship. His anger, in part a defense for his strong feelings of loss, was initially difficult to break through.

The treatment plan for RJ included the following goals:

1. Education about chemical dependency as a family disease, recognizing family survival roles, and encouraging acceptance of chemical dependency as a disease that kids can't cause, control, or cure.

2. Encouraging identification and appropriate ventilation of feelings of loss, anger, guilt, shame, and fear.
3. Reducing aggressive behavior with sibling, reducing acting-out behaviors at home, reducing anxiety, and improving coping skills.
4. Improving socialization skills, enhancing self-image, and encouraging participation in self-esteem-enhancing activities.

RJ was initially seen every week for a period of 6 weeks. For 12 consecutive weeks, he attended the multifamily substance awareness group, the psychoeducational program component. This serves as a powerful tool in reducing the level of denial for families affected by chemical dependency. Often, parents present the acting-out child for treatment after separation or divorce from the actively addicted spouse, not recognizing their own alcoholic family of origin and the impact that this may have had on relationships. The parent may identify the addict as "the one with the problem" and fail to see ways in which the entire family could have been hurt by the disease. The multifamily substance awareness group also begins to reduce the sense of isolation and shame that the chemically dependent family invariably experiences.

By the end of 12 weeks, Mrs. Sanders was convinced that she had done the right thing in separating from her spouse, although she continued to wish for his recovery in order to resume the relationship. She also maintained denial around her father's alcoholism. RJ, on the other hand, had gained a framework with which to begin to understand the confusion that had defined his family for several years.

In individual sessions, I sought to reinforce the knowledge base around family chemical dependency related to content that RJ and his mom were receiving in the group. Since RJ had expressed interest in artwork, I used the modality of art to engage him in the treatment process and explore his extreme sense of loss related to recent parental separation and the deaths of two family pets.

Third Play Therapy Session

The plan for session 3 included the viewing of a 10-minute film by the Johnson Institute, "A Story about Feelings," portraying a chemically addicted man, John, his family, and his pet cat, Z. My hope was that RJ could identify with the format of the film, which was actual children's drawings made into live animation. Most children experience a sense of excitement and power through seeing the artwork actually "come alive!" I had the film set up in our movie room, and I had stocked the office with markers and paper as well as animal puppets. At the beginning of the session, RJ and I took a closer look at the family portrait he had drawn and reflected upon it. It revealed an intact family, a cat, and a dog. RJ soon admitted, as I questioned him about the picture, that this was the family he *used* to have. He was clearly angry.

Content of Session	Rationale/Analysis
THERAPIST: RJ, I notice that you put two grown-ups in this picture and two smaller people.	
RJ (*impatiently pointing*): Yeah, my mom, my dad, me, my brother, my dog, "Casey," and my cat, "Special," OK? So what else is there to do today? I *hate* this place!	
T: It's so hard to talk about all these things you don't have in your life any more. Everything in that picture is just about gone now.	
RJ: (*Mulls this one over; the wind seems knocked out of his sails—his facial expression shifts.*) My cat and my dog are dead. I loved them so much. I loved my cat, Special, so much. . . . Do you know what my daddy did to Special once?	No wonder he is angry.
T: What?	
RJ: (*Suddenly, the shame returns. His voice becomes angry.*) Never mind! What do you care about it, anyway? (*His hands are on his hips now, and he is up from his chair.*)	
T: It is such a sad thing to lose your best pal.	I must be careful not to push. Let child proceed at his level.
RJ: It is! My cat, Special, used to sleep by me every night. (*Sits back down.*) He would lay in my bed at night and stay by me. (*Puts his head down on the table, arms folded.*) Sometimes it makes me feel very sad . . .	
T: It *is* very sad. You loved him so much.	Shall I show my own disapproval, give a strong-feeling response based on fear, or ask for more information?
RJ: He was my best friend in the whole world! My dad threw him across the room when he came home late one time. I was afraid he was dead, but he wasn't, you know. Special had nine lives. But he ran out.	
T: What happened?	
RJ: (*Becomes fearful again.*) None of your business! I told you I hate coming to this place. You make me think about sad things and watch sad, stupid movies! (*Gets up, goes to door, opens it.*) I'm leaving	Has he trusted too much?
T: I cannot let you leave right now.	Should I let him go? What is he running from? Maybe I will get to his level, and he will feel less threatened.
RJ (*getting up*): You are not the boss! Leave me alone. I can do whatever I want! (*At this point, he is nearly screaming.*)	

T (*picking up the panda puppet and talking in a squeaky voice*): RJ, please stay a few more minutes. I hate talking about this stuff, too. Wanna watch a movie with me?

RJ (*sighing*): I'll watch it, but then I am leaving this place.

T: You got it, RJ! OK, let's you and I and Panda go into the movie room. (*We go down the hall; I indicate a chair to him, and I turn on the projector.*) This movie's about a guy named John who has a disease. It might make you feel a little sad. (*RJ appears to accept this, and we watch "A Story about Feelings."*)

Comment

When RJ's level of discomfort with his own feelings seemed to overwhelm him, his instinct was to flee. It was in the presence of his overwhelming sadness and loss that he became belligerent and oppositional about everything. I had yet to learn how far I could go with him.

Later, I learned to structure each session in lengths of no more than 25 minutes, with careful containment of his feelings and their ventilation. For many children of alcoholics, the identification of feelings is very difficult, but RJ had not yet closed himself off to the feelings completely. He was certainly able to identify sad and angry feeling states within himself, but he was unable to ventilate appropriately, resulting in oppositional behaviors at home.

Mrs. Sanders, feeling unable to cope with her own feelings of loss and separation, was unavailable to RJ. As Mrs. Sanders began to become hopeful about change for her family after her psychoeducational experience, she was more receptive to attending psychotherapy sessions for herself. She began almost immediately to become more available to RJ and to recognize his acting-out behaviors as symptomatic of his unresolved losses. She was eager to assist in the grief process and the healing that would have to take place for the family to begin to feel better and to function more effectively.

Family Session

I asked Mrs. Sanders and RJ to attend a joint family session after 10 weeks of individual treatment. RJ had made progress in sessions, little by little, in identifying chemical dependency as a disease that affected his family. We read *The Brown Bottle* (Jones, 1983) together, and RJ drew a picture of his dad stuck in the bottle. He also drew a picture of his dad dead under the ground. It was after that that I scheduled the family session.

In preparation for the family session, I asked Mrs. Sanders to bring some photographs of the deceased pets. The full story unfolded during that family session, as RJ blamed his mother for the death of both pets as well as for the loss and separation from his father. Chemical dependency was involved again.

Content of Session	Rationale/Analysis

THERAPIST: Come on in (*indicating chairs*).
MOTHER: I brought those pictures we talked about. RJ, I have pictures of Special and Casey.

RJ (*arms folded across chest*): I don't care what you brought. I hate this place, and I don't want to come here anymore.

The recurrent negative theme.

T: May I look at these?

M: Sure. This one is a little blurry.

T: (*I take the two pictures from her. I barely look. I want an expert interpretation here.*) RJ, tell me about this picture.

RJ (*looking*): Mmmm—this is my dog, Casey, and my cat, Special, before they died!

T: They *died*! (*I turn toward Mrs. Sanders.*) Mom, this must have been very sad for all of you.

M· It was sad. But RJ, Casey was very old. I know how upset you were about Special, but there's nothing we can do about these things.

Mrs. Sanders's sense of powerlessness was evidenced in nearly every life situation, and her son's expression of feeling appeared to reinforce this.

RJ (*to therapist*): She gave Casey the bones, and Casey ate Special instead. She's so stupid! (*louder now*) And now I have no more cat, no more dog, no more family! I hate this place. (*Gets up, moves toward door.*)

I can't believe what I am hearing! The dog *ate* the cat??

T (*also getting up*): RJ, I know these things are so hard for you to talk about. You wish that Mom could have stopped all these sad things from happening. (*He sits; I hand him the panda puppet.*)

This is difficult to hear. How much *more* difficult it must have been for RJ!!

RJ: My dad threw Special across the room all the time. "Stupid cat, stupid cat!" (*Throws the puppet, then returns to his seat, puts his head down on the table, appears to be crying.*) I told you I hate this place! It makes me feel so sad! (*I allow silence and tears, and time to grieve.*)

T: How hard it must have been for you, RJ—Dad out most of the time, coming home mad and drunk—and big fights with Mom. Special was the only one there for you. (*At this point, Mrs. Sanders hears the reality of her son's experience in an actively chemically dependent home, and her eyes fill up. I turn to Mrs. Sanders.*) Mom, it would be

OK to feel sad together. This is *very* sad. (*I motion for her to move her chair closer to RJ, and she puts her arm around him, rubbing his back. He does seem to accept this.*)

M: RJ, I had no idea how upsetting this really was for you. I feel terrible for you.

RJ: (*Now that he has gotten an apology, RJ is going to see how much more he can teach her. Looking up, he reaches for a tissue, stops, wipes his eyes with his sleeve—real tough guy.*) You killed Special. It's your fault I don't have a cat anymore.

T: Can you guys tell me what happened to Special? You said he had nine lives, RJ. I wonder what you meant by that.

RJ: He had nine lives 'cause my dad threw him around so many times. And once he almost got run over. I thought he was dead once. He had a headache, though.

M: (*A helpless look is on her face; she appears guilty and ashamed.*) I *was* responsible in a way. We had a lot of company, and I forgot to feed the animals. After dinner, I took all the rib bones and gave them to Casey out in the yard. Casey got Special mixed up with the bones, and she was so hungry. (*She pauses.*) So Casey killed Special. I got the kids out of the way and tried to get Special, but it was too late.

T: What a tragedy this is!

RJ: I didn't even say good-bye to Special. *She* (*pointing at his mother*) just buried him. I don't even know where she put Special. (*He is angry.*)

M: Honey, I told you. I put him in the far corner of the yard, by the forsythia. (*to me*) It was pretty late, and I just didn't want the kids to see . . .

RJ: Yeah. Special got chewed up, prob'ly. (*Now he is almost cheerful.*)

T: I wonder how to say good-bye to Special. Could we write him a letter?

RJ: Special was a very smart cat, you know. I could write him a letter.

T (*getting paper and pencil*): How would the letter start? (*RJ likes this idea and picks up the pencil eagerly. Mrs. Sanders has returned her chair to its previous spot.*)

I wonder how much mother has comforted RJ through the years.

Mother assumes responsibility.

This is horrible! What a tragedy! Was mother drinking also? I have a tough time here believing the poor judgment this mother exercised. In some ways, I feel that RJ's name calling of his mother is accurate! This must have been an ordeal for *both* of them.

Trying to put some closure on this.

Mother seems to be withdrawing. She must feel exposed and guilty.

RJ (*writing*): Dear Special . . . Mom, how do you
spell "Special"?

M: S-P-E-C-I-A-L.

RJ (*continuing his writing*): You were the best cat
there ever was. . . . I love you so much. . . . What
a good friend. . . . Mom, how do you spell
"friend"?

RJ had not had an opportunity to say good-bye to Special, and the next few
sessions were about grief. We read *The Tenth Good Thing about Barney* (Viorst,
1971). This short story is about a dead cat who may either be in the ground
helping to make flowers or up in cat heaven eating tuna fish and drinking cream.
RJ then wrote a letter to Special, telling him how much he missed him, how he
hoped he was eating tuna in heaven, and how sad RJ was that he had lost not only
Special but also his father and his family.

In grieving the loss of his beloved cat, RJ was becoming aware of the many
losses he had experienced in his young life. Although RJ's violent behavior at
home directed against his little brother decreased, he remained somewhat oppositional, particularly with his maternal grandmother and his mother.

It was shortly after the family session that Mrs. Sanders approached me
about arranging weekly individual sessions for herself. She was beginning to
recognize the extent of her struggle to maintain her sense of self in the family
domicile and felt she needed support to implement some of the parenting
strategies we had briefly discussed during short periods at the end of RJ's
individual sessions. Individual psychotherapy with the mother began on a weekly
basis to assist her in learning to set appropriate limits and boundaries and to
maintain her parental role. We also discussed the issue of visitation and whether
or not RJ and his brother were safe. RJ continued in a role of parentified child
during these visits, as his father often went off to drink or take drugs, leaving RJ
and his 3-year-old brother in the care of another drug-addicted friend. Counseling
with Mrs. Sanders addressed the issue of safety for the children and the possibility
that she herself could face charges by Child Protective Services of inadequate
guardianship if she allowed the children to be released to their father for
visitation in a dangerous situation. She began refusing visitation out of the area in
favor of allowing it to occur at the paternal grandparents' home. This experience
of setting limits empowered Mrs. Sanders to begin to set limits at home also and
to begin to work toward financial independence and regain her role as mother of
the two young boys.

When RJ began school the following year, his teacher viewed him as sometimes sad and sometimes oppositional. He would frequently become antagonistic
with other children and bully them. My preliminary treatment plan had called for
work on improvement of socialization skills, and the modality of choice, our
latency-age children's group, was available for the fall. RJ would be the youngest
of the group, and I made the decision to offer him the group.

As previously mentioned, in the alcoholic family, the survival roles taken on by the children represent the attempt to cope with an often overwhelming situation and to maintain family homeostasis. RJ's role as the parentified child kept the family from experiencing the loss of the "normal" family life but also kept Mrs. Sanders under stress. Because of her own unresolved dependency needs, her grief, and other issues, she felt unable to regain the adult role of parent. Although the parentified behaviors in RJ at home had been reduced a great deal, I was concerned that as his mother moved toward financial independence and out of her parents' home, RJ would again seek to be the "little man" of the house instead of assuming role behaviors appropriate to his age. I was also concerned about his socialization skills. RJ had mentioned more than once that he wished he was the baby in the family and that he wished he had an older brother. In the planned latency-age children's group, RJ would be the only 7-year-old in a group of 8-, 9-, and 10-year-olds. I decided to weigh the risk factors of the behaviors becoming more regressive in such a setting against the hope that the benefits of this modality would be evident within the 12-week duration of the group.

Latency-Age Group

The group began with a definition of group purpose and goals. The common factor was that all the children had a chemically dependent parent. Most had parents who were already divorced or were in the process of being divorced because of the disease. I stated to them that we hoped that we would get to know some new friends who also lived with the disease of chemical dependency and to figure out how to deal more effectively with some of the feelings we experience in the chemically dependent household.

In the latency-age group for children of alcoholics, the overall goals are as follows:

1. To identify feelings of shame, guilt, and anxiety related to parental chemical dependency.
2. To encourage appropriate ventilation of those feelings.
3. To reduce the sense of isolation experienced by children of alcoholic parents.
4. To continue education about family chemical dependency: intergenerational impact; disease concept, chemical dependency as a disease that children cannot cause, control, or cure.
5. To improve socialization skills and encourage the use of positive peer support.
6. To enhance self-image.
7. To improve problem-solving skills and coping ability.

Self-image presented itself as an issue early in group, as it is an integral part of *The TAWK (Talk Alcohol with Kids) Game* by Paul White. Children each receive a blank figure as a "marker" and must fill it in in order to use it as a playing piece. Discussion then arises as to the children's unhappiness with their physical traits (e.g., "my hair is too red," "I'm too fat"). The therapist then validates the sad or angry or shameful feelings of not being happy with one's appearance, and this is modeled for the other group members. Instead of correcting the child's perception of him- or herself, the feeling attached to the belief is validated, paving the way for further discussion of feelings and beliefs that are accurate or inaccurate.

Second Group Session

In the second group session, I introduced *The TAWK Game* as a tool for improving our understanding about different situations. The goal of the game is to complete "puzzle people" and to coordinate the four parts of being a whole person: understanding, education, feelings, and decisions. Children have a path to follow, but there is no "correct" route, allowing for freedom of choice within reasonable limits. They choose color-coded cards and answer questions about each of these areas and receive a chip for any response that represents an effort to verbalize. RJ's poor self-image was reflected as he began to color his game piece.

Content of Session	Rationale/Analysis
THERAPIST: I see you chose yellow for your hair, RJ.	
RJ: That's the color I wish my hair was. (*Bill looks over at RJ, surprised.*)	
BILL: What are you, weird or somethin'? (*Looks at therapist quizzically; points to RJ.*) What's the matter with him, anyway? (*Points to own hair, which is bright red.*) I wish I had brown hair like you.	
RJ: (*Appears to take this in as he starts to color his eyes blue; his eyes are brown.*) Well, you can have it. And I wish I had blue eyes.	
T: What would happen if you had blue eyes and yellow hair, RJ?	
RJ: Then people would like me better. Brown is ugly.	I am not sure what this is about. Mother has blonde hair and blue eyes, whereas Father is darker in coloring. Perhaps he is trying to eliminate those physical parts of himself that are like Dad.
CAROLYN (*angrily*): It is not! I have beautiful brown hair. (*Tosses it around.*) You look fine the way you are. Now your piece is gonna be all messed up. It doesn't even look like you!	
RJ: (*Considers this. To me*) Can I get another guy to color? I don't want this one.	
T: You decided to be just the way you are, RJ, with that shiny brown spiked hair and bright brown eyes. (*handing him a new figure to color*) You can certainly be yourself with this game.	

The questions in *The TAWK Game* are designed to develop positive peer-group interaction as well as to cultivate education about the disease of chemical dependency. The learning experience that occurs in use of the game, however, is not contingent on the questions and reward chips but emerges in the process of the interaction.

Third Group Session

In session 3, we worked with the family roles. A film called "Soft Is the Heart of a Child" illustrates the survival roles in a chemically dependent family. Again, the isolation is reduced as the children see aspects of their own life situations occur in the story about an alcoholic family with Mom and Dad drinking too much. I followed the film viewing by assigning them family roles (the ones they played in their own chemically dependent families) and then having them pretend to perform a task together, such as eating dinner or doing homework. With only a few suggestions, they were able to stay in role, often with comical results. Since that worked well, I then reassigned the roles to ones they were unfamiliar with. That was uncomfortable for some of them. It is important for clinicians to recognize how difficult ingrained roles are to change.

The family heroes were anxious to set the table, cook dinner, get anyone an extra napkin. The scapegoat threw food. The lost child sat there and ate little. The mascot joked. In doing homework, scapegoats threw the paper across the room in a crumpled ball, whereas the family heroes erased constantly to make everything perfect. The lost child stared out into space, and the mascot wanted to tickle everyone. Clinicians interested in this game may refer to Moe and Perlman's (1989) *Kids' Power: Healing Games for Children of Alcoholics.*

Fourth Group Session

In session 4 of the group, with the engagement phase well under way, work began on problem-solving skills. On 10 3" × 5" index cards, I wrote out situations that might occur in chemically dependent homes. Each ended with two questions: "How do you feel?" and "What do you do?" I had the video camera set up and informed the group that we were going to be doing TV stories for taping. In small groups, they each took on roles in a dysfunctional family and attempted to solve the problems presented on the cards.

The situations included parental fighting, violence, sexual abuse, rejection by peers, sibling rivalry, safety, and academic difficulties. Group members were excited by this idea of "acting" and argued about who would get to play each scene. They were less concerned with their actual parts than they were with being in each scene. RJ, Carolyn, and Bill were in the scene about Dad coming home drunk and starting to yell at Mom. RJ took the part of the child, and Bill and Carolyn were the fighting parents. It is interesting to note that children of alcoholics especially love to play the role of the addicted parent. If they do not want this role, it sometimes indicates to me the extent of fear the child has of that parent.

The following is an excerpt from that scene, demonstrating how they attempted to problem solve.

Content of Session

Rationale/Analysis

BILL: OK, RJ, go over in that corner. You play with GI Joe guys or something. OK. Carolyn, I'm *wrecked. (Stumbles across the room.)* Hi, honey, I'm home.

CAROLYN: Where have you been? Dinner is cold now. And you're *drunk!*

B: Oh, all you do is nag, you b . . . *(At this point he looks over at me—is he allowed to say that word? I nod.)* You *bitch!* *(He giggles.)* You're always nagging me. Where's the kids?

RJ *(pretending to play in a corner)*: Hi, Dad. Can we go out to the park for a little while? It's still light out.

B: *(Begins to yell at Carolyn.)* Now he's telling me what to do when I get home, huh? Did you tell him Daddy would come home and take him to the park? I work hard, you stupid . . . *(looks up again)* bitch! I want to have a few beers when I get home and relax.

RJ: *(Gets up from his corner; the voices are louder now, and this is his cue.)* Dad, I'm sorry. How was your day?

What happens to *his* feelings?

(At this point, there is a comment from the "studio audience.")

DONNIE: Hey! It's not RJ's fault that the dad is drunk.

T: You're right, Donnie. Help out here.

D: That Mom is stupid. She should take him to the park herself.

T: That's one idea. Anybody else?

MELANIE: I hate when my parents fight like that. I cover my ears, but then they get madder.

CAROLYN: If I was *really* the mom, I wouldn't even talk to him. But my mom always does.

T: How does this feel for you RJ?

RJ *(brightly)*: Sad?

But you would not know it from his behavior!

T: Does anybody else feel sad in this scene?

C: I do! Sad and mad.

B: Well, I'm sadder than the whole world because I'm a drunk.

They are silent here. This *is* very sad for them. Bill has unknowingly reinforced the disease concept. they have validated the experience for one another through identification and offered support. Feelings of isolation and shame begin to be reduced.

In the group, RJ was able to receive the support and ongoing assistance from his older peers. For instance, his verbal skills seemed above age ability, and his reading was at the age level. When we sat together in a group of six to play *The TAWK Game*, RJ was able to ask for and accept help from several group members. He was accepted because he was so mature in his verbal productions and because, as the parentified child, he was a good listener who was eager to help out. The acting-out behaviors reported at school did not appear in the group.

CONCLUDING COMMENTS

Over the course of treatment we were able to assist RJ in coping with the many losses he has experienced and improving his ability to cope more effectively with difficult situations that arose as his mother attempted to become less dependent after a failed violent and chemically dependent marriage. Mrs. Sanders was eventually able to identify herself as an adult child of an alcoholic, with the understanding that this would imply the need for her own further treatment. One of the most important events occurring through treatment was the stabilization of a crisis situation. Although RJ was the identified patient, he was not allowed to be scapegoated in the family system because immersion in the psychoeducational group helped in reframing his behavior as functional for the chemically dependent family. When, during treatment, there was a relapse of RJ's strong oppositional behaviors, it then led the mother to explore what could be going on to make RJ revert to coping at his previous level. It turned out that his grandfather did some heavy drinking sometimes, too. It was RJ who was able to recognize this later on, using the framework we'd used to educate him about family chemical dependency. The grandfather's alcoholism created difficulty in the home, as Mrs. Sanders improved her self-esteem level and worked toward moving out. As she was increasingly able to appropriately parent RJ and David, she was more assertive with her parents in refusing to allow them to take over child rearing.

I had anticipated that with the ending of the group treatment phase and Mrs. Sanders's plan to separate from her family of origin, RJ would either regress to his previous level of functioning or else become depressed. The oppositional behaviors returned at home, but he did not become violent with his younger sibling, nor was he oppositional at school. He became slightly depressed, and we arranged a psychiatric evaluation as a precautionary measure because of his previous references to death and violence.

RJ was able to verbalize in the school setting about his feelings of sadness about his parents' divorce and the loss of his pets. This created some anxiety for Mrs. Sanders, but in several more family sessions we were able to discuss the importance of continuing to identify and verbalize feelings appropriately, something that had not been safe for Mrs. Sanders either in her family of origin or in her marriage.

As I reevaluate work with this family, I might have tried to involve the maternal grandparents, at least in the psychoeducational group. They had a profound influence on this reforming family and could have benefited tremendously. During one phone contact I had with the grandmother late in treatment, she spilled over in emotion about how difficult her life had been for all these previous months because of the two young children and her incompetent daughter who should have never married that awful man who was the father of RJ and David. In retrospect, there was a lot of "unfinished business" to be resolved.

Another aspect to treating this child could have been additional involvement with the other systems impacting on him, namely, his teacher and the new school system he had been thrust into at the time of his parents' break-up. Often a phone contact with a teacher to offer support in dealing with a difficult child can provide support and build a collaborative alliance. Aligning support on behalf of a young client models effective parenting for the beleaguered mother.

There were several key factors in the outcome of this case. One was Mrs. Sanders's decision to end the marriage to the chemically dependent spouse. Though she wavered many times, she did not send conflicting messages to RJ that could have confused him. The loss became a permanent one for him to begin to integrate into his life experience. Another important factor was the availability of a group for RJ's treatment as well as an exceptional mix of children. As mentioned previously, it is important to allow the child's survival role to remain in place and to cultivate the strengths of that role in the course of treatment. Courage and assertiveness can replace self-defeating behaviors.

Although treatment of RJ terminated after 2 years, Mrs. Sanders was referred for further help at an adult agency where she could deal with the impact of chemical dependency in long-term counseling. She was also referred to Alanon family groups for use of positive peer support. The ex-spouse continued to enter their lives and create difficulty from time to time, but Mrs. Sanders was more equipped to deal with him. This maintained a feeling of safety and security for RJ and his brother, David, so that they could get on with their normal developmental tasks and continue to heal from the devastating losses experienced in their young lives. This initial treatment paved the way for all of them.

PLAY THERAPY MATERIALS

Films
- "A Story about Feelings": The Johnson Institute, 510 First Avenue North, Minneapolis, MN 55441
- "Soft Is the Heart of a Child": The Kroc Foundation, Operation Cork, 8939 Villa La Jolla Drive, San Diego, CA 92037

Games and Puppets
- Puppets: Feelings Factory, Inc., 11-B Glenwood Avenue, Raleigh, NC 27603
- *TAWK (Talk Alcohol with Kids)*: Paul White, 3703 N. Main Street, Rockford, IL 61103; (815) 965-7608

Books
- Jones, P. (1983). *The brown bottle*. Center City, MN: Hazelden Foundation
- Viorst, J. (1971). *The tenth good thing about Barney*. New York: Atheneum

STUDY QUESTIONS

1. Discuss the pressure on the therapist when a child threatens to leave a session. Consider the therapist's alternatives when this happened in session 3. Critique her intervention and comment on the child's response.

2. Comment on the statement that changing the survival roles in the alcoholic family should not be considered a treatment goal. Do you agree or disagree? Give your reasons.

3. Comment on the child's need for an ongoing relationship with the chemically dependent parent. How was that handled in this case, and how do you envision the evolution of RJ's future relationship with his father? What role can the therapist play in assisting the child?

4. Do you agree with the therapist's concluding comments that the grandparents could have been involved in treatment? At what point might this intervention have been attempted, and what response might have been anticipated? Discuss, in principle, the issue of whether to include grandparents in children's treatment. What about inclusion of the siblings?

REFERENCES

Ackerman, R. (1983). *Children of alcoholics—A guidebook for educators, therapists and parents.* Holmes Beach, FL: Learning Publications.

Black, C. (1982). *It will never happen to me!* Denver: Medical Administration.

Jones, M. L. (1989). *Double jeopardy: Similarities in family dynamics of alcoholism and sexual abuse.* Garden City, NY: Adelphi University.

Jones, P. (1983). *The brown bottle.* Center City, MN: Hazelden Foundation.

Moe, J., & Perlman, D. (1989). *Kids' power: Healing games for children of alcoholics.* Deerfield Beach, FL: Health Communications.

Viorst, J. (1971). *The tenth good thing about Barney.* New York: Atheneum.

Woititz, J. (1982). *Adult children of alcoholics.* Deerfield Beach, FL: Health Communications.

PART IV

Medical/Health Crises

CHAPTER 15

The Crisis of Acute Hospitalization
Case of Seth, Age 7

SUSAN WOJTASIK
SALLIE SANBORN

Reviews of the literature in 1965 (Vernon, Foley, Sipowicz, & Schulman) and 1985 (Thompson) reveal some 500 articles and studies examining the psychological responses of children to hospitalization. These studies generally confirm the observations and insights of hospital workers and parents that hospital experiences cause emotional upsets and developmental regression that sometimes persist after the child returns home. The literature also stresses that developmentally based interventions can prevent or mitigate undue distress (Prugh, Staub, Sands, Kirschbaum, & Lenihan, 1953; Plank, 1971; Hardgrove & Dawson, 1972; Petrillo & Sanger, 1980; Thompson & Sanford, 1981; Bolig & Gnezda, 1984, Goldberger, 1988; Gaynard et al., 1990). The American Academy of Pediatrics (1986) in its *Handbook of Hospital Care for Children and Youth* recommends that all institutions with 10 or more pediatric beds create programs addressing the emotional and developmental needs of children.

The response to this heightened sensitivity to children's distress has had a profound effect on the shape and function of pediatric units in the hospital. Physical recovery that leaves emotional scars in its wake is now unacceptable in pediatric practice. General hospitals increasingly reflect sensitivity to children's need for emotional comfort through the provision of accommodations for parents, playrooms, school programs, and carefully planned environmental design. In January 1990, the Joint Commission on Accreditation of Healthcare Organizations for the first time in their accreditation manual included specific guidelines for the hospital care of children. These guidelines make specific reference to the need for family-centered psychosocial services.

The child life profession has developed during the past 25 years in response to the needs of children and families for developmentally specific psychosocial services in health care settings. The child life specialist joins the pediatrician, the child psychiatrist, the pediatric nurse, and the medical social worker as the newest member of the health care team offering comprehensive services to the sick or injured child and the child's family. The work of the child life specialist is rooted in the theoretical perspectives of child and family development. The importance of family bonds and the emotional and cognitive tasks, needs, and capacities of children from birth through adolescence constitute the bedrock of child life practice. The child life specialist advocates for consideration of the child as a rapidly growing, learning, feeling individual as well as a person in need of medical treatment.

Children need abundant opportunities for play when they are in the hospital, since play is the reservoir and wellspring of a child's fundamental capacity to assimilate and adapt creatively to life experiences. Before the child is able to organize his or her experience of the world in logical sequences, before rules and order become meaningful, symbolic and dramatic play serve to illuminate those aspects of life that are obscure and mysterious. The young child who is unable to play or whose play is impoverished is seriously disadvantaged in the face of troublesome or difficult situations. Indeed, throughout life, our ability to "play" with ideas to a large extent determines our ability to creatively address challenges.

The hospital setting subdues a child's natural capacity for social engagement and play. The crisis of hospitalization causes developmental achievements to be put "on hold" and frequently causes regression to earlier stages. In the hospital, babies typically babble less, exploring toddlers cling to their mothers more, and many children need stimulation with a variety of play forms before they are able to use play spontaneously.

Play unleashes the full potential of its healing power for diversion, for instruction, as preparation for frightening or painful medical procedures, and as a means of mastering feelings of anger and helplessness. "Therapeutic" play includes both unstructured and nondirective playroom activities with other children as well as the carefully focused and individualized use of hospital equipment and the playing out of medical procedures that permit children to experience the stresses of the hospital at a more manageable level.

In an environment in which many things are threatening and nearly everything is out of the child's control, helping children achieve and maintain a sense of comfort, safety, and well-being is a major challenge to the child life specialist. Whenever medical conditions allow, children are encouraged to spend time in the playroom. The only medical procedures permitted in the playroom are those initiated and carried out by the children themselves in dramatic play scenarios. Dolls become patients, and the child as nurse/doctor administers treatments. The playroom hospital corner is the site of intravenous infusions, spinal taps, the ever-hated and ubiquitous shots, major surgeries of trunk and limb, major traction and castings, as well as the measuring of temperatures and blood pressure.

The playroom offers a full range of play activities appropriate to the ages of the children using the room. Here the careful observations of the child life specialist uncover each child's unique strengths and coping strategies. This information greatly assists the medical team in planning methods of treatment that maximize the child's cooperation.

Perhaps the playroom's most salient feature for the child is its presence as a haven, a sanctuary, a place where it is safe to be a child. By extension, the child life specialist becomes a safe person. A trusting relationship with an adult who is not involved in medical treatment is enormously helpful to children and their families.

THE CRISIS OF HOSPITALIZATION

Illness, injury, and hospitalization are extremely stressful and have a tremendous impact on a child's emotional growth and development. The damaging effects of fear are pervasive and profound. Even though the child's actual pain or discomfort may be mild or even nonexistent, anticipation of the unknown may render the child helpless, particularly if parents are uninformed, overly anxious, or absent.

Golden (1983, pp. 214–216) identifies three major sources of stress in children who are ill and require hospitalization. These are related to (1) separation from parents and necessary relocation to a new environment, (2) loss of autonomy and control, and (3) fear of bodily harm and/or death. The anxiety connected with each of these specific stressors tends to relate to the age and developmental level of the child. Thus, the older infant, toddler, and young preschooler are especially vulnerable to separation anxiety; the Oedipal child (4 to 7 years) tends to be particularly fearful about possible bodily damage in addition to having concerns about autonomy and control; the older, latency-age child may struggle to understand the possibility and meaning of death.

All of these fears can be addressed both symbolically and directly through play. Piaget (1951) has stated that play "allows the ego to assimilate the whole of reality, to integrate it in order to relive it, to dominate it, or to compensate for it" (cited by Adams, 1976, p. 418). Play helps the child cope with the frustrations, fears, and disappointments rooted in his or her situation. It is the externalized expression of the child's emotional life and his or her natural vehicle for self-exploration and communication.

Although regression to more comfortable and familiar levels of behavior is common during hospitalization, some children show remarkable stability and even make substantial gains in maturity. For some children, the crisis of hospitalization affords opportunities for growth evident in surprising resilience and success. Such children are able to leave the hospital with a strong sense of having mastered a difficult series of experiences. One child at our hospital (Dorothy, age 13) expressed it this way (Morrow, 1985): "I thought I was *never* going to live through being in the hospital. But I did! Here I am! One week before I go home. I feel brave! Good old me! Now I can do *anything* if I've gone through all this!"

THE CASE: SETH, AGE 7

Seth is a 7-year-old boy admitted to a major metropolitan trauma center as a result of a fall from playground equipment in a public park.

He suffered a life-threatening injury to his spinal cord between the top third and fourth vertebrae (C_3-C_4). This injury not only rendered Seth quadriplegic but also compromised his breathing to such an extent that he required respirator assistance.

From the emergency room, Seth was admitted to the pediatric intensive care unit and spent the first 2 months of his hospitalization in this setting. Play interventions were begun on the day of his admission and continued on a daily basis throughout his 9-month hospital stay.

Family Information

Prior to his injury, Seth was in excellent health, very physically active, and extremely social and popular with adults as well as children. He had completed first grade and was about to enter second grade in a public school. His mother, Janine, age 27, had separated from Seth's father very shortly after his birth and had been living with a known drug dealer, Fredo, for most of Seth's life. Seth was very close to Fredo and called him Daddy. One week prior to Seth's accident, Fredo was shot and killed in an apparent drug altercation. The day of Fredo's funeral was the day of Seth's fateful fall.

At the time of the accident Seth was living in a housing project apartment with his maternal grandmother, Rita, age 48; Aunt Rose, age 28; cousin J, Rose's son, age 8, in a third-grade program for the gifted; mother, Janine, age 27; and brother, Carlos, age 9, who was repeating third grade. All adults in the home received public assistance and had no known job history outside of the home. There were drug abuse problems with both Rose and Janine. At the time of Seth's accident, Janine was 8½ months pregnant and experienced heroin withdrawal the evening he was admitted to the intensive care unit. The social worker involved managed to get Janine admitted to the methadone treatment program. She remained in the program throughout Seth's hospital stay.

Presenting Problem

Because of the severity of Seth's injury, he faced a prolonged stay in the acute hospital for stabilization of respiratory function and careful monitoring of other vital functions to forestall medical complications. A thorough evaluation of his injury was also undertaken to determine any possibility for the recovery of body function. The injury occurred so high in the spinal column that spontaneous breathing was seriously compromised. Life could not be sustained without respirator assistance. In the emergency room a surgical incision was made in Seth's throat, which permitted the introduction of a tube into his trachea (tracheostomy). This tube was connected to a mechanical respirator that essentially breathed for Seth. He became very conscious of his dependency on this machine and was often anxious about its reliable functioning.

Fine-tuning of Seth's mechanical respiratory levels comprised a major part of his medical care. If he could be weaned from the machine altogether, options for the course of his rehabilitation would be greatly expanded. This hoped-for goal was never realized. An intermediate goal was to reduce his assisted respiratory level to such an extent that he could speak with normal volume rather than a whisper. This goal was reached only after he was moved to the long-term chronic care facility where he currently lives. While at our facility he was never able to articulate above a whisper.

Seth required suctioning of mucous secretions through his tracheostomy two or three times an hour to keep the airway clear. When he was anxious, he asked to be suctioned almost continually.

Rehabilitation efforts at our center focused very little on physical movement and more on respiratory adjustment. Seth was in a Clinitron bed to reduce the possibility of decubitus ulcer formation. This bed was extremely heavy, requiring several people to move it. He was not moved to the rehabilitation area for physical therapy. Physical therapy at bedside was dependent on the schedule of an overextended staff and took place infrequently.

Play sessions in the hospital setting are often marked by informality and flexibility. Sessions are less time-bound than most play therapy sessions in other settings. There are many opportunities to lengthen or shorten sessions as the occasion demands. Sessions are often "interrupted" by treatments or routine daily care. These interruptions became opportunities for teaching and springboards for therapeutic interventions.

First Interview: Establishing Relationships

The first approach to working with Seth was through reading him stories. On the first day, a book requiring a lot of visual participation was offered. He gave little eye contact and little response.

Content of Session

THERAPIST: Hi, Seth. My name is Sallie. I work in the playroom. I brought some books to show you. This one, *Pancake Pie*, really tries to trick you. There are lots of little picture stories on each page, so we really have to look!

And we can also talk about some of the stuff that you've seen since you've been here. I work with kids to help them understand what all this stuff (*pointing to all the equipment in the room*) is so it's not so confusing.

A lot of kids wonder about what all these noises are and who all these people are and what kind of room is this anyway. Let me start with this room. This is called the ICU. There's always *initials* for everything here, too! So, just like your initials are SE for Seth Eberle, ICU stands for intensive care unit. This is where a lot of people come when

Therapist's Analysis

Take opportunity to engage Seth without verbal demands. Provide opportunity for choice, control, and the beginnings of interactive play.

Provide information about my role as well as addressing latency-age use of information-seeking behavior to gain control.

they first come to the hospital so that doctors and nurses can learn all about how *your* body works. That's why there are so many machines and noises, too. They're all to help doctors and nurses know how your body is doing and sometimes to help your body. Like this (*pointing to heart monitor and explaining how it works*). *Everyone* in the room has a heart monitor. And the IV—more initials!—stands for intravenous. That means it goes *into* your vein so your body can get the medicine it needs. Most people in the hospital have an IV too. And this (*pointing to his trach*) is to help you with your breathing.

(*Seth gives little direct eye contact, so therapist moves on with the book. As therapist reads book, Seth continues to give little direct eye contact but does appear interested in the story.*)

Respecting need to move slowly.

T: There's another book called *Annie and the Wild Animals* that is *so* amazing. It really tries to trick you, too. I'll bring it to show you tomorrow, and if you like, we can read it together.

The first session was kept deliberately brief in order to establish anticipation, engaging his interest without saturating it.

(*While Sallie is preparing to leave, Audrey, another therapist working with a younger child in the ICU, "knocks" on the imaginary door to Seth's "room" and asks if she may "come in" and introduce herself.*)

Provide modeling for staff in respecting Seth's privacy and control over his space even though he is in an open cubicle.

SETH: (*Shakes his head "no."*)

AUDREY: OK. Well, I'll stop by tomorrow and see how you feel about meeting me then. Bye!

Preliminary Assessment and Treatment Plan

Seth appeared to be a bright and engaging child. Although it was possible for him to whisper, he chose, on our first encounter, to remain nonverbal. He communicated quite effectively with his eyes. His ability to stay involved with the story (his eyes never left the page except to look at me; he did not look around the room or appear distracted) indicated that he could become engaged in activity.

For Seth, the challenge to restore developmental equilibrium was fraught with obstacles. He would need to learn how to utilize those around him to manipulate his world and thereby assist his communication, both verbally and nonverbally. Seth had to face a drastic change in status from that of an active, energetic 7-year-old interested in running, climbing, and building (Legos, Transformers, etc.) to his present and future reality of being quadriplegic. He needed to mourn his loss and adapt to his new identity.

Mourning the loss of body function can take the form for children of active resistance, such as crying, angry outbursts, or whining, or passive resistance, such as withdrawal, excessive sleeping, loss of appetite, or decreased interaction with the environment. The reactions of family and schoolmates can either help or hinder a child in the face of such a major readjustment. In Seth's case, his family, in spite of severe social problems, became quite consistently supportive. Janine especially was remarkably intact when it came to Seth. Although her visits were somewhat erratic while he was in the ICU, perhaps attributable to her adjustment to the methadone program and final trimester of pregnancy, after his transfer from the ICU to the general unit she was with him almost daily. Frequently she stayed overnight with him.

There was tremendous fighting among Janine, Rose, and Rita. As a result, the visits of Rose and Rita became less frequent. Seth's brother, Carlos, visited once or twice a week during the first few months and gradually tapered off to once or twice a month. Seth appeared to adjust well to the various visiting patterns of all family members except those of his mother. When she would fail to make an expected appearance, he would often withdraw, want the sheet pulled over his head, refuse to eat.

Seth's strongest peer relationships prior to his hospitalization were with his cousins. Because they were often not allowed to visit in the hospital, his interaction with them was considerably reduced. He tolerated this change well. His ability to make friends in the hospital appeared to compensate for this loss. Perhaps this also served as a defense against his disability. People in the hospital only knew him without movement and, therefore, adapted immediately to his present range of play. His former playmates would have to learn a new way of being friends with him.

The treatment plan developed by the child life specialist for her work with Seth included both short-range and long-range goals. Among the short-range goals were the following:

1. To help Seth and his family cope with the stress and anxiety of the hospital experience.
2. To promote normal growth and development while in the health care setting.
3. To help Seth recognize that he has some choices and that he can exert some control over his life.
4. To allow Seth to express his feelings of fear and anger about his disability.

Among the long-range goals are the following:

1. To help Seth move toward a sense of worthwhile personal identity.
2. To increase Seth's willingness to accept appropriate help from others.
3. To encourage Seth to renounce any lingering feelings of guilt or responsibility for the accident.

Play Therapy Sessions

Second Session

Content of Session	Therapist's Analysis

Content of Session

(Therapist brings *Annie and the Wild Animals* and a rabbit puppet as well as *Pancake Pie*.)

Therapist's Analysis

Always bring a familiar play item (one previously enjoyed) as well as other choices. This provides stability and continuity as well as opportunity for choice (control). Choices are limited so as not to overwhelm.

THERAPIST: (*holding puppet up*) Hi, Seth! Sallie brought me to meet you. How are you today?

Playfully engaging with indirect interaction, which is less threatening (and more fun). Also begins to introduce idea that there are a range of toys for me to bring.

SETH: (*Smiles and rolls his eyes playfully.*)

T: (*puppet*) Can I listen to the story with you?

S: (*Nods "yes."*)

T: (*Reads story that encourages Seth to describe the puzzles on each page of the story.*)

Beginning to introduce activities that elicit more response and thereby provide opportunities for increased interaction.

S: I liked the story. Do you have more?

T: What kind of stories do you like?

Accepting his interest and extending it to begin learning about one another.

S: I don't know. A lot of different ones.

T: How about if I bring a few different kinds and you can choose? We also have a lot of toys in the playroom for me to show you.

Respecting his hesitation, offers assistance as well as extending range of choice and introducing the hospital world beyond the ICU.

S: Can I go to the playroom?

T: Not just now, but soon you'll be able to. I'll ask your doctor when, OK? Usually when kids are in the ICU the doctors and nurses want them close by so they can learn exactly how their bodies work. That way they can take the very best care of you. When they've learned this and see that you're doing well with your trach and stuff, they'll move your bed to a room near where the playroom is. A lot of kids can't come to the playroom right away just like you. So I bring the playroom to them, just like I'm doing for you!

Acknowledge interest and show range of my role: liaison with medical staff; receiver and conveyor of information.

More explanation of the ICU and promise of movement beyond this space.

S: But why am I here? I've been in the hospital before. I was here for one week when I broke my chin. My father brought me cars and juice and cookies. I also got hit by cars before. I got hit once in the leg and once in the side, and I couldn't breathe. But why am I here now?

T: Well, do you remember what your family and the doctors and nurses have told you? You were playing on the monkey bars in the playground and, like lots of kids, you fell and got hurt.

Assessing his understanding of their explanation and providing a consistent response.

Universalizing the incident to reduce self-blame.

S: No! That was when I broke my chin!

T: You remember falling and hurting your chin, but you don't remember this fall when you hurt your neck. You know what? It sounds like you have a lot of questions about your fall and your reasons for being here.

S: I know I can't breathe or move now, but how come and for how long?

Supporting his feelings and clarifying need for more information.

T: You know, Seth, these are all important questions that we can talk about with your doctor. It's really important for kids in the hospital to know exactly what's going on and why, so that they don't have to be confused. So, when I don't have the answer to your questions, we'll find someone who does.

Highlight Seth's misconceptions and/or memory lapse. I need to clarify with medical staff what physical manifestations (swelling, etc.) could be causing memory loss as well as verifying what Seth has been told. Denial could also certainly be a factor.

S: Talking is the best thing!

I spoke to the social worker involved in the case, who said that Seth's fall could have caused some swelling in his brain that could possibly be causing memory lapse. The social worker would be meeting with Seth's mother to clarify what information she and the doctor had conveyed to Seth. She said that we would all meet with Seth later that day to assess his understanding and to attempt to clarify his misconceptions.

Third Session

The meeting took place with the care-giving team, and Seth was told that his injury would require the respirator for a *very* long time—maybe for all of his life. His body would not move on its own, but eventually he would have an electric wheelchair he could operate and could move around in. Seth made no immediate response; his mood was subdued. I remained after the meeting to provide an opportunity for Seth to respond either verbally or in play.

Content of Session	Therapist's Analysis
THERAPIST: Do you have any more questions about the meeting?	
SETH: No.	
T: OK. Well, if you think of anything, you can just ask, OK? You know I'll see you every day, so we can talk about these things whenever you're ready. It's kind of a lot to think about all at once. I brought two new books and a coloring book and crayons.	Do not force discussion but provide opportunity to bring up issues on his own terms and in his own time. Introduce new way of playing.
S: I can't color!	
T: We're going to color *together*. You can tell me which picture to color and exactly what colors to use where. I'm just your assistant. You'll be making all the choices.	Modeling new ways of playing and interacting as well as showing Seth ways to play and have control.
S: (*Rolls his eyes, but smiles and agrees.*) Let's draw the frog picture! I can make a frog sound. (*Makes clicking noise—well!*) But I can't whistle any more.	Establishes people as extension of his intention; learning to direct another's activity as if it were his own.
T: That's a great sound! It really is like a frog. I can whistle, but I can't do *that*!	Encourage and support his very real abilities.

Fourth Session

Seth received a new neck brace over the weekend and, according to nursing, had been anxiously complaining of breathing difficulties. Perhaps opportunity for preparation for this "minor" adjustment could have reduced his anxious reaction.

Content of Session	Therapist's Analysis
THERAPIST: I see you have a new neck brace. How does it feel?	Acknowledgment of new apparatus and possibility of adjustment reaction.
SETH: I hate it.	
T: What bothers you about it?	
S: It hurts under my chin, and I can't move my head so much.	
T: Did you tell the doctors and nurses?	Assess his ability to verbalize concerns to other staff with whom he felt less comfortable.
S: No! They don't listen to me. They can't understand me.	
T: Well, how about if I ask them if it can be adjusted or if it's something it takes a bit to get used to and soften, like new shoes.	Establish his sense of control, that is, asking questions as well as clarifying what may or may not be possible with regard to his

S: (*Nods "yes."*) But first what books did you bring?

neck brace. Also identifies the sensations of the neck brace with something familiar—new shoes.

Later the doctor came in, and I asked her to explain about the neck brace. She did so and then reminded Seth that he would be going to the operating room the next day for a trach adjustment. I remained throughout the medical visit and then prepared Seth for the OR procedure.

Content of Session	*Therapist's Analysis*
THERAPIST: I will be going with you to the OR too, OK? So if you have any questions you can ask, and if I don't know, what will I do? SETH: You'll find someone who does!	Reaffirming familiarity with known role and confirming his ability to get information he needs.
T: Now, you know that when you come out of the OR you'll still have the trach. They're just adjusting it, making it better for your breathing, but they're not taking it out, OK? S: I know.	Addressing fantasy that surgery will restore to preinjury state.
T: OK. So (*in sign language signs, "See you to-morrow!"*). Do you know what sign language is? S: (*Nods "yes."*) It's how deaf people talk. T: Right! Well, I just said to you, "See you tomorrow" in sign language. I'll teach you more tomorrow.	Introducing a new way of communicating metaphorically enlarges Seth's vision of how people with disabilities can compensate for them.

I accompanied Seth to the OR and remained with him throughout induction of anesthesia. He did very well. He returned to the ICU from the recovery room, and in our next session (5) he remained very engaged in "drawing" pictures. He did not wish to discuss the OR experience.

In the interval between the post-OR session and the following session (6), which included a weekend separation, Seth stopped eating. We considered this to be a response to both the OR experience and that which it reaffirmed: his lack of physical control. Therefore, he controlled what he could: his eating.

Sixth Session

Content of Session	*Therapist's Analysis*
(*Therapist brings book on planting seeds and farming as well as the rabbit puppet.*) SETH: I wish I could plant some seeds. THERAPIST: You can! We can make our own garden! What's your favorite vegetable?	Introduce the idea of relationship between growth and food in a fun and nonthreatening way. Concrete application of control and a sense of accomplishment

S: I like corn.

T: Well, I'll find some corn seeds, and we'll plant them.

(*Seth's mother comes in with tacos, which he had said he wanted. She attempts to persuade him to eat. He refuses.*)

S: I didn't promise that I'd eat!

MOTHER: Then no TV. And I'm leaving.

S: (*Still refuses.*)

NURSE: Let me try (*to Mother, who leaves the room*). Listen, Seth. Do you want to die? If you don't eat you'll die!

(*Seth still refuses, and the nurse leaves angrily.*)

T: (*using puppet*) Can I bug you about eating, too? I think you need *one* more person to bug you about eating.

S: (*Smiles and rolls his eyes.*)

T: You're being fed through your IV and through the nasogastric tube. There's no way you can die from not eating. No one would let you die from not eating. But it would be better for you and for your body if you would eat. Then the nasogastric tube could come out. And I *know* you would like that a lot. (*puppet*) Can we *please* finish our farming book now? I want to know how to make a corn plant grow.

S: (*Nods and smiles.*)

T: (*Continues puppet play to address eating and planting seeds.*) OK. Now tomorrow I'll need to bring *what* things to plant seeds?

Encouraging verbalizing his frustration in indirect way to facilitate expression of anger and possible motivation for not eating.

Addressing threat of dying without removing the need and motivation to eat.

Seventh Session

This was the seed-planting session. I brought a puppet along. Audrey, another child life specialist who also works in the ICU, asked if her puppet could visit my puppet. The two puppets had a silly interaction and acted out some anger. This session provided a passive play opportunity for Seth, which can be very beneficial when a child is too sick or too worn out to engage actively in play.

Eighth Session

Seth was still unresponsive to food but was very teasing and playful with me.

Aunt Rose met me at the elevator to say that Janine's baby had been born (a girl), and she and the baby were here in the hospital on the maternity floor.

Janine told Rose to say that Seth had said he was not eating because something was on his mind.

Content of Session	Therapist's Analysis
THERAPIST: You know, kids tell me that sometimes they don't feel like eating when they're worried about stuff, and I'm wondering if you're worried about your mom?	Universalizing feelings.
SETH: *(Shrugs with his eyes.)*	
T: Well, I'm going to go see her and come back and tell you exactly what's going on, OK? Would you like me to tell her anything?	Establish control and ability to effect some change for himself.
S: Tell her I love her.	
T: I will tell her. *(And then, using sign language, says "See you later.")*	

I took a Polaroid picture of Janine and the baby to bring to Seth, reassuring him that his mother was all right. Janine asked Seth if he would like to name the new baby. He named her Jean.

CONCLUDING COMMENTS

In general, we felt that the treatment goals were achieved, and by the time Seth was transferred to the long-term facility where he was to live, he was ready for the next steps in his rehabilitation. These steps included using a wheelchair operated by a mouth stick and changes in his respiratory levels, which allowed for audible verbalization. His confidence in his ability to breathe and function was stabilized, and this allowed him to tolerate the adjustment to his respirator. He no longer needed to use food refusal as a method of controlling his environment, as he had audible speech and mobility for the first time in almost a year.

Although Seth's disability is devastating and overwhelming, he has the innate capacity to tolerate it. His intelligence and humor have allowed him to compensate for the many losses he has experienced. Although it was difficult for many staff members to see him as anything but a tragic figure, I found myself completely engaged by his charm and courage. I could, therefore, ally myself not with his disabilities but with his capacities.

His developmental stage in conjunction with his humor and social skills were key factors in the success of his treatment and his overall positive adjustment to his disability.

Today Seth is mainstreamed in a public school outside of his hospital residence. He continues to meet life's challenges with humor and intelligence.

PLAY THERAPY MATERIALS

- Puppets: rabbit, dog
- Crayons, coloring book
- Seeds, planting materials
- Polaroid camera
- Books
  Brett, J. (1985). *Annie and the wild animals*. Boston: Houghton, Mifflin.
  Nordqvist, S. (1985). *Pancake pie*. New York: Morrow Junior Books.

STUDY QUESTIONS

1. Seth's mother's introduction to the ICU medical and nursing staff was not a positive one. How might this have been more effectively resolved?

2. Diagram a basic genogram of Seth's nuclear family. Based on this, where can you see potential problems for other family members? What issues has Seth's injury raised for each individual family member? How might these be addressed within the family and within the health care team?

3. How would you explain Seth's condition to the other children as well as prepare Seth for their questions? What questions might they ask?

4. Seth was transferred after 9 months to a long-term chronic care facility that had a ward of respirator-dependent children. Prior to this Seth was the only child on a respirator. Now he was one of many. How would you prepare him for the change?

REFERENCES

Adams, M. A. (1976). A hospital play program: Helping children with serious illness. *American Journal of Orthopsychiatry, 46*(3), 416–424.

American Academy of Pediatrics Committee on Hospital Care. (1986). *Handbook of hospital care for children and youth*. Evanston, IL: Author.

Bolig, R., & Gnezda, M. T. (1984). A cognitive-affective approach to child life programming for young children. *Children's Health Care: Journal of the Association for the Care of Children's Health, 12*, 122–129.

Gaynard, L., Wolfer, J., Goldberger, J., Thompson, R., Redburn, L., & Laidley, L. (1990). *Psychosocial care of children in hospitals: Clinical practice manual from the ACCH child life research project*. Washington, DC: ACCH.

Goldberger, J. (1988). Issue-specific play with infants and toddlers in hospitals: Rationale and interventions. *Children's Health Care: Journal of the Association for the Care of Children's Health, 16*, 134–141.

Golden, D. B. (1983). Play therapy for hospitalized children. In C. E. Schaefer & K. J. O'Connor (Eds.), *Handbook of play therapy* (pp. 213–233). New York: John Wiley & Sons.

Hardgrove, C. B., & Dawson, R. B. (1972). *Parents and children in the hospital*. Boston: Little, Brown.

Joint Commission on the Accreditation of Healthcare Organizations. (1989). *Accreditation manuals for hospitals, 1990*. Chicago: Author.

Morrow, N. (1985). *I wish to see a friendly face.* Unpublished collection of art and writing from Bellevue Pediatrics.

Petrillo, M., & Sanger, S. (1980). *Emotional care of hospitalized children.* Philadelphia: Lippincott.

Piaget, J. (1951). *Play, dreams and imitation in childhood.* New York: W. W. Norton.

Plank, E. N. (1971). *Working with children in hospitals.* Cleveland: Press of Case Western Reserve University.

Prugh, D. G., Staub, E., Sands, H. H., Kirschbaum, R. J., & Lenihan, E. A. (1953). A study of the emotional reactions of children and families to hospitalization and illness. *American Journal of Orthopsychiatry, 23,* 78.

Thompson, R. H. (1985). *Psychosocial research on pediatric hospitalization and health care: A review of the literature.* Springfield, IL: Charles C. Thomas.

Thompson, R. H., & Sanford, G. (1981). *Child life in hospitals.* Springfield, IL: Charles C. Thomas.

Vernon, D. T. A., Foley, J. M., Sipowicz, R. R., & Schulman, J. I. (1965). *The psychological responses of children to hospitalization and illness.* Springfield, IL: Charles C. Thomas.

CHAPTER 16

Diagnosis of Childhood Cancer
Case of Tim, Age 6

ROBIN F. GOODMAN

When parents hear the word "cancer" associated with their child they are devastated. Children and families confront the ordeal of cancer with varying premorbid states that are newly stressed by the diagnosis of the disease. In my role as a psychologist and art therapist, I help the child and family get through the "crisis" of cancer by finding a way for everyone to incorporate the disease and related experiences into the routine fabric of their lives. A preliminary assessment identifies behaviors that are reactive to the disease, those that are unique to the individual's personality style and way of functioning, and the strengths that can be bolstered and the weaknesses that will need protection.

My guiding principle in working with the children is to help them continue to grow, develop, and play as their peers do. Children typically live in the present moment and can readily adapt to a changed environment. A 22-year-old survivor of childhood leukemia told me that having cancer became such an intrinsic part of her life that she could never conceive of, nor answer, a question about how her life was different from others because she had cancer. Having cancer was an *integral* part of her growing up, integrated into who she was, just as having a brother and being on the swim team. Having long hair, losing it, and having it back again all contributed to her identity. This is not meant to minimize the experience but to demonstrate how resilient children can be and how they can sucessfully cope with the "crisis" of growing up with cancer.

Interest in the emotional impact of cancer has burgeoned since the late 1970s, partly because of the increasing survival rates of pediatric cancer patients. "Cancer is the leading cause of disease-related death among children, second only to trauma as the leading cause of death in children between the ages of 1-15 years" (Hockenberry, Coody, & Bennett, 1990). Prior to 1966 only 10-15% of the children with leukemia survived 5 years past diagnosis (Bearison & Pacifici, 1984). Today over 50% of the children diagnosed with acute lymphoblastic leukemia, the most common childhood cancer, survive 5 years following initial diagnosis, with a majority of these patients considered "cured" (Pizzo et al., 1989-1990). Researchers have been studying survivors of childhood cancer both to determine their present psychological functioning and adjustment and to determine retrospectively what factors from their disease contributed to their present status.

However, the research reveals conflicting results concerning the emotional adjustment of survivors of childhood cancer.

Dobkin and Morrow (1985-1986) report that survivors were socially as well adjusted as their healthy peers with respect to education, vocation, and marriage. However, others have found leukemics to have more behavior problems and to score lower on "measures of overall competence, and competence at school" (Sawyer, Crettenden, & Toogood, 1986, p. 204). In one of the major comprehensive studies of survivors, O'Malley, Koocher, Foster, and Slavin (1979) report that 59% of a sample of survivors with a mean age of 5.7 years at diagnosis were "judged to be impaired psychologically" (p. 162). Adjustment of survivors depended on age at diagnosis and time elapsed since diagnosis; the younger the child at diagnosis and the further away from diagnosis, the better. Retrospective studies also have linked emotional adjustment to self-esteem, verbal ability (Koocher, O'Malley, Gogan, & Foster, 1980), honest communication about the disease (O'Malley et al., 1979; Slavin, O'Malley, Koocher, & Foster, 1982), social relationships, and the use of denial as a coping mechanism (O'Malley et al., 1979).

The inherent conundrum of retrospective studies is the difficulty of detecting causation. The literature provides evidence that the entire family is affected by the disease (Dobkin & Morrow, 1985-1986; Eiser, 1979; Futterman & Hoffman, 1973; Van Dongen-Melman & Sanders-Woudstra, 1986) and influences the child's emotional state. Blotcky, Raczynski, Gurwitch, and Smith (1985) found that hopelessness among children with cancer was correlated with high distress among both mothers and fathers. Observations of fatally ill children aged 5 to 12 by Natterson and Knudson (1960) revealed that distress in pediatric cancer patients was related to such things as mother's absence, traumatic procedures such as venipunctures and bone-marrow aspirations, and the death of fellow cancer patients. Thus, a child's use of denial, anxiety, or access to social relationships may be dependent on the parents' handling of the situation more than on the disease itself. The interaction among the individual, the family, and the disease variables is complex at best.

The physical events of the cancer experience itself have been shown also to have a profound effect on the child. When compared to children with other chronic illnesses, leukemics showed "a greater preoccupation with threat to their body integrity and functioning, greater anxiety in their general out of-hospital life, and a lack of adaptability to the necessity of clinic visits" (Spinetta & Maloney, 1975, p. 1037). If, in fact, impaired adjustment is inevitable, research is still trying to answer the question of what accounts for impaired adjustment:

> the experience of cancer *per se*, aversive treatment . . . disruption of children's accustomed and expected daily routines . . . and social relationships, cultural attitudes toward having cancer, how children understand the uncertainties associated with having cancer, the financial burdens on the family, the chronic condition of cancer survivorship, or some combination of these inherent and exogenous factors. (Bearison & Pacifici, 1984, p. 268)

Many of these influences might be categorized as derailments of developmental tasks, but how severe these are and whether the effects are permanent are still open to question. There is a danger of inappropriately assuming that all cancer patients react pathologically or abnormally to their disease. Van Dongen-Melman and Sanders-Woudstra (1986) point to the fact that criteria used to assess pathology and normalcy in healthy populations cannot be transferred in a wholesale fashion. The so-called "pathological behavior" of a cancer patient may in fact be adaptive.

DEVELOPMENTAL CONSIDERATIONS

It is evident that the age of the child and the stage of the disease have bearing on the psychological tasks facing the child. We know that at different ages a child is likely to have specific fears related to hospital and illness experiences. In general, through age 6, a child's biggest fear is separation. This can lead to feelings of abandonment, withdrawal, and mistrust. From age 6 to 9 or 10, the fears of intrusion, mutilation, and punishment are dominant. The range of reactions at this age can include feelings of rejection and isolation from peers and family, guilt, inadequacy, insecurity, and loss of a sense of mastery. From age 9 or 10 to 12 the primary fear is loss of bodily functions and the "adult" fear of the possibility and permanence of death. Some consequences of illness disruption at this age are feelings of social isolation, difficulty with intimate relationships, increased dependency, body-image concerns, and religious questioning (Astin, 1977–1978; Cook, 1973, Easson, 1974; Holland & Rowland, 1989; Lonetto, 1980; Spinetta, 1974).

Two psychological issues figure more prominently for children with cancer: separation/loss and control/competence (Brunnquell & Hall, 1984). Loss associated with death has often been the focus in the literature on cancer, at times overshadowing other significant losses (Van Dongen-Melman & Sanders-Woudstra, 1986). Children with cancer must also cope with other real, concrete losses such as the loss of hair or limbs, or less observable losses such as loss of relationships or independence. Although dealing with separation is a developmental task, having cancer can bring this issue into focus because treatment necessitates prolonged or frequent separations from family and friends that may encourage heightened dependence on a parent. As a consequence of the disease, it is not unusual for a child to feel as if his or her life is in the hands of others. Decreased mobility secondary to the cancer also impacts on a child's ability to feel in control. Whereas loss of control "may disrupt both social and emotional development . . . control strategies can facilitate emotional adjustment during times of stress" (Worchel, Copeland, & Baker, 1987, p. 26). The interaction between the psychological and the physical is difficult to differentiate.

CHILDREN'S UNDERSTANDING OF DEATH

Childhood cancer remains a potentially life-threatening disease, and although death is still a taboo topic, children do think about and work with the concept.

There is some consensus on the stages children traverse on their way to a mature understanding of death. Yet, there is disagreement over whether age, cognitive ability, emotion, or experience is the main determinant of this understanding (Bibace & Walsh, 1979; Childers & Wimmer, 1971; Goodman, 1989; Jenkins & Cavanaugh, 1985; Kane, 1979; Kastenbaum, 1967; Koocher, 1973; Reilly, Hasazi, & Bond, 1983; Orbach, Gross, Glaubman & Berman, 1985; Safier, 1964; Schilder & Wechsler, 1934; Speece & Brent, 1984; Spinetta, 1980; White, Elsom, & Prawat, 1978).

Children typically proceed through specific stages in their development of a mature concept of death. The 3- to 5-year-old is at the preoperational stage of cognitive development; he or she is egocentric in his or her thinking and does not recognize that death is irreversible. At this age, death is experientially and emotionally equivalent to separation. In the second stage, with the advent of concrete–operational thought, death is understood in terms of the specific and the concrete. The 5- to 9-year-old may accept the existence of death but views it as linked to certain causes, such as violence or wrongdoing; this age child may also "personify" death (e.g., belief in the "boogey man"). By age 9 or 10, a child is on the way to the stage of formal operations and is able to think abstractly and to generalize from one person's death to everyone's, including his or her own. At this age, most children can comprehend the four main components of the adult understanding of death: that death is irreversible, inevitable, universal, and results in cessation of bodily functions (Anthony, 1971; Nagy, 1948; Wass, 1984).

Much has been written about how children with cancer become specifically socialized about their disease and its fatal potential. Researchers have studied the process whereby specific experiences influence a child's knowledge about disease. According to Bluebond-Langner (1978), children with cancer go through five stages on their way to becoming socialized about their illness. They progress from learning that their disease is serious to knowing that death is possible if the medicine does not work. Bluebond-Langner (1978) also believes that a child's self-concept corresponds to the different stages. For example, at the stage when children learn the names of the drugs they take and their side effects, they may consider themselves seriously ill but also conceptualize that they can get better.

A comparison of healthy children, suicidal children, and cancer patients concluded that cancer patients had negative feelings about life and were more attracted to death than healthy children (Orbach, Fesback, Carlson, & Ellenberg, 1984). This suggested that cancer patients confront death and deal with it in a specific disease-related manner in order to relieve their unpleasant physical experiences. Spinetta and Maloney (1975) found that cancer patients had an awareness of the seriousness of their illness and had greater anxiety than a control group of patients who had nonfatal chronic illness. However, a caveat is in order: one must avoid making generalizations about the child with cancer; individual variability influences adjustment and long-term psychological survival. We must always ask what *this* set of circumstances means to *this* particular child at *this* particular time.

MANAGEMENT OF THE ILLNESS

Over the years, experience has shown that children with cancer do best when involved in open, honest discussions about their disease and death (Bluebond-Langner, 1978; Goodman, 1989; Vernick & Karon, 1965; Koocher & O'Malley, 1981; Spinetta, 1974; Slavin et al., 1982). Historically, adults have tended to "shield" and "protect" children from discussion about cancer and illness. This seems to be a function of the anxiety in the adult rather than the child's rejection of discussion. Children can become lonely when they are aware of their diagnosis but their parents keep things secret and sugar-coat reality (Binger et al., 1969). As a result, there is little or no meaningful communication (p. 415). Professionals, disturbed about a child approaching death, may unwittingly become remote or unapproachable just at the time when support, information, and contact are needed most (Bluebond-Langner, 1978; Binger et al., 1969; Katz & Jay, 1984).

"Mutual pretense" (Bluebond-Langner, 1978) has been used to describe the adult stance toward death of looking the other way, which encourages the child to do likewise. Results, however, have not demonstrated any value in keeping children in the dark. In working with children with a potentially life-threatening illness, the more accurate question yet to be answered is not *what* to tell children about death and illness but *how* to tell. The answer lies in understanding a child's developmental level and then providing information appropriate to the child's ability to understand, clarifying misinformation, picking up cues about feelings and fears, and responding to these rather than avoiding them.

Much of our knowledge about what children with cancer think, know, and fear comes from investigative and clinical work based on projective assessments, play, and fantasy techniques. Adams-Greenly (1984) refers to Sourkes, who "pointed out that children often have two versions of an illness; the medical version, which they can repeat verbatim, and their own private version . . . play, art, drama, and casual conversation are all useful tools in ascertaining the child's private perceptions" (p. 63). Because the distinction between fantasy and reality, action and thought, can become blurred for children, it may be necessary to use methods that reveal fantasy in order to understand the totality of a child's understanding (Adams-Greenly, 1984). Then one can help a child cope with his or her illness by clarifying reality and dispelling fantasy.

"Finding an acceptable outlet for feelings of anxiety, anger, and fear and gaining a sense of mastery over the environment have been identified as important coping tasks among seriously ill children" (Koocher & O'Malley, 1981, p. 10).

> Giving patients and families the opportunity to talk about their concerns and receive information about their experiences is critically important. Being able to anticipate stressful events . . . can lessen the emotional drain even though the actual experience has not been altered. . . . Supportive information-giving, facilitation of communication among family members, and encouragaing discus-

sion of emotional issues [were deemed extremely important to patients and families.] The patient and family members must feel cared about and must know that all their questions will be answered directly and honestly. (Koocher & O'Malley, 1981, p. 175)

USE OF NONVERBAL THERAPY TECHNIQUES

Children learn through action as well as through words, and they can communicate about their internal world in a nonverbal manner through art and play. Providing the child with the opportunity to express feelings rather than holding them in lets the child turn the passive into the active and sublimate unacceptable feelings of anger and fear.

Therapeutic work with the child often takes the form of creative endeavors. According to Petrillo and Sanger (1980), play and art "deal with emotional release by offering rich and significant channels for expression" (p. 160). It allows for reorganization and reexperiencing problems and anxiety. The child is able to find solutions and enact feelings without fear of criticism. This does not deviate from the standard theory and methods recommended by nondirective play therapists such as Axline (1947). According to Kübler-Ross (1981),

> we receive from the child a picture of his world that is often clearer and more direct than what the artist portrays, because the child has little formal knowledge of art. When a child is investing his feelings and ideas in his drawing, the process unfolds without any critical forces to accuse him. . . . It appears that the child's feelings and thoughts . . . flow freely and directly onto drawing paper. (p. 65)

Art can be a powerful tool in discovering a child's concerns. By creating art, ill children are being constructive in the midst of a life that entails destruction of the part of them that has disease. Children can create their own artistic symbols to express feelings in contrast to taking a ready-made play object and projecting feelings onto the toy. The art work is more personalized and allows the therapist to talk in a nonthreatening way using the child's own metaphor (Kramer, 1971). Diagnostically, drawings may reveal how a child is coping with such physical changes as loss of hair or an amputation, and therapeutically, drawings can be used as a method of intervention. Of course, throughout the therapy, interpretation of drawings and assessment of a child always include more than one piece of art. One must consider the body of work and the context in which it was produced.

Common themes emerging in the art work of children with cancer include illustrations of disease-specific issues, especially those related to loss and change (Sourkes, 1982). Once diagnosed with cancer, children may feel they have lost their identity, and their self-image may be altered to accommodate aspects of their disease. Figure drawings by children with cancer can provide clues to how they feel about being labeled sick. Children feeling a loss of control may portray their anger in the form of superhero battles or attempt to regain a sense of control by realistically depicting various medical situations.

Once diagnosed, children often experience lost or changed relationships. Time with peers and family members is frequently altered because of the temporary effects of treatment, and fellow patients may die from disease. Thus, they may fear the loss of their own life. Children may feel helpless or hopeless in reaction to, and as a way of coping with, their feelings about death and loss. Their art may reveal renewed religious beliefs or faith that parents and staff can help them in their struggles.

THE CASE: TIM BRADLEY, AGE 6

Family Information

Tim Bradley is a 6-year-old boy in first grade, the second child of a white, middle-class family. He has one sister, Rebecca, age 9, who is in the fourth grade. Both parents are college educated. Mrs. Bradley, age 35, stopped working when her daughter was born, and Mr. Bradley, age 37, is an attorney. Both paternal grandparents are alive and are involved with the family. Although living in a nearby state, when Tim was diagnosed, they moved in with the family for 4 months to help out. The maternal aunt also routinely provides babysitting and companionship for the children.

Presenting Problem

Tim was diagnosed with leukemia at age 5, after a month of easy bruising and flu-like symptoms. Up until that time he was in good health and had suffered only the usual childhood ailments such as sore throats and chickenpox. Until Tim was diagnosed with leukemia, the family had not experienced significant stressors or traumas. There were no signs of previous familial psychopathology. The diagnosis challenged the family system, and weak links in the parents' communication patterns emerged. In addition, the child and his family had to deal with the tangible, technical aspects of the treatment regimen and the concomitant emotional reactions and fears surrounding the disease.

First Interview

I first met Tim on the fifth day of his initial hospitalization, at the beginning of his chemotherapy treatment. During his hospitalization he had a steady stream of visitors and family members, coming in shifts, to stay with him. He was already quite knowledgeable about his disease and knew his diagnosis. His hair had begun to fall out from the medicines, and although he was not quite sure why this happened, he was not particularly upset by it. For our first session I arrived with an assortment of drawing materials and hospital play supplies. I explained that I was a different kind of doctor, that I came to find out how he was feeling, see if he had any questions or complaints, and said that sometimes it helped to talk or draw to feel better.

When I arrived he was looking for the box he had been using to save his hair. Being unable to find it, I offered to wrap up strands of his hair in a paper towel. Then I suggested he decorate the box so everyone would know it was special and would not mistakenly throw it out. He drew a happy face on the toweling and then went on to color another picture. He talked about all the "sticks" (blood tests and intravenous lines) he was getting and what he did to get through them. He explained that his mother was at home sometimes to take care of his sister, and if he was alone at night and got scared he could call his father. When Tim was hospitalized, Mr. Bradley slept at the hospital or with friends nearby, coming to the hospital whenever he was summoned by Tim. Knowing how to get help can be extremely important for a child's well-being. Confidence and trust in parents have been associated with positive adaptation in the child with cancer (Worchel et al., 1987).

Tim had tremendous physical and psychological strength and made a rapid adjustment to treatment. His parents met with the school staff to ensure a smooth transition after discharge. Indeed, Tim returned to school in a month, with no apparent problems. All of his chemotherapy was given on an outpatient basis, which clearly encourages the resumption of normal activities. He was friendly with all the staff he encountered, from secretaries to nurses, and managed quite independently. His positive attitude was a reflection of the philosophy his parents displayed. They were careful to shield Tim from their own anguish and doubts. This mutuality between the parents and their ability to maintain stability in the early stages of the disease can reduce the child's fear and hopelessness (Rowland, 1989).

Tim had learned to cope by being in control of his situation and preparing himself for whatever events he experienced at the clinic. However, evidence indicating that he was a scared little boy erupted in his laughing and joking when others discussed medical procedures. Using denial and reaction formation he defended against his feeling afraid. In addition, he became upset one day when he had an unexpected bone-marrow test. This led to a joint effort on the part of his mother and me to help him feel in control. Tim dictated to me all the things he did to help him get through difficult procedures. Tim's list is a very good summary of coping procedures for children with cancer and their families. It illustrates some of the main principles and techniques of therapy used with this population. In particular, it supports the conclusion that children do best when involved in decision making about their treatment (Worchel et al., 1987).

Content of Session	Rationale/Analysis
Tim's tips:	
1. Calm down when the doctor wants to help you.	Belief in power of doctor to take control and cure. Guilt that some-

	thing you do could jeopardize outcome.
2. Find out what is going to happen and why.	Information seeking in order to master the situation. Knowing what to expect increases feeling of control.
3. Take deep breaths.	Relaxation and distraction aid coping.
4. Get hugs from Mom and Dad.	Need to feel safe; increased dependence on parents; fear of separation and abandonment.
5. Count while the needle is in.	Distraction; active participation to decrease feeling helpless.
6. Think of nice things.	Reaction formation; imagery used for distraction and to minimize negative associations.
7. Think about getting better.	Positive attitude as a way to feel in control and be a partner in cure.
8. It's OK to cry, but never say no!	Appropriate expression of feelings; limit setting on behavior. Doctor and parents are still in control.
9. Drink something or do something else.	Need for nurturance, distraction.
10. When you feel sad, talk to Mom or Dad or someone who is there.	Need for outside support; need for verbalization and expression of feelings.
11. Tell your friends to ignore that you are sick.	Coping with changed identity and need for normalizing childhood experiences and socialization.

Preliminary Assessment and Treatment Plan

When first diagnosed with leukemia, patients usually go through a month or two of intense chemotherapy to induce remission. This necessitates frequent trips to the doctor for medicine and procedures. This can be one of the most difficult stages to get through (Clements, Copeland, & Loftus, 1990; Rowland, 1989). The family had developed a routine whereby Mr. Bradley took time off from work to accompany Tim, and Mrs. Bradley kept up the usual activities for the children. When treatment required particularly painful procedures (e.g., a bone-marrow and spinal tap), both parents joined Tim.

Because of the frequency with which Mr. Bradley was with Tim, he was the first to discuss with the doctor some side effects that Tim was having. This resulted in Mrs. Bradley feeling left out and sparked the beginning of a difficult time for the family. In addition to the parents struggling with sharing their responsibilities, Tim was having temper tantrums at home in which he would get into fits of anger and be unable to calm himself down. Tim was bothered by his tantrums, and he felt guilty about his behavior. This was highly unusual behavior for him and was probably caused by a combination of the side effects from a medication, a course of radiation therapy, and general increased frustration with doctor visits.

This scenario illustrates some of the typical problems children and families must confront when the child cancer patient's "efforts at autonomy are thwarted [and] anger, repression, and withdrawal may result. The drive to reexert control can lead to increased oppositional behavior (stubbornness) and tantrums" (Rowland, 1989, p. 528). At the same time, parents can be confused about how to handle the situation and require assistance with their tendency to overindulge the child. It is best to encourage social autonomy appropriate to the child's age combined with reasonable limit setting (Rowland, 1989).

Tim had handled his disease well, but the signs of stress were becoming evident. In retrospect, his previous "good" grown-up behavior was just as much an indication of a brewing problem as was his "bad" (Rowland, 1989). He needed to release some of his pent-up anger and learn about the side effects of his medication. Additionally, the parents had not yet dealt with their own fears, the stresses the disease had placed on their family and marriage, and the role they each wanted to play in Tim's treatment. Tim would get confused when the parents suggested different techniques to help him during his behavior "crisis." Another significant precipitating factor in beginning treatment was that Mr. Bradley had developed ulcers and had been told by his internist that he was not handling his stress effectively.

Thus, about 3 months after Tim's diagnosis, psychological intervention was planned. Immediate intervention required seeing child and parents together to discuss Tim's outbursts and how they could be managed. With Tim and his parents together, I explained that Tim's episodes were not completely under his control and that they were partially caused by his medication. This was intended to relieve Tim's feelings of guilt and empower the parents to take control. They had wanted to be supportive of him when he was angry, but he did not respond to their efforts, and they were exhausting themselves. The mutual decision was that his frustration and anger should be acknowledged; then they would leave him alone to calm down. Later, they all could talk about what was upsetting him. With everyone in agreement, there was a sense of working together and mutual problem solving. At this point a plan for the family took shape. Tim would be seen individually for therapy, and the parents would be seen together for counseling sessions. What follows is a synopsis of a 6-month segment of therapy with Tim.

Play Therapy Sessions

Tim was routinely silly and even talked baby talk at times when he came for treatments or was asked questions about medical procedures. To explore his underlying feelings about these topics, I decided to have a session focused on hospital play.

Content of Session

THERAPIST: Tim, I wondered if you would like to play with some doctor equipment?

(*Tim giggles.*)

T: I brought this "patient" [a gingerbread-type stuffed doll]. Maybe we could work in one of the examination rooms.

CHILD: OK.

(*Once in the room Tim draws a face on the doll with markers and calls the patient doll "Tim." I show Tim all of the needles, gauze, swabs, etc., that I have brought.*)

C: First he has to curl up in a ball; then I have to wash his back with soap; then there's a needle.

T: Does it hurt? Is he going to cry?

C: It does hurt for a minute, but if you lie still it goes faster. Now he gets a band-aid and has to lie still for 45 minutes.

T: How was that?

C: Good, he didn't even need help.

T: Why does he need those shots and medicines anyway?

C: To get rid of the leukemia, so it doesn't come back.

T: How did he get sick?

C: No one knows; he just did, but he can't give it to anyone else. I want to leave "Tim" here and give him more shots next time.

Rationale/Analysis

Tim was waiting for a marrow and spinal tap, and I wanted to prepare him so he would not be upset or move around, which can interfere with the procedure.

Since it was an individual session, I let him use some small, real needles, being careful not to show him particularly large ones, which frighten children. Although I have a policy of being honest with patients, I have found that children become overwhelmed by the sight of actual bone-marrow and spinal tap needles. Tim was very familiar with the steps for the procedure and was in control while working.

I wanted to verbalize what may happen for him in the same situation. Practicing with me was safe and nonthreatening; ideally, the behavioral rehearsal and his sense of calm will generalize to the actual situation.

I wanted to know if Tim had any misconceptions or irrational fears about his disease. In his role play, he identified with the aggressor. He symbolically externalizes his fears, and his rehearsal promoted mastery.

Comment

We played with the doll twice more in the following weeks. At times the sequence of procedures accurately approximated his own experiences; at other times, he gave the patient doll numerous extra injections. At the end of the last session with the doll he declared that the "patient" could get a year off from treatment. Tim had also wanted to bring the doll to school so that his classmates would know what he went through. These sessions allowed me to explore, with Tim, his concept of his disease. I was able to find out that Tim was accurate in his knowledge about his leukemia, to the point of being sure that no one knows why people get it. It is interesting and expected that this factual information coexisted with more primitive thinking. Weeks later, his parents told me that Tim once said he was glad he got cancer now, when he was young, because he knew that everyone would get it someday. Mr. and Mrs. Bradley corrected his misunderstanding, but it demonstrates how the 6-year-old mind, needing answers for questions, will find them. Thus, Tim found relief in his rationalization for getting cancer. Also, it was significant that Tim had always been completely cooperative with his treatments, had not voiced any resistance, and had a positive outlook on life in general. It was only through the doll that I suspected that he too may have harbored a wish for "time off" from treatment.

Parent Counseling

At the same time I was seeing Tim individually, couples sessions with the parents continued on a regular basis. While discussing Tim's and his sister's behaviors at home, I also focused on pertinent parenting and marital issues. When so much of the child's care is taken over by medical personnel, parents can feel helpless and not needed. It is important to remind them that they know their child best, that they have skills, that as parents they can not be replaced by doctors and nurses, and that they are entitled to have their needs addressed.

Tim's parents went through some of the stages typical of parents of a newly diagnosed child. Individually Mother and Father had to confront the reality of not being able to protect their child from bad things. It highlighted both their own fallibility and their vulnerability. Because these fears are so basic and existential, they are difficult to discuss. Parents can be afraid of verbalizing and admitting their fears to each other, leaving them to feel alone in their grief and struggle at a time when adult, spousal support is needed the most. It is not uncommon for parents to respond to and cope with their crisis in seemingly opposite ways. For example, one parent is often the emotional one, carrying the burden of containing and/or displaying the emotions, and may cry or become depressed or even distraught for a period of time. The other parent may take charge, appear to be in control, and intellectualize about the disease. It is a complementary system whereby one person feels free to enact a certain role because the other provides balance or ballast. Together they successfully exhibit and confront the conflicting emotions stimulated by the crisis.

The parents usually go through an initial period, during the first few months, of preoccupation with the day-to-day tasks of treatment such as doctors' visits, blood counts, and oral medications at home. This period of heightened disease-specific activity enables them to pull together by handling concrete details. Slowly, as the medical aspects are routinized, a new period of unsettling feelings may emerge, when the reality of the cancer reappears with new virility. Thus, somewhere between 6 and 12 months, the parents begin to think about the "Why me?" and go through a stage of renewed anxiety about their child's chances of survival. It is at this point that, ideally, the child and family learn to put the disease in perspective. They realize they can never go back in time and can never live without knowing that it is possible for their child to die. They learn that life is precious, and "you take one day at a time," that the unpredictable is predictable, and they make choices about how to live in their changed world.

Sessions with Tim

Over the next month, Tim continued to have temper tantrums and developed sleeping spells, labeled "postradiation somnolence." He would doze off at unannounced times and could not be easily aroused. These episodes were usually preceded by irritability and crying without any apparent cause. While he was being evaluated neurologically, we worked on these problems in therapy.

Content of Session	*Rationale/Analysis*
CHILD: I think I need to talk to you about my sleepy spells.	Whenever possible I take my lead for sessions from the child rather than impose my agenda.
THERAPIST: OK. Tell me what's been going on.	
C: I think I want to make a journal.	Turning passive into active.
T: That's a great idea.	
C: I don't know how to spell all the words. Can you write it?	
T: I'll help you. You can tell me what to write. By telling me what bothers you we might be able to figure out what will help it.	

(*Tim chooses some colored paper for the cover of his journal and staples white sheets inside. He starts by drawing a picture of his brain being all confused, then tells me his story.*)

C: When I have the prednisone I get so cranky and I wanted to talk about it so I wouldn't be so cranky. Last night I had a fit because I wanted my treatment in Wilton; then I wouldn't have to drive into the city every day. It's so far, and it takes longer, and I miss school that day. I miss my activities, gym and art. And I miss my teacher too, and I miss my class. Sometimes I don't want to come at all because I can't go outside and play in my back yard. Wilton hospital has a better gift shop and better food, and it's easier. But the doctors are better here than at Wilton hospital.

T: If you could make it better, what would make it better at *this* hospital?

C: My first choice is to come here before school. My next choice is to come here at 4:15 so I don't miss school.

Encouraging problem solving to increase sense of control, decrease feeling victimized.

T: I know sometimes kids wish they didn't have to come here at all. They don't have to like coming for their medicine.

Validating his feelings and giving him permission to be upset and frustrated.

C: It's OK if I don't like coming here sometimes. When I have my sleepy spells I get very tired and mad. My brain doesn't get the signals out that good.

Comment

It was quite an accomplishment for Tim to express his negative feelings about his disease, doctors, and hospitals. He had been a trooper throughout the first 5 months of treatment but was feeling the strain of his new responsibilities. It gave him a tremendous sense of control when the doctor agreed to Tim's request to be seen after school. No one had considered that continuing to do the usual 6-year-old activities was so important to him. In Tim's world, gym and art were equally, if not more, important than being cured of leukemia.

Another significant theme in the session was Tim's ambivalence about negotiating for what he wanted. In a parallel fashion, in the parents' therapy we dealt with their difficulty confronting people, asserting themselves, and making their individual needs known to each other. Tim was a spokesmen for an unconscious family rule, and he was now a model for how to speak up.

Tim's tantrums waxed and waned. One of the focal points in sessions with the parents involved how they could be united in dealing with his outbursts. During one particularly bad incident, Tim impulsively screamed, "I'm no good, I'm dumb and stupid, I don't know my numbers; it's my chemo." He had also recently written a letter to Jason Gaes, the author of *My Book for Kids with Cansur* [*sic*]. He ended the letter, "I hate leukemia." With the parents I discussed the strains children and families encounter and their responsibility to reinforce everyone's strengths and not take anyone, child or spouse, for granted. The incident also suggested goals for my individual sessions with Tim. He needed to deal not only with the reality of his cancer but also with his perception of himself.

Content of Session

Tim agreed to have a session while he waited for his bone-marrow and spinal tap. I had some new drawing materials out for Tim to try.

Rationale/Analysis

Scheduling for our sessions varied. Some were planned, but others occurred spontaneously. This was because I see him according to his medical treatment schedule. I had regular weekly appointments with Tim's parents. I am aware of occasionally bringing special things into sessions. Tim is a capable and mature child, and I have more freedom to experiment and use sophisticated art materials with him. Also, I want to give him good things to counteract the fact that he has to go through so many painful, disruptive things. This is part of my countertransference.

CHILD: These are great! I get to use these in school. But this is different, because in school I get all the broken ones.

THERAPIST: Why?

I wondered about his self-esteem and if he felt left out or different from his peers.

C: I get there last because the others run up and get them, but they're not supposed to run up.

I wanted to address the issue of his needing to be good all the time, especially if he felt in any way responsible for his disease. I also wondered about his trying to fit in with his peers.

T: So you do the right thing but don't get the good ones?

C: It's OK because they have to share. (*Tim begins to work on a picture with white Cray-Pas but stops, saying it will not show up. He begins coloring in the sky with blue. He then draws a green line, a yellow circle, and black dot, saying it is a flower.*) Guess what it is.

He has a well-developed sense of morals and strong, positive superego.

T: I need a hint.

C: It's two words.

T: Does the second start with S? I don't know.

C: It's a black-eyed susan. I'm gonna add leaves. Now I'm gonna start another flower using all different colors. I'll call this one beautiful-eyed susan [see Figure 16.1].

I encouraged interaction with me so we would be able to develop a strong relationship and support his need to feel competent.

This raised the question of his use of splitting as a defense. Thus, he sees the world or himself as either good or bad. In some instances, it is likely that a child relates to each part of the picture. Thus,

FIGURE 16.1. A black-eyed susan and a beautiful-eyed susan.

T: How do they get along?

C: Great.

T: How do they like being different?

C: Good, because one's the child and one's the adult.

T: What are they doing?

C: Holding hands underground with their roots. I need to draw the roots and color in the dirt. If there is some aspect of himself represented in both flowers.

I wanted to explore how he integrated his good and bad selves and also how he may perceive relationships among people, whether family members, peers, or staff.

Trying to have him expand on the meaning of being different or special because of his cancer. I was reminded of his feeling guilty about his tantrums.

there was another black you could help, but I'm almost finished.

T: They're holding hands?

C: They can't go anywhere; they're always together. There's a girl in my class, Lizbeth, who draws lots of things; she does the best tulip in the class.

T: What are you best in?

Exploring his need for nurturance and perception of parental figures. He has age-appropriate dependency needs and expresses this in the content of the picture as well as by his veiled request for help with coloring in the roots.

Encouraging reality testing and assessment of his self-esteem and confidence level.

C: People, I'm pretty good at them. I'll show you how I draw different kinds of people. I didn't even know how until I was 5. (*He draws a large stick-like figure on the left side of the page first, then a smaller figure on the right.*) I like the small one better because it has shoulders and a neck [see Figure 16.2].

The two figures are somewhat similar to the two flowers in that they look like parent and child. I wondered if he identified with either figure. The figures are well formed and age appropriate, but the drawings in Figures 16.1 and 16.2 are linear, and Tim does not fill in the shapes, use all of the space, and one figure has no arms, suggestive of some tentativeness.

T: How are these two different? Maybe one's on prednisone and one isn't.

Making a connection to his real experience.

(*Tim decides to experiment with the special watercolor crayons I have brought. He makes stripes.*)

C: I'm gonna do lightning. (*He makes green and yellow zig-zags. He tries out different techniques such as holding a fistful of colors and drawing lines.*)

Talking about prednisone may have stimulated thoughts about his illness; thus, the change to a stormy theme.

T: It's fun to experiment sometimes.

C: Little kids do scribble scrabble.

Encouraging his exploration and loosening of restrictions.

T: Sometimes I do too. (*While he continues to work, I check to see if the doctor is ready for him. When I return he asks if it is his turn.*) Do you know what you're getting today?

Supporting his need/desire to be regressive in his play sometimes.

C: If my counts are low I won't get my bone-marrow and spinal tap. But that means it's bad because then I couldn't go to camp.

T: So there's a good part and a bad part about it.

C: Yeah.

It is not unusual for these children to be aware of the details of their illness and how it effects their lives.

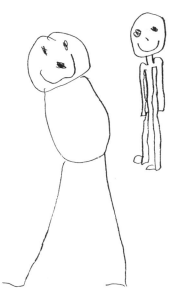

FIGURE 16.2. A parent and child.

T: What do you like best about camp?

C: When it's hot I get special permission to do my favorite activities, hobby and wood shop.

T: Any secrets this week?

C: Maybe, but I'm not telling.

T: Like what?

C: Can't tell; maybe with kids at camp, or parents, or babysitter. (*He begins to talk in a babyish manner.*)

T: If you could make a secret deal with Dr. Mandel, what would it be?

C: To skip a few treatments so I wouldn't have to have them every day, because I don't like to come sometimes.

T: What would your part of the deal be?

C: I would give him all the Ninja Turtle band-aids he wants.

T: What would happen if you missed some treatments?

They too like to plan ahead and be prepared for events. The discussion also points out his ambivalence toward treatment: there are good things and bad about cancer. When in the midst of his tantrums at home, he would come to session saying he had a secret to talk about. It was important for him to know that he had a safe place to talk about his problems.

I wondered if something about his impending procedures was upsetting him. Also, the last time he told me a "secret," it was about not wanting to come for treatment anymore.

When a child is feeling well, it is difficult for him to continue to believe he is sick. This is especially true for leukemia because there are no visible signs of disease, only signs of side effects. This se-

C: It would take longer to get better.

T: It's OK not to want to come; it's hard to get medicine when there's other things to do.

(Tim's counts were indeed low, and he left without getting medical treatment that day.)

quence also reveals how Tim would like to bargain. It is not uncommon for patients to want to have a just world and even try to make a deal with God. Here Tim wants to find a way to be rewarded and spared, as if being good enough or generous enough would make bad things or his cancer disappear. It is also clear that he is able to be quite realistic in his thinking and knows that missed treatments mean longer treatment. It is necessary to acknowledge this conflict, knowing something is good for you but not liking it.

(Six weeks later Tim did a pastel drawing, Figure 16.3.)

C: I am in the middle, on prednisone which is why I'm so big, Dad is on the left, and Mom is on the right . . . they have spinal needles.

He now spontaneously refers to his medical treatment, represents his anger by the needles, and portrays a relationship with his parents.

(Tim was now reportedly "back to his old self.")

FIGURE 16.3. Cacti: A mother, father, and son.

Comment

This excerpt from a portion of the therapy spotlights the normal stresses confronting the child and family and points out typical intervention strategies mentioned in the research and clinical literature about childhood cancer (Holland & Rowland, 1989). It must be emphasized that there is no right or wrong way to treat the disease-related emotional problems. A father of a 6-year-old daughter with leukemia once asked me how he should discipline her. He wanted to guard against spoiling her yet also make up for the real disappointments and pain in her life. I began by admiring the fact that he was aware of the problem and had questioned what to do. Herein was the key to the answer. Being conscious of internal responses, looking squarely at issues, and having the courage to take action go a long way toward finding solutions.

CONCLUDING COMMENTS

Tim and his family recognized that they could not handle all components of his disease alone. There was a shared ethic that one could enlist my services as readily as those of the oncologist in order to improve survival. Tim once coolly suggested to his sister, who was belaboring an issue during a family outing, that she should "go talk to Dr. Robin." The idea is not to foster unwarranted dependency on yet more "specialists" or "experts." Rather, childhood cancer is an experience for which most parents and children are ill prepared. Psychological treatment should be geared toward guiding them to manage their own lives their own way. In contrast to support from friends and extended family members, the on-site professional "knows," on some level, what the family's "cancer life" entails. The staff becomes a part of the family, a partner in the care of their child. This engenders a sense of trust and hope that strengthens the treatment alliance.

Although there are similarities between other cases and that of Tim and his family, there are no standardized, expected behaviors. Tim was a confident, engaging boy who continued on his developmental path almost independent of his illness. Some of his strengths were surely related to his good preillness functioning and the support of his cohesive family system. He had the normal fears and anger that any child would have going through painful and at first confusing experiences. When Tim was first diagnosed, Tim's father had left for the night after Tim got his intravenous line put in. Later, in need of a new one, he called his father. Tim was in tears, wanting his father to come back to the hospital. When Dad arrived, Tim asked him "Where's God now?" His father, having his own difficulty with the question, told Tim he would need to find his own answer. After being discharged, Tim announced one night at dinner that finally he knew a reason why God gave him leukemia: it was so he would know what it was like to be sick so he could help other kids. Some children and families can come through the experience stronger, changed, clearer in their vision about the meaning of life. For many patients and families, the crisis can be an opportunity rather than an obstacle.

PLAY THERAPY MATERIALS

- *Art Supplies*: pastels, markers, crayons, Cray-Pas, water colors, tempera paint, paper
- *Puppets*: variety, including dinosaurs and family puppets
- *Medical Supplies*: syringes, gauze, alcohol, band-aids, stethoscope, tongue depressor
- *Sources for Purchase*
  Childcraft: 20 Kilmer Rd., Edison, NJ 0881-3081
  Discovery Toys: Martinex, CA 94553; (800) 425-4777
  New York Central Supply: 62 Third Ave., New York, NY 10003
  Pam's Anatomical Puppets: 23 Hawthrone Circle, So. Burlington, VT; (802) 864-5085

STUDY QUESTIONS

1. Discuss the stress on the therapist of working with children who have a potentially fatal diagnosis. How can therapists effectively deal with their own feelings about death and dying?

2. Comment on the possible value of a play therapy group with Tim. What would be some of the pros and cons of group therapy compared to individual therapy in a situation of medical crisis such as cancer?

3. There are inevitable stresses on the siblings. Discuss how you might have conducted therapy sessions with the sister, how the initiation of sibling therapy would be discussed with the patient and parents, the issues that need to be addressed, and the goals of treatment for the sister.

4. Discuss the impact of the stress of illness on a child's ego development, especially with regard to the use of defenses. Evaluate Tim's developing sense of self and predict any possible future difficulties you may envision in reference to his emotional well-being.

REFERENCES

Adams-Greenly, M. (1984). Helping children communicate about serious illness and death. *Journal of Psychosocial Oncology, 2*(2), 61–72.

Anthony, S. (1971). *The discovery of death in childhood and after.* New York: Basic Books.

Astin, E. (1977–1978). Self reported fears of hospitalized and non-hospitalized children aged 10–12. *Maternal Child Nursing Journal, 6–7,* 17–24.

Axline, V. (1947). *Play therapy*. Boston, MA: Houghton Mifflin.

Bearison, D., & Pacifici, C. (1984). Psychological studies of children who have cancer. *Journal of Applied Developmental Psychology, 5*, 263-280.

Bibace, R., & Walsh, M. E. (1979). Developmental stages in children's conceptions of illness. In G. Stone, F. Cohen, & N. Adler (Eds.), *Health psychology* (pp. 285-303). San Francisco: Jossey-Bass.

Binger, C. M., Ablin, A. R., Feurestein, R. C., Kushner, J. H., Zoger, S., & Mikkelsen, C. (1969). Childhood leukemia: Emotional impact on patient and family. *New England Journal of Medicine, 280*, 414-418.

Blotcky, A. D., Raczynski, J. M., Gurwitch, R., & Smith, K. (1985). Family influences on hopelessness among children early in the cancer experience. *Journal of Pediatric Psychology 10*(4), 479-493.

Bluebond-Langner, M. (1978). *The private worlds of dying children*. Princeton: Princeton University Press.

Brunnquell, D., & Hall, M. D. (1984). Issues in the psychological care of pediatric oncology patients. In S. Chess & A. Thomas (Eds.), *Annual progress in child psychiatry and child development* (pp. 430-447). New York: Brunner/Mazel.

Childers, P., & Wimmer, M. (1971). The concept of death in early childhood. *Child Development, 42*, 1299-1301.

Clements, D. B., Copeland, L. G., & Loftus, M. (1990). Critical times for families with a chronically ill child. *Pediatric Nursing, 16*(2), 157-162.

Cook, S. S. (1973). Children's perceptions of death. In S. Cook (Ed.), *Children and dying* (pp. 1-15). New York: Health Sciences Publishers.

Dobkin, P. L., & Morrow, G. R. (1985-1986). Long-term side effects in patients who have been treated successfully for cancer. *Journal of Psychosocial Oncology, 3*(4), 23-51.

Easson, W. H. (1974). Management of the dying child. *Journal of Clinical Child Psychology, Summer*, 25-27.

Eiser, C. (1979). Psychological development of the child with leukemia: A review. *Journal of Behavioral Medicine, 2*(2), 141-157.

Futterman, E. H., & Hoffman, I. (1973). Crisis and adaptation in the families of fatally ill children. In E. J. Anthony & C. Koupernik (Eds.), *The child and his family: The impact of disease and death* (pp. 127-143). New York: John Wiley & Sons.

Gaes, J. (1987). *My book for kids with cansur*. Aberdeen, SD: Melius & Peterson.

Goodman, R. (1989). *Development of the concept of death in children: The cognitive and affective components*. Unpublished doctoral dissertation, Adelphi University, Garden City, NY.

Hockenberry, M. J., Coody, D. K., & Bennett, B. S. (1990). Childhood cancers: Incidence, etiology, diagnosis, and treatment. *Pediatric Nursing, 16*(3), 239-246.

Holland, J. C., & Rowland, J. H. (Eds.). (1989). *Handbook of psychooncology*. New York: Oxford University Press.

Jenkins, R. A., & Cavanaugh, J. C. (1985). Examining the relationship between the development of the concept of death and overall cognitive development. *Omega, 16*(3), 193-199.

Kane, B. (1979). Children's concepts of death. *Journal of Genetic Psychology, 134*, 141-153.

Kastenbaum, R. (1967). The child's understanding of death: How does it develop? In E. Grollman (Eds.), *Explaining death to children* (pp. 89-108). Boston: Beacon Press.

Katz, E. R., & Jay, S. M. (1984). Psychological aspects of cancer in children, adolescents, and their families. *Clinical Psychology Review, 4*, 525-542.

Koocher, G. (1973). Childhood, death, and cognitive development. *Developmental Psychology, 9*(3), 369-375.

Koocher, G. P., & O'Malley, J. E. (1981). *The Damocles syndrome*. New York: McGraw-Hill.

Koocher, G. P., O'Malley, J. E., Gogan, J. L., & Foster, D. J. (1980). Psychological adjustment among pediatric cancer survivors. *Journal of Child Psychology and Psychiatry, 21*, 163-173.

Kramer, E. (1971). *Art as therapy with children*. New York: Schocken.

Kübler-Ross, E. (1981). *Living with death and dying*. New York: Macmillan.

Lonetto, R. (1980). *Children's conceptions of death*. New York: Springer Publishing.

Nagy, M. (1948). The child's theories concerning death. *Journal of Genetic Psychology, 73*, 3-27.

Natterson, J. M., & Knudson, A. G. (1960). Observations concerning fear of death in fatally ill children and their mothers. *Psychosomatic Medicine, 22*(6), 456-465.

O'Malley, J. E., Koocher, G., Foster, D., & Slavin, L. (1979). Psychiatric sequelae of surviving childhood cancer. *American Journal of Orthopsychiatry, 49*(4), 608-616.

Orbach, I., Fesback, S., Carlson, G., & Ellenberg, L. (1984). Attitudes toward life and death in suicidal, normal, and chronically ill children: An extended replication. *Journal of Consulting and Clinical Psychology, 52*(6), 1020-1027.

Orbach, I., Gross, Y., Glaubman, H., & Berman, D. (1985). Children's perception of death in humans and animals as a function of age, anxiety, and cognitive ability. *Journal of Child Psychology and Psychiatry and Allied Disciplines, 26*, 453-463.

Petrillo, M., & Sanger, S. (1980). *Emotional care of hospitalized children*. Philadelphia and Toronto: J. B. Lippincott.

Pizzo, P., Poplack, D. G., Magrath, I. T., Ungeruiar, R. S., Cazonave, L., Israel, M. A., Balis, F. M., & Miser, J. S. (1989-1990). Cancers in children. In R. E. Wites (Eds.), *Manual of oncologic therapeutics* (pp. 394-416). Philadelphia: J. B. Lippincott.

Reilly, T., Hasazi, J., & Bond, L. (1983). Children's conceptions of death and personal mortality. *Society of Pediatric Psychology, 8*(1), 21-31.

Rowland, J. H. (1989). Developmental stages and adaptation: Child and adolescent model. In J. C. Holland & J. H. Rowland (Eds.), *Handbook of psychooncology* (pp. 519-543). New York: Oxford University Press.

Safier, G. (1964). A study in relationship between the life and death concepts in children. *Journal of Genetic Psychology, 105*, 283-294.

Sawyer, M., Crettenden, A., & Toogood, I. (1986). Psychological adjustment of families of children and adolescents treated for leukemia. *American Journal of Pediatric Hematology/Oncology, 8*(3), 200-207.

Schilder, P., & Wechsler, D. (1934). The attitudes of children toward death. *Journal of Genetic Psychology, 45*, 406-451.

Slavin, L. A., O'Malley, J. E., Koocher, G. P., & Foster, D. J. (1982). Communication of the cancer diagnosis to pediatric patients: Impact on long-term adjustment. *American Journal of Psychiatry, 139*(2), 179-183.

Sourkes, B. (1982). *The deepening shade: Psychological aspects of life threatening illness*. Pittsburgh: University of Pittsburgh Press.

Speece, M., & Brent, S. (1984). Children's understanding of death: A review of three components of a death concept. *Child Development, 55*, 1671-1686.

Spinetta, J. (1974). The dying child's awareness of death: A review. *Psychological Bulletin, 81*(2-7), 256-260.

Spinetta, J. (1980). Disease-related communication: How to tell. In J. Kellerman (Ed.), *Psychological aspects of childhood cancer* (pp. 260-269). Springfield, IL: Charles C. Thomas.

Spinetta, J. J., & Maloney, L. J. (1975). Death anxiety in the outpatient leukemic child. *Pediatrics, 56*(6), 1034-1037.

Van Dongen-Melman, J. E. W. M., & Sanders-Woudstra, J. A. R. (1986). Psychosocial aspects of childhood cancer: A review of the literature. *Journal of Child Psychology and Psychiatry and Allied Disciplines, 27*(2), 145-180.

Vernick, J., & Karon, M. (1965). Who's afraid of death on a leukemia ward? *American Journal of Diseases of Childhood, 109*, 393-397.

Wass, H. (1984). Concepts of death a developmental perspective. In H. Wass & C. Corr (Eds.), *Childhood and death* (pp. 3-23). Washington, DC: Hemisphere.

White, E., Elsom, B., & Prawat, R. (1978). Children's conceptions of death. *Child Development, 49*, 307-310.

Worchel, F., Copeland, D., & Baker, G. (1987). Control-related coping strategies in pediatric cancer patients. *Journal of Pediatric Psychology, 12*(1), 25-38.

CHAPTER 17

AIDS in the Family
Case of Roberta, Age 7

STEVEN E. REID

AIDS (acquired immune deficiency syndrome) is a fatal disease that has reached epidemic proportions nationwide. The disease has spread to include the most innocent and defenseless victims—children. Recent reports indicate that over 1,000 cases of children with AIDS have been identified. However, this number is expected to increase dramatically over the next few years. Several authorities have projected that 10,000 to 20,000 children will have AIDS by 1992 (National Commission to Prevent Infant Mortality, 1987).

Children with AIDS and their families experience acute emotional and physical suffering as a result of the disease. Most children with AIDS are from lower socioeconomic, minority groups in which poverty and drug abuse are disproportionately high. Frequently, these families are already weakened by problems of overcrowded housing, poor nutrition and education, and family violence. Support services and resources for this population are inadequate to meet their needs.

Children with AIDS and their families face the stigma that is attached to their illness. Parents feel guilt and anger about transmitting the disease to their partners and children. Infected children suffer the ravaging effects of the illness. These children are chronically ill and are at constant risk for developing a life-threatening infection. Frequent hospitalizations and painful medical treatments are common for these children. Furthermore, most children with HIV or AIDS are expected to become more symptomatic and ultimately to die of complications from the disease (Quinn, 1987). The specter of death is ever present in the lives of children with AIDS, causing untold mental anguish, fear, depression, and grief for the children and for their caretakers and loved ones.

Thus, the clinical picture of children with AIDS is unique, complex, and challenging. Recent efforts to study this population provide important information regarding the physical, psychological, and sociocultural characteristics of children with AIDS.

DIAGNOSIS AND TRANSMISSION

Approximately 80% of children diagnosed with HIV or AIDS are infected prenatally or perinatally from the mother. Dekker (1988) delineated the distribution of pediatric AIDS cases by transmission categories: 46.3% resulted from the mother's use of intravenous drugs; 14% from transfusions of contaminated blood to the baby; 12.3% from mothers born outside of the United States (the prevalence of AIDS is much higher in women in other areas of the world); 10.9% from mothers whose sexual partner was an intravenous drug user; and 16.5% from unreported sources. In a study of 66 HIV-positive children and 57 of their mothers, 98% (54 of 57) of the mothers were found to have used drugs before giving birth (*Pediatric AIDS Foster Care Network Bulletin*, 1990).

Not all HIV-infected mothers transmit the disease to their children. Approximately 60% to 70% of infants born to HIV-infected women serorevert to HIV-negative by 2 years of age (Mendez, 1988). Testing for AIDS involves measuring the infant's antibodies to the HIV virus in the blood. Many infants first test "false positive" because current tests cannot distinguish the mother's antibodies from those produced by the child in response to infection. As the child's immune system becomes more developed, the mother's antibodies disappear, and the child may then test negative for the presence of antibodies.

Diagnosis of HIV in infants and young children is further complicated by other factors. Some infected infants are asymptomatic until they reach latency age. The symptoms of HIV and AIDS are not unlike common childhood illnesses in that they may respond to short-term treatments. Therefore, pediatricians may fail to diagnose a pattern of acute infections. Earliest physical symptoms include failure to thrive, chronic upper respiratory infections, otitis media (middle ear infections), lymphadenopathy, chronic diarrhea, and neurological impairment resulting in developmental delays.

Diagnosis of HIV is sometimes delayed by poor or inconsistent caregiving, whereby parents seek pediatric care in a disorganized, episodic fashion. It is necessary to receive informed consent of the parent before testing a child for HIV. Since many parents fear the possibility of their child being diagnosed with AIDS, they may refuse to give consent. Some mothers are unaware of their own HIV status and may resist or deny the possibility of having HIV.

PHYSICAL AND DEVELOPMENTAL CHARACTERISTICS

Many children with AIDS come from disadvantaged families that provided little or no prenatal care. The majority of HIV-infected young children were exposed to drugs while *in utero* through maternal drug abuse. Thus, it is often difficult to distinguish the effects of HIV from the effects of drug abuse or other environmental factors on the early development of infected children. Research findings, however, indicate that most children with HIV or AIDS suffer from significant developmental delay, failure to thrive, and/or neurological impairment. Early reports painted a gloomier picture, with severe central nervous system damage such as progressive encephalopathy found in up to 50% of cases (e.g., Belman et al., 1985; Epstein et al., 1986). Other commonly found anomalies include low birth weight and height and microcephaly. Several researchers have found some facial stigmata—protruding, box-like foreheads (frontal "bossing") and a bluish tinge in the whites of the eyes (blue sclerae)—associated with HIV-infected children.

More recent research, however, suggests that many babies born with HIV do not experience significant neurological insult during fetal development. These children may have mild or nonexistent neurological problems at birth. A study of HIV children placed in foster care found that at least 91% of the children had delays in one or more developmental areas of gross motor, fine motor, or speech and language functioning (*Pediatric AIDS Foster Care Network Bulletin*, 1990). However, many of the children studied had only mild or moderate delays; for example, the average IQ score for the infected children in foster care was 75 (borderline intellectual development), compared to 83 for noninfected children. The areas least affected were personal and social skills.

Many clinicians recognize that children with AIDS may be affected by the crises of repeated hospitalizations, separation from caregivers, and social isolation stemming from infection control procedures (see Ultmann et al., 1985). These events by themselves often result in delayed development.

CULTURAL AND FAMILIAL FACTORS

AIDS is proliferating among children and families with the least support and resources in our society. In the majority of these families the mother is the head of the household and has more than one child. These families not only must deal with a child who has AIDS but also frequently must cope with the illness or death of one or both parents. Many families simply cannot handle the added stress of a child with AIDS, and the infected child may be placed with extended family or in foster care. Thus, at a time when stability would provide support, relationships terminate or change. Much of the work with families with a child with AIDS is crisis oriented and concerns the immediate concrete needs of the family such as home care or support services.

Other more subtle but nonetheless significant issues faced by families of children with AIDS include dealing with guilt and self-blame for their child's condition. Some parents must cope with the knowledge that their behavior directly resulted in their child's affliction.

Parents of school-age children with AIDS must also decide whether to inform the child of his or her diagnosis. Most parents choose *not* to disclose this information to the child because of the stigma associated with the disease. Parents fear that reverberations created by disclosure could disrupt all areas of their child's life, including friendships, education, and family relationships. The issue of disclosure grows in magnitude as the child becomes older and the illness progresses.

PSYCHOLOGICAL INTERVENTION
FOR CHILDREN WITH AIDS

Psychological treatment for children with AIDS usually occurs in hospital settings in conjunction with medical treatment. Most hospitals that provide treatment for a large number of patients with AIDS have counseling, outreach, and educational programs for families. A growing number of large-scale, family-oriented treatment programs are being developed to serve the multiproblem, drug-involved population that overrepresents the population of children with AIDS. Project WIN (see *Zero to Three*, 1989) is one such program. It provides direct services for families in the form of support for the parents' recovery from addiction, identifying and supplying home-based early intervention for the children's developmental needs, and helping the family find and use support services in their community. Project WIN consists of teams led by a case manager with a background in education, social work, or counseling and two other professionals from either the family counseling, speech, or physical therapy disciplines. Case managers see families in their homes and have a limited caseload of 8 to 10 families. Case managers coordinate the implementation of community services to ensure that families and children receive all necessary supports.

Although ambitious treatment programs such as Project WIN seem appropriate in light of the pervasively destructive effects of drug abuse and AIDS on children and families, there are few published reports describing individual psychological treatment of children with AIDS. This may reflect the fact that the majority of children with AIDS are diagnosed when they are infants and toddlers. Although preschool-age children suffer the physical effects of the illness, their emotional adjustment is largely defined by the parents' ability to help deal with the inevitable separations, hospitalizations, and medical treatments.

Older children with AIDS may have mild to severe neurological problems that prevent them from assimilating into the sociocultural mainstream and comprehending the diagnosis and its ramifications.

Nevertheless, there exists a population of intellectually intact school-age children who have AIDS. The risk for psychological suffering among these children is self-evident. Hospitalized children or children with terminal illness experience considerable anxiety, regression, and depression (Adams, 1976; Chan, 1980; Clatworthy, 1981; Harvey, 1980). The use of play therapy with this population has an established history (Golden, 1983). Many hospitals have play programs designed to help children cope with the loss of control and fearful fantasies associated with hospitalization.

But a child with AIDS typically has much more to cope with than his or her medical treatment. A 6-year-old may suspect the diagnosis of AIDS, particularly if either or both parents have the disease. The issue of secrecy is crucial for the family and places additional stress on family members who keep this secret. Thus, family support may falter for the child when he or she needs it the most.

Children with AIDS must deal with the issue of death, their own or that of a loved one. Children in early latency often appear egocentric regarding a loss of a loved one, typically showing more concern about their own immediate concrete needs than a sense of grief (Kübler-Ross, 1983; Schaefer & Lyons, 1986). Children often experience the death of someone close as abandonment. The permanency of death may be difficult for them to grasp despite a matter-of-fact curiosity about death.

The literature on play therapy supports a directive approach with children who are seriously ill. For example, Adams (1976) reports that comprehensive hospital treatment programs, which often include family counseling, complete recreational services, opportunities for free play, and educational programs, may be ineffective in reducing the fear, regressive or withdrawn behavior, and defiance of terminally ill pediatric patients. McEvoy, Duchon, and Schaefer (1985) emphasize the importance of *repeated* expression of anxieties and feelings regarding medical procedures and sickness for children with terminal illnesses. This approach recalls Levy's (1938) "release therapy," which is based on Freud's notion of the repetition compulsion. This approach involves creating conditions in which a child replays a traumatic event, or series of psychological insults, over and over until he or she can assimilate and master the associated negative thoughts and feelings. A more directive therapeutic approach appears to befit the sense of urgency created by a disease that threatens the life of a child.

Others, however, have persuasively argued that the inherently expressive, healing, and creative aspects of play are lost when the therapist becomes too directive (Guerney, 1983; Laughlin, 1990).

My own experience with play therapy for children with AIDS has confirmed my beliefs about the healing powers of play. Generally, I have found that these children more readily project their inner psychological life into the play than do children with lesser emotional problems. I have developed a style in which my level of directiveness varies depending on the play process. I am less likely to allow defensive avoidance to continue to play; whereas many therapists working from a nondirective standpoint might choose to comment and reflect on the child's feelings, I find that I am more likely to actively attempt to change the play process in order to reengage the child in fantasy expression. When the child begins to express more emotionally laden material, I tend to become reflective.

THE CASE: ROBERTA, AGE 7

Family Information

Roberta, age 7, is in second grade. Roberta had been retained in first grade because of absences related to her illness. Intellectual testing found her to be of normal intelligence. Roberta contracted AIDS from her mother during the pregnancy.

Felicia, age 32, is the biological mother of Roberta, also diagnosed with AIDS. She contracted AIDS through intravenous drug use.

Jose, the biological father of Roberta, died of AIDS about 2 years before the onset of play therapy for Roberta. He also became infected with AIDS through intravenous drug use. Jose and Felicia were never married, and Jose was an inconsistent presence in the household.

This family lived on welfare in a lower socioeconomic suburban area of New York City.

Presenting Problem

Roberta had been receiving ongoing pediatric care through a large local hospital. Her physical health had deteriorated over the previous year, requiring numerous hospitalizations and resultant prolonged absences from school. At the time of referral, however, Roberta's health had been relatively stable for about 2 months. Nevertheless, her school performance had worsened dramatically, and she began to exhibit symptoms of school phobia. Her mother also reported that Roberta seemed depressed and had become extremely clingy with her. Roberta received group therapy at the hospital, but Felicia requested individual play therapy specifically to help Roberta with these problems.

First Interview

The initial session lasted 1 hour and was conducted in two stages. The first half-hour was spent alone with Felicia to gather more information about Roberta's background and symptoms. The second part was a short play assessment of Roberta.

Parent Interview

The problem of clinginess immediately came to the forefront and at times seemed overwhelming for Felicia. She reported that she felt "trapped" by Roberta, in that when she even so much as left the room Roberta would scream for her. Felicia also disclosed that her illness had taken a turn for the worse and that she had recently been hospitalized. She believed that Roberta was frightened by her absence, and that is why she became so clingy with her. Felicia received ongoing counseling through the hospital, although she nonetheless felt very depressed lately. She described Roberta as a very sociable and energetic youngster who had always enjoyed school.

Felicia was very concerned about Roberta's sudden changes of mood and about her reluctance to leave the apartment to get on the bus for school. Reportedly, Roberta's teacher sent home several notes describing her mood changes: at times she was belligerent, and at other times withdrawn. Felicia informed me that she had never told Roberta about AIDS and was not planning to do so. To Felicia's knowledge no one in the school knew of Roberta's condition.

Initial Play Assessment

As a general rule, during initial play therapy sessions, particularly for children whose need for therapy is evident and unquestioned by the parent, I focus on engaging the child and observing his or her capacity and preference for different types of play. I do not attempt to evaluate the child's psychological functioning rigorously during this initial assessment because I know that, once engaged in play, the child will eventually project aspects of his or her psyche into the play.

With Roberta, I immediately observed that her demeanor in the presence of her mother was much different from that when apart from her. She seemed sullen when I approached her and her mother in the waiting room and chatted for a few minutes. I assumed that her mood reflected trepidation regarding therapy. However, once inside the playroom, Roberta became animated and very playful. She presented as a very cute, small-for-age girl who, aside from her pale complexion and somewhat frail appearance, did not manifest any overt signs of illness. She had a delightful squeaky voice, a high level of energy, and a rather tough, assertive self-presentation. Roberta did not hesitate to engage herself in play, without waiting for permission from me to handle materials. She immediately picked up a doll, then proceeded to pick up numerous other toys and play materials, only to play briefly and superficially with each.

At that point I moved closer to her and attempted to join her play. Roberta accepted my presence, and together we played with dolls and with "GI Joe" figures in the sandbox. One clear theme emerged from this initial play session: Roberta associated themes of sickness and vulnerability in her play more toward an authority figure than toward herself. The larger and more powerful figure elicited Roberta's sympathy and protectiveness. This theme also surfaced during a brief storytelling sequence. Typically I encourage children to embellish their play by telling stories about the characters; in this case Roberta's story described a little girl walking through the woods to meet her aunt (undoubtedly a derivation of "Little Red Riding Hood"). In this story, the little girl had to hurry to get to her aunt's house because the aunt was having a heart attack. The girl arrived just in time to save her.

Preliminary Assessment and Treatment Plan

The first session revealed some significant information: it appeared to me that Roberta had become, on some level, a mothering presence for her own mother. She seemed to sense her mother's weakened state. Roberta's clinginess, therefore, may have reflected a mothering urge as well as insecurity about her own safety. Initially, I planned to explore further the issue of parentification individually with Roberta in the play sessions. I also recognized that I might need to work with Felicia either alone or conjointly with Roberta to encourage a healthier balance in their relationship.

The other important theme that arose during the first play session was sickness. Even though Roberta ascribed sickness to a character other than the one she identified with, I assumed that she had significant reactions, feelings, and fearful fantasies about sickness that she would express over the course of therapy. I believed that her clinginess and mood changes reflected a general breakdown in her ego functioning as a result of considerable life stressors. Thus, I anticipated that Roberta would use play as a vehicle for expression of threatening feelings and, I hoped, as a means of gaining mastery over these feelings.

In all, I felt that this first session was an auspicious beginning, mostly because of Roberta's motivation to play and ability to engage in fantasy play.

Play Therapy Sessions

The first full session saw elaboration of the theme of sickness. Roberta seemed to focus her concern on the heart. At that time I did not know if her preoccupation with that part of the body was associated with her own experience or whether it was a focal point for her general fears regarding her own physical integrity. Her fears were expressed symbolically through the use of dolls and in drawings.

The session included block play and drawing with crayons and some painting. Roberta's figure drawing contained a big shaded-in area near the location of the heart. I attempted to talk about her drawing, but she was not responsive at this time. Later we engaged in play with dolls, and Roberta carried on the following conversation with me through the medium of doll play:

Content of Session	*Rationale/Analysis*
CHILD: (*holding large female doll with toy coffee cup*) I can't drink anything because the juice will come right out the hole in my heart.	
THERAPIST: (*talking through the doll*) You mean you have a hole in your heart? Does that hurt?	At this point I realized she was starting to express important material, so I reminded myself to be patient and stay within the metaphor of play.
C: Yeah, and when I drink juice it comes out right through here (*she points to the area near where the heart would be*) and makes a big mess! Yuch! It hurts! But I can eat carrots. (*Roberta then picks up an orange block from the floor and "feeds" the doll.*)	I was impressed that Roberta followed with a positive, self-affirming statement ("I can eat carrots").
T: (*still through the doll*) Oh, you must have a big boo-boo right there (*touches her doll*). Ouch! Here, here's a tissue in case you cry.	I had hoped to stay on the subject of physical illness and pain.
C: (*taking the tissue and wiping doll's nose, now talking to the doll instead of through it*) It's OK, it'll be OK, don't cry any more (*makes boo-hoo sounds for the doll*). Here, let's put a band-aid on it.	
(*For the next several minutes, Roberta and I use Scotch tape and tissue paper to construct and place a band-aid on the doll's chest, play-acting a nurse's role with the doll—I have dropped my doll in the meantime.*)	At this point I hoped to move from metaphor to reality and to elicit her reactions to her painful experiences. I knew from experience not to question the child

T: I hate it when I get hurt and have to go the doctor. (*Roberta says nothing.*) Sometimes I get cuts on my arm. (*I then pretend to have a cut on my arm, and I touch my arm and say, "Ouch."*)

C: Sometimes I go to the hospital and sleep there.

T: In a bed?

C: Yeah, a big bed that moves! (*She seems very excited about this.*)

T: Wow, that sounds like fun. Do you have fun at the hospital?

C: Yeah, except when they put all those needles in me. That hurts a lot.

T: Yeah, those darn doctors are so mean!

C: Yeah, I hate 'em all (*said with little emotion*).

directly. This is usually too threatening and only results in silence.

One strategy is to make a self-statement and include anticipated or appropriate emotional responses.

Here again, instead of questioning Roberta, I modeled the feeling to see if she would elaborate. However, she did not, and I did not push the issue at this early stage of therapy. Roberta seemed tired, and it was near the end of the session.

The fact that this sequence occurred near the end of the session influenced my interventions. If it had occurred near the beginning, I would have had more time to shift back into the less threatening metaphorical play after finding that my attempt at realistic discourse failed. For example, I might have picked up another doll and identified it as a doctor and then encouraged Roberta to vent any underlying anger or frustration onto the doll. Also, given more time, I would have encouraged Roberta to play with the toy medical kit in the hope that she would continue to express her anxieties regarding medical procedures and her own physical condition.

The next several sessions were relatively uneventful although important in the ongoing strengthening of our relationship and building of trust. Roberta continued to express anxiety and fear regarding her own body. Roberta expressed tactile hypersensitivity through doll play. She repeatedly poked the "skin" of the doll and said "ouch" or nonverbally expressed pain. She enacted sequences in which she was the doctor inflicting pain on the patient, the doll. At the same time, fears of abandonment began to be expressed metaphorically. My original hypothesis regarding Roberta's need to nurture and protect her own mother appeared to be correct as Roberta connected themes of sickness with abandonment. For example, "we" told a story, a derivative of a drawing, involving a family of whales in which the "mother" whale is attacked by sharks and is seriously injured. The child whale has to stay home from school to take care of the mother.

I immediately connected this material with Roberta's school phobia. The ending of this story, however, was somewhat unexpected. The child whale helps nurse her mother back to health, but as a result, the child whale changes color. Fantastically, the child whale is now red and white, not gray like all other whales. When the child whale returns to school, she is ridiculed by the other whales, becomes extremely upset, and runs away from home, never to return again. Despite the many interpretive possibilities of such rich psychological material, I attempted to stick to the most parsimonious ones. First, her mother's sickness requires her to adopt a parental role. Second, the mother's sickness eventually leads to separation, although, ironically, the child initiates the abandonment. And third, Roberta's self-image is tinged with inferiority and "differentness." This latter interpretation further suggested to me that, despite her often tough and self-confident exterior, Roberta perceived herself as fundamentally different from other children, possibly because of her own physical problems or because of more generalized shame regarding her family's illnesses.

The following excerpt from the fourth session (the same session as the one including the whale story) illustrates how even a seemingly innocuous play sequence often leads to significant revelation of deep-seated feelings and fears. In this case, parentification and fear of abandonment and death were the operative themes.

Fourth Session

This session involved sand play. Roberta wanted to go outside and find some insects to play with in the sandbox. We brought several insects in a jar back up to the office and put them in the sandbox. She watched them for several minutes in silence, seemingly enrapt with their attempts to crawl out of the sandbox.

Content of Session	Rationale/Analysis
CHILD: (*identifying the large "daddy long legs" spider*) Look! This one has a broken leg. (*The insect in fact looks intact to me.*) Aw, it's hurt. It needs to go to the doctor.	
THERAPIST: It needs help?	
C: Yeah, maybe its baby can help her.	
T: Its baby?	
C: Yeah, see? (*She points to the ant.*) That's the mommy, that's the baby.	
T: Do you think the baby wants to help the mommy?	
C: What is she going to do? She'll have to lay down and rest. (*Roberta tries to use a pick-up*	I did not know to whom she was referring at this point.

stick to move the spider, presumably to lay it down as she said.)

T: Well, maybe the baby could give her mommy a hug and a kiss. What do you think?

C: Yeah, but I still think the mommy is dead.

T: She's dead? But she still is moving around.

C: Yeah. (*then silence*)

T: So, what do you think?

C: I think this mommy's going to die. Isn't she?

T: Well, everybody dies some time. Even your mommy and my mommy will die some time. I think that will make me very sad.

C: If my mommy dies I'll live with my aunt. She lives in Brooklyn.

T: Will you miss your mommy if she dies?

I felt she was struggling between her intrapsychic urges and the limitations of physical reality. I tried to keep the play in fantasy form for the time being in order to elicit continued self-expression. At this point Roberta's usually "up" mien changed: she suddenly became serious, and I sensed she was ready to discuss deep-seated fears.

At this point Roberta looked directly into my eyes, and her eyes filled with tears. I said nothing, but I put my arm around her and said, "I know, you love your mommy very much." I felt Roberta struggling with her feelings, and I said, "You know, it's OK to cry in here, because I understand. This is our own private place. No one knows what we talk about but us." Roberta continued to sit with me in silence on the floor, but she didn't cry. She eventually turned her attention back to the sandbox. Roberta started to grab handfuls of sand, hold her hand above the spider, and let the sand sift through her hand like sand in an hourglass. The effect was to stun the spider but not truly maim it.

Content of Session

CHILD: I know my mommy is going to die.

THERAPIST: How do you know that?

C: Because she has AIDS. That'll kill you.

T: Did she tell you that?

C: No.

T: You know what AIDS is?

C: Yeah, it's a disease that kills people. We have it at school.

T: So your mommy is going to die?

C: Yeah. I won't be able to hug or kiss her any more. I won't sleep with her any more either.

T: You'll be very sad. But maybe other people will love you. You think?

Rationale/Analysis

At this point I was genuinely flabbergasted that Roberta not only knew this but also told me. It was clear she had no intention of revealing to me how she knew this. I did not know what she meant by the school reference; I presumed she learned about it there.

I wanted to emphasize that Roberta would still be loved and

C: My aunt loves me. She's nice to me. Did you talk to her?

T: No, I never met her. Do you love her too?

C: Yeah, I guess so. My mother will be in heaven. Then she'll be happy. Heaven is beautiful. It's peaceful.

T: Yes, I've heard that. Do you think you'll go to heaven too when you die?

C: Oh yeah, I'll go to heaven too. I'll be a spirit, like Santa Claus.

T: I guess everybody dies some time, don't they? Even you and me, right?

C: Yeah, but not until you're a grandmother I'll bet. I mean a grandfather.

T: How about you? When are you going to die?

C: When I'm 66. How about you?

T: I don't know really.

cared for even if her mother died. I felt that focusing on her continued existence even after her mother died would help her cope with her fears regarding her own mortality aroused by her own illness as well as the prospect of her mother's death.

I thought it quite significant that she expressed a form of mourning for her mother but not for herself. In fact, she did not pick up on my references to her own mortality, nor did she reveal nonverbally any sense of dread.

I believe there were several connections between the whale story that began the session and the later dramatic sequence with the insects. By revealing her awareness of her mother's diagnosis, Roberta also revealed her own fears about losing her mother. Moreover, although this was never clearly expressed by her, I sensed that Roberta also experienced feelings of shame related to her mother's diagnosis. I did not know how much she knew about AIDS. Yet the fact that she kept secret her knowledge of her mother's diagnosis suggested that she associated something negative, perhaps shame, with the disease. This hypothesis explains Roberta's whale story in which her mother's illness directly causes her to experience social rejection (perhaps the whale turned red from embarrassment).

One might also expect Roberta to experience anger toward her mother for being sick and for "threatening" to leave her. When she was dropping sand onto the spider (which clearly hurt the spider), I strongly sensed repressed anger surfacing, but Roberta did not express this in play. I also felt that Roberta could have been using the safety of the play situation to experience some control over life and death, as often occurs in play, especially with sand (Weinrib, 1983). Both of these hypotheses would be borne out in subsequent sessions.

The session itself was illustrative of several important play therapy processes. First, the session moved from more distant, fantasy material toward more consciously expressed feelings and thoughts, a general process that is often viewed as the ultimate goal of nearly all play therapy approaches (Schaefer & Reid, 1986). Second, the session saw the use of mutual storytelling. I adapted Gardner's (1971) mutual storytelling technique. The traditional use of mutual storytelling involves the child first making up his or her own story, then the therapist making up his or her parallel story, which contains adaptive solutions or perspectives on the basic conflict of the story.

I used a modified form of this technique in which Roberta and I created a story together. I found that I needed to use this approach because Roberta typically had difficulty organizing and expressing her thoughts in complete stories—usually she started out well but then couldn't finish. My contributions to the story were purposefully neutral and as minimally leading as possible. To illustrate, she stopped her story after relating that the child whale had to stay home from school to help her mother. I then said, "Oh, I see, so then what happened? Maybe she got all better, or maybe she got sicker? Did the little whale go back to school?" Still, Roberta didn't continue her story, so I offered, "OK, so let's say the mommy whale gets all better, then what happens?" Roberta then finished her story.

Over the next two sessions Roberta continued to express themes of sickness and death in her play. She continued to associate this material with parental figures. She seemed compelled to play with string, doll figures, and tissue in the sand box (making quite a mess, I might add!). A sequence repeated frequently involved the string becoming snakes, which strangle the human figures (sometimes GI Joe figures, sometimes Playmobil figures, and sometimes small dolls [6–8 inches tall]). Roberta then adopts a parental role, chastising the snake, then soothing and "nursing" the victim. Tissue was used by her to represent a pillow, blanket, etc. Sometimes the victim dies, and Roberta would then bury the figure in the sand. Sand often pulls for burial themes, but the significance of her burials was unquestioned because they were the endpoints in a series of representational events. Her repeated burials seemed to reflect an exercise in control over death. Often, Roberta and I would express sympathy (with "pretend" tears) for the deceased people and verbalize how much we would miss them. Our play remained in metaphor during most of these sequences. These play sequences appeared to help Roberta gain some mastery over her feelings regarding impending loss.

At this point in the therapy, I believed the sessions had been very productive for Roberta. Her mother reported positive changes at home, primarily in terms of Roberta's affect, which Felicia said improved greatly. Felicia also reported that Roberta still was clingy, but the intensity of her clinginess had decreased. During therapy, I was struck by the intensity of her play and by the frequency with which she used play to channel psychologically significant material. This seemed to me to be a clear demonstration of the expressive and cathartic properties of play. I was also aware that Roberta rarely expressed concerns about her own sickness in play. I was reluctant to probe for this material. Her apparent "shield" against anxiety or fears regarding her physical vulnerability probably reflected a healthy defense mechanism. She had a very concrete, matter-of-fact approach to death. Yet, as the following exchange reveals, she had already been deeply touched by death at her young age and in fact did harbor hidden fears regarding her own mortality.

Eighth Session

This session witnessed a subtle change in Roberta's choices of play materials. She shifted away from the more inviting, perhaps less threatening, expressive materials such as sand and Play Doh toward more realistic toys such as dress-up clothes and props and a toy medical kit. It was while playing with these materials that Roberta began to decompensate somewhat.

Content of Session	*Rationale/Analysis*
CHILD: (*referring to the doll, which she "dressed up" with a hat and jewelry*) Ooh, I hate you, you stinky doo-doo! There, you aren't a lady anymore, you're a man. (*With this she takes off the jewelry and puts a necktie around the neck of the [female] doll.*) There. You stink! (*She then throws the doll across the room.*)	
THERAPIST: Uh-oh, you're really mad at him!	
C: Yeah, Daddy. Here, Daddy. (*She retrieves the doll and hands it to me.*)	Roberta clearly called me "Daddy," not the doll; this appeared to be a manifestation of transference. Perhaps the doll also represented a father (the "bad" doll was first identified as a man, not a boy).
T: I'm Daddy?	
C: Here, Daddy, spank the bad boy for making doody in his pants. (*She then doesn't wait for me and begins to spank the doll.*)	
T: He made a mess?	
C: Yeah, a bad mess, he's in big trouble now! He's gonna get spanked real bad now. He's a real bad boy! (*She begins to spank him again—I say nothing, seeing her need to release this emotion. Roberta hits me several times in her rage, which I perceive to be purposeful intent to hurt me. Roberta hits the doll so hard that she apparently hurts her hand. She shakes her hand and nearly screams in pain and begins to cry and complain loudly that she hurt her hand. She begins to sob.*)	Perhaps this was a father-related memory.

This appeared to be a function of transference; Roberta appeared to displace onto me emotion related to a painful memory or series of psychological insults. |
T: Ouch, you hurt your hand. Here, let me see. (*I gently take her hand and rub it a little.*)	I risked feeding her transference by being nurturant, but, quite frankly, I did this on instinct and figured I could recover any damage my response might cause.
C: My daddy's dead. (*Roberta scrunches up her face in a concerted effort to keep from crying again.*)	
T: That's sad, isn't it?	
C: (*recovering herself*) He has AIDS too. He died a long time ago. One time he went to the hospital and didn't come out. A snake inside of himself filled with blood. Then it wrapped around his	I did not make too much of her wrong tense here.

I assumed that this explanation was mixture of something she was |

heart and exploded his heart. He had a heart attack. (*Roberta relates this with a very matter-of-fact tone of voice.*)

T: You miss your dad, don't you? (*Roberta only nods her head.*) I'll bet you loved him very much.

C: Nobody cares that he died. I didn't cry when he died. My mother cried. My daddy was very tall, taller than you. He put me on his shoulders.

T: Then you must have been very tall too.

C: Want to play Uno?

T: OK. (*While setting up the game, I attempt to continue this discussion, but she appears to turn me off at this point.*)

T: So did you ever play cards with your daddy?

C: Yeah. (*prolonged silence*) One time he took me to Adventures. We went on the big ship. I laughed so much, then I threw up on myself. He didn't get mad at me.

T: I'll bet he loved you a lot.

C: Oh yeah, then why did he get AIDS? He just didn't love me too much, did he? (*She appears genuinely angry now.*) He just loved his AIDS more, didn't he?

T: You mean . . .

C: He is always in the hospital. He does drugs. He shoots crack. He's a piece of shit!

T: You're very mad at him.

C: Yeah, shit on him! (*She then hits doll again.*) Now my mommy has AIDS, and she's gonna die too. Then what will I do? (*She has regained her composure somewhat.*)

T: I guess you'll have to live without them. Do you think you can do that?

C: No. I'll kill myself so we can all be together in heaven. (*silence*)

T: It's so hard to be without the people you love. (*silence*) Are you afraid to die?

C: No. I don't even know what it means!

T: What do you think it means?

C: It's when you go to heaven. (*She points up, grabs the doll.*) Let's ask Daddy. Daddy, what do you do in heaven all day? (*Roberta looks at me.*)

told and her own embellishment. Regardless, I immediately understood her prior references to the heart and to snakes.

I quickly recognized her avoidance of this emotionally laden topic. I reminded myself to be patient!

I sensed that the small point of calling her father "Daddy" (as she had been doing) as opposed to "Dad" triggered in Roberta a feeling of identification and perhaps a relaxing of her guard.

I was at a bit of a loss for words here. Possibly she was repeating what her mother told her.

I knew I needed to tread lightly. I knew she could turn this discussion off at any moment.

T: (*through doll*) Well, it sure is different than
being on Earth. I'm a spirit, like the wind.

C: Can you call me on the telephone?

T: No, but I can hear you. (*At this point Roberta*   Roberta had had enough!
asks to finish the Uno game and shows no inter-
est in returning to the discussion.)

In this session Roberta revealed her sense of grief over her father's death as
well as fear of losing her mother. Because these concerns were elevated to the
level of realistic discussion between us, I was able to refer to them over the next
several sessions in the hope of continuing and deepening the discussion. However, Roberta was not open to these inquiries, as she either responded with
silence or avoidance. It was as if she needed some time to reestablish her defenses,
which had succumbed to the eruption of unconscious conflict during the session
described above. Roberta preferred to engage in solitary play in the form of
drawing and painting. In recognition of her need to recuperate, I fell back on a
more nondirective style of interaction and hoped that her play would lead her
back to conflictual material.

Eventually, Roberta once again began to use play to express strong emotion
and to discuss recurrent themes of sickness and loss. However, her expressions
lacked the same urgency found in the sessions described above. The carthartic
effect of these initial outpourings appeared to provide Roberta with greater
equilibrium. I found that she was able to openly discuss her mother's illness and
her father's death with more frequency, but only for brief moments of time. She
seemed to be assimilating the painful feelings associated with these events into
her consciousness.

Roberta's mother reported to me that Roberta asked her if she (Felicia) were
going to die. Felicia said she felt very uncomfortable with this question and told
Roberta that she wasn't going to die. Felicia feared she "lied" to her daughter and
asked me what she should say. I informed her that Roberta knew she had AIDS
and had discussed it with me. Felicia was not surprised; she had sensed that
Roberta knew. I suggested to Felicia that she be honest with Roberta and attempt
to talk about AIDS with her. I told her that Roberta had made significant progress
in her ability to understand and deal with the fearful prospect of losing her
mother. Felicia later reported that she did have an open discussion with Roberta
and was surprised at how well Roberta dealt with the issues. Felicia remained
adamant, however, about Roberta not finding out about her own diagnosis. Felicia
said that some day she might tell Roberta, and with that in mind I gave her a copy
of a booklet entitled *Jimmy and the Eggs Virus* (Tasker, 1988). This publication
was written on a child level to demystify AIDS and HIV and help children cope
with the fears and misunderstanding associated with the diagnosis.

Further discussion with Felicia revealed that she continued to have trouble
separating from her daughter. She described other problems in setting limits—as
Felicia remarked, she just could not say "no" to Roberta. Felicia was already aware

of how her own feelings of guilt and grief regarding Roberta's disease made it difficult to demand too much of her daughter. Yet she also knew that being too indulgent was not good for Roberta. I suggested that Felicia join Roberta and me in the play therapy sessions for a few weeks. My objective for the conjoint sessions was simple: I wanted Felicia to "practice" setting limits. Modeling by the therapist and review of the parent–child interactions following the sessions are two advantages to using play therapy sessions for this purpose (Griff, 1983).

For three consecutive sessions, I extended the session length 15 minutes and divided the time accordingly: Roberta and I would play alone for 40 minutes and then be joined by her mother for the remaining 30 minutes. These sessions were revealing in several ways. Felicia had a tendency to be overinvolved in Roberta's play; that is, she often "took over" for Roberta and did not allow her to experiment (or struggle) on her own. She seemed to have difficulty allowing Roberta the autonomy to engage in spontaneous play, as illustrated in the following sequence:

Content of Session	Rationale/Analysis
FELICIA: Roberta, what are you making?	
CHILD: I don't know.	
F: Looks like a TV set. See, here's the knobs, and here's the picture tube.	
THERAPIST: What is it Roberta?	
C: I don't know, what's yours?	
T: I don't know yet; what's it look like?	
C: Here, mine's a big horse. See, here's the tail, here's the head, here's the body.	
F: Here, you should color this in brown, not blue, horses aren't blue.	At this time I felt that Felicia was applying her own standards to Roberta's expression instead of just showing respect for her daughter's work.
C: My horse is blue.	
F: No, that's not right!	
T: (*to Felicia*) I think she likes it this way. It's pretty, no?	
C: I don't know. Let's do something else. Let's play pick-up sticks.	

This rather uneventful sequence highlights a pattern that emerged rather quickly in the conjoint sessions, that of Felicia subtly rejecting her daughter by not accepting her play productions. Blau (1988) describes how this type of parent–child interaction can affect the child's development of autonomy and self-esteem. As gently as I could I brought Felicia's behavior to her attention. She seemed to grasp the concept and interpreted her development as overprotectiveness. I also pointed out that the subtle messages of nonapproval embedded in Felicia's responses might lead to insecurity and dependency on the part of Roberta, which could account in part for her clinginess. Roberta's need for closeness and approval already were heightened by her illness and her mother's illness. Yet her mother's behavior may have exacerbated Roberta's neediness.

I asked Felicia to observe how I approached Roberta in the play session, specifically with respect to how I showed approval and acceptance of whatever Roberta expressed in her play. These behaviors included (1) showing interest and nonjudgment toward any form of spontaneous play produced by Roberta, (2) praising Roberta's efforts, not just the outcome of her efforts to produce something, and (3) allowing Roberta to go at her own pace, that is, not attempting to direct or control the outcome. Felicia attempted to put these behaviors into practice in the home, with some reported success in the form of longer and more enjoyable periods of play with Roberta. After 3 weeks, Felicia reported that Roberta was less clingy and much less moody in the home.

The original goal of the conjoint sessions was not met because it was based on an erroneous assumption regarding the problem at hand, clinginess. I had assumed that Felicia had difficulty setting limits because of her sense of guilt. Yet I observed no difficulty on the part of Felicia in setting limits. However, the conjoint sessions revealed a family dynamic that otherwise would not have been discovered or worked on.

Individual play sessions resumed and lasted only for another month because the family moved to another state to be closer to extended family. These remaining sessions were difficult for Roberta, as she undoubtedly experienced the termination of our relationship as another loss. Yet her ability to cope seemed to be stronger. Her mother reported that she was actually very excited about moving to Georgia because she would be living in a house. I assisted Felicia in locating a mental health center in the area and encouraged her to resume play therapy for Roberta as soon as possible.

CONCLUDING COMMENTS

Play therapy for Roberta appeared to provide for her a much needed conduit through which she expressed considerable pent up emotions. Her need to discharge strong feelings was evident immediately during the initial assessment session. During subsequent sessions she readily utilized an array of play materials, from expressive arts to concrete medical-oriented toys, to express her fear of dying, fear of losing her mother, anguish over the death of her father, and anxiety about the medical treatments she received. My interventions remained true to my eclectic theoretical orientation: I used a combination of directive techniques and nondirective responses to elicit fantasy material and to encourage conscious mastery and assimilation of painful psychological material. At times I was content for Roberta to remain in the metaphor of play, recognizing the theoretical rationale of the healing and actualizing potential of spontaneous play. At other times I encouraged Roberta to discuss painful material realistically in the hope of strengthening her overall ego functioning and attaining a more realistic perspective on her situation. I also was pleased about the outcome of the conjoint sessions. Although their benefit was somewhat serendipitous, I felt that I had contributed to a potentially significant change in the relationship between Roberta and Felicia.

From time to time over the course of therapy I was troubled by Roberta's relative lack of fantasy expression regarding her own mortality. At the start of therapy I had assumed that this issue would surface, yet Roberta apparently did not harbor fears of her own death, unless these fears were simply too deep-seated to emerge. She was clearly much more involved in the prospect of losing her mother. Perhaps this reflected developmentally appropriate concerns on her part. It was never clear to me whether or not Roberta knew of her own diagnosis. I had to respect Felicia's wishes regarding informing Roberta of this fact.

In closing, it should be remembered that my treatment of Roberta was in actuality an adjunct to comprehensive services provided by a local hospital. Both Roberta and Felicia received group counseling on a regular basis. Social work and case management services were also provided to the family. These programs seemed to help keep the family together and provided much needed support.

PLAY THERAPY MATERIALS

- Sand box
- Medical kit
- Dolls: small, bendable
- GI Joes
- Playmobil figures

- Scotch tape
- Tissues
- Band-aids
- Insects
- String

STUDY QUESTIONS

1. Discuss the understanding about death of a typical 7-year-old. How do you evaluate Roberta's reactions to her father's death and to the prospect of her mother dying? How do you think she will respond when she learns of her own diagnosis, and how can therapy help her at that time?

2. How would you have responded to Roberta's whale story? As with many children's stories, this one expresses several themes. Identify these and indicate which you would have pursued and why.

3. Comment on the conjoint sessions with mother, child, and therapist. What are some of the potential advantages and disadvantages of using this approach? Criticize the therapist's intervention in the conjoint sessions, indicating why they were successful and/or how they might have been more successful.

4. Discuss the termination process when a child and family relocates. In this case, what issues would you have emphasized, had you been the therapist?

REFERENCES

Adams, M. (1976). A hospital play program: Helping children with serious illness. *American Journal of Orthopsychiatry, 46*(3), 416–424.

Belman, A. L., Ultmann, M. H., Horoupian, D., Novick, B., Spiro, A. J., Rubinstein, A., Kurtzberg, D., & Cone-Weston, B. (1985). Neurological complications in infants and children with acquired immune deficiency syndrome. *Annals of Neurology, 18,* 560–566.

Blau, B. (1988). Pre-play: A modality to foster parent–child interaction with developmentally disabled infants. *Association for Play Therapy Newsletter, 8*(11), 1–3.

Chan, J. M. (1980). Preparation for procedures and surgery through play. *Paediatrician, 9,* 210–219.

Clatworthy, S. (1981). Therapeutic play: Effects on hospitalized children. *Journal of the Association for the Care of Children's Health, 9*(4), 110–113.

Dekker, A. H. (1988). The impact of AIDS in the pediatric and adolescent populations. *Journal of the American Osteopathic Association, 88,* 629–635.

Epstein, L. G., Sharer, L. R., Oleske, J. M., Connor, E. M., Goudsmit, J., Bagdon, L., Robert-Guroff, M., & Koenigsberger, M. R. (1986). Neurologic manifestation of human immunodeficiency virus infection in children. *Pediatrics, 78,* 678–687.

Gardner, R. A. (1971). *Therapeutic communication with children: The mutual storytelling technique.* New York: Jason Aronson.

Golden, D. B. (1983). Play therapy for hospitalized children. In C. E. Schaefer & K. J. O'Connor (Eds.), *Handbook of play therapy* (pp. 213–233). New York: John Wiley & Sons.

Guerney, L. F. (1983). Client-centered play therapy. In C. E. Schaefer & K. J. O'Connor (Eds.), *Handbook of play therapy* (pp. 21–64). New York: John Wiley & Sons.

Harvey, S. (1980). The value of play therapy in the hospital. *Paediatrician, 9,* 191–197.

Kübler-Ross, E. (1983). *On children and death.* New York: Macmillan.

Laughlin, C. D. (1990). At play in the fields of the lord: The role of metanoia in the development of consciousness. *Play and Culture, 3*(3), 173–192.

Levy, D. (1938). Release therapy in young children. *Psychiatry, 1,* 387–389.

McEvoy, M., Duchon, D., & Schaefer, D. (1985). Therapeutic play group for patients and siblings in a pediatric oncology ambulatory care unit. *Topics in Clinical Nursing, 7*(1), 10–18.

Mendez, H. (1988, June 9). *AIDS and the preschool child.* Paper presented at AIDS and the Preschool Child Conference, New York University, New York.

National Commission to Prevent Infant Mortality. (1987). *Perinatal AIDS.* Washington, DC: Author.

Pediatric AIDS Foster Care Network Bulletin. (1990). Revealing data collected on HIV-postive children. *Pediatric AIDS Foster Care Network Bulletin, 2*(1), 1–5.

Quinn, T. C. (1987). The global epidemiology of the acquired immunodeficiency syndrome. In C. E. Koop (Ed.), *Report of the Surgeon General's workshop on children with HIV infections and their families* (DHHS Publication No. HRS-D-MC-87-1). Washington, DC: U.S. Government Printing Office.

Schaefer, D., & Lyons, C. (1986). *How do we tell the children?* New York: Newmarket Press.

Schaefer, C. E., & Reid, S. E. (1986). The psychology of play and games. In C. E. Schaefer & S. E. Reid (Eds.), *Game play: Therapeutic use of childhood games* (pp. 1–17). New York: John Wiley & Sons.

Tasker, M. (1988). *Jimmy and the eggs virus.* Newark: Children's Hospital of New Jersey.

Ultmann, M. H., Belman, A. L., Ruff, H. A., Novick, B. E., Cone-Wesson, B., Cohen, H. J., & Rubinstein, A. (1985). Developmental abnormalities in infants and children with acquired immune deficiency syndrome (AIDS) and AIDS-related complex. *Developmental Medicine and Child Neurology, 27,* 563–571.

Weinrib, E. L. (1983). *Images of the self: The sandplay therapy process.* Boston: Sigo Press.

Zero to Three. (1989). Drug exposed babies: Research and clinical issues. *Zero to Three, Bulletin of National Center for Clinical Infant Programs, IX*(5), 1–31.

CHAPTER 18

Life-Threatening Blood Disorder
Case of Daniel, Age 11

CAROL P. KAPLAN

The diagnosis of serious illness represents a crisis both for the patient and for the family. This chapter presents the case of Daniel, an 11-year-old boy living with his parents and 15-year-old brother. A well-developed and previously healthy youngster, he had recently been diagnosed with a relatively rare autoimmune blood disease. The disorder, pancytopenia, affects the patient in a variety of ways, including vulnerability to hemorrhages and extra susceptibility to infection. Life-threatening consequences of accidents and infectious illnesses are always a possibility. Thus, although he looked (and usually felt) like a healthy boy in late latency, Daniel's life suddenly changed after his diagnosis. He was restricted from engaging in certain contact sports that he had previously enjoyed, he began missing many days from school, and he was subjected to frequent and often painful medical procedures and to hospital stays of varying length.

The situation was complicated by uncertainties surrounding the course of the disease in a boy Daniel's age; that is, it might eventually either worsen or improve. Moreover, the team of physicians did not always agree about which activities ought to be prohibited, and Daniel was aware of these differences of opinion. Previously a cooperative and cheerful boy, he reacted to the whole situation with anger and negativism, insisting that he should be allowed to continue to play his favorite contact sports. His behavior at home and at school deteriorated, as did his schoolwork. Expectably, the family was affected in a variety of ways by the crisis, and in turn the parents' reactions impacted on Daniel.

This chapter focuses on the work done with Daniel and his parents (especially his mother) around conflicts precipitated by the illness in an effort to help them cope with this crisis so that Daniel could proceed with his development. Treatment was short term, consisting of 11 sessions over a period of about 5 months. Daniel was seen 10 times, either alone or with his mother, and both parents were seen together once. The 11 sessions were spread out over 5 months because of circumstances connected with the illness, such as emergency hospitalizations and doctor visits, in addition to a family vacation. In the intervals between sessions, the worker remained in telephone contact with the family.

Two issues among the many facets of this case are highlighted in this chapter: the development and treatment of children in late latency and the impact of a diagnosis of serious and chronic physical illness on the child's development. The main theoretical framework utilized for understanding developmental and treatment issues of late latency is that of Charles Sarnoff (1987a, 1987b). Authors whose work on physical illness has particular relevance to Daniel's case are Anna Freud (1952) and William Geist (1979).

Sarnoff's work on the late latency period (1987a, 1987b) illuminates the ways in which a chronic illness such as Daniel's magnifies the normal conflicts of this age. One of these conflicts is the "problem of passivity," described by Sarnoff as follows:

> This is a conflict between the wish of the child to be cared for and to remain a child, and resentment of the loss of independence that fulfillment of this desire brings. Moods, temper fits, withdrawal to rooms, and challenges of authority take center stage clinically when these conflictual areas are most intense. (Sarnoff, 1987a, p. 118)

An age-appropriate conflict between the desires for dependence and independence would certainly be exacerbated in a child like Daniel with a potentially life-threatening illness, because the normal thrust toward growing up is tempered by fears of unknown possibilities in the future.

Sarnoff describes heightened narcissism with self-preoccupation and manifestations of grandiosity as a common defense seen in children during late latency and early puberty. Even healthy children will inevitably experience potentially belittling and even humiliating events that can shatter their fragile self-image and self-confidence.

> Each surrender to the outside world cuts into narcissistic enhancement of the self and causes feelings of low self-worth. The negative and forceful reaction of young adolescents to positions of passivity may be explained on the basis of the humiliation felt by the loss of control to powerful authorities. (Sarnoff, 1987b, pp. 26–27)

It would not be surprising to find that serious illness amplifies the normal grandiosity of a child Daniel's age. Sick children must endure not only restricted activities but also traumatic medical procedures, both of which constitute assaults on their bodies and their growing sense of independence. For a boy, moreover, these can also represent a threat to the sense of masculinity. Grandiosity may also serve as a defense against the fear of growing up and becoming more independent, when the future (as for a child with a serious illness) may include fearful unknowns.

Sarnoff (1976, 1987a, 1987b) has written extensively about the "structure of latency," which enables children to utilize symbolic and fantasy play to discharge conflicts both on their own and in play therapy. Between the ages of 11 and 14 most children begin to enter puberty, and at this point many changes—physical, cognitive, and social—start to occur. These include the increased substitution of realistic, communicative speech for the earlier type of play in which fantasy provided a disguise for real people and situations in the child's life.

The work with Daniel illustrates a common feature of treatment with late-latency children: that children of this age tend to use symbolic play to a lesser extent. I have found that, like Daniel, children at this stage of development often play both to facilitate talking about current issues and, when intense feelings arise, to retreat from such material. The medium of play provides a comfortable milieu in which the child can hear and process the therapist's comments and interpretations even when he or she does not appear to be listening. At the same time, the presence of play materials enables the child to shift activities if the subject becomes intense or uncomfortable.

Finally, Sarnoff provides insight into an aspect of work with parents that, in conjunction with Geist's observations (discussed below), pertain to Daniel's case. As Geist points out, a therapeutic goal with chronically ill children is to help the parents hear the child's anger and complaints while continuing to make decisions involving the child's well-being. Yet Sarnoff notes that even when children are physically healthy, parent–child conflicts take on a certain coloration because of the child's stage of development. This, in turn, has implications for another important therapeutic issue that emerged in this case. Sarnoff writes that as children in late latency and early puberty become increasingly aware of their growing physical and social maturity,

> the children often reach beyond . . . the limits set by their parents. Battles between early adolescents and their parents ensue. The children defend their dawning independence. The parents watch for the safety of their children. Unaware that they are not at cross purposes, children and parents fight. Demonstration of the presence of shared goals can be a helpful intervention by the therapist. (Sarnoff, 1987b, p. 27)

In this case, the shared goals included the desire to have Daniel select as many enjoyable activities as possible for a boy his age without jeopardizing his health.

Anna Freud (1952), in her seminal paper on the emotional effects of physical illness on children, points to several outcomes that pertain to Daniel's case. In the first place, when children require nursing care and experience a loss of functioning or a weakened body state, they tend to regress to earlier levels of development. Some children do not resist such a backward pull, but those "who have built up strong defenses against passive leanings oppose this enforced regression to the utmost, thereby becoming difficult, intractable patients" (p. 72). In Daniel we see a youngster who demonstrated consistent opposition to passive compliance with medically and parentally imposed demands.

A second ramification of physical illness that Anna Freud discusses is the impact of restriction of a child's freedom of movement. She notes that such limitations on children on the part of adults have always carried punitive connotations; for example, children are frequently punished by being sent to their room or forbidden to go out to play. At the same time, children have a tendency to "defend their freedom of movement . . . to the utmost" (1952, p. 72). When under enforced restrictions on their mobility, children will discharge aggression by irritability, restlessness, bad language, and so forth. Such manifestations of aggression were evident in Daniel's behavior.

Finally, Anna Freud notes that just as the earliest bond between mother and child involves the mother with the child's body, the child in adolescence may unconsciously provoke her involvement by demonstrating "recklessness in matters of health" that results in power struggles with his mother. Daniel was approaching puberty, and his defiance of his mother's prohibitions can also be seen in this light.

Geist (1979), in an important contribution to the understanding of ways in which children react to the onset of chronic illness, delineates a number of processes that are relevant to Daniel. He points out that a chronic illness always represents at its beginning some kind of loss for a child, especially with regard to self- and body image. Children must therefore go through a process of mourning in order to integrate the new self-concept. Daniel's behavior could be viewed as representing such a mourning process.

Like Anna Freud, Geist recognizes that the onset of severe illness is accompanied by aggression in children. He believes that children experience such an event as an attack, a "narcissistic injury that frequently evokes ineffable rage, a primitive fury for which words have no expression" (Geist, 1979, p. 10). In discussing the sick child's fury, Geist describes it as being so terrifying that adaptation is rarely achieved by means of sublimation. Instead, children and adolescents turn to other protective mechanisms, including the acting out of their anger in order to "invite the environment to manage the patient" (p. 11). This certainly appears applicable to Daniel.

Moreover, children fear that their illness is evidence that they possess destructiveness powerful enough to cause family dissolution. Indeed, not unexpectedly, Daniel's family was adversely affected by the crisis of his illness, which only increased his underlying anxiety that he would destroy those very people on whom he depended for continued growth and development. What children need, according to Geist, is an atmosphere in which their feelings are accepted but they are not ceded control over decisions regarding their care. In fact, one of the goals of the work with Daniel's parents was to help them establish a climate in which they could allow him to express his feelings while at the same time they set firm limits.

Although Geist specifically addresses the feeling of anger, I have found that another issue that children with life-threatening conditions especially need permission to verbalize is the fear of death. As Geist points out, disease is extremely unfair, and children must realize that adults understand this fact. "Paradoxically, only then are the children free to accuse their elders of not knowing how it feels to be sick" (Geist, 1979, pp. 12–13). Such a confrontational event actually occurred at the culmination of Daniel's treatment.

Two additional points made by Geist can be applied to Daniel's case. Most chronically sick youngsters ask "Why me?" and think that their illness represents a punishment for prior actions, wishes, or thoughts. Their guilt must be handled not only by reassurances that they are not to blame but also by candid explanations of their disease and—where appropriate—statements about lack of knowledge about causes. Yet the ultimate goal of treatment of children who are chronically ill cannot be "cure," according to Geist, but rather must be adaptation to the illness.

THE CASE: DANIEL ROGERS, AGE 11

Family Information

This was a white, middle-class family of European Catholic extraction, living in the suburbs. In the home were:

Daniel Rogers, age 11, student in sixth grade in a public middle school
William Rogers, age 15, brother of Daniel, student in 10th grade in a public high school
Mary Rogers, age 41, biological mother of Daniel and William, housewife
George Rogers, age 42, biological father of Daniel and William and husband of Mary, an accountant in a large corporation

Presenting Problem

Mrs. Rogers made the initial telephone call about 2 months after the beginning of school, stating that Daniel had begun doing poorly in his school work and misbehaving in class. In addition, at home he had become oppositional, angry, and had developed an "attitude." She explained that the diagnosis of pancytopenia had been made 5 months ago and described the multiple medical procedures and hospitalizations Daniel had been undergoing since then. These included frequent blood tests, two spinal taps, and medications given intravenously to deal with infectious illnesses. Mrs. Rogers also reported that when Daniel went to his doctors' offices, he often saw children with leukemia and other malignant conditions who were suffering hair loss from chemotherapy.

The major stated reason for anger on Daniel's part, and the predominant theme in his conflicts with his parents, was the prohibition against playing contact sports. He was especially upset at not being allowed football, which he loved and had played in a league the previous year. The parents had tried to interest him in other activities and in sports that would be less dangerous (because they presented less of a threat of brain hemorrhage in case of injury), but he rejected these alternatives. Mrs. Rogers explained that of the three physicians in charge of Daniel's medical care, two had advised against football, while the third had taken a neutral stance. After considerable thought and discussion, she and her husband had decided that they would not be comfortable if they did not follow the conservative course in this matter.

Mrs. Rogers stated on the telephone that she and her husband were both in favor of counseling in general, and in particular they believed that Daniel might be holding back some feelings about his condition. She expressed the hope that talking with a counselor would help him come to terms with his restrictions and motivate him to do better in school. She stated that she and her husband were both willing to do whatever might be necessary to help Daniel. They were a very close family, she said, despite the fact that her husband had a very demanding job that frequently required long hours and trips out of town. Although matters of daily living with Daniel usually fell to her, her husband often took him out, especially to baseball, football, and hockey games. She indicated that William was accepting of his brother and supportive of him but was involved with school and other activities with his friends. She alerted me to the fact that she would be the one to bring Daniel for his sessions but that her husband would do everything possible to make himself available "if necessary."

First Interview

Content of Session	Rationale/Analysis
(Mrs. Rogers and Daniel arrive for the session on time. Both are dressed neatly in casual clothes. Daniel is tall for his age and well developed. I greet them in the waiting room.)	

THERAPIST: Hello, Mrs. Rogers, hello, Daniel. I'm Dr. Kaplan.

MOTHER: Hello, Dr. Kaplan. Daniel, say Hello to Dr. Kaplan.

CHILD: Hi. *(He looks ill at ease, avoids eye contact with me, and glances toward his mother.)*

T: Daniel, why don't we go into my office, and Mom can wait in the waiting room.

C: *(looking at his mother)* Mom, come in with me.

M: I'll be right out here Daniel . . .

C: *(more insistently)* Please, I said come in with me, Mom.

M: But Dr. Kaplan said she'd like to see you alone . . .

C: Mom, I told you I would rather go in with you . . .

M: But Daniel . . .

T: Why don't you both come in?

(They sit down in the office, and Daniel continues to direct his attention to his mother, avoiding looking at me.)

I decide to see them together both to decrease his resistance and to have an opportunity to observe the interaction between them.

T: Daniel, do you know who I am and why your mother brought you here today?

C: I'm not sure.

T: Well, I'm a person who helps children and their families. I gather there have been some problems lately. Who would like to tell me about it?

M: Well, Dr. Kaplan, lately Daniel has been getting into trouble in school. He's not handing his homework in, and some of his teachers have said that he has a poor attitude.

C: (*bursts out, with face reddening*) It's because you won't let me play football!

M: (*in a calm, controlled voice*) Now you know what the doctors said . . .

C: (*getting angrier*) Dr. Green said I could play football! You just don't want me to.

M: (*trying to reason with him*) That's not true. Dr. Adams and Dr. Freed said it's not a good idea. We want to do what's best for you.

C: (*yelling*) Then let me play football!

M: (*continues to speak in a rational, controlled manner*) We've been through all this, Daniel. Football has too much risk of injury, too much contact. We've offered you alternatives, like bowling . . .

C: (*continuing to yell*) I don't want bowling, that's for nerds! I want to play football!

(*Mrs. Rogers looks in my direction as if to say, "You see what I have to deal with."*)

T: (*commenting to no one in particular*) I guess it can be pretty confusing when such smart doctors have different opinions about what to do.

C: (*Briefly glances in my direction, then glances away and mumbles something inaudible.*)

(*Mrs. Rogers looks relieved that the battle has been interrupted.*)

T: I did hear certain things about Daniel's situation over the phone. It sounds like this whole business of being sick could be pretty scary to begin with, and then when the doctors don't agree a kid might feel even more scared. (*Daniel does not speak but looks over at me.*) I know only a little bit about Daniel's condition. I do know he

Sensing that beneath the power struggle over football there are feelings that need to be opened up, I begin to address these feelings in a neutral, nonthreatening manner with a conversational tone, speaking generally and not directly to Daniel, using the third-person "kid" and universalizing.

needs to have frequent tests. It would help me to have as much information as possible about it.

(*Daniel joins his mother in describing blood tests, bone-marrow tests, scans, hospital stays for IV medication, and so on. He is very knowledgeable and rather detached in his descriptions.*)

C: (*less vehemently than before*) Yeah, but Mom, I still think I can play football.

M: (*remains composed and controlled*) No, it really is not a good idea, and you know it.

C: (*grudgingly*) It's stupid not to let me play.

M: (*changing the subject*) Dr. Kaplan, I think we should talk about school. Daniel's teachers have said he is not completing his work, nor is he doing his homework, even though when we ask him about it he says it's done. And his math teacher has complained that he is disruptive in class . . .

C: (*defensively, shouting*) Mrs. Jones is a jerk, she hates me, it's not my fault!

M: But what about the homework? You tell us it's done, but apparently it isn't.

T: Sometimes it's helpful to make a plan about homework—when to do it, how much time to spend on it, and so forth. How does that strike you both?

M: That sounds like a very good idea . . .

C: (*angrily to his mother*) You just don't understand . . . those teachers are jerks . . . if you don't get it then you're stupid too . . .

T: (*addressing both of them, using a conversational tone*) You know, a lot of times when kids have confusing and scary things to deal with, it is not unusual for their school work to slip. In my experience, when kids have illnesses that go on for a long time and require a lot of tests and doctors' visits and hospital stays, this can be very scary. They can even be confused about what is wrong with them, especially when they are seeing doctors who are treating children with things like leukemia (*Daniel is now looking at me and listening.*)

M: But of course Daniel does not have leukemia. We have explained that to him many times.

Mrs. Rogers is attempting to remain in control and is highly intellectualized. Daniel is using the defenses of intellectualization and grandiosity. I join the family in this intellectualized approach but will try to open up issues that I sense are underneath and to express them in ways that permits them to be heard.

Daniel's negative response to my concrete suggestion indicates that a working alliance has not yet been formed, so that by staying with the topic of school work I convey the impression that I am allied with mother and criticizing him.

As I talk to his mother indirectly about concerns I suspect Daniel might have, he can absorb what is being said. I am also modeling for

T: Oh, I'm sure you have. But still it would be perfectly natural for a kid to worry that he might die.

M: (*Mrs. Rogers looks startled, but Daniel remains quiet and listens.*) Daniel's doctors have told all of us that he has an excellent chance of living a long life.

T: I'm sure that's true. He is getting fine medical care.

M: (*Nods in agreement.*)

T: (*addressing Daniel*) Daniel, our time is almost over, and I wonder whether we could talk alone for just a few minutes.

(*He agrees, and Mrs. Rogers goes out to the waiting room. Daniel gets up and investigates the games and play materials on the shelves. He does not stay long with any one.*)

T: What kinds of things do you like to play with?

C: Video games are my favorite. I also like to draw, especially horses, cars, and motorcycles. I can draw those pretty good. Oh, you have a Nerf ball—I like these. (*Begins tossing it.*)

T: You know, it seems to me there are a lot of things you are having to deal with lately. I think it would be good for us to get together again next week and talk some more. Then, if you want, you can also draw or play.

C: (*Shrugs.*) That's OK with me.

T: When we do talk together alone, everything you tell me will be private and confidential. And maybe sometimes we can include your mother, the way we did this time. Is anything else on your mind today?

C: Well, yeah. I really hate my math teacher, and also some kids in school. And I hate my father too.

T: How come?

C: He's always blowing his stack and yelling at me.

T: I've never met your father, but I'll probably be seeing him soon. Do you want me to discuss this business of yelling at you?

C: (*Shrugs.*) It's OK with me, but I doubt it will do any good.

his mother an openness about "taboo" subjects, especially fear of death.

His willingness to be alone with me leads me to think I have made some progress toward forming a working alliance with him.

T: Well, I can try. I think our time is up now.
Bye, Daniel, it was good to meet you.

C: Bye.

Preliminary Assessment and Treatment Plan

Daniel, a boy of 11 with a chronic blood disease, was reacting to the diagnosis and its consequences for his life with anger, negativism, and grandiosity. The underlying feelings appeared to include fear, helplessness, and confusion. Despite his oppositionalism, his response to the first session indicated that it might be possible to form a working alliance within which the issues surrounding his illness could be discussed. However, his need to have some control over the structure of the sessions, including the use of play materials, would have to be respected. The therapist would be required to be flexible with regard to such matters as including his mother during sessions. Also, approaching his concerns indirectly seemed to have worked, and this technique could be used in the future, although the ultimate goal would be to enable him to express his feelings.

Despite the fact that only Daniel's mother attended the first session, it was clear that some assessment of both parents was needed. Mrs. Rogers appeared to be handling her own anxiety about Daniel's illness, and his opposition to the physical restrictions, by remaining controlled, logical, and rational. She obviously wished Daniel's life to continue along as "normal" a path as possible. However, in the process she was unable to assist him in dealing with his painful feelings and his fears. Thus, treatment of Daniel would have to include her.

The nature of the marital relationship and the degree of support that Mr. Rogers could offer to both Daniel and to his wife were not known. An immediate goal, therefore, was to assess these issues in the next session, which was held with Mr. and Mrs. Rogers jointly.

Second Session

During this session, which the parents were able to schedule despite a heavy work load and a lot of traveling for Mr. Rogers, additional information was obtained. Mr. Rogers presented a definite contrast to his wife. Whereas she was calm and controlled, he was highly anxious. He revealed in the course of the interview that he felt very guilty. The source of his guilt was twofold. First, following the diagnosis of Daniel's illness he became so depressed that he left the family for about 1 month and stayed with his parents. Second, he acknowledged that he had a tendency either to give in when Daniel became insistent or else to lose his temper and "blow up." He revealed, in addition, that he had gone into therapy following his depressive episode and that recently his wife had been joining him for marital sessions. They both agreed that they were getting along better now and were working together in dealing with Daniel.

Mr. Rogers said that he was spending as much time as he possibly could with the family, and especially with Daniel. Even though his time was limited, he was trying to make it "quality time." Since the main problem in his relationship with Daniel was his tendency to explode, a number of strategies were discussed that might help him to set limits and handle conflicts in a more constructive way. He showed an interest in trying them and said that he would also discuss the issue further with his own therapist. Mrs. Rogers seemed satisfied that her husband was trying as hard as he could. We concluded by agreeing that he would make himself available in the future if it appeared to be indicated. Before ending I told the parents to let me know by telephone about any significant events (medical, behavioral, etc.) that might occur between sessions and also encouraged them to phone me about any concerns they might have regarding Daniel. They agreed to do so.

The information about the marital crisis that had been precipitated by Daniel's diagnosis and that was now stabilized, plus the fact that Mr. Rogers would be discussing his management of Daniel with his own therapist, reinforced the initial plan of keeping the focus of the treatment on Daniel, with his mother to be included as needed.

Third Session

Content of Session	Rationale/Analysis
(*Daniel walks slightly behind his mother into the waiting room. He looks ill at ease.*)	
THERAPIST: Hi, Daniel. Hi, Mrs. Rogers.	
CHILD: Mom, can you come in with me?	
MOTHER: (*glancing at me*) Well, I guess so . . .	
T: Sure.	I want to minimize Daniel's discomfort. In addition, I suspect that after a short while he will remain in the office alone.
M: (*in the office, settling into her chair*) This past week has been better. Daniel missed a day of school because of a stomach virus, but I can see he is making an effort to do his homework. Things have been calmer at home too.	
T: Does it seem that way to you too, Daniel?	
C: (*giggling, squirming in his chair*) Yeah, I guess everyone has been getting along a little better. But it won't really be good until they let me play football.	
M: Daniel, you know what we've been discussing about that . . .	
C: Yeah, yeah.	

T: Daniel, do you think we can spend a little time alone now?

C: OK.

(*Mrs. Rogers leaves for the waiting room.*)

C: (*leaning his chair back against the wall, balanced on two legs, which his mother had asked him not to do*) One of these days I know I'll get to play football again. It's so great, there's nothing like it.

T: You really do love football! You know, I saw your father the other day. He told me that you go to see football games pretty often with him.

C: (*nodding*) Sometimes I get players' autographs. I have a big collection. Also, I write to some of them, and they write me back personal letters. (*Gets up and takes paper and pencil from the shelf.*) I'm going to draw a motorcycle. (*Proceeds to draw it.*)

The subject matter of Daniel's drawings, as well as the discussion of football and his contacts with players, point to probable concerns involving masculinity and passivity. Since my immediate goal is to nurture our working alliance, I praise his proficiency in art rather than explore the meaning of his pictures.

T: That looks very real.

C: I'm good at cars and horses too. (*Draws a car and a horse.*)

T: (*watching him draw, commenting on the details*) That looks like a racing car. Is it? (*He nods.*) And that horse is very lifelike.

(*As Daniel draws and I admire his pictures, he appears increasingly relaxed. We continue to chat, and Daniel begins to doodle rather than to draw in a formal way.*)

C: Sometimes I draw stuff like this in school.

T: How are things in school these days?

C: Well, there are these kids who are mean. They tease other kids.

T: Do they ever bother you?

C: Yeah, sometimes. But me and my friends, we stick up for each other. Don't tell my mother, but I had a fight in school.

T: Remember what I told you about confidentiality! How did you feel about the fight? Were you afraid you might get hurt?

C: No way! I stick up for myself! Only a nerd would walk away from a fight. (*Proceeds to give examples of boys who are "cool" and others who are "nerds."*)

I suspect Daniel is indeed afraid of fighting, especially since he understands his disease and also that

T: I guess I can see your point.

(*Daniel continues doodling with pencil and Magic Markers, chatting about various aspects of school including subjects he likes and those he dislikes. He also describes amusing things that happened during the day. He seems surprised when the time is up.*)

he is ambivalent about his mother knowing about the fight. I decide not to interpret this conflict involving dependency and passivity directly because we have just begun treatment.

Fourth Session

Once again Mrs. Rogers came in with Daniel for a brief time at the beginning of the session, during which she reported that he had not had any health problems that week. Things were continuing to go better at home and with regard to school work. This time when he brought up the issue of football, she indicated that they would have to wait and see what the doctors decided. Then she left and waited outside.

Daniel had brought a number of glossy camp brochures with him, which he was eager to show me. The entire session was devoted to going over these brochures, discussing the activities that were pictured and described, and weighing the advantages and disadvantages of the different camps. Even though the summer was many months away, Daniel seemed to have no doubt whatever that he would be attending one of them. His attention was drawn not only to the sports but also to such activities as arts and crafts and camp performances. My comments generally related to the range of interests Daniel had and how exciting it was to look forward to camp. When I mentioned that sometimes kids also felt a little nervous about going away, he denied having any such concerns.

I reinforced Daniel's hope and optimism, since he was doing better. I gave him an opportunity to discuss separation anxiety, but he did not pick up on it.

Interval in Treatment

Following the fourth session, Daniel was not seen for 6 weeks. Initially he could not come to sessions because his medical condition had deteriorated so that he had to see his doctors frequently for careful monitoring. Then he improved and the family went away on a previously planned vacation. After they returned, however, he had to be hospitalized for a surgical procedure. In order to maintain our contact, I spoke to him over the telephone whenever possible, even though he was not particularly verbal under these circumstances and our conversations tended to be brief.

During this period I also had a number of telephone contacts with Mrs. Rogers. The first of these phone calls was for the purpose of Mrs. Rogers reporting on the medical situation and canceling our appointment. Even though she did not complain, I empathized with how difficult this must be for her. Not only did she carry the major responsibility for Daniel's ongoing medical care, the fact that she was the one who spent so much time with him meant that she was the one to whom he turned for support as well as for setting of limits. Yet the medical crises must surely make her feel worried and anxious. I wondered to whom *she* could turn for support. She was stoical and said that she and her husband were communicating much better and were able to help each other through these episodes now. Nevertheless, her response to my concern was evidenced by her continuing to keep in telephone contact with me.

When Mrs. Rogers reported in one of these conversations that Daniel had reverted to certain of his previous patterns of behavior, particularly the tantrums at home, I reminded her of some of the issues we had addressed in our very first meeting. I focused on the feelings he must be experiencing, such as confusion, fear, and anger. She was able to empathize with him and said that as hard as this was for the family, she realized it must be especially hard for him to endure the pain, confinement, and isolation from friends.

Fifth Session

Content of Session   *Rationale/Analysis*

(*This is the first session following a break of 6 weeks. Daniel has just been released from the hospital after a surgical procedure. As he and his mother enter the waiting room, Mrs. Rogers asks if she can come into the office with him for a few minutes. He appears angry and irritable.*)

MOTHER: I've just received an unsatisfactory report from school . . .

CHILD: (*shouting*) I don't want to talk about that! (*He holds his hands against his ears.*)

THERAPIST: Maybe it would be better if Daniel and I spoke alone. (*Mrs. Rogers nods and leaves the office.*) It seems you felt pretty mad when your mom told me about school . . .

C: (*interrupting, angrily*) I'm not going to talk about that!

T: In here you have the right to decide what you want to talk about. (*Daniel goes over to the shelf and picks up a Nerf ball, which he tosses up and down.*) I know you've just been in the hospital . . .

C: (*vehemently*) I had a *disgusting* roommate!

T: What do you mean?

C: That kid just cried all night. I couldn't get any sleep.

T: That must have been very hard.

C: (*snapping*) I don't want to talk about it!

T: OK, it's up to you. Want to play catch?

(*Daniel throws the ball at me as hard as he can, laughing. I throw it back, and we begin a humorous game of catch. As we play, Daniel seems to calm down.*)

T: (*casually*) You sure were mad just before.

C: Yeah, how would you feel if kids came up to you in school and asked you if you have cancer!

T: I guess that could be really upsetting. What did you say?

C: I told them I don't have cancer.

T: It might be natural, though, for a kid to think that's what he has when he's sick a lot and everyone gets so worried. Especially if that kid is around kids who do have cancer, he might even worry that he could die. (*Daniel does not reply but continues throwing and catching.*) I know that what you have is not cancer, but it is a disease that can cause a lot of problems. Luckily you have good doctors . . .

C: I know, I know. Let's do something else. (*He takes out paper and crayons and begins to doodle. The doodle becomes a mountain.*) I'm drawing a guy skiing.

T: Do you like to ski?

C: (*with bravado*) Yeah! I like to ski very fast, out of control, straight down!

T: Gee, that sounds risky. People can get hurt doing that.

C. I *want* to break my leg!

T: (*jokingly*) I guess then you wouldn't be able to go to school, and you'd have to stay home and get taken care of until you got better. That would be awful!

C: (*Laughs heartily.*)

It appears that he is overwhelmed with his feelings, and I am hoping that if we defuse the intensity it might be easier for him to verbalize his concerns. Playing might serve this purpose.

I assume that his grandiosity and bravado are counterphobic attempts to compensate for the narcissistic assaults he suffered during his recent hospitalization as well as for his sense of vulnerability and fears of the unknown and of growing up. Accordingly, I indirectly interpret the wish to remain dependent.

Sixth Session

Content of Session

(*This week Daniel is in a good mood. He announces he wants his mother to come in with him to tell me something.*)

Rationale/Analysis

CHILD: I got my report card, and I went up in all my subjects.

MOTHER: That's true. And although we know Daniel can do even better, we are very proud of him.

THERAPIST: Well, that is certainly good news.

(*We discuss Daniel's grades in his various subjects, and then Mrs. Rogers goes to the waiting room. Daniel remains in his chair for a little while, chatting. He then gets up, takes the Nerf ball, and begins tossing it up and down.*)

C: Yesterday I went to the doctor for a blood test.

T: Gee, it must be pretty painful and unpleasant to have to go through that all the time.

C: (*emphatically*) No way, not for me! It's *fun* to get blood drawn!

T: Well, it sure wouldn't be fun for *me*. But it seems as if you can handle it.

(*We play a game of catch until the end of the session.*)

Once again Daniel uses grandiosity and bravado as a defense. Again I do not directly confront the defense, but I am attempting to reinforce his sense of autonomy and mastery.

Seventh Session

Content of Session

Rationale/Analysis

(*The previous week Daniel had missed his session because he was hospitalized for 2 days. He immediately comes into the office alone and takes paper and crayons. He begins doodling and humming.*)

THERAPIST: Your mom told me about you being in the hospital.

CHILD: (*noncommittal*) Yeah.

T: She told me you had to have a lot of tests and an IV.

C: That's nothing. I'm used to it.

T: Well, I know that I myself would find all those procedures pretty unpleasant . . .

C: Hey, you want to hear what I had to eat in the hospital?

T: Sure.

Daniel is using the drawing as a means of avoiding difficult material. His description of getting any food he wants illustrates his defensive grandiosity. My comments about my own negative reactions

C: It's great. They order in anything I want. My favorite is Chinese. Want me to draw all the different dishes I had? (*He proceeds to illustrate the Chinese dishes he ate. We compare notes on the subject of Chinese food. Shifting to doodles*) You know, in school a lot of kids get into fights.

T: How do you feel about fighting.

C: I'm not afraid to fight; I'm just afraid to get into trouble. It's *good* to have a blood disease! You don't get into trouble, and your friends protect you.

> to painful procedures seem sufficient, in view of his resistance.

> I do not challenge his rationalization, which is a way of dealing with his fear of fighting. This is a loaded issue, involving concerns about passivity and dependency as noted above.

T: Well, I guess every cloud has a silver lining.

C: (*suddenly notices that one of the office chairs has several loose screws*) Next week I'm going to bring in a screwdriver and tighten those screws.

T: Do you like fixing things?

C: Sure, and I'm good at it too. I help my dad a lot around the house.

> I am reinforcing his sense of competence and masculinity, as expressed in a more adaptive form than fighting.

T: That's a really useful skill to have.

Eighth Session

Content of Session

Rationale/Analysis

(*The following week Daniel marches directly into the office carrying a screwdriver and proceeds to tighten the loose screws on my office chair.*)

THERAPIST: Thanks very much!

CHILD: (*Seems pleased, then mood changes; picks up Nerf ball and begins tossing it in the air.*) I'm so mad. I can't play football.

T: I can imagine how bad it must feel for a person not to be able to play a sport he loves.

C: (*Does not reply, but is listening.*)

T: I know your father takes you to see football games quite often. Maybe in one way he is trying to make up for the fact that you aren't allowed to play.

C: (*Nods, looking and sounding sad.*) But it's not the same.

> I note that this time he has expressed his feelings without as much anger.

T: I guess it's really a drag to have this kind of restriction.

C: (*casually continuing to toss the Nerf ball*) I know two kids who have leukemia. I met them at a picnic to raise funds for children with blood diseases.

T: I wonder whether you ever worry that you have leukemia.

C: (*Shrugs.*) Nah.

T: You don't have it; what you have is a different problem with your blood. But it would be natural for a kid to worry that he might have leukemia too, or even to worry that he might die.

C: (*quickly*) I never worry about that. Hey, you know I got two more autographs for my football collection.

Despite his denials, I suspect that Daniel *is* afraid and that this issue needs to be addressed on a continuing basis.

Ninth Session

Content of Session

(*The previous week Daniel had missed his session because he was hospitalized following abnormal results on one of his routine blood tests. This week he arrives at the office carrying a skateboard.*)

CHILD: Can I bring my skateboard into the office?

MOTHER: Daniel, you might damage Dr. Kaplan's office . . .

THERAPIST: It's OK, my office can take it.

C: (*Enters the office, where he demonstrates the use of the skateboard, showing me various maneuvers and describing how he and his friends play with skateboards on the street; as he jumps on and off, he actually does not appear to have very good control over it.*)

T: Gee, I'm surprised the doctors allow you to do this on the street.

C: Sometimes they do, and sometimes they don't. It depends on my blood. [Note: He is referring to his platelet count, which determines whether the blood will clot properly or whether a danger of hemorrhaging exists.]

T: That sure looks like fun. I think I might be afraid of hurting myself, though.

C: (*vehemently*) Not me! (*Continues skateboarding around the office.*) Guess what. On my street, me and my friends built a jump. Jumping is really

Rationale/Analysis

I choose not to comment, nor to remind him of his similar bravado about skiing in an earlier session, because I want to encourage him to feel comfortable about expressing his fears.

cool. (*Pauses.*) Although I *am* a little afraid of heights.

T: (*Nods.*)

C: (*after a little more skateboard demonstration*) Can my mother come in for a minute?

T: Sure, just go and get her.

C: (*to mother*) Mom, in school I had a bloody nose. I forgot to tell you.

M: We'll have to let the doctor know.

C: (*Does not comment.*)

It now appears that the act of skateboarding in the office may have been a grandiose defense against feelings of vulnerability and passive dependency. Perhaps, too, he is trying to impress me with his skills (both small and large muscle).

Tenth Session

Content of Session

(*Daniel follows his mother into the waiting room with an angry expression.*)

CHILD: Mom, you better come in with me!

MOTHER: Daniel, I . . .

C: (*shouting*) I want to play football! Why can't I play football?

THERAPIST: (*ushering them into the office*) Why don't we talk in here?

M: (*calmly*) Daniel, every time this issue comes up, we go over the same things. You know the reasons . . .

C: (*yelling*) What you're saying is stupid!

M: (*still calm*) We just don't want to take any chances . . .

C: (*Starts to cry and continues yelling.*) It's my fault I have this blood problem. I must have done something wrong. Why am I being punished?

M: Honey, you haven't done anything wrong. This isn't your fault . . .

C: (*still crying*) Yes it is! Why can't I play football? I want you to let me play football!

T: (*addressing Mrs. Rogers*) You know, I think this whole situation is scary and kind of confusing for Daniel. I've discovered that sometimes when kids feel scared because their lives seem to be out of control, they tend to think that they have done something bad and deserve punishment. I suspect they may think so because it is easier in a way than feeling helpless.

Rationale/Analysis

I am addressing Daniel's concerns indirectly as I speak to his mother.

M: Daniel, you know how many times we have suggested that you could join a bowling league. You've always enjoyed bowling . . .

C: (*enraged, yelling*) I *told* you bowling is for nerds!

T: (*addressing Mrs. Rogers*) It seems that Daniel prefers football because it is a more manly sport than bowling.

M: But he knows football is not possible . . .

C: (*Jumps out of his chair and shouts at his mother.*) You just don't know what it's like to be a kid my age! (*Runs out of the office to the waiting room.*)

T: (*to Mrs. Rogers*) I think Daniel has made an important statement today. (*going to the waiting room and addressing Daniel*) So long, Daniel. I can see you feel very upset today, and I'm sorry we have no time left to talk it over. Let's talk about it next week, and you can also call me if you want.

Eleventh Session

Content of Session

(*Immediately after the previous session, Mrs. Rogers had telephoned me to relate the events that had followed. Daniel had left the office angry and had refused to go into the house. Instead he had gone to the garage, where he remained for about an hour. When he finally returned to the house he was quiet. This incident, and the fact that he had seemed to be out of control, had upset the whole family, she said. Now, according to Mrs. Rogers, Daniel was saying that he no longer wanted to come for treatment. I said I could understand his feeling but suggested she tell him that I wanted to see him one more time because I had something to tell him. She agreed to bring him in. When Daniel appears for the session, he seems more hesitant than at any time since the beginning of treatment.*)

THERAPIST: (*after he and I are in the office alone*) Daniel, your mother told me that you didn't want to come any more.

C: (*Nods.*)

Rationale/Analysis

I am uncertain who is really resisting treatment at this point, Daniel or the family.

T: I can understand how you feel. You really got very upset here last week. I can't blame you in a way for not wanting to come back. After all, I can't make you well. Still, I'm glad you came one last time to talk some things over.

C: (*Looks uncomfortable.*)

T: You have often found things in the office to play with while we have talked. Maybe you'd like to choose something now.

C: OK. (*Selects paper and Magic Markers.*)

T: (*Watches while Daniel draws and doodles.*) You and I have talked about your disease a lot, and I understand that you have an excellent chance of living a long life. But I also realize that there are a lot of unknowns about your illness. The doctors have to watch you closely, and often you have to have tests. Many times when kids have diseases that contain unknowns, they feel afraid to grow up because they are afraid of what the future might hold. That is a perfectly normal reaction.

C: (*Continues drawing and doodling; does not interrupt.*) Do you want to play catch?

T: Sure. (*We play with the Nerf ball and chat for the rest of the session.*) I think our time is up now. Bye, Daniel, best of luck.

C: Bye.

Regardless of whether the resistance actually stems from Daniel himself or from the family, I must assume that this will be my last opportunity to see him.

Daniel draws and does not seem to listen, but his responses indicate that my remarks have been heard.

CONCLUDING COMMENTS

At the time treatment concluded, I was uncertain about the efficacy of the work with Daniel. This was especially true because of the abrupt way in which treatment came to an end. I thought more work might have been done with Mrs. Rogers, and also with Mr. Rogers, to help them tolerate Daniel's expression of feelings. I was also concerned about whether Daniel had resolved the issues with which he was clearly struggling. I told Mrs. Rogers that I would like to keep in touch, and she agreed.

Approximately 6 months later I telephoned the Rogerses to follow up on Daniel's progress. Mrs. Rogers was extremely pleased to hear from me. She told me that Daniel was doing very well despite the fact that he had suffered some complications and been hospitalized several times. He had started bicycle riding in a serious way and was no longer obsessed with football. He even was able to live with limitations on the bicycle riding at those times when his blood results were abnormal. She said she attributed this greater acceptance on his part to the fact that she and her husband were able to be more open and accepting of his feelings regarding his illness, and they encouraged him to express himself. She said, "Now we listen to Daniel!"

Furthermore, Mrs. Rogers reported, despite the frequency with which his diagnosis had been explained to him, Daniel had come right out and asked his parents directly whether he had leukemia. This had enabled them to explain that, despite the fact that so much was unknown about his illness, he did not have cancer. She felt that finally he understood and believed this. The most important concrete gain, Mrs. Rogers said, was that Daniel's attitude and school work were now markedly improved. She added that if the situation were to deteriorate again, she would not hesitate to contact me.

I therefore concluded that a key factor in the positive outcome was that I had enabled Daniel to express his feelings and had also been able to provide support for Mrs. Rogers so that she could tolerate these feelings. Formerly taboo issues, such as death and cancer, were now open for discussion and clarification. Thus, the deteriorating relationship between Daniel and his parents—which, prior to the onset of his illness, had been a generally positive one—was strengthened, and they were no longer adversaries. Daniel could now proceed to engage in activities that increased his sense of autonomy and growing masculinity.

PLAY THERAPY MATERIALS

- Paper, pencils, crayons, Magic Markers
- Nerf ball

STUDY QUESTIONS

1. Were the issues surrounding Daniel's illness resolved? To what extent can children achieve resolution of issues in the case of a chronic illness with an uncertain course?

2. How might one account for the fact that children with illnesses and disabilities that are either congenital or diagnosed in early childhood may present very differently from Daniel (e.g., with less anger)?

3. How should peer relationships be evaluated in Daniel's situation? Note that even though he was not healthy, he did not identify with very sick children either.

4. How might a family therapy approach have affected the outcome of this case?

5. Why did Daniel's treatment actually terminate so abruptly?

REFERENCES

Freud, A. (1952). The role of bodily illness in the mental life of children. *Psychoanalytic Study of the Child, 7,* 69–81.

Geist, R. (1979). Onset of chronic illness in children and adolescents: Psychotherapeutic and consultative intervention. *American Journal of Orthopsychiatry*, 49(1), 4-23.

Sarnoff, C. (1976). *Latency*. New York: Jason Aronson.

Sarnoff, C. (1987a). *Psychotherapeutic strategies in the latency years*. Northvale, NJ: Jason Aronson.

Sarnoff, C. (1987b). *Psychotherapeutic strategies in late latency through early adolescence*. Northvale, NJ: Jason Aronson.

PART V

The Crisis of Natural Disasters and Other Catastrophes

CHAPTER 19

A Crisis Play Group in a Shelter following the Santa Cruz Earthquake

JILL HOFMANN

PAM ROGERS

Project COPE—Counseling Ordinary People in Emergency—is a federally funded crisis counseling program for people who have been victims of a disaster. COPE is an emergency response mental health team that provides individual, family, and group counseling to the residents of Santa Cruz County (a small coastal county in central California). Project COPE originated after storms and floods in 1982, when it provided services for 18 months. After the October 17, 1989, Loma Prieta earthquake, COPE reemerged to provide services again to disaster victims and workers in Santa Cruz County. The project's staff is composed of five full-time employees who are psychologists and social workers in addition to approximately 40 independent contractors from the local mental health private practice community.

BACKGROUND ON THE DISASTER

The "San Francisco" earthquake of 1989 actually originated in Santa Cruz County, where the epicenter was the Nisene Marks State Park in Aptos, California. This earthquake registered 7.1 on the Richter scale and lasted a total of 15 seconds. The aftershocks continued even 7 to 8 months after the original quake, with over 2,000 in the first 6 weeks. The earthquake damaged or destroyed over 10,000 homes and left three to four thousand businesspeople out of work. There were six deaths and approximately 300 injuries.

In the first few hours after the quake, people were evacuated into shelters because of gas leaks, damaged or destroyed homes, or fire hazards. Shelters were created by the Red Cross all over the county in converted school gymnasiums, church community centers, and city auditoriums. They housed up to 300 people during the day and had beds for 30 to 100 people at night.

The October 17 earthquake brought with it chaos and confusion in its aftermath. For the people who were emotionally affected by the quake it created a strong sense of helplessness and inability to cope. People in a natural disaster often experience a number of conflicting emotions because their lives are thrown

379

into disorder. Homes that are not destroyed often have cosmetic cracks, broken dishes and glasses, and crumbled chimneys. Streets are often buckled and impassable, concrete is torn up, bridges are out, power poles are down. The possibility of additional quakes kept the anxiety high for the residents of Santa Cruz County in the immediate aftermath of the quake.

For the *children*, the earthquake was even more traumatic because of their lack of knowledge and previous experience. They often mirrored the terror and anxiety of their parents. The particular children we worked with were displaced from their homes and lived temporarily in shelters with other children and adults.

LITERATURE ON CHILDREN IN DISASTER

The professional literature related to children in disaster is quite limited, since most reports focus on the reactions of adults. Sugar (1989) points out this omission, which was also reflected in the absence of posttraumatic stress disorder as a diagnosis applicable to children prior to the American Psychiatric Association's revision of the third edition of the *Diagnostic and Statistical Manual of Mental Disorders* (DSM-III-R) in 1987. The operating principle has been to provide crisis intervention to *parents* who, in turn, are expected to reassure their children in crisis situations.

Although assistance to parents to help their children may constitute a valid first step, Sugar (1989, p. 163) maintains that "treatment should be individualized, since children's improvement is not determined by parental response." Sugar believes that individual psychotherapy is essential for some troubled children in disaster and that crisis-oriented group and family therapy also should be available.

A range of treatment techniques also is recommended by Frederick (1985), who includes structured and unstructured drawings, the coloring storybook, instruction booklets, and play and group therapy among recommended approaches to helping children traumatized by catastrophic situations.

In an earthquake, the physical ground shakes, and children experience loss of protection from their parents and other adults. All of this leads to shaky emotional grounding. Galante and Foa's (1986) epidemiological study of child earthquake victims in Italy found a wide range of disturbed behaviors in the first days after the earthquake. Sugar (1989) listed children's responses to disaster as including phobias, sleep problems, loss of concentration, loss of appetite, violent behavior, and dissociative reactions. Galante and Foa (1986) found that first-through fourth-grade elementary school children eagerly participated in monthly sessions designed to help them discuss and work through their fears and disaster experiences. Earlier work with children after the San Fernando (California) earthquake also demonstrated the value of community outreach plus counseling to help children who manifested symptoms (Howard & Gordon, 1972).

Berren, Beigel, and Ghertner (1986) state that provision of crisis intervention and follow-up support after disasters is crucial. Services may take the form of direct mental health intervention for individuals who require grief counseling related to loss of homes and loved ones as well as services that provide less intensive intervention in the form of clarification of facts and discussion of the survivors' feelings about the disaster. In Santa Cruz both types of services were necessary. The recurring aftershocks kept anxiety levels high about possible future losses, and this sense of continuing vulnerability made it difficult to put closure on the crisis that had been experienced.

CRISIS GROUP TREATMENT

This chapter is devoted to the use of a children's group in the crisis of a disaster, specifically, an art play group that took place in one of the temporary shelters following the earthquake. Play groups were founded as a means of (1) diffusing the fear of the trauma, (2) helping children discharge their feelings about the traumatic experience, and (3) giving parents much-needed respite. Staff was composed of trained psychotherapists of various mental health disciplines who had the help of volunteers ranging in age from 17 to 80. The location of the particular shelter we describe was in the center of town two blocks from the hardest hit area of downtown Santa Cruz.

As mental health workers we had choices to make with the limited personnel available in the first few days. We chose to have one "rover" to see children and family individually and make assessments, and one group therapist who would address the children's needs in a group treatment modality. We also had a core of volunteers who came in and out in 4-hour shifts to relieve the primary group therapists and to escort children to the bathroom.

We decided to have the group in an open space divided from the rest of the shelter by large long tables rather than selecting a more secluded room. This was because parents could see the group in process and the children were not isolated from their parents and friends by a closed door. (Safety and accessibility were both important factors, since the one room that was available had shelves that could topple over if we had a major aftershock.) Unfortunately, there was an endless stream of people who came in at the front of the building where the group was located. The large 3' × 6' tables became the physical boundaries of the group.

The task of the mental health workers initially was to provide structure out of chaos. We sought to provide a frame for the play group by establishing boundaries between us and the environment. Quite literally this meant shielding the children from the constant movement, sounds, and distractions of the shelter. By initially establishing specific tasks for the children to engage in and supporting the completion of each task, we provided a point of focus.

Beginning Phase

The initial task for all children entering the play group was to tell their story. The clinicians engaged the children in a dialogue of introduction (name, age, where do you live?, with whom?, how did you get here?). Then we would ask the children to describe where they were during the earthquake and what they had experienced. Most of the children provided short responses and required support to discuss details. The majority of the stories focused on what the children had experienced *visually* during the earthquake, for example, "I saw my mom running toward me," or "I saw the chimney fall." A logical intervention based on this was to have the children convey their experience visually. We asked them to draw what happened to them during the earthquake. As the drawings began to emerge, the children remembered more and more details of their experiences. The therapists suggested that children make books for themselves of their experiences (see Figure 19.1), thus providing some continuity to their series of pictures.

Most of the children responded positively to this exercise. They were able to focus on a specific task for an extended period of time. A few of the children found the experience anxiety provoking because they felt unable to convey their experiences adequately. For example, a 7-year-old girl struggled for some time with a picture of herself and her mother under a table. She reported that the figure in her drawing did not appear to be frightened. With the help of a therapist, written words were added to the picutre to convey her feelings.

The active involvement of the therapist, spending time in a one-to-one exchange with the individual children, assisted the formation of an alliance, thus reinforcing the frame of safety. Another asset of this process was that it generated data about each child. The therapist elicited information about the level of trauma experienced by the child and gained some awareness about the child's coping skills. Also in this initial "interview" process, the therapist was able to achieve some limited insight into the individual dynamics and ego strength of the child. This information emerged through the drawings, which revealed information about their families and their past history of traumas. For the children, the task of making the "earthquake books" was a tool to integrate their experience as an essential step toward a sense of mastery. For the therapists, this task provided important diagnostic information.

This early stage of the group also provided the children with a parallel-play experience. They were able to observe the activities of the other children, yet were able to maintain some control over their experience through the focus of their own books. The task for the therapist was then to move the group from a parallel-play mode to group interaction.

Shift to Group Process

The groundwork was set for this shift by the children sharing with the group their earthquake books and their experiences and by the accompanying spontaneous dialogue between the youngsters. Responses to other children's stories varied from empathy ("Yeah, our cat is missing too) to competition ("*All* our dishes broke"). By the end of this exchange, the children were better acquainted with their new playmates.

The ground shakes and
it scares me. My mom says
that it could hurt my house and
where I live.

FIGURE 19.1. Sample page from one child's "earthquake book." Courtesy Naomi Jacobson.

Another tool utilized to facilitate the shift to group play was the Scribble Game (Winnicott, 1971). The children were directed by the therapist to sit in a circle. Crayons were placed in the middle. Each person had a blank piece of paper in front of him or her. The youngsters were directed to select their favorite color of crayon and then scribble on the paper. When this was completed, each was told to pass his or her scribble to the person sitting on his or her right. The person receiving the scribble was to look at it and find a picture within it. They were then asked to outline the image they saw and could enhance it in any way they wanted. This game was repeated several times with variations on passing the scribble. (It should be noted that this was among the more popular activities with the children. Throughout the course of the next several days, the children repeatedly requested this game and often played it after leaving the group.) This task also provided another diagnostic opportunity for the therapist. The emergence of an image from the scribble was much like a projective test, allowing the unconscious process to come forth. The images the children discovered fell broadly into two categories. The first, quite understandably, were "scary" images such as monsters, witches, broken things, crooked houses. The second set of pictures were of simple, everyday-type objects such as birds, fish, and flowers. This task provided information regarding the continuing anxiety of the children, since there appeared to be a correlation between the level of loss or impact of the earthquake experience and the "scariness" of a child's images; the more severe the loss, the "scarier" the image.

The Scribble Game was a structured interactive exercise. Other activities provided similar structured experiences. Board games with clear and simple rules helped the group interaction. The first game selected was Sorry. (Two games were set up simultaneously to accommodate the children from the play group, the therapist, and any children joining the group at this point.) This game allows for success, setbacks, disappointments, and the possibility of mastery over all the elements.

Structure and Evaluation of the Group

The group would last for several hours at a time, 4 hours in the morning, 5 hours after lunch, and 3 hours at night. After the first day, we chose to take a break during meals, as the throngs of people descending on the shelter during mealtime made it far too difficult to focus on any given task. In general, structured activities continued over the 4 days.

However, the children were not all expected to play together after the first day. Smaller groups were formed, depending on the previous group experiences of the children. As new children joined the groups, they were asked to make an earthquake book, for assessment purposes, before joining other activities. The children were grouped together by age and the degree of trauma from the earthquake. The children with the largest degree of fear were grounded with a therapist working on a highly structured activity such as board games. Children with less evident anxiety were paired or grouped together to participate in play with clay, cars, action figures, and dolls. Many younger children, both boys and girls, would spontaneously "adopt" a doll to care for. The children with more aggressive expression of their anxiety often chose to play with the action figure and cars, creating war games.

Ground rules were important to give the children the structure missing in the chaos around them. The rules were as follows: (1) not to draw on another child's drawing without permission, (2) not to hit or yell while in group, (3) to remain quiet when another person is talking, (4) to ask permission to go to the bathroom (volunteers always escorted children to the bathroom).

We always encouraged the children to talk about their drawings if they wanted to. Most importantly, we encouraged the therapists not to make assumptions about the child's drawing; for example, something that resembled a cat to a therapist could be a collapsing bridge to a child. We would ask "what" and "how" questions: "What is that?" "How did that figure get in there?" We avoided "why" questions that put children on the spot, since quite often they could not come up with an answer.

We used a wide variety of board games; the ones we found most useful were those in which the children could either gain mastery over someone else on the board or show aggression in a nonpunitive way (several of these board games are listed at the end of the chapter).

Several case examples from the play group are presented. Each illustrates how the degree of trauma, together with the assessment of the individual, provided the therapists with tools to assist the child toward resolution of the crisis. As discussed previously, this demonstrates two facets of the work. First, the content of a child's play material provides a window for understanding the child. Second, the experimental tasks and process of the group guide the children toward mastery and control.

CASE EXAMPLES

Bob, Age 9

Identifying Data

Bob was a 9-year-old boy brought to the play group by his mother, a single parent in her early 30s. The mother's office was in an old building in downtown Santa Cruz, and they resided in a mobile home. He participated in group for 4 days.

Presenting Problem

The mother reported that she wanted "support" for her son, who had been home alone during the earthquake. She further reported that both of them were fearful of staying in their home, as it had been partially knocked off its foundation. They were unable to cook and came to the shelter for meals.

Initial Contact

After information had been gathered from his mother and the introductions, Bob was invited to draw. He appeared anxious and looked to his mother for cues. She, too, appeared anxious and looked to the therapist for reassurance. The mother was invited to sit nearby and observe the group. She seemed quietly relieved by this.

With the guidance of the therapist, Bob began to draw pictures of his experience of the earthquake. His first picture was of the mobile home, half off its foundation and resting at an angle. He drew a picture of his face in the window, frowning. The second picture was of him on his stomach crawling toward the door of the home. The final picture was of Bob standing outside looking at a bridge that had cracked and a broken water main.

Throughout the process of drawing, Bob engaged openly with the therapist. He reported being frightened and crying for his mother. His affect significantly shifted when he talked about the picture of the cracked bridge. His voice sounded weak, and his mood was helpless, as he reported he did not know how his mother would get to him if the bridge was "broken."

While Bob recited his experience, his mother provided herself with a parallel process. She drew a picture of *her* experience on the second floor of an office building, watching furniture fall and windows break. Both drew their immediate earthquake experience. The therapist then asked them to draw a picture together of how they were reunited. Bob asked his mother questions about how she had gotten across town, how she had known to go around the bridge, and how she had found him. She asked him questions about what he had done until she arrived, and so on. It was clear that so much had occurred in the first day that they had not shared their experience with one another, leaving each with doubts and unanswered questions. As this process unfolded, a new understanding was achieved by each, and an initial step toward mastery was taken.

Assessment

Bob was a 9-year-old boy who appeared clean and well groomed. His speech was soft but clear. He was overtly frightened when recounting his experiences in the earthquake but appeared calm most of the time. His affect was appropriate. Both judgment and impulse control were within appropriate range for his age. He did not experience hallucinations or delusions and was oriented in all spheres.

Group Progress Summary

Bob continued in group for the next 4 days. He was compliant and readily engaged in the activities. His mother accompanied him to group for 2 days. On the second day, she assisted with setting-up and cleaning-up activities. By the afternoon of the second day, she assisted with conducting board games and structured activities, and she spoke with other parents as they brought their children to the group. On the third and fourth days, she volunteered with the Red Cross, helping to cook meals. First, as Bob was actively engaged in the process, so too was his mother. Her process paralleled Bob's as they moved through their fears toward a sense of understanding and mastery. Each person, following the earthquake, sought out his or her own way to regain a sense of control: the therapists through their work, the children through their play, and the parents through their assistance.

Siblings, Ages 11, 8, and 6

Identifying Data

Three siblings were brought to group by their oldest sister. Judy was an 11-year-old girl, Lynn was an 8-year-old girl, and Sam was a 6-year-old boy. The mother was a single parent, and the family resided in a communal-living situation with two other families. The mother was unemployed at the time of the earthquake. The children attended the play group for 4 days.

Presenting Problem

Their home was severely damaged by the earthquake and was considered uninhabitable. The oldest girl, Judy, reported that the younger children had been quite frightened by the earthquake and were upset because they could not find their cat. They were staying with friends but came to the shelter for meals.

Initial Contact

Because it was the oldest child who initially contacted the group, the therapist asked to speak to her mother. The family was informed about the nature of the group and about the tasks specifically focused on dealing with earthquake-related issues and trauma. Before the mother had an opportunity to respond about whether the children would attend, Judy replied, "We need that!" She looked to her mother for agreement. The mother nodded and left. Judy gathered her siblings together and asked the therapist what they were supposed to do. The drawing exercise was explained. Judy proceeded to arrange crayons and paper for her siblings. As the therapist questioned the children during the drawing, Judy listened intently and frequently responded to questions asked of her brother and sister, and she sometimes reworded the therapist's questions to them. Under their sister's watchful eye, both Lynn and Sam readily participated in the task and engaged with the therapist. The story of the earthquake that emerged was of the three youngsters alone at home watching television. As the earthquake began, Judy told her siblings to get under a table. The three of them stayed there until it was over and then left the house. In addition to this sequence, Sam's picture focused on him crying. He drew a picture of himself with tears falling with the caption "Help!" (Judy assisted with the writing.) Lynn's picture focused on things falling past them, under the table, and crashing on the floor. She also drew a picture of the cat crying. Judy's picture focused on the events of getting under the table and out of the house. She finished quickly and continued to draw on her own until her siblings finished their pictures.

Assessment

Sam was a 6-year-old boy whose appearance was somewhat unkempt, and his clothes were dirty. His speech was moderately blunted and slow. His mood was timid and pensive, with affect being mood congruent. He was frequently distracted by external stimuli and required reminders to stay on task. He appeared oriented in all spheres and did not experience hallucinations or delusions.

Lynn was an 8-year-old girl. Although her clothing was appropriate, she appeared disheveled and unkempt, with uncombed hair and dirty clothing. Her speech was often quiet except when speaking to her sister. Her mood was one of sadness, and her affect showed this quality. She was oriented in all spheres and did not experience hallucinations or delusions.

Judy was an 11-year-old girl who was also somewhat unkempt. She had a cast on her arm from a playground accident. Her speech was clear and unremarkable. She was well defended against inquiries about her feelings and focused her energies externally. Her mood and affect shifted as her relationship with the therapist deepened. Initially she was suspicious, but she appeared more angry as the group progressed. Judy was easily distracted by external stimuli but was able to focus on a task when prompted to do so. She was fully oriented.

Group Progress Summary

Sam and Lynn were brought in each day by their older sister. The younger children responded well to the structure of the board games and enjoyed playing Sorry, Chutes and Ladders, and Candy Land. Judy often initiated these games for her siblings and then would choose to draw independently. Her pictures were of unicorns, hearts, and flowers. The drawings appeared to have a "magical" quality for Judy, transporting her beyond her caretaking responsibilities. Judy greatly enjoyed the scribble game and asked the therapist to play with her on a couple of occasions. Again the images that emerged had a magical quality, including fairies and animals. If Judy experienced fear as a result of the earthquake, she did not readily express it. She did, however, return to group one day to report that the cat had been found. She was obviously relieved and happy.

The family history and past traumatic experiences of these children provided each of them with a mental set for dealing with the earthquake. The displacement from their home was not a new experience, nor was survival independent of parental support. In group, these children quickly found a structure for themselves and a level of safety that allowed them to examine (at least superficially) their earthquake experience. Dealing with experiences on an affective level, however, was not part of their repertoire, and they clearly defended against it.

This family was referred to follow-up groups at the clinic, but, unfortunately, they never attended.

Ray, Age 9

Identifying Data

Ray was a 9-year-old boy who was staying at the shelter with his mother, in her mid-30s, and his grandmother, in her late 50s. The family had resided together in a single-family home prior to the earthquake. Ray's mother worked full-time, and his grandmother part-time.

Presenting Problem

The family home sustained major damage and was considered uninhabitable. Ray's grandmother reported that he had been increasingly aggressive and angry since the earthquake. She further reported that both she and her daughter had been very anxious and unable to sleep.

Initial Contact

As with the other children, Ray was initially invited to draw. He had difficulty settling down and staying in his seat. He was easily distracted by the activities of the shelter, and he frequently got up and moved about the area. With the assistance of a therapist, Ray was able to complete two drawings. The first one was a picture of himself playing ball outside a house with a neighbor. In the second picture the scene was replicated except that the chimney had fallen and the house had cracks in it. Ray described watching the house move and the chimney fall. He further reported his grandmother running up the street toward him.

Although Ray had difficulty concentrating on the drawing task, he actively participated in the group task of telling his story. He was very competitive with the other youngsters and strove to have the "best" story. As other children reported their experience, he typically responded, "Yeah, but *I* saw the chimney fall," or "Our house was totaled!" He was also very interested in the reports of individuals injured in the earthquake and shared these stories with great detail.

Assessment

Ray was a 9-year-old boy whose appearance and clothing were age appropriate. His speech was often pressured and loud. Although he was visibly anxious, there seemed to be an underlying quality of sadness. Ray demanded attention from his peers as well as the therapist. His behavior was often provocative and aggressive. He was oriented to person, place, and time and did not report delusions or hallucinations.

Group Progress Summary

Ray participated in the group all day the first day, and half a day on the second and third days. He did not participate on the fourth day because his family left the shelter. Ray was eager to engage in the group activities despite the fact that he sometimes found the experience frustrating to him. When, during the Scribble Game, he was unable to locate an image to outline, his response was to mark over the scribble with black crayon. For another scribble, when he was able to identify an image, he outlined a distorted face that he reported was a picture of Freddie Kruger. Because of Ray's aggressive behavior, the therapist attempted to channel his aggression into play activities that could also provide mastery experience related to the earthquake. The therapist engaged Ray in a mutual storytelling exercise using action figures. Ray's story focused on opposing characters that destroyed each other. The therapist retold the story with the characters working together to overcome adversity. Ray responded positively to the therapist's version of his story. Ray also played with clay and engaged in war games with figures over extended periods of time.

Although Ray's anxiety continued to predominate his experience in the group, after several days he was able to focus on a task without constant supervision. His earthquake block play exhibited a decreased level of destruction to the structure. Ray was developing skills and activities for himself where he could have some control.

Amy, Age 7

Identifying Data

Amy was a 7-year-old girl brought in by her father on the second day of the group. She lived with her father and stepmother. Their home had sustained minor damage, and they were able to remain there.

Presenting Problem

Amy's father brought her to the group because he was concerned about her initial reaction to the earthquake. He reported that she was frightened to the point that she refused to be left alone for even a brief period. He reported that she was excessively clingy and tearful.

Initial Contact

Amy was hesitant to join the group but agreed to try with her father's support. She watched him carefully as the therapist asked them questions. Amy was reluctant to draw, seemingly afraid that if she focused her attention elsewhere, her father would leave. The therapist suggested that she draw the book with her father. Amy drew the pictures, and her father wrote the text. She appeared to enjoy this activity and was then more willing to try something else. Her father stayed for most of the first day of group.

Assessment

Amy was a 7-year-old girl of slight stature. She was well groomed. Her speech was quiet, and she rarely made eye contact when speaking. Her mood was timid and fearful, and her affect was occasionally inappropriate, laughing when upset. She was oriented in all spheres and did not express any thought disorders.

Group Progress Summary

Amy participated for a full day on the second day of the group and again for a half day the following day. After the initial contact and activity, Amy was introduced to the Scribble Game. She played this with another young girl and a therapist sequentially. Most of her images were of animals, although she outlined two images she reported were objects broken during the earthquake. Amy was unwilling to move on to another activity when the game concluded and sought out a doll. Amy spent some time caring for the doll. When Amy was asked if her doll would like to participate in the games, she rejoined the activities accompanied by the doll.

When Amy arrived for group on the second day, she sought out the doll immediately. Again she participated in the activities with the doll. When it came time to leave, the therapist gave the doll to Amy. It had become a transitional object, representing Amy's ability to care for and control something outside of herself.

CONCLUDING COMMENTS

The case vignettes illustrate a variety of issues presented by the children in the play group as well as several intervention techniques utilized by the clinicians. Aside from the aforementioned process issues, two additional elements significantly impacted on the play groups. These were the environmental intrusiveness of the shelter and the ongoing aftershocks from the earthquake. Both factors added to the stress of the children, the families, and the staff.

Because the play area was a common one of the shelter, privacy was unavailable. Constant distractions bombarded the children and the therapists. People were continually asking questions regarding shelter procedures and needed to be referred to the Red Cross staff. Observers were interested in the activities of the group and would intrude to ask questions. Adults who themselves were distraught would seek out the therapist for assistance in dealing with their own issues. All of these situations required the therapists to approach these individuals delicately, not to exacerbate their anxiety. Despite our best efforts, however, conflicts were inevitable and did occasionally occur, particularly in situations where the therapist felt that the intrusion was adversely impacting the children in the group.

In one situation a doll that had been adopted by a young girl (Amy in the preceding vignette) was missing. It was learned that a woman had taken the doll from the table. When confronted by the therapist, the woman became hostile and refused to relinquish the doll. She reported that she needed it, as it represented her children. After a lengthy discussion, she agreed to return the doll to the child. The intrusion created yet another crisis for the girl (and, possibly, for the woman as well).

The aftershocks created new crises for everyone. Each time the earth began to move and the shelter building shook, new waves of panic shot through the children and adults alike. The aftershocks provoked new memories of the original quake. As this information surfaced, the therapists assisted the children with processing these memories, and these were incorporated into their mastery experience. In time, people became more accustomed to the aftershocks, which, although frightening, also could be endured and survived. This provided individuals with a sense of control over their own reactions, which is an empowering experience.

As demonstrated in the case examples, the groups offered the children the opportunity to express and externalize their feelings and to gain support from others who had undergone similar experiences. The families also benefited from the groups to the extent that parents participated with their children or observed group process. In some instances we felt that the children would benefit from ongoing treatment, and referrals were made.

SUPPORT FOR THE THERAPIST: STAFF DEBRIEFING

In this earthquake the therapists were themselves victims. All the people in the area who were working were themselves stressed. They too were affected by the emotional aftermath of the quake. They had suffered the same effects of (1) erratic shaking of the earth, (2) unknown welfare of their families, (3) natural gas leaks, (4) damaged homes and property, and (5) chaotic environment. In addition, they were working with children who were traumatized by the event. They were surrounded by chaos and were constantly needing to provide and reconstruct a safe frame wherein the children could release their fear and anxiety.

In order to work effectively it became imperative that the therapists themselves be able to discharge tension. "Debriefing" groups were organized to provide a forum for the therapists to discuss the traumatic event. A "debriefing" included a facilitator, who was there to ensure that each person had the opportunity to ventilate essential details of where, how, and what happened to him or her during the actual earthquake. The purpose of the facilitator was to acknowledge each person and to actively listen. No interpretation or formal interventions were made. It was important that each person be able to talk about his or her own earthquake story and its effect on his or her emotional well-being. These groups were formed two times a day (a.m. and p.m.) so that therapists had the flexibility to attend either one. Although not mandated, they were clearly emphasized as important to attend.

This opportunity provided the therapists with a chance to talk with each other about their reactions to the earthquake, thus normalizing the experience while discharging some tension. They could hear the similarities in the experiences of their peers and acknowledge their differences. In discussing the content of the events a multitude of feelings would arise; fear, anger, sadness, confusion, and laughter were common as people discharged the tension. The two most common themes brought up in the debriefing were issues of loss of control and vulnerability.

Therapists often returned every day to the debriefing groups and would often retell their story. As did the children, adults also experienced a need to *retell* their story many times. In the case of the disaster, it was found to be vital to have a support system for staff. Without support for staff, they may experience loss of focus and impaired concentration, a sense of confusion, and sleep disorders. Exhaustion sets in with the passage of time. We were fortunate in that volunteers from the National Center for Post-Traumatic Stress in Menlo Park staffed the debriefing for many of the therapists. Whenever possible, it is important to have staff that have *not* been victimized do the debriefing in order to safeguard emotional distance and objectivity (Webb, 1990).

When therapists work under such intense circumstances, lunch breaks and bathroom breaks get forgotten, and debriefing may seem incidental. However, for the welfare of the therapist it is vital to build in attention to his or her own needs. Time for debriefing (at least one per day), time for exercise, time off away from the crisis area, and food breaks are essential. In crisis, help for the helpers may be the first thing that is forgotten, but it is the most important resource to be remembered.

PLAY THERAPY MATERIALS

Our supplies were donated by large drugstores and hardware supply stores. We received over 20 pounds of clay, a hundred coloring books, and hundreds of packages of crayons. We utilized the crayons well but found that having the children create their own coloring books was much more empowering for them than simply using standard coloring books. They drew both to express their own experiences and to show other children who had not been in the quake what one was like. The motive of educating others empowered them because it implied that they had information and could impart knowledge. They prided themselves on their books, and we had instant art shows on the walls of the shelter. A second gain was a sense of hominess and ownership of their temporary surroundings. We used butcher paper for drawing, and when we ran out we used cut-up brown paper bags. A word of caution: crayons or drawing utensils that stain or that need water to be washed off should be avoided, since in a disaster there is often very little water available, and this earthquake was no exception.

The clay worked well, but we had too little of it to engage children *en masse*, and we also felt that we knew too little about their individual histories to work with clay. Clay was used for individual treatment and diagnostically as assessment. Board games came in many varieties, and the ones we found most useful were the ones in which children could either gain mastery over someone else on the board or show aggression in a nonpunitive way.

Art Supplies for Disaster (Keep in Storage)
- Roll of butcher paper, colored construction paper
- Newsprint, 18" × 24" or bigger
- Magic Markers, nontoxic, nonstaining, water base if possible
- When painting, be aware of acrylics, as they need to be washed immediately; if water is not a problem get bright-colored acrylics
- Oil-base pastels such as Pentel (be aware of cleaning problems)
- Clay, white or gray, in small 5- to 10-pound bags; this stores well

Additional Resources
- Yogi Bear comic books and coloring books ("After Quake," Los Angeles Department of Mental Health, Hanna-Barbera Productions)
- Yellow Bird Earthquake tapes (video) accessible through your local Office of Emergency Services
- Board games such as Sorry, Candy Land, Chutes and Ladders
- Stuffed animals, dolls (they act as transitional objects), and animal and people puppets

STUDY QUESTIONS

1. How can therapists maintain their own equilibrium and cope with their own stress when working in an environment surrounded by chaos?

2. What are typical behaviors of children in situations of extreme stress? Identify these responses in the specific case examples. How does the therapist distinguish between "normal" (reactive) and severe, "pathological" stress reactions in children?

3. What indicator(s) would point to a diagnosis of posttraumatic stress disorder (PTSD), and what is the time frame for making this diagnosis?

4. In what ways could the crisis group format be adapted to use in loss situations such as toxic spills, fires, or school bus accidents?

REFERENCES

American Psychiatric Association. (1987). *Diagnostic and statistical manual of mental disorders* (3rd ed., rev.). Washington, DC: Author.

Berren, M. R., Beigel, A., & Ghertner, S. (1986). A typology for the classification of disasters. In R. H. Moos (Ed.), *Coping with life crises: An integrated approach* (pp. 295-305). New York: Plenum.

Frederick, C. J. (1985). Children traumatized by catastrophic situations. In S. Eth & R. S. Pynoos (Eds.), *Post-traumatic stress disorder in children* (pp. 71–99). Washington, DC: American Psychiatric Press.

Galante, R., & Foa, D. (1986). An epidemiological study of psychic trauma and treatment effectiveness for children after a natural disaster. *Journal of the American Academy of Child Psychiatry, 25*(3), 357–363.

Howard, S. J., & Gordon, N. S. (1972). *Mental health intervention in a major disaster.* NIMH Research Grant MH 21649-09, Child Guidance Clinic, San Fernando, CA.

Sugar, M. (1989). Children in a disaster: An overview. *Child Psychiatry and Human Development, 1903*, 163–179.

Webb, N. B. (1990). Consultation in crisis situations: Behind-the-scene help for the helpers. In H. J. Parad & L. G. Parad (Eds.) *Crisis intervention, Book 2: The practitioner's sourcebook for brief therapy* (pp. 293–312). Milwaukee, WI: Family Service America.

Winnicott, D. W. (1971). *Playing and reality.* New York: Basic Books.

CHAPTER 20

Individual, Group, and Family Crisis Counseling following a Hurricane
Case of Heather, Age 9

CATHY DODDS JOYNER

At midnight on September 21, 1989, the eye of Hurricane Hugo, a category 4 storm with sustained winds of 135 miles per hour, crossed Charleston Harbor. Over 200,000 people had sought safety in Red Cross shelters. Countless more fled inland to hotels, motels, and homes of friends and family. Four days later, 46,000 people were housed in the 280 shelters that remained open. Twenty-four South Carolina counties were declared federal disaster areas because of widespread destruction. At the final tally, property losses ranged from $5 to $8 billion. Five thousand homes had been destroyed, and an estimated 18,000 were severely damaged. Approximately one quarter million people lost their jobs or workplaces. Twenty-six South Carolinians died Hugo-related deaths (Hugo, 1989).

As a result of Hugo, there were estimated losses of $1.04 billion in timber, $100 million in crops, and $222 million in farms and machinery. The projected losses from tourism range from $400 million to $1 billion. The proportions of physical loss in South Carolina were overwhelming (Hugo, 1989).

While many agencies were responding to the physical needs of South Carolinians, the South Carolina Department of Mental Health responded to the emotional needs of the people. The Department requested a grant from the National Institute of Mental Health to provide outreach crisis counseling. Funding for the grant was provided by the Federal Emergency Management Administration (FEMA). Because of the large numbers of people affected and the degree of physical devastation, emotional recovery lagged behind that which could have been expected from studies of previous natural disasters. The grant was funded through January 15, 1991, almost 16 months after Hugo struck.

The National Institute of Mental Health grant provided for outreach crisis counseling services to the 24 affected South Carolina counties. Outreach counselors were hired from the respective communities and had varying degrees of counseling experience. Training in identifying and treating posttraumatic stress reaction was provided. Ongoing training was a provision of the grant and was fitted to the emerging needs of the victims and counselors alike. Vulnerable populations were targeted in the grant. Providing services to these populations was limited only by the creativity and ingenuity of the crisis counseling teams.

Providing mental health services to communities post-Hugo presented numerous obstacles. Large numbers of people were affected in a variety of ways. Some lost everything they had; others were left with bare necessities. Grief over physical loss was compounded by the less tangible loss that accompanies natural disaster. This intangible loss, least understood by those who experience it, is easily denied. Intangible loss, which cannot be measured in dollars, wreaks havoc on individuals and families as they attempt recovery. There is the loss of community as families and services are disrupted. Those who are joyful at returning home find their communities changed. Those who are displaced grieve the loss of physical property and community bonds. To children, displacement or disruption in home communities affects peer relationships. They lose the support of friends at a time when it is desperately needed and lose a significant arena in which their development takes place, all at a time when their parents may be emotionally unavailable.

Disaster robs its victims of time. Hours, weeks, and months may be spent in survival. This is time lost from family and friends, time lost from the simple pleasure of living. Parents, caught up in the need to survive, may not be in tune with their children's emotional needs. Providing food, water, shelter, and clothing takes priority. As basic survival needs are met, and as recovery progresses, parents must deal with their own emotional responses, leaving little energy to confront the emotional needs of their children.

The sense that we have some control over our lives is also lost. We could not control the fury of nature. There is little that can be done to control the pace of recovery. Looking at the surrounding devastation over and over again reminds the disaster victim of his impotence.

An even more subtle loss is the loss of a sense of security in life's predictability. The realization that one's life can be drastically changed in a few short hours leaves the victim feeling open and vulnerable to further capricious events. This vulnerability and the need to survive postdisaster contribute to resistance to mental health services (Hugo Outreach Support Team, 1989).

RESISTANCE TO MENTAL HEALTH SERVICES

Following natural disaster, community and individual energies are involved in meeting basic survival needs. There is no time to deal with emotional issues. The outreach worker must be present at the survival level, working in shelters and in soup kitchens, riding down dirt roads into isolated areas to deliver food and water. He must develop a working relationship with church and community leaders and with those who provide services to disaster victims. The outreach counselor's presence slowly chips away at resistance.

Resistance to mental health services stems in part from the vulnerability of disaster victims. Certain emotional responses are normal and predictable following natural disaster. Lacking understanding of what he is experiencing, the disaster victim may feel "crazy." The accessibility of the outreach worker in the community allows disaster stories to unfold naturally. The counselor can normalize the victim's experience, thereby reducing his anxiety. A conversation in a soup kitchen over a sink filled with dirty dishes can be very therapeutic and carries none of the stigma of seeking agency-based mental health services.

THE PHILOSOPHY OF OUTREACH

Being actively involved in community recovery can be likened to building rapport in a clinical setting. It is necessary if a level of trust is to develop between outreach counselor and the client community. Community involvement also exposes the outreach counselor to the values and way of life of the community. This understanding is valuable as the outreach counselor assesses and tailors interventions for his clients. Even when the outreach counselor is a member of the community he serves, the dynamics of disaster force him to deal with mistrust and denial on the part of communities and individuals. He must, in his role as a professional, weave himself into the fabric of the community.

Another obstacle to providing mental health services is inherent in the mechanisms individuals use to survive natural disaster. Being strong, acting as if nothing is wrong, and not thinking about one's experiences are useful in surviving the event itself. Utilizing these denial mechanisms in recovery, however, can create dysfunction. All of these mechanisms prevent the individual from dealing directly with his emotional reactions to the disaster.

The denial that stems from these mechanisms is present in both individuals and communities. The assumption is that the absence of strength signals weakness; that acting as if everything is OK will make it so; that not thinking about one's experience will minimize it. In truth, repressing the emotions that accompany disaster causes them to fester, and this creates dysfunction.

THE PHASES OF RECOVERY: GRIEVING THE LOSS

Emotional recovery from natural disaster is a process that proceeds in phases over a 1- to 2-year period. Each individual's recovery is unique. The time frame for recovery depends on the individual's perception of loss and on the coping skills employed in recovery (Bergman & Barnett-Queen, 1989).

Death, injury, and destruction of homes and the environment are physical manifestations of disaster loss and must be grieved. More difficult to define and perhaps more difficult to grieve are the intangible losses. These are losses so personal they are sometimes difficult to share for fear they will be misunderstood. It is the loss a mother feels when she relates the story of forgetting her son's birthday in the days after the storm. "I didn't even remember," she says, "until I found a message written in the mud on the floor of his room—'Dick is 9 today.'" It is the old woman who sits on her porch and says, "There used to be a pecan tree out there. My mama planted it. All my kids played in it. Now it's gone."

Both types of loss, the tangible and the intangible, must be grieved. The manner in which individuals deal with the grief imposed by natural disaster is not very different from the stages of grief Elisabeth Kübler-Ross delineated in *On Death and Dying*. The dying person moves from the first stage of denial and isolation through stages of anger, bargaining, depression, and, finally, acceptance (Kübler-Ross, 1969).

On impact and immediately following a natural disaster, victims are in shock. They are at once confused and numb. They cannot begin to deal with the enormity of the task they face as they survey the destruction. To survive, they must deny—deny that the disaster has really changed their lives, deny their need for help. They may even deny the reality of their situation.

When the victim can no longer deny, he becomes angry. There is no relief in being angry with an act of nature. Anger with God is cloaked in guilt and silence. But anger demands an outlet. It may be displaced onto family, friends, and co-workers, creating relationship problems. Anger may be turned inward and result in physical symptoms.

The victim's anger may become so exhausting that he may begin to bargain. "Things will be back to normal by Christmas." "I'll have my family back home by the end of the month." "Soon as I get all this debris removed, I'll feel better." When these expectations are not met, he creates another deadline and another in an effort to bring closure. He continues to place stipulations on achieving normalcy. What the victim finds is that no amount of physical recovery can compensate for dealing with the grief inherent in disaster.

To recover fully, the disaster victim must go into his grief. He must acknowledge his loss and the consequences of that loss. To do so is so frightening that the victim often chooses to remain at an earlier stage. He continues to deny or remains angry with no resolution. Substance abuse is common among victims who choose to remain at these levels. Alcohol and drugs keep unwanted feelings at bay and make it easier to blame while accepting no personal responsibility for recovery.

If the disaster victim is able to acknowledge and grieve his loss, he can move toward acceptance. He knows his life will never be quite the same. He will always be touched by the event and by the realization that he has survived his loss.

Through each stage of the mourning process, it is the role of counselor to support the victim. He must acknowledge the victim's feeling of loss, listen nonjudgmentally, and gently confront when necessary. He must be a lifeline as the victims sinks into his grief. The counselor can teach skills and offer information, but it is the victim who must do the work of grieving.

TYPICAL RESPONSES OF CHILDREN IN DISASTER

Each child's reaction to natural disaster is unique. The child's direct experience of disaster, his perception of his parents' responses, and his developmental level at the time of trauma are key factors contributing to the child's response to natural disaster (Newman, 1976). Although each child is unique, certain responses are typical to each developmental level.

The very young child may respond with passivity and helplessness as the predictability of his world is disrupted. He is unable to differentiate the reality of the event from his fantasy. The event and reminders of the event may take on magical attributes. The child must depend on the parent to provide reassurance, to reconstruct reality.

Becoming overly anxious and clinging are typical of young children after disaster. The child is confused and frightened by the destruction and loss he sees around him. He fears losing his parent, his base of reality on whom he relies for his very existence.

Not being able to identify his feelings and lacking the skills to verbalize his discomfort, the child may respond in a number of ways. He may act out his frustration in aggressive or repetitive traumatic play. If he perceives his feelings as "bad," he may withdraw in shame. Regressive behaviors such as thumbsucking, lapse in toilet training, regressive speech, and sleep problems (nightmares, night terrors, fear of being alone at bedtime) are other ways young children alert us to their anxiety (FEMA, 1989).

Latency-age children are more in touch with the frightening reality of the event. They may be confused and even frightened by the feelings they experience. These feelings may be overwhelming at times and impair learning and concentration.

Because they are more aware of reality, these children develop concerns about the safety of their families and other victims. Experiencing the disaster has awakened them to the vulnerability of their world. They may develop specific fears around reminders of the event and may fear being left alone.

Latency-age children are more aware of their roles in the event and recovery. They may become preoccupied with their behavior during the traumatic event. Much as adults, they may experience guilt or responsibility for certain outcomes. Cognizant of their parents' recovery, they may choose not to verbalize their anxieties in an effort to spare their parents.

Sleep disturbances, somatic complaints, and traumatic play are common responses in latency-age children. Behavior may be altered, becoming aggressive or reckless. Some children become inhibited. Events that trigger memories of the traumatic event appear to evoke responses from both younger and latency-age children (Bergman & Barnett-Queen, 1989).

ASSESSMENT IN A DISASTER

Working with children following a natural disaster requires a multifaceted approach. Since reaction to trauma is unique to the individual and a function of numerous variables, careful assessment is necessary to develop effective intervention attuned to the needs of each child.

The level of family functioning pre- and postdisaster, the degree to which the family felt prepared for and secure during the event, and the degree of perceived and actual loss are important variables affecting recovery. The number and type of posttraumatic reactions displayed by the child will also determine the types of interventions to be used.

THE CASE: HEATHER, AGE 9

The following case is a composite of many children seen over a period of months in Charleston County. The posttraumatic stress reactions displayed are not universal but were frequently seen in latency-age children. Damage in the community was extensive and widespread. Some members of the community faced near-death experiences as a tidal surge of over 15 feet inundated the area. The guidance counselor in the elementary school developed a student referral list based on actual loss, degree of life threat, and/or family displacement. Referrals were also made by teachers who noted changes in a child's classroom behavior and/or falling grades. The approach utilized in this composite case involves one-to-one sessions, group work, and work with the child's family.

Family Information

Heather Simmons is a 9-year-old third grader who lives in a community heavily damaged by Hurricane Hugo. Prior to the storm, she lived in a one-story brick home with her father (John), mother (Susan), brother ("Bubba," age 11), and sister (Sarah, age 4). Her father was self-employed, and her mother worked part-time.

Presenting Problem

Heather, her mother, and siblings spent the night of Hugo with Heather's maternal grandmother. Water rose several feet into the house. On returning home the next day, the Simmonses found their home damaged by tidal surge. Mr. Simmons, who had spent the night in the rafters of his place of business, was safe but had lost much of his machinery.

Classes in Charleston County resumed October 7, 3 weeks after Hugo. Since returning to school, Heather's grades had fallen because of an inability to concentrate. A later interview with Heather's parents revealed that she had begun wetting the bed several times a week, a behavior Heather had exhibited when she was younger and under stress. They also reported that Heather had difficulty falling asleep, making it difficult to get up for school in the morning.

First Interview

The goals of this first session with Heather were to build rapport, to begin the debriefing process, and to normalize for her much of what she and her family were experiencing. The interview took place in the school guidance office. Written permission had been obtained by the guidance counselor in response to a letter notifying parents of the counseling services to be offered. I had been introduced to Heather's class on a visit with the guidance counselor. She told the class that we were friends and that my job was to talk to children about their Hurricane Hugo experiences. This session was my first face-to-face meeting with Heather.

It is important to allow the child some control in this session as to what she is willing to share. There are several reasons for this. Only the child is aware of what she can emotionally manage to deal with at this point. It is also important that the child not respond according to what she feels are your expectations as the adult/therapist. Finally, as a victim of natural disaster, the child feels her life is out of control. Allowing her control of the interview begins to reaffirm for her that she is able to master some elements of her life. She also begins to master "Hugo" as she retells her story.

Content of Session	Rationale/Analysis
THERAPIST: Hi, Heather. I'm Mrs. Joyner. I'm a friend of Mrs. Jones [guidance counselor].	
HEATHER: Hi.	
T: I visit lots of schools and talk to kids about what happened to them during Hurricane Hugo. I'd like to talk to you if that's OK?	Normalize the session.
H: I guess.	
T: I'm going to be asking you some questions about yourself and your family. So, it's only fair that I let you ask me some questions about me. What would you like to know?	Create a level of comfort for Heather by disclosing information about myself.
H: Um. Do you have kids?	
T: Yes. I have two daughters and one son.	Child may be wondering if I can possibly understand *her* experience.
H: Where do you live?	
T: I live on Sullivan's Island.	
H: Did your house get messed up?	
T: Yeah, it got messed up some.	
H: (*Pauses.*) I can't think of anything else.	
T: Well, if you think of anything later, you can ask me then. OK?	
H: OK.	
T: Heather, could you tell me a little bit about where you were and what happened the night of the storm?	Begin debriefing.

H: (*Looks down and takes a deep breath.*) We went to my grandma's—Mom, me, Sarah, and Bubba. Dad stayed at his work 'cause he said we'd be safe at Grandma's and he'd need to take care of things at work. He said he'd see us the next day.

T: That must have felt scary leaving your dad.

Validate and normalize feelings.

H: Yeah, but my mom said it would be all right too. It was fun at first at Grandma's. Then the lights went out and it was raining and the wind was blowing hard. It sounded like rocks were hitting the windows.

T: That's pretty loud.

H: It was, but Sarah went to sleep anyway. I could hear it even when I put my head under my pillow.

T: The wind was so loud, there was no way to escape hearing it.

H: Uh huh. (*pause*) After a while the water started coming under the door. We put towels down 'cause we thought it was just rain blowing in. I went in the kitchen with Bubba to get some Coke. I had my flashlight. Then we heard a loud noise. When we tried to run to the living room there was water coming in the door.

Total loss of safe environment.

T: The wind blew the door open and the rain was coming in?

H: No. It smelled like the ocean, and it was coming on the floor. Mama was screaming 'cause Sarah was on the bed in Grandma's room. She ran to get her. Grandma wouldn't let us go with her. She told us to get on the kitchen table. She had to yell 'cause it was so noisy. (*Pauses and looks down*)

Child observes mother's panic.

T: Sounds like you were real worried about your mom and Sarah?

H: So was Bubba. But Mom came back with Sarah and sat on the kitchen counter. Me and Bubba touched the water. It was cold. (*Pauses and grins.*) You know there was fish in the water!

T: Wow! During the hurricane there were fish swimming in your grandma's house?

H: Yeah. I wish I had my fishing rod then. It was home.

Listening to Heather, my feelings are sadness and anger that such a precious little human being should have had to experience such terror. I also realize that to be helpful, I have to maintain my objectivity. Heather needed both my feeling and my objectivity.

T: Where's your fishing rod now?

H: I don't know. Lots of our stuff is gone 'cause of the water.

T: So the water came in your house too?

H: Yeah.

Heather related that her father had come the next morning, and they returned home to find their house and possessions damaged by the tidal surge. She said they were now living in a trailer.

Content of Session	Rationale/Analysis
THERAPIST: It sounds like the hurricane was really scary for you and your family, Heather. And it feels really *sad* when your house and clothes and toys are messed up. (*Heather nods.*) Sometimes, after a hurricane like Hugo, what happens to kids is that they're so *sad* and *mad* it's *hard to concentrate* in school. Their grades may not be as good as before. And their moms and dads are so busy cleaning up and getting their homes back together, they don't seem to have time for kids. Sometimes they're so busy and so sad themselves, they get angry and yell at their kids. That doesn't mean the kids or their parents are bad people. They're just sad. They have lots of things on their minds after the storm. They don't feel happy any more. (*pause*) What I do is talk to kids about ways they can feel better. I'd like to come back and talk to you if that's OK.	Normalize feelings and experiences around Hugo.
HEATHER: I guess.	

T: Then I'll come back next week this time. Bye.

H: Bye.

Preliminary Assessment and Treatment Plan

Heather's debriefing revealed the complete loss of safety she and her family had experienced the night of Hugo. It also revealed that the family had suffered extensive tangible loss. The guidance counselor reported that Heather's self-esteem was suffering because of repeated failures in the classroom. She also informed me that most of Heather's friends were displaced, disallowing support and self-esteem enhancement from the peer group. On the basis of this information, a preliminary treatment plan was formulated. Individual, group, and parent sessions were indicated. The time frame for treatment would be largely dependent on the coping mechanisms already in place and on the degree to which these mechanisms allowed the individual to move effectively through the recovery process.

Individual sessions would provide a safe environment for Heather to ventilate. These sessions would also establish the therapist as part of Heather's support system and provide a setting for self-esteem enhancement.

Incorporating Heather into a group, I hoped, would reduce isolation and provide opportunities for positive peer interaction. New coping skills would also be introduced in group.

The initial session with Heather indicated a need to debrief her parents because of the severity of their Hugo experiences and the degree of loss. It would be important to assess the perceptions of their roles in preparation for and during the hurricane. Further interventions would be determined by initial debriefing and assessment.

The treatment plan would also involve working with the teacher to provide opportunities for success and positive peer interaction in the classroom.

Session 2

The goals of this session, held 1 week later, were to continue rapport building, to assess Heather's present living situation, and to learn more about the child.

Content of Session	Rationale/Analysis

THERAPIST: Hi, how are you?

HEATHER: OK.

T: Are you still staying with your grandma?

H: No. We got a camper in our yard. (*pause*) Me and Mama and Sarah sleep in there. Bubba and Daddy sleep in the house on sleeping bags.

T: You all are getting the house cleaned up?

H: I'll be glad when we finish.

T: Sounds like you're ready to be back in your house and in your own room.

H: The camper's OK for now.

T: Sure it is. But everybody likes to have their own place with their own things where they can be alone if they want to be.

Relieve feelings of guilt Heather may be experiencing.

H: Yeah.

T: Heather, sometimes when things get a little too much for me to handle, I just close my eyes and imagine that I'm somewhere else. I've made a whole place in my head where I can relax and be content. And when I've been there a few minutes, I open my eyes again, and I feel like I can handle things a little better. (*I describe in detail my place.*)

H: That sounds pretty.

T: And I can leave it just like it is or change it if I want because it's my special place.

H: That's neat.

T: Would you like to have your own special place?

H: I guess.

T: I'll help you. I'll even write it down so you can read it over and remember it.

H: OK. (*Heather describes a forest scene for me. I ask her for details. Would it be cool or warm? Would there be flowers? Would the trees be full, or would it be fall? When she has finished, I ask Heather to close her eyes, and I read what she has described in a soft, soothing voice.*)

T: How did you like it?

H: Good.

T: Think you might want to practice going to your special place this week? (*handing her what I have written*) Take this with you and read it over if you need to.

H: OK.

T: You've got to go back to class now. Can I come back to see you next week?

H: Sure.

T: I'll see you then.

Session 3

Heather and I talked about her going to her special place. She related that it had worked "good" except when Sarah cried. "She's very noisy," Heather said. Heather had drawn a picture of her special place for me. I complimented her, and she told me that sometimes people teased her because her pictures looked "different."

Content of Session	*Rationale/Analysis*
THERAPIST: Sometimes being called "different" doesn't feel good.	
HEATHER: Yeah, they mean my pictures are weird.	
T: Do you like your pictures?	
H: Sure, but I want other people to like them.	

T: Have you ever heard of Picasso, Heather?

H: No. (*showing interest*)

T: Some people thought his pictures were weird. Let's go into the library and see if we can find some art books on Picasso.

(*Heather and I spend 20 minutes in the library looking at books on modern art. She is amazed at Picasso's art and sculpture and even more amazed that people pay millions of dollars for his work. I tell her that much of the art we are looking at had been considered weird in the artist's day but that he continued to paint and sculpt that way because it seemed "right" to him.*)

H: You mean people didn't like his pictures.

T: That's right. But he believed in what he did even when other people didn't.

H: Sorta like my pictures.

T: Sorta. It makes you feel happy to draw, right?

H: Yeah.

T: Could you draw some more pictures for me next week? We could make a book if you like.

H: That'd be fun.

T: OK. Now scoot on back to class.

Peer acceptance is important to Heather. Just as important is cherishing her individuality. Opportunities for peer acceptance and approval are provided in group as well as in the classroom.

Session 4

This individual session followed several group sessions. I began by asking Heather how things are going. She reported that they were still working on their house and that it was hard for her to concentrate in school sometimes.

Content of Session

THERAPIST: Sometimes, after storms like Hugo, it's really hard to concentrate in school. We're sad and even mad. There are so many changes in our lives, and we really wish that things could be like they were before. Sometimes, parents are so busy and worried they forget to tell kids how special they are. They even yell at them sometimes when kids haven't done anything wrong.

HEATHER: (*Looks down at her lap.*)

T: When these things are all happening at once, we start feeling bad about ourselves. It's like there's a tape recorder in our heads that's sending

Rationale/Analysis

Normalize.

us bad messages about who we are. What I'd like to do today is to help you make some new tapes for you. Some good tapes.

H: How do you do that?

T: Well, first, I want you to tell me four special things about you.

H: Four things? (*pause*) I'm funny. My dad says so. And I like to draw.

T: You're a good artist.

H: I think so.

T: You're funny, and you're a good artist. That's two.

H: I'm good at figuring out things.

T: One more.

H: I'm nice.

T: Great. That's four. "I'm funny. I'm a good artist. I'm good at figuring out things. I'm nice." Now let's make the tape. Close your eyes. Imagine there's a tape recorder in your head. (*Heather giggles.*) Now turn it on and repeat after me. "I'm funny. I'm a good artist. I'm good at figuring out things. I'm nice."

H: (*Opens eyes.*) Is that all?

T: No. Now you have to play the tape. I want you to play it at least four times a day.

H: When?

T: Well, you put your shoes on and take them off every day. How about playing your tape every time you put a shoe on or take one off? Let's practice. (*I have Heather repeat the four positive self-statements as she takes her shoes off and puts them on again.*) Now, I want you to do that every day.

H: Can I do it more than four times?

T: Sure. You can do it as many times as you like. Sometimes, when you're getting bad tape messages, you might want to play the good tape messages a little louder. Time to get back to class.

H: OK. Bye.

T: What are the good tape messages?   Reinforce.

H: I'm fun. I'm a good artist. I'm good at figuring out things. I'm nice.

T: Great. See you next week.

Heather told me at a later session that her head was getting crowded. I asked her to explain. She said that she had decided to put a trash can up there to throw away the bad messages.

Group Sessions

For children of disaster, a group becomes a support system. In a small way, this takes the place of the community peer system, which for some children is displaced as a result of storm damage. Group also provides an environment for learning new coping skills and for the children to develop and share their own unique coping mechanisms.

A group had been formed with several children in Heather's class. These children had had similar experiences but were functioning more effectively in the classroom than Heather. Heather was incorporated into these group sessions. The hope was that sharing in group with children who had similar experiences would help her feel less isolated. She would also come to understand that there were other children whose parents' emotional reactions were making life scary and uncertain for them. Her family was not abnormal.

First Group Session

A core group of three children was established based on similarity of experiences. As assessments were made, new children were added. Whenever a new member was brought into group, we did a minidebriefing so that each child would be aware of the others' experiences. Group met for approximately 30 minutes every other week.

The focus of this session was on understanding our bodies' responses to feared events and on learning a coping skill to help master these physiological responses.

Content of Session	*Rationale/Analysis*
The session began with each child sharing how his or her body felt the night of Hugo: "Icky feelings in my stomach," "My heart was beating so fast I could hear it," "I was shaking." I then told the story of the caveman who left his cave early one morning to be confronted by a huge tiger with very long teeth. I asked the children what they would do if they were the caveman. "I'd beat him up!" "I'd run." "I'd call the police." Together we determined that we would have to either fight or run. Whichever choice we made, we would need lots of energy. I then explained in simple terms how our bodies respond to a feared event and pointed out that all the physiological responses we'd had the night of Hugo were normal.	Sharing reduces isolation. Normalized physiological responses. These feelings were not a result of some fault or inadequacy in the child.

After all, we couldn't hit a hurricane or run away from it! This provided a framework for teaching a progressive muscle relaxation they could utilize when they had fearful memories of the storm or when there was a thunderstorm, an event that caused dread in some children. This exercise was practiced in other group sessions.

Progressive muscle relaxation exercises enable children to *control* their responses, although they cannot control the precipitating event.

Some children in this group reported having nightmares or other sleep difficulties, that is, not being able to fall asleep at night, waking up frightened and not being able to go back to sleep. Dealing with these issues became the focus for the next several sessions.

Second Group Session

Content of Session

This session began by relating frightening dreams or other scary feelings the children were having when they awoke. I also told them one of my hurricane dreams and of my anxiety when I awoke. We shared ideas about why we were having these dreams/sleep problems and concluded that this was normal after what we'd experienced. We discussed ways we were presently dealing with these issues and whether or not these were helpful. Most children were going to the beds of parents or siblings. "Homework" for next week was to come back with a plan for dealing with these feelings when the children awoke.

Rationale/Analysis

Sharing reduces isolation.

Bringing dreams into the light diminishes their power.

Adults can have scary dreams too.

Put control back in child's hands.
Builds sense of mastery.

Third Group Session

Content of Session

Focus for this session was on sharing dreams and sharing plans. I reminded the children that it takes practice to make our plans work and that we might need to make some changes as we found out what works for us and what does not. Everyone is different. Some of the plans were as follows: get up, turn on light, and go to the bathroom to wash face and get a drink of water; turn on light and write the dream in a book; turn on light and listen to music; turn on flashlight under the covers and read a book or color.

Rationale/Analysis

Guard against failure.

The following sessions focused on assessing the effectiveness of the plans and reworking them when necessary. Children provided support for one another. A deep-breathing technique and a simple meditation for children were taught as skills that could be incorporated into the children's plan.

During the school year, groups continued to meet on a bimonthly basis. The needs of children provided a changing focus for the groups.

A final group session was held at the end of the school year. I debriefed the children again, and we discussed how things had changed since the first time we met. We went over the techniques we had practiced (progressive muscle relaxation, deep breathing, self-designed techniques) and talked about using these in the event of another hurricane threat. We also brainstormed ideas on how the children could help their families prepare for another possible storm. This gave them some tools to utilize if there were a hurricane watch in the future.

Parent Counseling

Working through issues and feelings on a one-to-one basis and/or in group counseling is sufficient for some children following a natural disaster. Families that have a high level of predisaster functioning and who communicate openly without denial about their experience are generally able to provide the support their children need. Intervention that provides literature about the normal and predictable responses to trauma, on life-style changes that may help reduce stress, and on ways parents can help children cope may be all these families require to withstand the stress of disaster and to recover adequately.

If, after debriefing and work on developing new coping skills, children still exhibit posttraumatic stress reactions, it may be necessary to engage the parents directly. Such was the case with Heather. Her teacher related that Heather was still having difficulty staying on task and that she was in danger of failing. In an individual session with me, Heather related a story of her father becoming frustrated over his problems with putting on a new roof. He threw his hammer and let all his frustration out on her. "He's not like my daddy anymore," she said. "We aren't even like a family." To Heather, the loss she was experiencing went beyond the physical loss of her house. She felt that she had lost her "family" and with that her support and security.

First Family Session

Content of Session	Rationale/Analysis
I dropped by the Simmonses unannounced one afternoon to introduce myself. Mr. Simmons was home. Mrs. Simmons was at work. Mr. Simmons had not been able to resume his business at that time. I told him I was working with the school guidance counselor to help children deal with	Informal visit is nonthreatening. By focusing on large number of children, Heather was not singled out.

their fears and stress over the hurricane. I also told him I had talked with Heather several times and that she had told me about the night of the storm and their loss.

He offered to show me the storm damage and described the plans he had for repair. As we walked through the house, I talked to him about some of the problems I was seeing in children as a result of Hugo, problems such as difficulty concentrating in school, storm fears, regression behaviors, acting out, and of the changes the storm had forced on their lives.

As we walked to my car, I asked Mr. Simmons about his experience the night of Hugo. He related spending the night in the rafters of his business, not knowing whether he would live or die, not knowing if his family was safe. His story was punctuated by an occasional laugh. He finished by saying, "Yeah. It was tough. But we're making it." I asked if I could come back and see him and his wife. He invited me back the following week to talk with both of them. He thanked me for my interest in Heather.

Normalize Heather's experience.

Debrief. Identify coping style used by parent. Assess where father is in process of recovery.

Second Family Session

Content of Session

Both parents were present at this meeting. Since they had been at separate locations the night of Hugo, their experiences had been different. I asked them separately to related their experiences. At various points I asked them to identify for me how they were feeling. What emerged was each spouse's anxiety for the other the night of the storm. Mrs. Simmons also felt anger that her husband had decided to remain at his business.
Mr. Simmons expressed guilt over what his family experienced. He felt he should have done better for them. He reluctantly admitted anger over not being able to recover faster.

I then discussed with them, in general terms, what needs to happen in order for families to recover. The use of general terms is important to avoid any perception of blame. People are vulnerable around parenting in normal times; following natural disaster, parents are *especially* vulnerable.

Rationale/Analysis

Debrief. Identify coping styles. Assess where parents are in the recovery process.

Begin process of identifying and sharing feelings.

.

Normalize feelings using generic statements.

I pointed out the importance of sharing feelings with spouses and children. Children need to know that their parents can be frightened or anxious or angry and that these feelings are OK even if they do not feel comfortable. Parents can help their children by telling them what they as adults do with these feelings.

Reestablish parent as support system for child. Reestablishes communication. Provides tool for parent to feel good about his or her parenting.

Another suggestion for the family was to set up a routine. Natural disaster throws family life into chaos. Reestablishing a routine provides children with a sense of security and predictability that is important to healthy functioning. I also told them they needed to take time to have fun—a difficult thing to do when people are engrossed in survival.

THERAPIST: You all had a really rough time these past few months. The night of the storm was just the beginning. You both have been working so hard that at the end of the day you don't have the time or energy for each other or the kids. I can tell how much you care about one another and your children. I think it's very important to set aside some time for each other and the kids. You all need time to be quiet with one another, time to listen. And you need time to laugh together. But, you're going to have to plan it or you'll find something "important" to do, like finishing the sheetrock.

Focus on what family has working for them, their caring.

Both the Simmonses agreed. I asked them to make a plan with me present. They settled on alternating bedtime stories with the children—something they had quit doing since Hugo—and a Saturday picnic. The picnic was to last exactly 1 hour, and there was to be no mention of the work they "should" have been doing. I reminded them that they also needed to find couple time.

This family needed to know they were not alone in their experience. Mr. and Mrs. Simmons also needed the opportunity to vent their feelings in a supportive environment. These feelings, though normal and predictable, were getting in the way of their being a couple and of being effective parents to their children. Finally, the family needed permission to be a family again. The stress of surviving a natural disaster and the prolonged recovery often precludes familial activities.

I left some information on posttraumatic stress and recovery for the Simmonses to read at their leisure. I continued contact by phone and visited several times while I was in the area to assess their ongoing needs and progress.

CONCLUDING COMMENTS

In counseling Heather and other children of disaster, it is important to "debrief." Debriefing involves telling one's story in as much detail as possible, reliving the sights, the sounds, the smell, the feel of the event. This allows the individual to integrate the experience and come to view him- or herself as a survivor. Debriefing can and should occur more than once so that the counselor can assess the child's progress and so that the child can place the event in the past. With Heather, initial debriefing was extensive. She had good verbal skills, and she and other children in the community had had previous opportunities to relate their stories to the media. During other sessions Heather was debriefed less extensively as opportunities arose, for example, in relation to dreams and family issues. Normalization of feelings and experiences is important in relieving anxiety. Heather needed to know that what she was feeling was normal even if it didn't feel comfortable. Providing her with skills to utilize when things felt uncomfortable helped her feel more in control. Since recovery from disaster is a process that takes from 1 to 2 years, I hoped to provide Heather with skills she could utilize in meeting future problems.

Self-esteem is an important component in being able to deal with stress. Helping Heather make her personal tapes and teaching her to use them promoted positive self-worth. I also worked with Heather's teacher to create situations in the classroom in which Heather could experience some successes.

In session, I tried to create an environment for Heather where she could recapture her specialness. I listened nonjudgmentally and with respect for her feelings. At home, her parents did not hear what Heather was trying to tell them. Her performance in school was just another problem heaped on the existing pile. I believe a key component in helping a child master an event like Hugo and the resultant crises is to offer the child your belief in her importance as a person.

Placing Heather in a group reduced her isolation by allowing her to share with other children who were having similar experiences. These children replaced her peer support system, which had been disrupted. Group was a place to learn, to develop new skills, and a place where a kid could be a kid. Many children victimized by Hugo didn't have much to laugh about, but group was a place to giggle.

Spending time with Heather's parents was very important. They needed someone to listen to their frustrations, someone to tell them they weren't crazy, someone to support them when their world had dissolved under them. Heather's parents needed to understand what Heather was experiencing and to be relieved of any guilt they were feeling.

Recovery for Heather and her family and for others like them is not complete. It is a process. There are times during the process when, for every proverbial step forward, victims of disaster take two steps back. The job of the counselor is to help the client develop the skills to survive and the belief in self that will allow him to risk utilizing these skills. There is no way to solve all the problems that flow from natural disasters. What the counselor hopes to do is help the disaster victim come to view himself as a disaster survivor.

PLAY THERAPY MATERIALS

- Magic Markers and paper
- Books
  Davis, L. (1989). *Kelly bear feelings.* Lafayette, AL: Kelly Bear Books.
  Hugo Outreach Support Team. (1990). *Are you ready?* Charleston, SC: South Carolina Department of Mental Health.
  Gethers, R. (1989). *Hugo rap.* Charleston, SC: Hugo Outreach Support Team.

STUDY QUESTIONS

1. Discuss the fine line between "normalizing" children's reactions after a disaster and minimizing them. Critique the therapist's interventions in the first interview in terms of where you believe she helped Heather feel relief and where she might have explored Heather's *individual* reactions more.

2. Comment on the therapist's sharing of personal information with children. Do you agree that this makes the child more comfortable with the therapist? How does the therapist decide about how much personal information to disclose? How could the therapist refrain from answering personal questions without offending the child?

3. What are the implications of the therapist talking to the parents separately after several individual sessions with the child? Is confidentiality an issue in this situation, and how can the therapist handle this, both with respect to content the child has shared with the therapist and also related to matters the parents have chosen to share?

4. Discuss the use of guided imagery techniques with children. In what situations do you believe it is particularly appropriate? How can the therapist help an inhibited or anxious child participate in a guided imagery experience?

REFERENCES

Bergman, L., & Barnett-Queen, T. (1989). *Facilitating post-trauma recovery.* Unpublished manuscript, Counseling and Readjustment Services, Columbia, SC.

FEMA (Federal Emergency Management Agency). (1989). *Coping with children's reactions to hurricanes and other disasters.* Northridge, CA: San Fernando Valley Child Guidance Clinic.

Hugo. (1989). *The State*, Columbia, SC.

Hugo Outreach Support Team. (1989). *Dealing with stress.* Charleston, SC: Author.

Kübler-Ross, E. (1969). *On death and dying.* New York: Macmillan.

Newman, C. J. (1976). Children of disaster: Clinical observations at Buffalo Creek. *American Journal of Psychiatry, 133*(3), 306-312.

CHAPTER 21

The Aftermath of a Plane Crash— Helping a Survivor Cope with Deaths of Mother and Sibling

Case of Mary, Age 8

VICTOR FORNARI

"Excuse me—may I please ask you a question . . . am I going to die?"
—Mary, age 8, 3 hours after having survived an airplane crash,
   while she was in the Pediatric Intensive Care Unit

On January 25, 1990, Avianca Flight #052 en route from Bogota, Colombia, to JFK airport in New York, crashed in Cove Neck, Long Island. Of the 158 passengers aboard the plane, 85 survived, among them 21 children and adolescents. This chapter discusses psychotherapy with a survivor of that plane crash, an 8-year-old girl who will be called "Mary."

Lenore Terr, in her book *Too Scared to Cry: Psychic Trauma in Childhood* (1990), states that "psychic trauma occurs when a sudden unexpected overwhelmingly intense emotional blow or a series of blows assaults the person from outside" (p. 8). Certainly, the sudden crashing of an airplane, with its devastation of injury and losses, qualifies this experience as one where psychic trauma occurred. Terr elaborates that "traumatic events are external but they quickly become incorporated into the mind; a person probably will not become fully traumatized unless he or she feels utterly helpless during the event or events" (p. 8). Historically, Terr reports, most adults have tended to minimize reports of young children about traumatic events. She suggests that it is helpful to assist children to recall their memories of a terrifying event close to the time that the trauma actually occurred.

Work with 8-year-old Mary gives us the opportunity to examine the emotions of childhood psychic trauma as well as the mental work associated with

Dedication: I would like to dedicate this chapter to the victims of the Avianca airline disaster: those who perished, those who survived, as well as all of their families.

Acknowledgments: I would like to thank Sunny Hernan for the preparation of the manuscript and Jared Fuss, M.D., for his editorial suggestions.

traumatic life experiences. The emotions of terror, rage, denial, and unresolved grief as well as repeated memories and dreams about the crash remained vivid to Mary in the immediate aftermath of the trauma. Because of early intervention, Mary was given repeated opportunities to describe her traumatic experiences in an effort to regain some understanding and control over the overwhelming and devastating experience she had endured.

E. James Anthony (1988) states that community reactions following disasters of various types are similar. During the period of impact, between 12% and 25% of people usually remain calm and capable of purposeful action; another 10% to 25% are likely to become psychiatric casualties, manifesting extreme anxiety and tremulousness; a large proportion of the community, perhaps 75% seem immobilized by inertia. Individual reactions closely parallel those of community response. Among the victims of a disaster, many survivors tend to be overlooked amid the chaotic conditions because they are immobilized and in a stunned state. These may include child onlookers and families waiting anxiously for information. Anthony reminds us that the reactions of children are inclined to mirror the reactions of their parents, and generally there is an increase in attachment behavior in both.

According to Frederick (1985), the effects of a catastrophic situation on children depend on (1) the child's developmental level at the time of the trauma, (2) the child's perceptions of the family's reaction, and (3) the child's direct exposure to the trauma. Typical reactions of children in catastrophic situations include the following psychological and behavioral symptoms: sleep disorders (bad dreams), persistent thoughts of the trauma, belief that another traumatic event will occur, conduct disturbances, hyperalertness, avoidance of situations similar to the event, psychophysiological disturbances, and, in younger children, regression to enuresis, thumbsucking, and dependent behavior (Frederick, 1985). We see many of these symptoms in the case of Mary.

Recommended treatment techniques include the use of coloring storybooks, drawings, instruction booklets, play therapy, group psychotherapy, and incident-specific treatment (Frederick, 1985).

Sugar (1988) emphasizes the importance of providing help to child as well as adult victims of a disaster. The case presentation illustrates the particular importance of direct work with the child in a situation in which family members are too overcome by their own grief to provide adequate support to the child.

THE CRISIS SCENE: JANUARY 1990

Immediately following the crash of Avianca Flight #052, nine children were brought to North Shore University Hospital-Cornell University Medical College for emergency medical care. The emergency room on the evening of January 25, 1990, had been evacuated and then prepared to receive an unknown large number of injured crash victims. All of the patients who had previously been receiving treatment in the North Shore–Cornell emergency room were either transferred to the cafeteria, where a temporary emergency room was set up, admitted to the hospital, or discharged home. Prior to the arrival of any of the crash victims, several hundred physicians, nurses, social workers, and other health care providers were called in as part of a disaster plan to prepare for receiving the crash victims.

There was a high degree of anxiety and uncertainty in the emergency room prior to the arrival of the first crash victim. No one knew quite what to expect. No one had ever experienced the emergency room in this heightened sense of readiness. As the first crash victims were helicoptered to the landing pad and wheeled by stretcher through the emergency room, the grim reality of the crash became vivid to all who heard the cries, moans, and screams of the injured survivors. The helpless injured were covered with blood and were wheeled on stretchers to examining rooms surrounded by five or six health care professionals. A sense of helplessness pervaded in the emergency room.

Despite the large number of staff, the emergency procedures went quite smoothly, and each staff member seemed to find his or her role. As the first child was wheeled into the emergency room, it seemed clear that one of the roles that would be critical was to speak to each conscious child and try to calm him or her down in an effort to ease his or her anxiety while the emergency medical care was being provided. Many of the children sustained fractured bones and were in a high degree of pain.

To complicate the situation further, these frightened youngsters were unsure of the whereabouts of their family members. A plane crash, physical injury, and the fear that their family members might be dead caused all of those involved in caring for these children to be moved by the emotional anguish of these youngsters. The staff reassured and supported one another. They felt relieved whenever they learned that someone arriving to help in the Pediatric Intensive Care Unit (PICU) could speak Spanish. As the psychiatrist and social worker approached one child, Mary, in the far corner of the unit, they saw a frightened child with her left leg in traction and her right leg splinted. Mary seemed terrified and in pain.

THE CASE: MARY, AGE 8

Family Information

Mary, an 8-year-old girl, was traveling from Colombia to the United States with her mother and 5-year-old brother. They were to reunite with her father, who had come to New York 10 days earlier on business. He worked for a pharmaceutical company. This was to be their first trip to the United States. They were anticipating 5 days in New York and then 1 week in Orlando, Florida, where they were to visit Disney World, the anticipated highlight of their trip.

Presenting Problem

Mary reported that she had some apprehension about her trip, as this was her first ride on an airplane. Throughout the 9-hour flight, she and her brother played, ate, and rested in preparation for their reunion with their dad. Just before the plane crashed, Mary reported that the lights went out. There was a lot of screaming as the plane lost altitude and ultimately crashed. Mary recalled being awake and seeing her mother and brother either asleep or dead.

First Interview

This meeting occurred 3 hours after the crash.

Content of Session	Rationale/Analysis
(*Mary was lying in bed in the PICU with both of her legs in traction and an intravenous line in her left arm. There were bruises on her face with crusted dried blood.*)	
DOCTOR: (*in Spanish*) Hello, my name is Dr. Fornari. I speak Spanish. What is your name?	I felt some apprehension, not knowing how, or if, the child would respond.
MARY: Mary.	
DR: How do you feel?	
M: Oh, Doctor, may I please ask you a question?	
DR: Of course!	I thought, how polite and poised.
M: Am I going to die?	Moved beyond words, I had chills.
DR: No, Mary. You will be fine.	
M: May I ask you another question, please?	I realized how terrified this child was.
DR: Of course, Mary.	
M: May I go to sleep? I am so tired.	Moved by her delicacy and grace.
DR: Of course.	I thought, what a delightful kid!
(*Mary went to sleep.*)	

Comment

I reassured Mary, as there was no issue of a life-threatening injury. I noted with interest that she did not ask about other family members. I considered that she might be in a state of emotional shock and numbness.

Preliminary Assessment

Mary was an 8-year-old girl who sustained multiple fractures of her legs but no other serious injuries and no apparent loss of consciousness in an airplane crash where she witnessed much horror. Mary worried about her own survival as well as the uncertain condition of her mother and brother, whom she feared dead.

It appeared that Mary was a mature, sensitive, and particularly polite girl.

Play Therapy Sessions

Session 2

This session occurred 12 hours after the crash, in the PICU.

Content of Session	Rationale/Analysis
(*The morning following the crash, Mary was in good spirits, and her clinical condition was stable.*)	
DOCTOR: Good morning, Mary. Do you remember me?	Eager to see her response.
MARY: Yes, I think so.	
DR: How are you feeling?	
M: I am in much pain. (*seeing toys on her bed*)	
DR: (*speaking through a stuffed animal*) Did you sleep last night?	
M: Yes, but I am still so upset. I saw my mother get hit in the head by a rock. I am so worried about her.	Moved by her fears.
DR: It must have been so frightening.	Worried that her mom might be dead. I was trying not to discuss her mom too much.
M: I saw some children who were dead! (*with terror*) I never saw dead people before, but they weren't breathing—they must have been dead.	
	Mary appeared terrified.
DR: What a terrifying experience!	
M: I was talking with them one moment, and then they were dead.	How courageous to be able to put words to such a traumatic experience.
DR: How are you feeling? (*holding her right hand*)	
M: I am in so much pain! (*grimacing from pain*)	
DR: Were you able to sleep?	
M: I think so—I was so tired. They must have given me some medicine to make me sleep.	This child seemed so mature.
DR: I will come to see you every day. I talk to children and their families about their worries.	
M: Doctor, please help me. I am so scared for my mommy. I think my brother was hurt badly.	
DR: Did you see him?	Cautiously.
M: Yes, I don't think he was moving—unless he was sleeping . . .	

DR: As soon as we have information, I will tell
you. Here is my name (*handing her my card*)—
this is my phone number. If you want to see me
or talk to me, ask the nurse to call me. (*signaling
over to the nurse*) Nurse, if Mary wants me, call
me. Here is my home number too!

M: OK.

DR: I will come back later today.

M: Thank you, Doctor!

DR: Bye-bye.

I felt like someone needed to give
her the sense of being looked
after. I wanted her to feel as safe
and cared for as possible.

I felt moved by her gratitude.

Session 3

Twenty-four hours after admission to the hospital, Mary was transferred from the
PICU to a general pediatric bed. Her condition was stable. Surgery was necessary,
but her father was not yet in contact. Although her father was aware of her
survival, he remained occupied with the search and identification of his wife and
son. A family friend called to say that the father would be by to visit 12 hours
later. When I arrived, Mary was in surgery. I introduced myself to the family
friend.

Content of Session

FRIEND: Oh, doctor, her mother and brother are
dead, but she does not know.

DOCTOR: I am so sorry.

FRIEND: Her father does not want her to know—
he is worried about her, but I am worried about
him. He has not eaten in 24 hours and he cannot
sleep. He blames himself and wishes he was dead.

DR: Can I talk to him?

FRIEND: He is in the waiting area. My family is
with him; we will not leave him alone. He will
not speak to anyone now.

DR: I will come back tomorrow. Here is my card.
Call me any time. Can I write down your name
and phone number?

FRIEND: Of course, here it is. Thank you.

DR: Oh, thank you. I will do what I can to
help Mary and her dad. They will need your help,
too.

Rationale/Analysis

I had chills thinking about this
girl's sweetness and her profound
loss.

Worrying about him.

How fortunate he has some social
support.

Give important information *in
writing*.

Filled with emotion and wanting
her to know I understood the situation.

Session 4

Content of Session	Rationale/Analysis

(Sixty hours after the crash, I met with Mary, her dad, and some family friends. Mary was 24 hours postoperative and in excruciating pain.)

DOCTOR: Hello, I am Dr. Fornari. (*approaching Mary's dad*) I am pleased to meet you. You have a wonderful daughter.

I shook his hand for a long time, as he knew that I knew about his loss and Mary still did not know.

DAD: (*looking exhausted*) Thank you. It is nice to meet you. (*He looked so sad.*)

DR: (*turning to family friends*) Hello, I am happy Mary has such good friends (*without too much enthusiasm*).

FRIEND: Thank you. We are here to do what we can—this little angel needs us.

Moved by the analogy of Mary as an angel.

DR: Mary, how are you today?

MARY: Bad (*crying*). I am in too much pain. I can't stand it. (*Mary was in what appeared to be a very uncomfortable position with both legs in traction with pins through each knee area.*) I am afraid I will never walk.

DR: (*turning to Dad*) Have they given her pain medicine? (*turning to Mary*) You will walk Mary—you will be fine! Don't worry.

DAD: Yes, but I don't want her to take morphine. I do not want her to become addicted.

DR: I encourage you to allow the pediatricians to give her pain medicine. The bone surgery she had is very painful, and the medicine will help her to recover. Addiction will not be a problem.

Worried that this child will suffer more than necessary.

DAD: Oh, OK.

DR: Would you like me to get a nurse to ask for pain medicine?

DAD: OK.

MARY: Oh, Doctor. I can't stand the pain!

DR: We will help you. The nurse will come soon.

DAD: Doctor, may I speak to you outside?

I was hoping he would ask to speak with me.

DR: Yes, of course.

DAD: (*Mary's dad was a thin man of 30 who looked distraught and spoke softly. We spoke in a room across from Mary's.*) Doctor, my daughter does not yet know about her mother and brother. When should I tell her?

DR: (*Before speaking, I put both of my hands on his right hand.*) I am so sorry for your loss.

DAD: (*With his head hung low, he nodded without words.*)

(*We stayed silent together for 5 or 10 minutes. He cried profusely. I was moved to tears.*)

DR: This is a terrible loss.

DAD: I cannot go on.

DR: I know that this is hard, but you must find the strength.

DAD: Doctor, I am worried.

DR: Of course.

DAD: I want to die. (*softly*)

DR: I understand how you feel, but you must find the strength to live. Your daughter needs you very much.

DAD: I know, but I don't know if I can. (*pause*)

DR: I am sure that you do not feel up to it today. You must take one day at a time. I will help you and Mary if you let me.

DAD: (*silence, it seemed so long*) What can you do? You can't bring back my wife and son! (*mix of anger and sadness*)

DR: No I cannot. I wish that I could—that some one could! Do you feel unsafe?

DAD: I don't know—I want to die!

DR: You must promise me that you will not hurt yourself.

DAD: I can't.

DR: Unless you can, you may need to be hospitalized.

DAD: No—I will be fine.

DR: May I see you every day?

DAD: If you like, but when do I tell her?

DR: For now, she is in too much pain and, because of the morphine, in and out of sleep. I would wait 1 or 2 more days until her pain is eased and she is fully alert and awake.

I was moved by his position. I thought that he could be me—a wife and two children one day and then this terrible tragedy. I felt so vulnerable.

Now moved and anxious.

Feeling helpless. I know anger is justified and is an expected part of the grief process, but I hope he does not turn against me.

Worried that he might be suicidal.

Worried that he may need to be hospitalized.

Was he honest?

Hoping to be reassured.

DAD: OK. (*nodding in despair*)

(*We sat together for over 1 hour. One of the other psychiatrists joined us. Mary's dad was comforted by our concern and was relieved that we spoke to him in Spanish. When we returned to the room, Mary was asleep. I shook his hand and left.*)

DR: I will return tomorrow.

DAD: Thank you. I know that I must live for Mary.

Moved beyond words. I was overwhelmed and exhausted. How could he be gracious?

On the subsequent 2 days, I met with Mary's dad. He gradually began to seem more at ease. Mary continued in pain and on morphine.

Session 7

Content of Session	Rationale/Analysis

(*Six days after the crash, Mary was off the morphine and fully alert and awake. When I entered the room, she was watching television. Her bed was filled with stuffed animals and surrounded by balloons.*)

MARY: Hello, Fornari! (*She exclaimed in an animated way.*)

Surprised by her good humor.

DOCTOR: How are you feeling?

M: Better, thank you.

Pleased!

DR: Is your dad around?

M: Yes, he just went to get coffee.

DR: What are you up to?

M: Television. I still have some pain. Will I ever walk again? (*We played with her stuffed animals for quite a while.*) Look at a picture of my mommy and brother. Aren't they sweet? (*looking at the pictures*)

Wondering whether Mary would bring up the topic of her mother or brother—or is she expecting *me* to bring it up?

DR: Yes. They are sweet, just like you!

M: I am tired . . . I am sorry . . .

DR: I will go now. Say hello to your dad. I will stop by tomorrow.

M: Bye-bye Fornari!

(*Outside in the hallway I met Mary's dad with his coffee in hand. He greeted me warmly.*)

DR: How are you today?

DAD: So-so.

DR: Can we talk?

DAD: Of course.

DR: How is Mary?

DAD: She is a little angel—so sweet, so beautiful.

DR: How are you?

DAD: I am half dead!

DR: You are brave.

DAD: No—I must be strong for Mary. (*He cried.*) When do we tell her? (*pause*)

> I was touched by his ability to share his sadness.

DR: Do you think that she doesn't already know?

DAD: Doctor, will you tell her? I cannot.

DR: You will not have to tell her with words. Sit with her, and she will tell you. Cry together.

DAD: I was thinking of telling her that I just found out, so she isn't angry that I haven't told her for the past 5 days. (*He paused and put his arms around me and his head on my shoulder and cried.*) Will you be here when I tell her?

> Bargaining.
>
> I was so moved but pleased that he was able to feel safe with me and trust me.

DR: Do you want me to be?

DAD: (*pause*) No, I think I will tell her later, after you have gone.

DR: Call me if you like. I will be by in the morning.

DAD: Thank you.

DR: No—I thank you for allowing me to share your experience with me. You are a very special man.

DAD: No, I feel dead.

DR: You have a very special daughter.

DAD: Thank you. (*We shook hands for about a minute and I left.*)

Session 8

This session occurred 1 week after the crash.

Content of Session

Rationale/Analysis

DOCTOR: (*entering the room*) Good morning, Mary.

MARY: Oh, Doctor, have you heard the terrible news?

DR: What do you mean, Mary?   I decided to let her tell me.

M: My mother and brother have died. I am so sad. I never expected this. I was so worried that I would never walk again. I was even worried that I might die. But I never considered that I might live and that my mother and brother might die. This is worse than my worst fear. I am in so much pain (*pointing to her heart and crying heavily*). This hurts too much. (*pause*) I will be   Awed by her strength.
OK you know. My mother always taught me to be strong.

DR: (*I smiled through my tears, and we held hands.*)

M: (*cried and cried*) I can't believe my mother is dead.

DR: You must have had a very special mother— she had a very special daughter.

M: Oh, Fornari! (*crying*)

(*Mary and I sat together for 30 minutes. Later that day, I met with Mary's dad.*)

DR: How did it go?

DAD: She is so special—my little angel.

DR: Tell me how it went when you told her.

DAD: It was as you said. Few words. I said I have just learned that your mother and brother have died. She exclaimed, "Oh, Daddy—this is so pain- ful." I told her that the family in Colombia was worried. I asked her whether she would call them   Moved by his strength.
and make the announcement, even though I knew that they already knew. Mary called them. She said, "I am very sad—my mommy and brother have died." Then we cried together on and off all night.

DR: You are a loving father, and you are more important to her now than ever.

During the days following Mary's disclosure to me of her mother's and brother's death I met with her daily. Mary regularly greeted me with enthusiastic and energetic exclamations—"Fornari!"—as though she was rooting for a team at a football game. Ten days after the crash, Mary's dad left for Colombia to accompany the remains of his deceased wife and son. Mary's separation from her dad during this critical period in her recovery and mourning process intensified her attachment to me.

Session 12

Content of Session	Rationale/Analysis
MARY: Hello (*without the enthusiasm of previous visits*).	
DOCTOR: How are you today Mary?	What's up? Is her denial wearing thin?
M: Bad—very bad (*crying*).	
DR: I can understand. This is such a difficult time in your life.	Wanting to empathize with her situation.
M: I miss my mommy so much, I can't believe she is dead. I am so sad, sadder than I thought I could ever be.	
DR: You are entitled to be sad. It is so hard to believe that she is dead.	
M: I am so sad (*crying*).	
FRIEND: But look, Mary, at all of the balloons and toys on your bed! (*with the message to cheer up!*)	
DR: I think Mary is sad for a good reason. Do not cheer her up. If you try to, she will think that you don't understand her.	
M: (*listening attentively*) My mother was so sweet (*crying*).	
DR: Over the days and weeks to come you will think a lot about Mommy: how special she was and how much you miss her. That is normal, Mary. It is important. Cry as much as you need to. I will bring you plenty of paper handkerchiefs.	I wanted her to know that mourning was normal and necessary.
M: Will you come every day? I miss my daddy too!	
DR: I will be here every day. When you want to talk, you can also call me. My number is by the phone.	

Mary never did call, but I wanted to convey the comfort and knowledge of her being cared for. Mary's dad and friend did call me on many occasions in addition to my daily visits. I visited Mary nearly every day. I introduced her to several of my colleagues, who visited with her as well. I did not have fixed appointment times but usually visited with her in the mornings.

Session 18

Content of Session	Rationale/Analysis

(Dad had returned from Colombia.)

MARY: Fornari—guess what? My father is back *(with a big smile).*

DOCTOR: Hi, Mary, that's wonderful. How are you?

M: So-so.

DR: What have you been up to?

M: Television, television, and television—what else would you like me to do?

DR: Have you been reading?

M: No—I'm not too much in the mood. My daddy can read to me now, though.

DR: Are you interested in school work?

M: *(looking at me as though I were a monster)* School work—are you crazy?

DR: Maybe, but I think it's time to do something besides TV. What do you think?

M: Like what?

DR: I can ask the teacher to come and speak to you.

M: *(pause)* OK.

Although Mary survived a plane crash, lost her mother and brother, and remained in bed with her left leg in traction, I decided to see whether Mary was ready to normalize her life. In the days that followed, Mary met regularly with a tutor and a child life specialist, who facilitated her play through games and art work. In addition, she began reading on her own. I met with Mary's dad and encouraged him to mourn with Mary, because he had been in Colombia during the initial phase of Mary's mourning for her mother and brother. He reported that he described to Mary, in detail, the events in Colombia, including the plane ride home, the funeral, and the burials. Mary remained in the hospital for 50 days.

Session 30

This session occurred 5 weeks after the crash.

Content of Session	Rationale/Analysis

MARY: Fornari, I had a bad dream last night. I've had it before, but I never remember the whole thing.

DOCTOR: Tell me about your dream.

I encouraged her to speak with me, using an "open-ended" directive.

M: I am on a plane. I see God's face. I think he's wearing a long white beard. I ask to see my mommy. I don't remember any more.

DR: What do you think about your dream?

M: I don't know why I was on a plane. I will never take a plane even if I have to walk back home to Colombia.

DR: The idea of taking a plane must be very scary.

M: It is. (*pause*)

DR: What else about the dream?

M: I remember seeing God's face.

DR: What about God's face?

M: I wonder if my mommy is with Him. I want to tell Him to take care of her and ask Him how she is. I miss her so much. It's not fair that He has her and I don't.

Moved by her loss.

DR: You are right, it isn't fair. Sometimes terrible things happen that we cannot explain, and they aren't fair.

M: Fornari, do you know if you can drive from New York to Colombia? I'm never going to fly!

DR: Right now flying seems so scary, but you don't have to decide about this now.

M: (*pause*) No, I will never take a plane. When I grow up, I want to be a child psychiatrist. Will you teach me how?

DR: If I can. Why a child psychiatrist, Mary?

M: Because I want to help children the way you help me.

DR: How will you get here if you won't fly?

Testing her attachment.

M: I don't know—maybe by car—or couldn't you come and teach me near my house?

Bargaining.

The intensity of Mary's fear of airplanes became apparent (now 5 weeks after the crash), as she could think about her long-awaited release from the hospital and eventual return home to Colombia.

During the weeks that followed, much time was spent reviewing the crash, talking, and using crayons and paper to begin to help her to master flying and the crash.

Session 38

After 50 days in the hospital following the airplane crash, Mary was to be released. Mary was apprehensive about losing the security of her friends and routine. She was to go to a home in the community with her dad for several months for further rehabilitation. Separation and loss remained as sensitive themes.

Content of Session	*Rationale/Analysis*
MARY: Look at my new casts. In 2 weeks my casts come off. I can't wait!	
DOCTOR: I am glad you are healing. You are a special girl, Mary.	
M: Fornari, will you come to see me?	
DR: Mary, we can speak by phone, and you will come with Dad to see me. I will try to come and visit you also.	I was so pleased with her progress.
M: Look at my new TV and Nintendo—my own Nintendo!	
DR: That's great, Mary. Remember that you can call me, and we can talk?	Pleased at her enthusiasm.
M: I know. I am scared. I don't know how I'll go home.	
DR: We have time to work on this, Mary.	

Mary had made many close friends while in the hospital. Her kindness and gentle innocence attracted caring and concern. Mary was discharged to a home in the community. Mary and her dad resided there for nearly 2 months before their return to Colombia 4 months after the crash.

Session 40

I accompanied Mary, her dad, and the family friend to the orthopedist's office when Mary was to have her casts removed. Mary would walk for the first time in 10 weeks.

Content of Session	*Rationale/Analysis*
MARY: (*screaming in fear*) I'm scared. How do they take them [her casts] off?	
DOCTOR: Don't worry Mary—they won't hurt you.	
M: Will I be able to walk? Will it hurt? Will I know how?	

Content	Rationale/Analysis
DR: After having your legs in casts for several months, moving your muscles may be sore. Little by little, with physical exercises, you will walk and run like before.	I offered her reassurance, preparing her for gradual recovery.
M: I am so scared. I never thought I would walk. Do you remember, Fornari? I never thought I would walk! I never thought my mother and brother would die . . . (*crying*)	
DR: You will walk, and you will be fine. I know that your progress and recovery must remind you that Mommy and your brother died.	The orthopedist assured me that Mary would be fine.
M: (*crying*) I'm scared.	Survival guilt.

The casts were removed; Mary flexed her legs and complained of much pain. Despite physical therapy, Mary refused to walk for over 2 weeks.

Session 44

In the physical therapist's office, I met with Mary, her dad, family friend, and physical therapist. Mary was walking and pleased with her progress.

Content of Session	Rationale/Analysis
MARY: Look, Fornari—I can jump!	
DOCTOR: (*I watched Mary jump up and down; I applauded.*) That's great! Mary you are doing great!	I was so proud of her accomplishments.
M: I can also hop—watch!	
DR: (*I watched Mary hop, skip, jump, and run.*) You are doing great. You must be so proud!	I was pleased with my own work with her.
M: I am.	
DR: I bet you're getting ready to go home soon.	
M: I am, but I am scared. I don't want to take a plane.	
DR: Do you think you can?	
M: I guess, with my father there I can, but I don't want him to die!	Fear of loss of the surviving parent.

Two days later, Mary and her Dad left for Colombia. We shared a warm good-bye. I hugged Mary and gave her some chocolate candy kisses as a token of affection. I told her, "Mary, I know you will never be the same after the plane crash. I, too, will never be the same after meeting you. You have taught me so much about strength, courage, and love. I thank you for letting me get to know you and for giving me so much." We hugged. Mary's dad put his arms around me; he cried. Mary said, "Good-bye, Fornari. Thank you. I will miss you."

I later heard conflicting stories about the return trip to Bogota. First I had heard that Mary had refused to fly. A family friend called to say that they had taken a train from New York to Miami, Florida. From there, they went by boat to a South American port, where they could continue their return to Colombia by train, bus, and then car.

Subsequently, I was told that the trip proceeded differently. In actuality they drove by car from New York to Miami. The reason, I was told, was that Mary's dad had not made the necessary arrangements in time to fly. Perhaps *he* was afraid to let Mary fly. Once in Miami, they flew by plane to Bogota. Mary expressed fear about flying, but after being comforted by her dad while on the plane, Mary was able to relax during the return flight home.

SUMMARY

During an emergency, it is important to remain calm and be able to think clearly. The primary role of health care providers, including rescue workers, emergency room staff, and hospital workers, is to be able to administer emergency medical care and not become immobilized by the terror of the disaster. While providing emergency services to children and adolescents, it is essential to convey a sense of safety, support, and reassurance to diminish their anxiety and allow the necessary care to be administered. During this process, empathy with the victims offers them the comfort of knowing that the health care providers understand their condition. This was demonstrated during the early work with Mary.

As this work progressed, empathy facilitated the therapeutic alliance between Mary and me; it was necessary for me to establish this connection with the child and her family and support system. In Mary's case, working closely with her father and the family friends facilitated the therapeutic alliance with Mary.

During therapy immediately following a disaster, it is critical to take the child's lead once the therapeutic alliance has begun to develop. The victims of psychic trauma will often offer many signals that they are ready to begin to discuss their traumatic experiences as well as their losses.

In reviewing traumatic experiences with child or adolescent victims, it is helpful to reconstruct the trauma as completely as possible and to review it many times using different modalities. These may include play, drawing, mutual story-telling, looking at family photo albums, reviewing newspaper coverage of the trauma, or other visual material such as television or video coverage of the event.

Children, like adults, bring their fantasies, dreams, and associations into the therapy, often stimulated by the techniques utilized in prior therapy sessions. An important guideline is to take the child's lead when utilizing these techniques so as not to retraumatize the child by being too confrontational before the child is prepared to review the painful memories and experiences.

Psychotherapeutic work with child victims of psychic trauma may go on for many months and years following the traumatic event. As the child reaches new developmental stages, these traumatic experiences and their associated losses may take on new significance, and the child may develop new symptoms. These may manifest as new fears, sleep disturbances, nightmares, or almost any kind of symptom. It would be naive to assume that symptoms that develop long after the trauma are unrelated. A more sensitive and thoughtful view would be that children are *never* the same after psychic trauma. Their lives are marked by their traumatic experiences as before or after the event. All subsequent life experiences, symptoms, and major decisions may contain elements that are remnants or derivatives of their earlier psychic trauma.

CONCLUDING COMMENTS

Working with the child survivors of psychic trauma soon after the traumatic event offers us an opportunity to observe the initial coping responses of these children. This allows the therapist to experience the trauma with the child rather than to have to reconstruct it in the consulting room many years later, which more commonly happens. This offers the therapist a unique opportunity to prevent a variety of symptoms that might otherwise develop.

The premorbid psychological status of the child, the child's temperament, and the family's psychosocial supports all have a profound impact on the child's ultimate adaptation. Mary offers us the unique and compelling opportunity of examining an 8-year-old girl following her survival from an airplane crash; we see her initial coping style and the way in which she began to integrate her experiences as well as mourn her tremendous losses. Mary represents an example of extraordinary courage and adaptation in the face of disaster. It appears that early, regular, and repeated opportunities to discuss her experiences allowed her the opportunity to begin to work through her devastating psychic trauma.

When originally informed that Mary had refused to fly home, I wondered what else I could have done to help her to overcome her fear of flying in an airplane. More desensitization of airplanes might have allowed her the possibility of getting on the plane. Perhaps I should have been satisfied to have her travel by train, boat, bus, and car at this time. Mary had overcome so many obstacles that flying, at this time, was not the most important goal. Mary can choose to master flying at a later time if and when she decides to.

Later, I learned that Mary had indeed traveled home to Colombia by plane. I was surprised, pleased, and impressed with Mary's resilience.

PLAY THERAPY MATERIALS

- Puppets/stuffed animals
- Drawing paper and markers
- Photographs of family members
- Newspaper reports of the crash

STUDY QUESTIONS

1. Discuss the normal grief process of an 8-year-old child. How would you evaluate Mary's mourning process? What kinds of responses might be predictable in the year following the traumatic loss of a mother and a brother?

2. Comment on the stress faced by the therapist in having to cope with tragedies, as in this case. How can the therapist best deal with his or her feelings? Can you envision a role for staff debriefing in a group format for all crisis workers?

3. Discuss the delicate matter of timing the disclosure to the child of the death of a family member. Do you agree with the way it was handled in this case? Why, or why not?

4. How could Mary be helped to overcome her fear of planes? If you had been the therapist, would you have focused more on this fear prior to her departure? If so, what methods would you use?

REFERENCES

Anthony, E. J. (1988). The reactions of children and their parents to disastrous and violent circumstances. In E. J. Anthony & C. Chiland (Eds.), *The child in his family; Perilous development: Child raising and identity formation under stress* (pp. 425–427). New York: John Wiley & Sons.

Frederick, C. J. (1985). Children traumatized by catastrophic situations. In S. Eth & R. S. Pynoos (Eds.), *Post-traumatic stress disorder in children* (pp. 73–99). Washington, DC: American Psychiatric Press.

Sugar, M. (1988). Children in a disaster: An overview. In E. J. Anthony & C. Chiland (Eds.), *The child in his family; Perilous development: Child raising and identity formation under stress* (pp. 429–442). New York: John Wiley & Sons.

Terr, L. (1990). *Too scared to cry: Psychic trauma in childhood.* New York: Harper & Row.

Afterword:
The Crisis of War

Afterword
The Crisis of War

NANCY BOYD WEBB

Less than 2 months after completion of the manuscript of this volume, war erupted in the Persian Gulf. In a short space of time children's television viewing changed from cartoons to real battle scenes, images of Israeli children wearing gas masks, and oil-soaked birds struggling to survive.

Frightening as these realities appear, however, war does not automatically precipitate crises for child (or adult) witnesses. As detailed in Chapter 1, it is the *perception* of the event that determines an individual's crisis state. For example, a child who believes that the purpose of war is to fight a "bad man" bully will probably react very differently from the child whose mother has been called into active duty. Moreover, the adjustment of the child with the soldier mother depends on numerous factors in that child's current and past life, besides the mother's recent war involvement. These other factors, comprising the tripartite crisis assessment (Chapter 1), include the child's age, past experience with separation and violence, and the nature of available support from the family, school, and community.

Each person's unique history results in a distinct profile upon which the assault of war stamps a different imprint. The reactions of two 8-year-old children in the same third-grade class illustrates the mediating influence of past life events on individual responses to the current stress of war.

Case of Drew. Drew, age 8, and his sister, 2 years younger, had been living with their mother since their parents' divorce 2 years earlier. Their mother, a medical technician, had joined the Army Reserve following the divorce, as a step toward career security. The family had moved to the community where the maternal grandparents live to facilitate contact and frequent babysitting with them. Drew and his sister have attended the same school since he was in first grade. They see their father during two vacations each year, since he has remarried and has also moved; he provides child support and maintains contact on birthdays and holidays.

Soon after the war began, Drew's mother was sent to the Persian Gulf. Prior to leaving, she made arrangements for the children to move in with her parents. They continue in the same school, and although somewhat anxious when they see television accounts of the war, they tell their friends that they are proud of their mother's role in the war, "taking care of sick soldiers."

Case of Donald. Also age 8, Donald is in the same class as Drew in the same Army base community. Donald has a stepbrother, Robert, age 13, who bullies him when his parents leave the boys together. Their father, an Army sergeant, has a very authoritarian style and frequently becomes physically abusive to Donald's mother when he has been drinking. The father favors Donald and usually punishes Robert severely when the boys argue.

When the father's unit was sent to the Persian Gulf, Donald began having severe nightmares, resulting in his spending most of the night in his mother's bed. In school Donald has become withdrawn and preoccupied. He speaks about his worries that Saddam Hussein's terrorists could poison their water or explode a bomb near the Army base.

Clearly, these cases illustrate the significance of past experience impacting on a current stressful separation. Both Donald and Drew had to adapt to the loss of a parent, but the overall *meaning* of that loss related to the context of the child's past and present vulnerabilities and strengths.

It is sadly ironic that consideration of children's responses to the crisis of war summarizes many of the theoretical underpinnings of this book. The major section headings of the book—The Crisis of Violence, The Crisis of Loss, Medical/Health Crises, and The Crisis of Natural Disasters and Other Catastrophes—all apply grimly to the situation of war. However, for children ages 3 to 11, who have been the focus of this book, one of the most confusing and disturbing aspects of the war is witnessing adults deliberately killing each other because they cannot solve their problems by talking. Adults who bomb residential neighborhoods and families sleeping in shelters now are perceived by children as both aggressors and victims. Certainly their role as "protectors" has weakened in the eyes of children.

War destroys the innocent childhood belief that the world is safe and that they are protected by adults who solve differences in a rational way. As Anna Quindlen stated in *The New York Times* (February 10, 1991), "the children think the adults have lost it." Long-term effects on the children will depend on the unique pattern of pieces that comprise each individual's personal life mosaic.

Based on general knowledge about child development and reactions to stress, the following tentative predictions represent topics for future study:

1. Children with both parents in active service away from home are at high risk of future emotional disturbances.
2. Children who live in war-torn areas are at high risk of future emotional disturbances.
3. Children whose history includes past experience with violence and loss are vulnerable to future emotional problems based on the added stress of war.

4. Children whose lives are seriously disrupted by the war (family move, change of caretaker, change of school) will show future emotional problems.

AGE CONSIDERATIONS

The ability of children to comprehend the elements of threat and danger associated with war varies with the child's age and level of cognitive development. Concepts of distance, large numbers (of soldiers or bombs), and time factors (duration of war) are abstractions that elude the comprehension of the average preschool and young latency-age child. *All* children, however, have some first-hand experience with fighting, arguments, angry feelings, and frustration, and this may be the level on which children interpret war.

Preschool Children

Many view the Gulf war as a real-life fairy tale involving a greedy king who unfairly took someone else's kingdom. Like the fable that begins, "in a far, distant land a long time ago," this current war may not seem stressful to preschoolers unless the adults around them are upset and convey a strong sense of danger and threat. Excessive television viewing, involving the witnessing of wounded and dead casualties, would probably prove overstimulating and upsetting to preschoolers and should be avoided.

Latency-Age Children

Since children between the ages of 6 and 11 tend to focus on issues of right and wrong, good and bad, friend and enemy, it is likely that many children of this age subscribe to a rather simplistic view of war. They may, in fact, channel some of their own normal aggressive feelings into pleasure associated with eliminating the "enemy." At the same time, latency-age children have more ability to understand the concept of biological and chemical warfare and to appreciate and fear the "unseen" danger.

The issue of protection and safety is crucial for *all* children, and adults must find ways to offer reassurance. Some specific techniques for helping children deal with their war-related anxieties are outlined below.

PLAY THERAPY TECHNIQUES

Virtually *all* of the play therapy methods demonstrated in the cases in this book can be adapted to helping children cope with the stress of war. Furthermore, many play therapy methods can be used either *individually* (with a child who has already developed some symptoms) or in a *family* or *group* context either after or before war-related anxieties convert to symptoms.

The chapters on working with children following natural disasters demonstrate a variety of art, storytelling, and behavioral techniques appropriate to helping children deal with the feelings stimulated by war.

Lenore Terr's letter in *The New York Times* (February 22, 1991) stressed the importance of giving children the chance to *speak* about their war-related concerns. The logical place for this to occur is in the family and school settings where children live their daily lives. However, since children's speech often converts symbolically into the "language of play," adult helpers (e.g., parents, school social workers, child therapists) must understand and communicate with children in both their symbolic language of play and verbally.

Art

This play therapy modality has wide applicability for children of all ages and is particularly useful for children whose language skills cannot convey the subtleties and intensities of their feelings. Children can obtain tremendous relief by drawing their fears and wishes. The process of "externalization" of feelings, discussed in Chapter 2, enables the fearful child to destroy a perceived enemy on paper, thereby achieving some relief from the fear that the enemy will destroy him or his entire family.

Storytelling

This method, relying on verbal, rather than visual, images allows a child's imagination to create scenes of punishment and reward, anger and love. The storytelling format may use props such as family dolls (Chapter 3) or war toys (Chapters 11), or it may take the form of filling in a *Desert Storm Workbook* as designed by the National Childhood Grief Institute (1991). This workbook consists of "exercises" designed to help children integrate war and global events. It contains sentence-completion blank pages intended to provide children with an outlet for expressing in story and artistic form their responses to war-related topics.

Puppets

In the hands of a creative and responsive play therapist, puppet play offers an ideal arena for playing out war and battle themes. Indeed, many children instinctively select an "aggressor" and a "passive" puppet, whether or not war is a factor in their current life experience. Some school classes may elect to enact a puppet show representative of world events, in a dramatized, symbolic format. This could offer the class an outlet for their feelings of helplessness about world events at the same time as providing the possibility of problem-solving an outcome of their invention (diplomacy, retribution, peace).

Dolls

The young child who fears danger may try to obtain mastery of this fear through doll play that enacts scenes of comforting and nurturing. The child identifies with the doll that is comforted, thus simultaneously permitting expression of the fear (crying baby) and its surcease (bottle and soothing). Doll play frequently takes the form of the child simultaneously identifying with both baby and nurturer.

The older (latency-age) child may elect more representational war games, either with puppets or soldier play.

Clay

The possibilities of doing and undoing implicit in the media of clay make it useful for symbolic acting out of aggressive impulses (and identification with the aggressor). Bombs and guns take on three-dimensional forms in which enemy and ally can be obliterated with a blow of a child's palm. This element of realism possible with clay might create anxiety for a child with a parent at the front, yet it simultaneously offers the child a fantasy means of controlling the outcome.

Board Games

The competitive attribute of many board games lends special significance to their use with children responding to the stress of war. While winning and losing is *always* an issue for children (and many adults), the role of winner takes on special significance in times of war. Can the therapist hold to the same perspective about winning and losing when playing Battleship with a latency-age child whose parent is in the Gulf as in peacetime? Even children whose parents are not active servicemembers have a heightened sense of right and wrong, winner and loser in times of war. This can lead to meaningful discussion between moves during a board game.

CONCLUDING COMMENTS

War simulates many of the feelings and behaviors of a couple in the midst of divorce, with the fallout spilling onto the children, who feel awed and helpless by witnessing their parents' anger and contempt for one another. Young children are not capable of understanding two opposing viewpoints simultaneously, either in their own family or on the international battlefield. It is the role of the play therapist to help such children express their frustration, while also offering hope for a more secure future.

REFERENCES

National Childhood Grief Institute. (1991). *"My desert storm" workbook: Firstaid for feelings.* Minneapolis, MN: Author.

Quindlen, A. (1991, February 10). Out of the mouths. *New York Times*, Section 4, p. 17.

Terr, L. A. (1991, February 22). First, how do children feel about the war? *New York Times* [Letter].

Play Therapy Resources

Play Therapy Resources

TOY CATALOGS

Chaselle, Inc.
New England School Supply
P.O. Box 1581
Springfield, MA 01101
1-800-628-8608

Childcraft, Inc.
20 Kilmer Road
Edison, NJ 08818
1-800-631-5657

Childswork Childsplay
Center for Applied Psychology, 3rd floor
441 N. 5th Street
Philadelphia, PA 19123
1-800-962-1141

Constructive Playthings
1227 East 119th Street
Grandview, MO 64030
1-800-225-6124

Learn & Play
Troll Associates
100 Corporate Drive
Mahwah, NJ 07498
1-800-247-6106

Ther-a-Play Products
P.O. Box 761
Glen Ellen, CA 95442
1-800-333-5979

Toys for Psychotherapy with Children
Play Therapy Associates
1603 9th Street, Suite 400
Greeley, CO 80631
1-800-542-9723

Toys to Grow On
P.O. Box 17
Long Beach, CA 90801
1-800-542-8338

SELECTED TRAINING PROGRAMS

A comprehensive directory of play therapy training programs may be obtained for a fee from the Center for Play Therapy, Denton, Texas. The programs listed here represent a small selection in different parts of the country from a total of approximately 85 programs nationwide.

Boston University
Counseling Psychology Department
Dr. Eileen Nickerson
605 Commonwealth
Boston, MA 02215
613-353-3276

California School of Professional Psychology
Dr. Kevin O'Connor
1350 M Street
Fresno, CA 93721
209-486-8420

Center for Play Therapy
Dr. Gary Laudreth, Director
University of North Texas
Denton, TX 76203
817-565-2909

Fairleigh Dickinson University
Psychological Services Department
Dr. Charles Schaefer
139 Temple Avenue
Hackensack, NJ 07601
201-692-2649

Pennsylvania State University
Human Development and Family Studies
Dr. Louise Guerney
University Park, PA 16802

Postgraduate Certificate Program for Child and Adolescent Therapy
Dr. Nancy Boyd Webb, Director
Fordham University
Graduate School of Social Service
Tarrytown, NY 10591
914-332-6000

Reiss-Davis Child Study Center
Carol Silbergeld, Director of Social Work
3200 Motor Avenue
Los Angeles, CA 90034
213-204-1666, ext. 349

The Therapy Institute
180 North Michigan Avenue, Suite 1100A
Chicago, IL 60601
312-332-1260

Index

Index